THE THEOLOGY OF RABBINIC JUDAISM
Prolegomenon

by

Jacob Neusner

Scholars Press
Atlanta, Georgia

THE THEOLOGY OF RABBINIC JUDAISM
Prolegomenon

by
Jacob Neusner

©1997
University of South Florida

Cover Art by Suzanne R. Neusner

Publication of this book was made possible by a grant from the Tisch Family Foundation, New York City. The University of South Florida acknowledges with thanks this important support for its scholarly projects.

Library of Congress Cataloging in Publication Data

Neusner, Jacob, 1932–
    The theology of Rabbinic Judaism : prolegomenon / by Jacob
Neusner.
        p.   cm. — (South Florida studies in the history of Judaism ;
no. 153)
    ISBN 0-7885-0386-3 (cloth : alk. paper)
    1. Rabbinical literature—History and criticism.　2. Talmud—
Theology.　3. Midrash rabbah.　Ruth—Theology.　4. Judaism—
Doctrines.　I. Title.　II. Series.
BM496.5.N4825　1997
296.3'09'015—dc21　　　　　　　　　　　97-26845
　　　　　　　　　　　　　　　　　　　　CIP

Printed in the United States of America
on acid-free paper

THE THEOLOGY OF RABBINIC JUDAISM

Prolegomenon

SOUTH FLORIDA STUDIES IN THE HISTORY OF JUDAISM

Edited by
Jacob Neusner
Bruce D. Chilton, Darrell J. Fasching, William Scott Green,
Sara Mandell, James F. Strange

Number 153
THE THEOLOGY OF RABBINIC JUDAISM
Prolegomenon

by
Jacob Neusner

TABLE OF CONTENTS

Preface

Rabbinic Judaism is the Judaic religious system that appeals to the myth of the dual Torah, oral and written, and finds its authoritative writings in the documents comprised by Scripture and the writings that set forth the originally-oral Torah. Here begins a quest for the cogent structure that sustains, and system that animates, the Oral Torah in its formative age, the first through the seventh centuries of the Common Era. Viewed synchronically, how do the documentary components of the Oral Torah cohere? At issue is theology, by which I mean, the governing rationalities, of the foundation-documents of Rabbinic Judaism. In response to the distinctive traits of those documents I propose three distinct and complementary approaches to discerning the modes of thought, the category-formations, that impart cogency and proportion to that Judaism.[1] On what basis do I undertake to ask questions of cogency and coherence to the Oral Torah? The foundation of the claim that theology sustains and imparts cogency to the Oral Torah and its writings comes to expression in a simple principle, a single fact of intellection:

there can be no rationality that governs in one document of a given corpus of kindred writings that all together are identified and privileged by a determinate religious system but not in another component of the same authoritative corpus.

Upon that rock I propose to build the work of descriptive, historical theology that commences with this Prolegomenon. Chapter Two fully spells out what I mean in that simple statement of principle.

We move, then, from the parts to the whole, the documents to the system that the documents adumbrate. That is because that religious system — a generative theory of the world-view, way of life, and theory of the social entity comprised by the faithful — comes to concrete expression, here and there, in this detail or that, whole and complete. The detail recapitulates the main point of the whole, as the system repeats itself interminably and unashamedly. But it follows that — again to state with heavy emphasis — *it is not the system that recapitulates the documents,*

---

[1] I use the word "rationalities" in line with Marshall Sahlins, *How "Natives" Think. About Captain Cook, for Example* (Chicago, 1995: The University of Chicago Press), p. 148-190.

but the documents that recapitulate the system.[2] The writings constantly refer
back to, take for granted, acknowledge the presence of, the coherent, generative
system, comprised by a set of interlocking paradigms. That is, a symbolic structure
and a precipitating myth, a system of ideas that transcends the texts and forms the
matrix of the texts demands articulation. Then what we do when we ask the
theological question of the writings is undertake a search beneath the surface of
their particular messages to uncover that statement that, all together and all at
once, wherever and whenever the documents speak, the system sets forth in its
own behalf.

To ask a corpus of religious writings to reveal what holds those writings
together and makes them cogent, we raise the question of theology — the interior
logic of reasoned discourse about the knowledge of God. In the case of Rabbinic
Judaism knowledge of God comes to Holy Israel through God's self-manifestation
in the Torah revealed by God to our rabbi, Moses, at Sinai, in two media, Oral and
Written. Here I propose to examine the entire corpus of authoritative documents
of Rabbinic Judaism — the writings of the Oral Torah — in quest of their inner
logic, their collaborative rationality, their common system and shared structure of
ideas.

This I do by identifying the three modes of theological discourse that I
am able to distinguish in the writings classified as the Oral Torah. These are, first,
paradigms or models that everywhere define structure, system, order, and proportion,
second, their modes of making self-evidently logical connections and drawing
conclusions therefrom, and, third, their vocabulary of symbols conveyed in opaque
words formed into lists. Accordingly, in this initial statement of method I spell out
how to identify the systemic structure of Rabbinic Judaism as set forth in its writings
of the formative age, from the first through the seventh centuries of the Common
Era. I propose to find out how the documents of the Oral Torah recapitulate the
system — the coherent substrate of ideas — of the Oral Torah, of what principal
components that system is comprised, and where and how we recognize those
building blocks of generative thought and argument and the consequent doctrine.

What justifies presenting such a question to the Oral Torah? It is the
simple fact that the writings of the Oral Torah, portrayed as the anonymous statement
of a consensus, speak for a small and unified group of sages, in the phrase of Brian

---

[2] The category, "canon," is not native for this literature and — I now realize — does not
apply. The reason is that "canon" refers to a complete and closed collection of authoritative
writings, while the oral Torah remains open to new documents. In the Judaism under study
here, teachings of the latest generation, even to our own time, fall into the category of "oral
Torah." Not only so, but we also do not know, for the formative period, for whom the
documents were authoritative, apart from the circles that authored and sponsored them.

Stock, "a textual community."[3] This community in composing its writings constantly appeals to consensus, e.g., by omitting the names of authorities behind those rules or opinions that are deemed authority, by tying a name to a position so as to label the position schismatic.[4] Hence the community's most basic mode of expression presupposes a unity of viewpoint and a harmony of perspective, a point to which we return in Chapter Two.

That is a merely formal argument. As to matters of substance, these documents, from the Mishnah, ca. 200 C.E., through the Talmud of Babylonia, ca. 600 C.E. all together and all at once set forth a religious system and structure. That is not only the position of the Talmud of Babylonia, a definitive recapitulation of the whole.[5] It is also the fact yielded by internal evidence. Specifically, everyone of the documents appeals to a common set of paradigms or models or patterns and a single symbolic system, particular to these writings and found in no others produced by any other Judaism. They all share through these paradigms fundamental principles and generative convictions both unique to the set and also common to them all, e.g., all concur on the privileging of certain parts of the Hebrew Scriptures ("Written Torah," "Old Testament"), and all take for granted the authority of named figures within a chain of tradition to Sinai, "our sages of blessed memory," that is, sages or rabbis. A single myth permeates the whole. A limited symbolic vocabulary pervades, and, as a matter of fact, it is a different symbolic vocabulary from that exhibited in synagogue decoration.[6] So, it follows, I refer here not to the lowest common denominator, still less to a set of self-evident but systemically inert convictions (e.g., God is one, God revealed the Torah, and the like), which most Judaisms can have affirmed. I speak of a set of differentiating paradigms, modes of making connections, and corpus of verbal symbols, that are altogether particular, if not in definition then in proportion and use, to the writings at hand and characteristic of them all.

Some suppose that, while these writings are uniform in certain rhetorical preferences, they cannot be described as systematic. Isolated opinions conflict, so we may find everything and its opposite and therefore define the Judaism of the

---

[3] Brian Stock, *The Implications of Literacy* (Princeton, 1987: Princeton University Press)
[4] So Mishnah-tractate Eduyyot 1:6: Said R. Judah, …why do they record the opinion of an individual against that of a majority to no purpose? So that if a person should say, 'Thus have I received the tradition,' one may say to him, 'You have heard the tradition in accord with the opinion of Mr. So-and-so [against that of the majority].'"
[5] See below, note 17.
[6] I demonstrated that fact in *Symbol and Theology in Early Judaism.* Minneapolis, 1991: Fortress Press, which forms the basis of Chapter Eight.

whole any way we wish. But in the pages of this book, I shall propose the hypothesis, for systematic testing in the future, that the documents refer to a single mythic and symbolic system throughout, and by identifying in detail the principal components of the encompassing paradigm, I shall further lay out the way of accurately and proportionately describing that system as a whole. This I propose to do by a detailed and complete survey, explained here and executed in future work, that specifies the native categories of the Oral Torah, their relationships and balance and order. The system then will tell us what theological questions we may proceed to investigate: the topical program, the logical structure, and the system through its documentary expressions will also tell us where to look and how to assess the importance of what we find: the category-formation, locations, and proportions of the entire body of writings. The result dictates what we can know and how we can find it out.

I cannot over-stress that in these pages I do not set forth a new claim but recapitulate in a critical framework one that for the entire history of Rabbinic Judaism has accompanied these writings from their very origin. Those who produced these writings clearly insisted upon the harmony and coherence — the continuity — of all their statements, read all together, as nearly every page of the two Talmuds demonstrates. Disharmony, incoherence, contradiction — these imperfections immediately attracted attention and demanded harmonization. It follows that those who received and valued these same writings from the beginning to the present take for granted that any sentence chosen from one document may be shown to cohere with any sentence chosen from any other; the entire corpus — and all that would flow from it for centuries to come — constituted one whole Torah of Moses, our rabbi. Hence the traits imputed to the writings deemed by the sages and masters of those writings over nearly two millennia to fall into the category of Torah, traits of coherence and cogency, validate this inquiry into the nature of that pervasive, active and effective rationality, the character of that ubiquitous logic.

Then how are we to describe the system that animates in varying ways and dimensions the deep structure that sustains the normative documents of Rabbinic Judaism in their formative period, from the Mishnah through the Talmud of Babylonia?[7] These writings I propose to learn how to read as a continuous, coherent statement, from start to finish, with the proviso that — as in the pages of this book

---

[7] I have done one work of constructive (though not systematic) theology, which is *Judaism's Theological Voice: The Melody of the Talmud.* Chicago, 1995: The University of Chicago Press. I have no plan to pursue the still more intimidating problem of a *systematic, constructive* theology. In this century the systematic and constructive theologies that demand close study are those of Abraham J. Heschel and Eugene Borowitz. Eliezer Berkowitz clearly aimed at a constructive system, though he did not realize his goal. Much work remains to be done on elucidating the system and construction that they put forth in their *oeuvre.*

I show — at least three distinct approaches to the description of governing rationalities work together to identify the bases for coherence and the paths to continuity. How do I do so? To test the conviction of those who value the documents that they belong together and share in the same standing, to speak in one voice a single truth, I seek to identify what to the faithful is self-evident. I mean that logic that forms those paradigms characteristic of them all, that reason, the self-evidence of which the faithful acknowledge and ubiquitously affirm. The upshot is, by their nature and definition the authoritative writings point us toward the system to which the corpus gives expression, and which the kindred documents embody in detail. That rationality or logic or self-evident reason or pervasive model[8] that speaks in the documents both severally and jointly will define that single theology common to them all. Hence identifying the governing paradigms, recurring points of stress and tension, category-formations and the connections between and among them, symbols uniformly invoked — that is what will form the centerpiece of the ultimate account of the theology of the Oral Torah to which this Prolegomenon points.

Specifically, I see three necessary, complementary approaches to the theological reading of the documents of the Oral Torah, [1] the quest for paradigms that govern, [2] the inquiry into rules for making connections and drawing conclusions, and [3] the search for the rules that validate the specific symbolic vocabulary inherent in Rabbinic Judaism and its meanings. Taken all together, our tripartite task is to learn how to think in the manner in which the framers of the holy books conduct thought. But many years of work separate from its successful conclusion this initial definition of the Oral Torah's logic, the connections the Oral Torah deems self-evident, the besought conclusions that part of the Torah finds inexorable and inescapable. Indeed, as I shall explain, the initial, but protracted task is simply on the basis of the methods sketched here to identify the facts that pertain: the correct category-formations, the locations where these find definition, the rules for assessing the proportionate balance that assigns centrality to one, peripherality to another, such formation. So a vast labor of collecting facts, correctly assessed, awaits.

All that we now know with certainty is that prevailing modes of inquiry have not served us well. For at the moment we find ourselves in the situation of Foucault, as cited by Marshall Sahlins: all we know with certainty is what does *not* make sense of the data in hand. Sahlins frames matters in this language:

> Better to adopt the attitude of Foucault when presented by Borges with a zoological classification from a certain Chinese encyclopaedia, in which it is written that 'animals are divided into (a) belonging to the Emperor, (b) embalmed, (c) tame, (d) suckling pigs, (e) sirens\ (f) fabulous, (g) stray dogs, (h) included in the present classification, (i) frenzied, (j)

---

[8] I use these terms interchangeably, though in time to come will have to differentiate among them.

innumerable, (k) drawn with a very fine camel hair brush, (l) et cetera, (m) having just broken the water pitcher, (n) that from a long way off look like flies. In the wonderment of this taxonomy, the thing we apprehend in one great leap, the thing that, by means of the fable, is demonstrated in the exotic charms of another system of thought, is the limitation of our own, the stark impossibility of thinking *that*.[9]

Connections we shall observe in Chapter Seven, classification-schemes we shall survey in Chapter Eight, prove as jarring as the items joined in the odd zoological classification scheme before us. We find ourselves in a comparable position. Faced with the classification-system that forms the foundation of the documents of the Oral Torah, our own system of thought — based as it has been on the categories of Protestant dogmatic theology — leads us to cognitive dead-ends, as I shall explain in Chapter Three, and defines a category-formation that simply has to be abandoned. What has gone wrong is not the poor execution of a serviceable method, witless Urbach's incapacity to do more than publish his card-files, Moore's persistent power of mere paraphrase. What is not working is the category-formation that told Urbach and Moore how to set up their files. They found themselves unable to do more than collect and arrange sayings, meaning, they invoked no program of analytical questions that served the documents at hand. That failure explains why the starting point for describing a theology within a determinate body of writings requires that we take up the matter of rationalities, the identification of principles of self-evidence and the consequent modes of classification.

For confronting a body of legal, exegetical, and theological writings that undertake a mode of thought and consequent manner of discourse that is anything but systematic, dogmatic, and, in the context of the philosophical foundation of theology in Western religious civilization, theological at all, where do we now stand? The present descriptive-theological accounts of Rabbinic Judaism prove intellectually vulgar. That is because those accounts prove categorically inappropriate to important parts of the data, the results asymmetrical and disproportionate to the evidence, and, alas, the consequent accounts, when right, at best prove merely paraphrastic — but mostly, simply vacuous. For presently influential works present to the documents of the Oral Torah a questionnaire of dogmatic theology deriving from Protestant hands[10] and yield an implausible result, one incapable of defining the native categories or of explaining how they cohere.

---

[9] Marshall Sahlins, *How "Natives" Think*, p. 163, citing Michel Foucault, *The Order of Things* (N.Y., 1973: Vintage Books), p. xv.

[10] Ephraim Urbach's systematic discussion of whether the law is autonomous or heteronomous responds to a question posed by Kant but unlikely to have found comprehension among those whose writings Urbach claims to describe and interpret, a classical example of a misplace category-formation. But that is only one blatant instance of the intellectual vulgarity characteristic of his work.

I undertake to raise the theological question of the Oral Torah because my completed work on the literature, the history, and the history of the religion, of the formative age of Rabbinic Judaism has prepared me to do so. I have translated and analyzed the documents, compared and contrasted them with others of the same classification, and set forth the documentary history of the ideas of the Judaism set forth in the Oral Torah. While from the beginning, in the mid-1950s, of my study of Rabbinic Judaism, to which I have devoted my entire adult life, I have been a long time in coming to this problem, forty years, really. Before asking the final, the synchronic, question, I first had to describe the literary and formal traits of the documents of the Oral Torah, then analyze their history, and finally to interpret their respective religious systems.[11] Building on literary, historical, and religions-historical results, this inquiry into theology forms the logical next step in a systematic study of the formation of Rabbinic Judaism in its principal writings, from the several documents, through their interrelationships, and now onward to their coherent statement. But until now, I have not attempted to take a sighting on them as a coherent statement, in continuity.

Yet as I have stressed, no one who knowledgeably practices the Judaism of the dual Torah, Oral and Written, will find the theological question puzzling. For it is as a continuity that all of these books, along with the entire corpus of writings produced afterward and in dialogue with these books, have been read by the Judaism that privileges them. By those who practice the religion, Judaism, in its classical system, all are deemed to form quite interchangeable parts of a single whole statement. They constitute the written down form of the originally oral part of the one whole Torah of our rabbi, Moses, received from God at Sinai.[12] The great Rabbinical sages for all time have found proper the linking of what they find in one of these writings with what they find in some other, forming a combination by using the language, "the Torah teaches...," (or, in contemporary parlance, "Judaism says...,"). In the synagogue, on the Sabbath just passed and the one

---

[11] That is to say, I have already examined in its own terms each free-standing component of the Oral Torah ("book," "document"), translating and describing them all one by one. Through exercises of comparison and contrast, I have further investigated the relationships between and among groups of kindred documents, e.g., the Mishnah, Tosefta, Talmud of the Land of Israel, and Talmud of Babylonia, Leviticus Rabbah and Pesiqta deRab Kahana, Tractate Abot and Abot deRabbi Nathan. So the documents have been read as autonomous statements and also as writings in some ways connected with one another. The bibliography of these various studies of translation, then description, analysis, and interpretation, encompasses hundreds of volumes and does not have to be reproduced here. The set of items covering only Ruth Rabbah, given below, stands for the whole, for each document has been treated in the same systematic way.

[12] A study of the sense of the claim of orality in the Rabbinic context awaits; outside of the Mishnah, where matters are made explicit, precisely what people meant by that mythic allegation is hardly clear. But that study will carry beyond the limits of the formative age, the first through seventh centuries.

coming next, the premise of all teaching of the Torah is the same. Accordingly, in line with the principle announced at the outset, insisting on a common logic among diverse documents identified by the faithful and privileged to form a single system — we therefore may well wonder what actual traits of mind and intellect or doctrine particular here and nowhere else, traits manifest in the writings themselves, validate the premise that the whole holds together.

All future study of the normative outcome of the formative age of Rabbinic Judaism depends upon the result. The blatant failures of prior accounts of the theology of the Oral Torah leave no doubt that theological investigation of the intellectual properties of the Oral Torah must demand the first priority in the study of Rabbinic Judaism. If we are to know more than how to paraphrase what the sources say, we shall have to understand more than we now do about the category-formations that will govern the work, the locations at which these categories are set forth and given definition, and the proportions and balance of the system as a whole that these categories comprise. If now we plan also to analyze, explain, and interpret the message, not merely this saying or that story read in no larger context, if we hope to identify the intellectual context of the textual allegation, if we intend to compare and contrast what we find on a given topic of religious thought in one text in its context with what we find in another in its setting — for all systematic work that awaits we have now to describe the context in rationality and encompassing logic that forms the matrix for all of the texts. That defines what is at stake in the study of the theology of the Oral Torah.

We come then to the book at hand. Here I set forth only a first word, a prolegomenon, on the systematic description of the theological structure of Rabbinic Judaism in its formative authoritative documents, from the first to the seventh century. I mean to make possible a sequence of particular studies of the main beams of the structure, their position in, and proportion of, the whole. These studies will move beyond my now-completed analytical, diachronic, and historical reading of the documents of the Oral Torah[13] and undertake a synthetic, synchronic, and descriptive, reconstructive theological one, as is clear. The plan and program of the book may be spelled out in a few simple statements. The first three chapters set the stage, and the next five form the shank of the book. The order of the chapters is dictated by the logic of the argument that the book is meant to advance, start to finish. I could not have dealt with any subject at any point in the exposition other than the point at which it occurs. But there is a constant interchange between one exposition and another, for while I set forth three distinct methodological approaches, each responding to the character of a different type of evidence, the approaches recapitulate the main premises of one another and sustain a single reading of the whole. If I had to summarize my problem, it is: how does the Oral

---

[13] The final statement of the results is in *The Transformation of Judaism. From Philosophy to Religion.* Champaign, 1992: University of Illinois Press.

Torah find its natural position within "the one whole Torah of Moses, our rabbi." But that problem will become clear only in context.

Chapters One through Three place the inquiry into historical and methodological context. Beginning with a diachronic reading of the documents of the Oral Torah, so setting the theological problem into its historical context, Chapter One describes the documentary history of ideas of the Oral Torah. Recapitulating a long series of monographs devoted to the documentary history of particular ideas, e.g., on the Messiah, on the definition of "Israel," on virtue, on the image of God, I spell out the main intellectual traits of the documents of the Oral Torah that come to light when these are read in their ordinal (and temporal) sequence. These documentary-historical stages I characterize overall, diachronically, as first philosophical, then religious, and finally theological, terms that are carefully defined in context. Accordingly, the chapter is meant to place into historical perspective the entire problem of synchronically describing the systematic theology that finds expression in the documents severally and jointly. I cannot conceive of a theological study that does not build upon a prior, historical inquiry: first we find out how in sequence things took shape, then to see them as a logical whole without regard to the accidents of history we ask how they hold together.

Chapter Two then spells out the issue of theology, why we should pursue the problem, what is at stake, and what obstacles stand in the way. I point to why the matter proves urgent even in the context of contemporary social and religious discourse: the issue of speaking in the name not of this isolated sage or that anonymous saying but of "Judaism," the religion.

Chapter Three carries us to the outer frontiers of the theological problem as presently construed. I address the two important efforts to answer the theological question and why they failed. I choose for that exercise the only truly original and important minds to take up the theology of Rabbinic Judaism as a labor of description, George Foot Moore and Ephraim E. Urbach. Here I review the problems that Moore and Urbach failed to solve. Of the two and all the other scholars of Rabbinic Judaism to offer a systematic statement of the whole, Urbach is the only one with an authentic mastery of the sources in their own language(s) (Hebrew, Aramaic) and (more to the point) in their original intellectual context. Unlike all the others — whether Schürer and Strack in German or Bonsirven in French or E. P. Sanders and Moore in English, Urbach could actually read a page of the Talmud. The best the others have done has been to pick out relevant sayings and paraphrase them, ignoring questions of the native category and context altogether. I ignore other, perhaps ephemerally-prominent accounts of Rabbinic theology, whether in French, German, Hebrew, or English, because I find them either derivative and mere exercises in paraphrase of other peoples' work, or simply impressionistic and ignorant, lacking depth of knowledge of the sources, relying upon examples that allegedly stand for we know not what, or both.

After the systematic introductory exposition, given in Chapters One through Three, I set forth my three distinct approaches to theological description. These are, first, the investigation of paradigms set forth as building blocks in specific documents, explained in Chapters Four, Five, and Six; second, the identification of systematic composites that define native-categories and even set forth propositions pertinent thereto, in Chapter Seven; and third, the definition of modes of symbolic discourse that, I maintain, are carried on in some of the documents as well, spelled out in Chapter Eight.

Of the shank of the book, Chapters Four through Eight, only Chapters Four through Six require a word of explanation. Chapter Four forms the methodological center of the book, my solution to the problem of theological description of the documents of the Oral Torah. This is spelled out in context. I define what I mean by paradigm or model or structure (I use the words interchangeably), how I think that category of inquiry functions and why it solves the problem before us.[14] I further spell out why I find in the paradigmatic structure that the documents reveal the keys to the category-formation of Rabbinic Judaism, the locations where specific formations are fully articulated in their classical formulation, and the proportions of the whole provided by each of these principal parts. Chapter Five then defines the method I use to point out the basic paradigms of a document, and Chapter Six executes the method for one document. Here, then, I show how I propose to define and identify governing paradigms in a given document.

The method I spell out in those three chapters (so tightly linked in conception that ideally they would form a single, simple chapter on its own) finds its bases in the character of the documents, seen in three measures, first, one by one, second, in their connections, and all at once, that is, as autonomous statements. I explain how the documents are to be read not only as statements unto themselves or statements that intersect or connect, but as a single continuous statement. The solution works out the logic of that three-dimensional reading of the sources as it pertains to [1] the construction of the correct category-formation, [2] the identification of the location of the data pertinent to the definition of a given theological category and its doctrine, and [3] the formation of a judgment on the place and proportion of a given category-formation within the structure of Rabbinic Judaic theology seen whole.

---

[14] I first invoked the category, "paradigm," in my *The Presence of the Past, the Pastness of the Present. History, Time, and Paradigm in Rabbinic Judaism.* Bethesda, 1996: CDL Press, and here I revise and recast part of the exposition of that work in order to expand the range of the concept. As is clear, as the context requires, I use, also, such words as model and system, and, in context, may speak of logic, reason, or rationality, all alluding to the same traits of mind and intellect that I claim to uncover in the documents. Chapter Six recasts some of the results of that work in this much larger framework.

Chapter Seven takes up the counterpart problem, for the halakhic sector, of identifying locations at which important theological expositions take place, at the same time addressing the issue of divining the logic of making connections and drawing conclusions. Chapter Eight, as is clear, addresses another kind of logic, the kind that emerges in symbolic discourse; here too the issue resolves itself into a study of how one thing connects to another and the lessons that the rules for making connections teach. I conclude with some appropriately brief remarks on a program of future inquiry into the theology of the Oral Torah: what can we now do that we could not do before, and how should we do it?[15]

While fundamentally new, this exercise in theory and method draws upon completed studies and established results of mine. That is because I work on a long trajectory, over formidable continuities of cumulative reflection and on-going self-criticism. In the nature of such an approach to a career of learning, each major project of mine therefore builds and improves on its predecessors, recasting established data and vastly revising prior approaches to problems that now appear in a fresh context, using established results in a new way. This tripartite way of framing approaches to solving the theological question is fundamentally new, but it continues a number of distinct lines of research of the past. Only one chapter is merely recapitulative, and one is entirely fresh. The former is my characterization of the documentary history of the Rabbinic Judaism in Chapter One, which summarizes the summaries of a sizable sequence of studies that are set forth in *The Transformation of Judaism. From Philosophy to Religion*;[16] *Rabbinic Judaism. The Documentary History of the Formative Age*;[17] and *Introduction to Rabbinic Literature*.[18] In my view readers will want to place the theological inquiry, which is by its nature synchronic, within its diachronic setting, and that work has been done in the specified summaries.[19] Chapter Two is entirely fresh. Chapter Three goes over my critique of Moore set forth in a systematic way and in proper context

---

[15] Once I am satisfied with the method I have devised, I shall exploit it in a series of systematic expositions of the principal paradigmatic structures of Rabbinic Judaism in its formative age and will then portray them whole and complete. That will constitute the entire statement that I can set forth of Rabbinic Judaism as a religious system of the social order.

[16] Champaign, 1992: University of Illinois Press.

[17] Bethesda, 1994: CDL Press.

[18] N.Y., 1994: Doubleday. The Doubleday Anchor Reference Library.

[19] In other work, not taken into account here, I argue that the Talmud of Babylonia made the definitive theological statement of the Oral Torah. See in particular *Judaism States its Theology: The Talmudic Re-Presentation*. Atlanta, 1993: Scholars Press for South Florida Studies in the History of Judaism. This work rests on a number of supporting monographs, especially *The Bavli's Unique Voice. A Systematic Comparison of the Talmud of Babylonia and the Talmud of the Land of Israel*. Atlanta, 1993: Scholars Press for South Florida Studies in the History of Judaism, in seven volumes. See also *The Bavli's One Voice: Types and Forms of Analytical Discourse and their Fixed Order of Appearance*. Atlanta, 1991:

in my *Judaism. The Evidence of the Mishnah*.;[20] and of Urbach in essays beginning in the mid-1970s. I reread chapters of Urbach's *Sages* in thinking through the present exercise and found that my memory understated the full intellectual vulgarity of his work; this I demonstrate in context.

Resting on considerable research as to the facts and prior reflection on their meaning, the three approaches to theological description have each come to preliminary, generally incomplete formulation, none in the present systematic context. Chapters Four through Six recast and greatly expand the notion of paradigm that I came upon and set forth in a much more limited framework in *The Presence of the Past, the Pastness of the Present. History, Time, and Paradigm in Rabbinic Judaism*.[21] I did not then realize the documentary dimensions of the notion of theological paradigms that I now claim form the heart of the Rabbinic system. Chapter Six draws upon the translation and introduction set forth in a sequence of systematic studies. These are *Ruth Rabbah. An Analytical Translation*,[22] and *The Midrash Compilations of the Sixth and Seventh Centuries: An Introduction to the Rhetorical Logical, and Topical Program. III. Ruth Rabbah*,[23] and the outline and analysis of the document presented in *The Components of the Rabbinic Documents: From the Whole to the Parts*. Volume III. *Ruth Rabbah*,[24] and finally in *The Documentary Form-History of Rabbinic Literature* V. *The Aggadic Sector: Song of Songs Rabbah, Ruth Rabbah, Lamentations Rabbati, and Esther Rabbah I*.[25] For its facts Chapter Seven depends upon the complete, analytical outlines of the

---

Scholars Press for South Florida Studies in the History of Judaism; *The Bavli's One Statement. The Metapropositional Program of Babylonian Talmud Tractate Zebahim Chapters One and Five*. Atlanta, 1991: Scholars Press for South Florida Studies in the History of Judaism' *How the Bavli Shaped Rabbinic Discourse*. Atlanta, 1991: Scholars Press for South Florida Studies in the History of Judaism; *The Law Behind the Laws. The Bavli's Essential Discourse*. Atlanta, 1992: Scholars Press for South Florida Studies in the History of Judaism; *The Bavli's Intellectual Character. The Generative Problematic in Bavli Baba Qamma Chapter One and Bavli Shabbat Chapter One*. Atlanta, 1992: Scholars Press for South Florida Studies in the History of Judaism; *Decoding the Talmud's Exegetical Program: From Detail to Principle in the Bavli's Quest for Generalization. Tractate Shabbat*. Atlanta, 1992: Scholars Press for South Florida Studies in the History of Judaism.But upon further reflection I have concluded that to limit the theological inquiry to the authoritative Talmud would exclude vast bodies of pertinent data and frame the question in an altogether too narrow and literary framework. That accounts for my recasting of matters in terms of paradigms and models and self-evident systems of classification, covering all of the documents.

[20] Chicago, 1981: University of Chicago Press.
[21] Bethesda, 1996: CDL Press.
[22] Atlanta, 1989: Scholars Press for Brown Judaic Studies.
[23] Atlanta, 1990: Scholars Press for Brown Judaic Studies.
[24] Atlanta, 1997: Scholars Press for South Florida Studies in the History of Judaism.
[25] Atlanta, 1997: Scholars Press for South Florida Studies in the History of Judaism.

Talmud of Babylonia that I published in *The Talmud of Babylonia. A Complete Outline,*[26] and then recapitulated in *Rationality and Structure: The Bavli's Anomalous Juxtapositions.*[27] Chapter Eight revises for the present purpose some of the findings of *Symbol and Theology in Early Judaism;*[28] here too the documentary framework places the earlier thought in a new perspective. But after Chapter One, because of the issue raised here for the first time, everything is either new or renewed in this fresh context.

The next phase of the work, as will be self-evident at the end of the final chapter, will take the form of a grammar, which I plan as follows:

A Theological Grammar of the Oral Torah.
I. *Vocabulary: Native Categories*
II. *Syntax: Constructions and Connections*
III. *Semantic Rubrics: Models of Explanation and Anticipation.*

That trilogy will then be followed by *The Theology of the Oral Torah.* Each project presents its own challenges and surprises.

I consulted a number of colleagues in the field of theology in general, and Patristic theology in particular, on how in other, kindred religious systems the same problem of systematic description of theology. I had thought that scholars of Patristics might already have found solutions to the problems of continuity, structure, and coherence, as a common theology might emerge among the writings of the Church Fathers in Greek, Latin, or Syriac. Though the character of the writings is different from the ones I examine — most are attributed to individuals, and most of these produced philosophically articulate theologies, with the logic clear and often explicit, I supposed that asking how the whole cohered — other than through creed and liturgy — co-workers in Patristic theology, historically described, might have found the way. So I solicited the guidance of a number of colleagues in kindred fields. Professors Maurice Wiles, Brevard S. Childs, William Shea, and Schubert Ogden were prompt in replying with their learning and wisdom, which, in reading over the years, I have come highly to value. Professor (and Dean) F. M. Young, University of Birmingham, wrote a long and exceptionally helpful letter, giving her sense for what is required for Patristic theology, which perspective I greatly value. She also was kind enough to send a copy of her lecture at the 1996 Oxford Patristic Conference, "From Suspicion and Sociology to Spirituality: on Method, Hermeneutics, and Appropriation with Respect to Patristic Material," a systematic reading of Torrance's *Trinitarian Faith.* In all, I found colleagues in Patristic and

---

[26] Atlanta, 1995-6: Scholars Press for *USF Academic Commentary Series.*

[27] Atlanta, 1997: Scholars Press for South Florida Studies in the History of Judaism.

[28] Minneapolis, 1991: Fortress Press.

Christianity theological studies in general to be remarkably generous with their learning and wisdom and eager to help a colleague in a neighboring field.

Alas, what I learned from the best in the English-speaking world in active Patristic and other theological studies was that models for what I hope to accomplish have not presented themselves in the kindred study of Christianity. It was clear from the correspondence that the problems I address find close counterparts across the border. Whether the character of the evidence sustains the kind of studies I propose here, and whether the methods I propose may in some way serve in the counterpart field, seems to me premature to assess. At this moment, so it seems to me, histories of doctrine inclusive of creeds, monographs on the theological system of this figure or that do not correspond to what I seek to find out. And my old and dear friend, Professor Brevard Childs, I was warned away from searching for models in Biblical Theology, which has tried to link within a single framework books that in no way correspond in their social foundations and perceived traits of intellectual coherence to the Rabbinic writings. So I find myself, as has often been the case in the past, pretty much on my own, but also among friends.

Perhaps the remarkably cogent character of the Rabbinic corpus renders the project feasible (so I suppose), while the diverse types of authorities, languages and cultures, and modes of thought and religious experience represented by the corpus of Scripture, on the one side, and Patristic writing, on the other, can never accommodate an account of a counterpart character. But those who were kind enough to counsel me unanimously affirmed that the work of councils and the formation of creeds do not constitute the equivalent of the sustaining paradigmatic structure that I here allege to have characterized the Rabbinic corpus. Whether my proposals help them solve problems in the theological description of catholic and orthodox Christianity in its formative age I cannot say. Professor David Satran, Hebrew University, listened patiently to my exposition and called my attention to Gerhart B. Ladner, *God, Cosmos, and Humankind. The World of Early Christian Symbolism* (Berkeley, 1995: University of California Press, and gave valuable and stimulating advice as well. It was in conversation with him that I realized Chapters Seven and Eight would be required and that Chapters Four through Six would not suffice.

As on nearly every systematic project I undertake, I found uncommonly helpful the observations of Professor William S. Green, with special reference to the other-than-canonical category that applies to the books of the Oral Torah.

Finally, I consulted at some length with Professor Donald Akenson, Queens University, editor of McGill-Queens University Press, on the present project, the planned *Grammar,* and the projected Theology, and I found him a remarkably astute counsel and critic.

My academic appointments as Distinguished Research Professor of Religious Studies at the University of South Florida, Tampa, and as Professor of Religion at Bard College, sustain all of my research activities. I am grateful for the opportunities for learning and teaching afforded by both remarkable centers of academic study of religion. My colleagues in Tampa and St. Petersburg and in Annandale-on-Hudson — teachers and friends — define a cordial and happy context for my work. I am glad to point, also, to students at both USF and Bard whom I have found stimulating and interesting.

JACOB NEUSNER
UNIVERSITY OF SOUTH FLORIDA, TAMPA
AND
BARD COLLEGE
ANNANDALE-ON-HUDSON, NEW YORK

I

The Documentary History of the Oral Torah

I. WHAT, EXACTLY, IS THE ORAL TORAH?

The Oral (part of the) Torah is comprised by a vast and voluminous corpus of documents of tradition that is set forth in addition to, and in completion of, Scripture. These are, by title, only a score in all, but in the original Hebrew and Aramaic or in English translation they cover many thousands of pages in print. Each title identifies a massive book; the Oral Torah contains little that is brief and nothing that is perfunctory.

To grasp the sheer volume of the whole, take the legal corpus, for example. The Mishnah, a philosophical law code is divided into sixty-two tractates, subdivided into more than five hundred and fifty chapters, averaging ten or more paragraphs of several hundred words; the Talmud of the Land of Israel subjects thirty-nine of these tractates to a minute, clause by clause inspections, the Talmud of Babylonia does the same for thirty-seven, each Talmud making its own selection of tractates for analysis. The second Talmud also amasses a huge corpus of topical miscellanies, large-scale compilations of free-standing compositions and even composites devoted to a single general theme — all in addition to its systematic exegetical and analytical work. A collection of supplementary legal sayings not included in the Mishnah but enjoying high standing, the Tosefta alone in volume competes in size with the Bible, Old and New Testaments together.

The mere outline of the Talmud of Babylonia that I made covers eight volumes of several hundred pages each, and that of only three-fourths of the Talmud of the Land of Israel, the second, third, and fourth divisions, a somewhat more elaborate outline, requires the same number of volumes. The outline that I made of the principal Midrash-compilation fills thirty-two volumes.[1] Genesis Rabbah

---

[1] *The Talmud of The Land of Israel.. An Outline of the Second, Third, and Fourth Divisions.* Atlanta, 1995-6: Scholars Press for South Florida Studies in the History of Judaism, in eight volumes; *The Talmud of Babylonia. A Complete Outline.* Atlanta, 1995-6: Scholars Press for *USF Academic Commentary Series,* in eight volumes; *The Two Talmuds Compared.*

devotes one hundred chapters to the exposition of the book of Genesis. Leviticus Rabbah sets forth thirty-seven systematic demonstrations of propositions, each in several thousand words. And so the numbers mount up.

To estimate the sheer volume of the authoritative writings of Rabbinic Judaism in the formative age, it suffices to state that my English translation of the corpus nearly whole — the Mishnah, tractate Abot, the Tosefta, the thirty-nine tractates of the Talmud of the Land of Israel, thirty-five of the thirty-seven of the Talmud of Babylonia, the Mekhilta Attributed to R. Ishmael, Sifra (three large books in English), Sifré to Numbers, Sifré to Deuteronomy (three hundred and fifty-seven chapters), Genesis Rabbah (three large books in English), Leviticus Rabbah, Pesiqta deRab Kahana (two volumes in English), Song of Songs Rabbah, Lamentations Rabbati, Esther Rabbah I, Ruth Rabbah, and Abot deRabbi Nathan — requires more than one hundred and ten megabytes. So we take up a mighty and complex writing.

The whole then forms the initial transcription of what Rabbinic Judaism calls the Oral or memorized (part of the) Torah revealed by God to our rabbi, Moses, at Mount Sinai. Why invoke the word Torah, and why introduce the matter of the traditional medium, oral or memorized? The definitive and indicative myth of Rabbinic Judaism requires that we do so. That is because, viewed all together, in line with the foundation-story of Rabbinic Judaism ("the Judaism of the dual Torah, oral and written"), that at Sinai the Torah was revealed by God to Moses, called "our rabbi" as a sage and model for all sages in the future, in two media, writing and memory, these documents enjoy the status of "Torah." They are universally held to constitute the oral part of that revelation. Moses wrote down the the written part, memorized and orally formulated and orally transmitted the other half. From Moses to the sages of late antiquity a chain of tradition stretched forward unbroken. So the teachings of the sages who took their place in the chain of oral tradition from Sinai ultimately reached written form in completed writings, which I call interchangeably documents or books.

These stretch out from the first document, beyond Scripture, of Rabbinic Judaism, the Mishnah, which reached closure at ca. 200 C.E., through the Talmud of Babylonia, concluded at ca. 600 C.E. Of those writings, the Mishnah alone stands on its own, setting forth its propositions as free-standing syllogisms, a systematic exercise in *Listenwissenschaft*. The Mishnah then does not take the form of a commentary. But all the others are presented as commentaries. These fall into two sectors, the one on norms of behavior or halakhah (law), the other on norms of belief or aggadah (lore). The Mishnah is subject to exegesis, in one form

---

Atlanta, 1995-6: Scholars Press for South Florida Studies in the History of Judaism, in thirteen volumes; and, for the Midrash-compilations, *The Components of the Rabbinic Documents: From the Whole to the Parts. Sifra.* Atlanta, 1997: Scholars Press for South Florida Studies in the History of Judaism, in thirty-two volumes.

or another, in the Tosefta, ca. 300, Talmud of the Land of Israel, ca. 400, and the Talmud of Babylonia, ca. 600.

Selected books of Scripture, particularly those prominent in synagogue liturgy, the Pentateuch and the Five Scrolls, are subjected to exegesis, whether conventional or propositional, in Sifra, to Leviticus, Sifré to Numbers, Sifré to Deuteronomy, Genesis Rabbah, Leviticus Rabbah, Song of Songs Rabbah, Ruth Rabbah, Lamentations Rabbati, and Esther Rabbah I. A compilation organized in exegesis of passages or themes of the synagogue's lectionary cycle, Pesiqta deRab Kahana, follows suit.

A small corpus of two books, tractate Abot and its talmud, Abot deRabbi Nathan ("The Fathers," "The Fathers According to Rabbi Nathan"), sets forth teachings of sages and, in the latter, exemplary stories about sages.

When did the documents of the Oral Torah come to closure? Three principal periods delineate the sequence of completed writings, the Mishnah's, in the first two centuries, concluded at ca. 200 C.E.; the Yerushalmi's, in the next, ca. 200-400; and the Bavli's, in the third, ca. 400-600. The high points of the former come with tractate Abot which is the Mishnah's first apologetic, ca. 250, the Tosefta, a collection of supplements ca. 300 C.E., the Talmud of the Land of Israel ca. 400 C.E., followed by the Babylonian Talmud. The exegetical compilations on the Pentateuch involve Exodus, in Mekhilta attributed to R. Ishmael and of indeterminate date, Sifra on Leviticus, Sifré on Numbers, and another Sifré, on Deuteronomy, all at a guess to be dated at ca. 300 C.E. The second period, that of the Yerushalmi, encompasses also Genesis Rabbah ca. 400 C.E., Leviticus Rabbah ca. 425 C.E., and at the end, Pesiqta de Rab Kahana. The third period, that of the Talmud of Babylonia, covers also Lamentations Rabbah, Song of Songs Rabbah, Esther Rabbah I, and Ruth Rabbah.

These documents, all together, form the Oral Torah as it had reached its statement at the end of late antiquity, on the eve of the advent of Islam. So in both volume and importance, the Oral Torah establishes a formidable presence in the history of the Judaism that appeals for its authoritative writings to Scripture and to the documents under consideration here and the writings that flow from them both. Indeed, within the Judaism that privileges these documents, the oral part of the Torah exercises decisive authority, its reading of the written part of the Torah determining the sense and standing of Scripture itself.

How is this claim that the teachings of the sages originated in a chain of oral formulation and oral transmission? It is the Mishnah in particular in behalf of which that claim is explicitly advanced. That is in two forms. First, the claim that the Mishnah derived from teachings transmitted by God to Moses at Sinai is implicit in the opening chapter of Mishnah-tractate Abot, which commences, "Moses received Torah at Sinai and handed it on to Joshua, Joshua to elders, and elders to prophets. And prophets handed it on to the men of the great assembly" (M. Abot 1:1) and concludes, in listing links in the chain of tradition, with authorities prominent in the Mishnah itself. What is alleged by linking the Mishnah's sages to Sinai in a chain of tradition then is obvious. The chain of tradition is comprised by the following names: Simeon the Righteous, Antigonos of Sokho, Yosé b. Yoezer, Yosé b. Yohanan of Jerusalem , Joshua b. Perahiah , Nittai the Arbelite , Judah b. Tabbai , Simeon b. Shatah , Shemaiah , Abtalion , Hillel , Shammai , Rabban Gamaliel , and Rabban Simeon b. Gamaliel. The key names are Hillel and Shammai, Gamaliel and Simeon b. Gamaliel; the latter are attested in Acts and in writings of Josephus, respectively. All four figure in important legal passages of the Mishnah, with Hillel and Shammai and the schools thereof playing major roles in numerous tractates. Their disciples then are principals of the Mishnah, some of them also named individually, e.g., Rabban Yohanan ben Zakkai, master of the authorities who figure in the age beyond the destruction of the Temple, such as Eliezer and Joshua, teaches of Aqiba, who taught Meir, Judah, Simeon, and others to whom the shank of the Mishnah is attributed. The clear connection to Sinai and its revelation of the Torah alleged in behalf of the contents of the Mishnah is therefore contained in these names, set forth as a chain reaching forward from God's revelation to Moses.

But more than this implicit claim, that the Mishnah itself is worded as God worded matters for Moses is explicitly spelled out in the following:[2]

> **I.43**   A.   *Our rabbis have taught on Tannaite authority:*
>
> B.   What is the order of Mishnah teaching? Moses learned it from the mouth of the All-Powerful. Aaron came in, and Moses repeated his chapter to him and Aaron went forth and sat at the left hand of Moses. His sons came in and Moses repeated their chapter to them, and his sons went forth. Eleazar sat at the right of Moses, and Itamar at the left of Aaron.
>
> C.   R. Judah says, "At all times Aaron was at the right hand of Moses."

---

[2] Following the procedures fully exposed in my systematic academic commentaries, I indent what I deem to be secondary or otherwise marginal to the initial allegation of a statement, and I further indent the later glosses and the like, so showing the lines of structure and order of the Talmudic and Midrashic discourses. These are *The Talmud of Babylonia. An Academic Commentary.* Atlanta, 1994-6: Scholars Press for *USF Academic Commentary Series*; *The Talmud of the Land of Israel. An Academic Commentary to the Second, Third, and Fourth Divisions.* Atlanta, 1998: Scholars Press for *USF Academic Commentary Series;* and *The Components of the Rabbinic Documents: From the Whole to the Parts.* Atlanta, 1997: Scholars Press for South Florida Studies in the History of Judaism. All citations of Rabbinic literature in this book are taken from these commentaries worked out through visual markings.

D. Then the elders entered, and Moses repeated for them their Mishnah chapter. The elders went out. Then the whole people came in, and Moses repeated for them their Mishnah chapter. So it came about that Aaron repeated the lesson four times, his sons three times, the elders two times, and all the people once.

E. Then Moses went out, and Aaron repeated his chapter for them. Aaron went out. His sons repeated their chapter. His sons went out. The elders repeated their chapter. So it turned out that everybody repeated the same chapter four times.

F. On this basis said R. Eliezer, "A person is liable to repeat the lesson for his disciple four times. And it is an argument a fortiori: If Aaron, who studied from Moses himself, and Moses from the Almighty —so in the case of a common person who is studying with a common person, all the more so!"

G. R. Aqiba says, "How on the basis of Scripture do we know that a person is obligated to repeat a lesson for his disciple until he learns it [however many times that takes]? As it is said, 'And you teach it to the children of Israel' (Deut. 31:19). And how do we know that that is until it will be well ordered in their mouth? 'Put it in their mouths' (Deut. 31:19). And how on the basis of Scripture do we know that he is liable to explain the various aspects of the matter? 'Now these are the ordinances which you shall put before them' (Ex. 31:1)."

I.44 A. *So why shouldn't everybody learn directly from Moses?*

B. It was so as to pay honor to Aaron and his sons and honor to the elders.

C. *Then why not have Aaron go in and learn from Moses, then his sons may go in and learn from Aaron, then the elders may go in and learn from his sons, and these in the end will teach all Israel?*

D. *Since Moses had learned from the mouth of the All-Powerful, the matter would work out better that way.*

BAVLI ERUBIN 54B

From the clear claim that the Mishnah derives from oral formulation and oral transmission of teachings in memory — hence formed "the Torah that is memorized" — came the classification "Oral Torah," which encompassed all of the authoritative documents produced by the same authorities who stood in the line of tradition from Sinai, their disciples, and the disciples of their disciples, through to the closure of the Talmud of Babylonia, the final and authoritative statement of the Judaism of the dual Torah, oral and written, that took shape in the first six centuries of the Common Era.

But that claim explains little about the other books of the collection. It suffices to allege that sages who stand in the chain of tradition to Sinai, that is, who have acquired their knowledge through discipleship to a master within that tradition, then are held to teach the Torah too, deriving, if not the particular law or saying, then the basic principle embodied in the concrete teaching, from that same chain of tradition. Quite how all of the documents, with their innumerable attributions of statements to sages of the first six centuries C.E., in every detail derive from oral tradition at Sinai need not detain us.

Nor do we need to dwell upon the anomaly that that single tradition of Sinai produced conflicting opinions on most topics, whether of law or of theology. The Talmuds and other compilations systematically show how the law may be derived by exegesis from the written Torah of Sinai (an implicit rejection of the claim that the Mishnah's law enjoys an autonomous standing, not deriving from exegesis at all). Conflicts of tradition or opinion in the exegetical literature are systematically harmonized or otherwise sorted out. But what is important is the consequence of the foundation-myth, which is, imputing the status of Torah-teaching to all statements, all collections of statements, all documents, wherever and however they originated, equally form normative statements of the Torah of Sinai.

The result of the Torah-myth not only validates, but makes necessary, this inquiry into the governing theological system. For each statement on the face of matters enjoys the same status, as to truth, as all of the others. None can be dismissed as enjoying lesser status, and every single statement has to be validated by appeal to a common criterion of truth: revelation by God to Rabbi Moses. That is why, on principle a sentence selected from one document on a given subject may intersect with one chosen from another document on the same subject, and both together contribute to a single picture of said subject. That conviction, characteristic of Judaic sages from the closure of the writings at hand to our own day, signals the certainty that the whole coheres. The sages of Judaism thereby testify to their conviction that theologically cogent positions — norms of belief, norms of behavior expressive of belief — unite the entire representation of the Torah, start to finish. On that basis, the inquiry into the theological coherence of the whole finds ample justification in the attitudes of the masters of the tradition and those faithful to it.

Not only so, but when we come to the substance of matters, an inner logic pertains as well. Since God cannot contradict himself, and since our sages exhibit ample acumen to detect disharmonies of thought and discontinuities of logic, the foundation-myth takes as its premise that a single coherent theology animates the whole. The claim that sages hunt out inconsistency finds its demonstration on nearly every page of the Talmud of Babylonia, which is sages' ultimate and definitive statement of the system whole and complete, both parts of the Torah, oral and rewritten, being recapitulated in its pages. So the generative question concerning the inner logos of the whole is provoked by the character of the literature and its reception over time. What makes answering the question difficult is the manifest contradiction and illogic that even a quick examination of the sayings on any given topic discerns. So much for the definition of the Oral Torah and its fundamental principles.

II. THE DOCUMENTARY HISTORY OF IDEAS

The documents that set forth the Oral Torah are to be read not only synthetically but also diachronically, not only systematically, as the statements of a single coherent system, but also analytically and therefore historically, in temporally-determinate phases. When the Oral Torah is dismantled and its parts are read diachronically and analytically, in the order in which the documents are assumed to have come to closure, there emerges a clear picture of the way in which the theological ideas of Rabbinic Judaism unfolded over time and in diverse circumstances. So we now ask, if we read the documents one by one in the temporal sequence of closure, start to finish, what sort of history of the ideas that comprise the theology of the Oral Torah emerges? It is the documentary history of the formation of Judaism.

The documentary history of the ideas of a religious system, through close attention to the intellectual circumstance and political context in which writing reached closure, relates the sequence of writings to the religious system(s) set forth therein as these unfold through time. It is accomplished, specifically, by assessing shifts exhibited by the mythic, symbolic, or even doctrinal indicative traits of a sequence of documents. The sequence is established by appealing, in explaining those shifts, to the generally accepted dates assigned to the closure of writings. In this way we may confront questions of cultural order, social system and political structure, settings to which the texts respond explicitly and constantly. For in Rabbinic literature we deal with writings that set forth an account of how the Jews are to constitute the Israel of which Scripture speaks, forming a kingdom of priests and a holy people. In that context, confronting writings of a religious character, we err by asking questions of a narrowly historical character: what did X really say on a particular occasion, and why. These questions not only are not answerable on the basis of the evidence in hand. They also are trivial, irrelevant to the character of the evidence, marginal to its manifest focus of interest. Even if we were to concede the historical accuracy and veracity of all the many allegations about what sages said and did, how little we should know — but how much we should have missed — if that set of questions and answers as to historical veracity were to encompass the whole of our inquiry![3]

If we are to trace the unfolding, in the sources of formative Judaism, of a given theme or ideas on a given problem, the order in which we approach the several books, that is, components of the entire corpus of official writings, gives us the sole guidance on sequence, order, and context, that we are apt to find. I know no way of demonstrating that authorities to whom, in a given composition, ideas are attributed really said what is assigned to them. A fair amount of evidence, in both the Tosefta and the two Talmuds, indicates otherwise, as reasons of logic require attributing to a given named authority not what is initially assigned to him but exactly the opposite opinion. Not only so, but sayings attributed to one authority in a given document are attached to the name of a different authority in another document. It follows that, assuming without corroboration that we have *ipssissima verba* merely because a saying is attached to a name not only contradicts the basic premises of all contemporary historical scholarship but also violates the character of the evidence before us. The writings in hand may assign the same saying to two or more authorities, explicitly invent a saying and impute it to a given authority, ignore considerations of anachronism in making up stories, recast a received saying and re-frame its main point in response to a problem of logic or disharmony, or otherwise show profound unconcern to issues of historical truth, narrowly framed.

What we cannot show we do not know. Lacking firm evidence, for example, in a sage's own, clearly assigned writings, or even in writings redacted by a sage's own disciples and handed on among them in the discipline of their own community, we have for chronology only a single fact. It is that a document, reaching closure at a given time, contains the allegation that Rabbi X said statement Y. So we know that people at the time that the document reached closure took the view that Rabbi X said statement Y. We may then assign to statement Y a position, in the order of the sequence of sayings, defined by the location of the document in the order of the sequence of documents. The several documents' dates, as is clear, all constitute guesses. But the sequence based on internal evidence that places the Mishnah before the Tosefta, the Tosefta before the Yerushalmi, and the Yerushalmi Bavli for the exegetical writings on the Mishnah is absolutely firm and beyond doubt. The sequence for the exegetical collections on Scripture, Sifra, the Sifrés, Genesis Rabbah, Leviticus Rabbah, the Pesiqtas and beyond is not entirely sure. Still the position of the Sifra and the two Sifrés at the head, followed by Genesis Rabbah,

---

[3] I spell out these matters in *Reading and Believing: Ancient Judaism and Contemporary Gullibility*. Atlanta, 1986: Scholars Press for Brown Judaic Studies. The contrary view is that we have historical knowledge that comes to us a priori. That position is explicitly adopted by critics of mine, which proves that the points made here are not commonplace at all.

then Leviticus Rabbah, then Pesiqta deR. Kahana and Lamentations Rabbati and some related collections, seems highly likely.

If we lay out these writings in the approximate sequence in which — according to the prevailing consensus — they reached closure, we gain "documentary history of ideas." This is, specifically, the order of the appearance of ideas when the documents, read in the outlined sequence, address a given idea or topic. The consequent history consists of the sequence in which a given statement on the topic at hand was made (early, middle, or late) in the unfolding of the Rabbinical writings. To illustrate the process, what does the authorship of the Mishnah have to say on the theme? Then how does the compositor of Abot deal with it? Then the Tosefta's compositor's record comes into view, followed by the materials assembled in the Talmud of the Land of Israel, alongside those now found in the earlier and middle ranges of compilations of scriptural exegeses, and as always, the Talmud of Babylonia at the end.[4]

So, in sum, this story of continuity and change rests upon the notion that we can present the history of the treatment of a topical program in the official writings of that Judaism. I do not claim that the documents represent the state of popular or synagogue opinion. I do not know whether the history of the idea in the unfolding official texts corresponds to the history of the idea as it was maintained among the people who stand behind those documents. Even less do I claim to speak about the history of the topic or idea at hand outside of Rabbinical circles, among the Jewish nation at large. All these larger dimensions of the matter lie wholly beyond the power of that approach to measure. The reason is that the evidence at hand is of a particular sort and hence permits us to investigate one category of questions and not another. The category is defined by established and universally held conventions about the order in which the Rabbinical writings reached completion. Therefore we trace the way in which matters emerge in the sequence of writings followed here.

We trace the way in which ideas were taken up and spelled out in these successive stages in the formation of the official corpus. Let the purpose of the exercise be emphasized. *When we follow this procedure, we discover how, within the formation of the Rabbinical writings, the idea at hand came to literary expression and how it was then shaped to serve the larger purposes of the nascent system as a whole.* By knowing the place and uses of the topic under study within the literary evidences of the Rabbinical system, we gain a better understanding of the formative history of that system. What we do not learn concerns what people were thinking

---

[4] A considerable body of completed work, both by myself and my students and now others as well, illustrates the working of this approach. For a single systematic presentation of the documentary history of an idea and its consequences, I recommend my *Judaism and its Social Metaphors. Israel in the History of Jewish Thought.* N.Y., 1988: Cambridge University Press.

or even what sages had in mind, beyond what they tell us in these writings. About other larger historical and intellectual matters we have no direct knowledge at all. Consequently we claim to report only what we learn about the official literature of a system evidenced b;y a limited factual base. No one who wants to know the history of a given idea in all the diverse Judaisms of late antiquity, or the role of that idea in the history of all the Jews in all parts of the world in the first seven centuries of the Common Era will find it here.

III. THE PUBLIC CHARACTER OF DOCUMENTARY IDEAS AND THE POSSIBILITY OF THEOLOGICAL DESCRIPTION

In order to understand the documentary method and its pertinence, also, to the possibility of theological inquiry into structures and systems, we must again underline the social and political character of the documentary evidence presented. We deal not with what an individual, however authoritative, maintained, but with the sum and substance of consensus: what the entire textual community of sages determined to be worth preserving and handing on as normative. The sources constitute a collective, and therefore official, literature. All of the documents took shape and attained a place in the corpus of documents of the Rabbinical movement as a whole. None was written by an individual in such a way as to testify to personal choice or decision.

Accordingly, we cannot provide an account of the theory of a given individual at a particular time and place. We have numerous references to what a given individual said about the topic at hand.[5] But these references do not reach us in the authorship of that person, or even in his language. They come to us only in the setting of a *collection* of sayings and statements, some associated with names, others unattributed and anonymous. The collections by definition were composed under the auspices of Rabbinical authority — a school or a circle. They tell us what a group of people wished to preserve and hand on as authoritative doctrine about the meaning of the Mishnah and Scripture. The compositions reach us because the larger Rabbinical estate chose to copy and hand them on. Accordingly, we know the state of doctrine at the stages marked by the formation and closure of the several documents. That is what permits us to speak of "Judaism" — that is to say, a theological system and structure. The documents' strength and weakness match. We know little about particular persons and their systems. We know much about the community and its consensus. So the documents allow us to allege that we can

---

[5] I began my scholarly career by working on biographies, *A Life of Yohanan ben Zakkai.* Leiden, 1962: Brill, *Development of a Legend. Studies on the Traditions Concerning Yohanan ben Zakkai.* Leiden, 1970: Brill, *The Rabbinic Traditions about the Pharisees before 70.* Leiden, 1971: Brill. I-III., and finally *Eliezer ben Hyrcanus. The Tradition and the Man.* Leiden, 1973: Brill. I-II. But after a decade I realized that the Rabbinic sources do not yield historical biography in any conventional sense, and I turned to two decades of work on the kind of history that the sources, properly analyzed, do yield.

describe what the entire body of sages set forth as a coherent statement, a rational and coherent system that in their view held together in a cogent and harmonious way.

In the diachronic mode — as distinct from the synchronic one that theology requires but also sustains — we follow the references that we find to a topic in accord with the order of documents just now spelled out. In such a study we learn the order in which ideas came to expression in the official writings. We begin any survey with the Mishnah, the starting point of the writings after Scripture. We proceed systematically to work our way through tractate Abot, the Mishnah's first apologetic, then the Tosefta, the Yerushalmi, and the Bavli at the end. In a single encompassing sweep, we finally deal with the entirety of the compilations of the exegeses of Scripture, arranged in that order that I explained at the beginning of this chapter.

The reason for that stress on the temporal order of closure of the documents is simple. In tracing the order in which ideas make their appearance, we ask about the components in sequence ("history of Judaism") so far as we can trace the sequence. Then and only then shall we have access to issues of *history*, that is, of change and development. If our theme makes its appearance early on in one form, so one set of ideas predominate in a document that reached closure in the beginnings of the writing down of the Oral Torah and then that theme drops out of public discourse or undergoes radical revision in writings in later stages of the corpus of official writings, that fact may make considerable difference. Specifically, we may find it possible to speculate on where, and why a given approach proved urgent, and also on the reasons that that same approach receded from the center of interest.

What do I conceive to be at stake in the documentary history of Judaism? It is to set forth the history of the formation of Judaism, as the Rabbinical writings of late antiquity allow us to trace that history. The ultimate system of Judaism itself formed during those seven centuries in three distinct stages, marked in each case by the distinctive traits of the literature that reached closure at the end of each successive stage, as I shall explain. More to the point, each stage produced a Judaic system. Formed in the first two hundred years and represented by the Mishnah and its associated writings, the first is utterly free standing. The second, taking shape from 200 to 400 and represented by the Talmud of the Land of Israel and its companions, is connected to the first but essentially distinct from it. The third, expressed in documents that reached closure between 400 and 600 within and around the Talmud of Babylonia, is connected to the second but in important traits distinct from it as well. When later on we turn from history to theology of ideas, we reconstitute the whole in yet another manner, from a completely different perspective.

IV. CATEGORY-FORMATION: PHILOSOPHICAL AND RELIGIOUS

Stated in documentary terms, the formative history of Rabbinic Judaism tells a story in three brief paragraphs.

[1] It shows, first, how the Judaic system emerged in the Mishnah, ca. 200 C.E., and its associated Midrash-compilations, ca. 200-300 C.E., as a philosophical structure comprising a politics, philosophy, economics. These categories were defined as philosophers in general understood them: a theory of legitimate violence, an account of knowledge gained through the methods of natural history, and a theory of the rational disposition (and increase) of scarce resources.

[2] This philosophical system then was turned by the Talmud of the Land of Israel and related Midrash-compilations, ca. 400-500 C.E., into a religious system. The system was effected through the formation of counterpart categories: an anti-politics of weakness, an anti-economics of the rational utilization of an infinitely renewable resource, a philosophy of truth revealed rather than rules discovered.[6]

[3] Then, finally, the religious system was restated or re-presented by the Talmud of Babylonia and its companions of Midrash-collection, ca. 500-600 C.E. In those writings it was given theological re-presentation through the recovery of philosophical method for the formulation of religious conceptions. In the great tradition, we may say, the formation of Judaism took place through [3] the final synthesis of [1] the initial thesis and [2] the consequent antithesis. That dialectical, Hegelian pattern helps make sense of the history of religious expression and ideas that the official books of Judaism expose.

Since I have used the terms "philosophy" and "religion" and suggested they be treated as distinct categories of thought, let me now spell out what I mean by "philosophy" and "religion." By "philosophy" I refer to the category-formation, inclusive of categorical definitions, put forth by philosophy in ancient times. By "religion" I refer to the category-formation put forth on a wholly-other-than philosophical basis in that same period. The one is secular and worldly in its data, utilizing the methods of natural history for its analytical work; the other is transcendental, finding its data in revelation, utilizing the methods of the exegesis of revelation for its systematic work. Both are exercises of sustained rationality, in the case of this Judaism, of applied reason and practical logic.

But the one begins in this world and its facts, which are analyzed and categorized through the traits inherent in them, and the other commences in the world above and its truths, which are analyzed and categorized by the categories of

---

[6] The characterization of the first two stages in the formation of Judaism is contained within these books of mine: *The Economics of the Mishnah*. Chicago, 1989: The University of Chicago Press; *Rabbinic Political Theory: Religion and Politics in the Mishnah*. Chicago, 1991: The University of Chicago Press; *Judaism as Philosophy. The Method and Message of the Mishnah*. Columbia, 1991: University of South Carolina Press; and *The Transformation of Judaism. From Philosophy to Religion*. Champaign, 1992: University of Illinois Press.

revelation. The one yields philosophy of religion, the other, religious statements, attitudes, convictions, rules of life; the one represents one way of knowing God, specifically, the way through the data of this world, the other, a different way to God altogether, the way opened by God's revelation and self-manifestation, whether through nature or beyond. Let me now spell out this distinction with reference to the systemic results of a reading of the Mishnah and the Yerushalmi.

The Mishnah set forth in the form of a law code a highly philosophical account of the world ("world-view"), a pattern for everyday and material activities and relationships ("way of life"), and a definition of the social entity ("nation," "people," "us" as against "outsiders," "Israel") that realized that way of life and explained it by appeal to that world-view. We have no difficulty in calling this account of a way of life an economics, because the account of material reality provided by the Mishnah corresponds, point for point, with that given in Aristotle's counterpart. The Mishnah moreover sets forth a politics by dealing with the same questions, about the permanent and legitimate institutions that inflict sanctions, that occupy Greek and Roman political thinkers. There is no economics of another-than-this-worldly character, no politics of an inner "kingdom of God." All is straightforward, worldly, material, and consequential for the everyday world. Then the successor-documents, closed roughly two centuries later, addressed the Mishnah's system and recast its categories into a connected, but also quite revised, one. The character of their reception of the received categories and of their own category-formation, emerging in the contrast between one set of documents and another, justifies invoking the term, "transformation," that is, of one thing into something else. That something else was a religious, as distinct from a philosophical, category-formation.

The first Talmud and associated Midrash-compilations attest to a system that did more than merely extend and recast the categorical structure of the system for which the Mishnah stands. They took over the way of life, world-view, and social entity, defined in the Mishnah's system. And while they rather systematically amplified details, framed a program of exegesis around the requirements of clerks engaged in enforcing the rules of the Mishnah, they built their own system. For at the same time they formed categories corresponding to those of the Mishnah, a politics, a philosophy, an economics. But these categories proved so utterly contrary in their structure and definition to those of the Mishnah that they presented mirror-images of the received categories.

The politics, philosophy, and economics of the Mishnah were joined by the Yerushalmi to an anti-politics, an anti-economics, and an utterly-transformed mode of learning. In the hands of the later sages, the new mode of Torah-study — the definition of what was at stake in studying the Torah — redefined altogether the issues of the intellect. Natural history as the method of classification gave way to a different mode of thought altogether. As a matter of fact the successor-system recast not the issues so much as the very stakes of philosophy or science. The reception of the Mishnah's category-formations and their transformation therefore stands for the movement from a philosophical to a religious mode of thinking. For the system to which the Mishnah as a document attests is essentially philosophical in its rhetorical, logical, and topical program; the successor system is fundamentally religious in these same principal and indicative traits of the media of intellect and mentality.

Given the definitions with which I began, how do I know whether a system is philosophical or religious? The answer is not subjective, nor the criteria private or idiosyncratic. The indicative traits in both instances, to begin with, derive from and are displayed by documents, for — I take it as axiomatic — the mode of the writing down of any system attests to both the method and the message that sustain that system. From how people express themselves, we work our way backward to their modes of thought: the classification of perceived data, the making of connections between fact and fact, the drawing of conclusions from those connections, and, finally, the representation of conclusions in cogent compositions. All of these traits of mind are to be discerned in the character of those compositions, in the rhetoric that conveys messages in proportion and appropriate aesthetics, in the logic that imparts self-evidence to the making of connections, the drawing of conclusions, and in the representation of sets of conclusions as cogent and intelligible, characteristic of writing and expressed in writing.

In the Yerushalmi (and the Bavli later on) scarce resources, so far as these are of a material order of being, e.g., wealth as defined by the Mishnah and Aristotle, are systemically neutral. A definition of scarce resources emerges that explicitly involves a symbolic transformation, with the material definition of scarce resources set into contradiction with an other-than-material one. So we find side by side clarification of the details of the received category and adumbration of a symbolic revision and hence a categorical transformation in the successor-writings. The representation of the political structure of the Mishnah undergoes clarification, but alongside, a quite separate and very different structure also is portrayed. The received structure presents three political classes, ordered in a hierarchy; the successor-structure, a single political class, corresponding on earth to a counterpart in Heaven. Here too a symbolic transaction has taken place, in which one set of symbols is replicated but also reversed, and a second set of symbols given instead.

The Mishnah's structure comprising a hierarchical composition of foci of power in the Yerushalmi gives way to a structure centered upon a single focus of power. That single focus, moreover, now draws boundaries between legitimate and illegitimate violence, boundaries not conceived in the initial system. So in all three components of the account of the social order the philosophical system gives way to another. The world-view comes to expression in modes of thought and expression — the logic of making connections and drawing conclusions — that are different from the philosophical ones of the Mishnah. The way of life appeals to value expressed in other symbols than those of economics in the philosophical mode. The theory of the social entity comes to concrete expression in sanctions legitimately administered by a single class of persons (institution), rather than by a proportionate and balanced set of classes of persons in hierarchical order, and, moreover, that same theory recognizes and defines both legitimate and also illegitimate violence, something beyond the ken of the initial system. So, it is clear, another system is adumbrated and attested in the successor-writings.

The categorical transformation that was underway in the Yerushalmi, signaling the movement from philosophy to religion, comes to the surface when we ask a simple question. Precisely what do the authorships of the successor-documents speaking not about the Mishnah but on their own account, mean by economics, politics, and philosophy? That is to say, to what kinds of data do they refer when they speak of scarce resources and legitimate violence, and exactly how — as to the received philosophical method — do they define correct modes of thought and expression, logic and rhetoric, and even the topical program worthy of sustained inquiry? The components of the initial formation of categories were examined thoughtfully and carefully, paraphrased and augmented and clarified. But the received categories were not continued, not expanded, and not renewed. Preserved merely intact, as they had been handed on, the received categories hardly serve to encompass all of the points of emphasis and sustained development that characterize the successor-documents — or, as a matter of fact, any of them. On the contrary, when the framers of the Yerushalmi, for one example, moved out from the exegesis of Mishnah-passages, they also left behind the topics of paramount interest in the Mishnah and developed other categories altogether. Here the framers of the successor- system defined their own counterparts.

These counterpart-categories, moreover, redefined matters, following the main outlines of the structure of the social order manifest in the initial system. The counterpart-categories set forth an account of the social order just as did the ones of the Mishnah's framers. But they defined the social order in very different terms altogether. In that redefinition we discern the transformation of the received system, and the traits of the new one fall into the classification of not philosophy but religion. For what the successor-thinkers did was not continue and expand the categorical repertoire but set forth a categorically-fresh vision of the social order — a way of life, world-view, and definition of the social entity — with appropriate counterpart-categories. And what is decisive is that these served as did the initial categories within the generative categorical structure definitive for all Judaic systems. So there was a category corresponding to the generative component of world-view, but it was not philosophical; another corresponding to the required component setting forth a way of life, but in the conventional and accepted definition of economics it was not an economics; and, finally, a category to define the social entity, "Israel," that any Judaic system must explain, but in the accepted sense of a politics it was not politics.

What is the difference between philosophical and the religious systems? What philosophy kept distinct, religion joined together: that defines the transformation of Judaism from philosophy to religion. The received system was a religious system of a philosophical character; this-worldly data are classified according to rules that apply consistently throughout, so that we may always predict with a fair degree of accuracy what will happen and why. And a philosophical system of religion then systematically demonstrates out of the data of the world order of nature and society the governance of God in nature and supernature: this world's data pointing toward God above and beyond. The God of the philosophical Judaism then sat enthroned at the apex of all things, all being hierarchically classified. Just as philosophy seeks the explanation of things, so a philosophy of religion (in the context at hand) will propose orderly explanations in accord with prevailing and cogent rules. The profoundly philosophical character of the Mishnah has already provided ample evidence of the shape, structure, and character of that philosophical system in the Judaic context. The rule-seeking character of Mishnaic discourse marks it as a philosophical system of religion. But, we shall now see, the successor-system saw the world differently. It follows that a philosophical system forms its learning inductively and syllogistically, by appeal to the neutral evidence of the rules shown to apply to all things by the observation of the order of universally accessible nature and society.

A religious system frames its propositions deductively and exegetically by appeal to the privileged evidence of a corpus of truths deemed revealed by God. The difference pertains not to detail but to the fundamental facts deemed to matter. Some of those facts lie at the very surface, in the nature of the writings that express the system. These writings were not freestanding but contingent, and that in two ways. First, they served as commentaries to prior documents, the Mishnah and Scripture, for the Talmud and Midrash-compilations, respectively. Second, and more consequential, the authorships insisted upon citing Scripture-passages or Mishnah-sentences as the centerpiece of proof, on the one side, and program of discourse, on the other. But the differences that prove indicative are not merely formal.

More to the point, while the Mishnah's system is steady-state and ahistorical, admitting no movement or change, the successor-system of the Yerushalmi and Midrash-compilations tells tales, speaks of change, accommodates and responds to historical moments. It formulates a theory of continuity within change, of the moral connections between generations, of the way in which one's deeds shape one's destiny — and that of the future as well. If what the framers of the Mishnah want more than anything else is to explain the order and structure of being, then their successors have rejected their generative concern. For what they, for their part, intensely desire to sort out is the currents and streams of time and change, as these flow toward an unknown ocean.

The shift from the philosophical to the religious modes of thought and media of expression — logical and rhetorical indicators, respectively — come to realization in the recasting of the generative categories of the system as well. These categories are transformed, and the transformation proved so thoroughgoing as to validate the characterization of the change as "counterpart-categories." The result of the formation of such counterpart-categories in the aggregate was to encompass not only the natural but also the supernatural realms of the social order. That is how philosophical thinking gave way to religious thinking. The religious system of the Yerushalmi and associated documents sets forth the category-formation that produced in place of an economics based on prime value assigned to real wealth one that now encompassed wealth of an intangible, impalpable, and supernatural order, but valued resource nonetheless. It points toward the replacement of a politics formerly serving to legitimate and hierarchize power and differentiate among sanctions by appeal to fixed principles by one that now introduced the variable of God's valuation of the victim and the anti-political conception of the illegitimacy of worldly power.

This counterpart-politics then formed the opposite of the Mishnah's this-worldly political system altogether. In all three ways the upshot is the same: the social system, in the theory of its framers, now extends its boundaries upward to Heaven, drawing into a whole the formerly distinct, if counterpoised, realms of Israel on earth and the Heavenly court above. So if I had to specify the fundamental difference between the philosophical and the religious versions of the social order, it would fall, quite specifically, — to state with emphasis — *upon the broadening of the systemic boundaries to encompass Heaven.* The formation of counterpart-categories therefore signals not a reformation of the received system but the formation of an essentially new one.

The first fundamental point of reversal, uniting what had been divided, is the joining of economics and politics into a political economy, through the conception of *zekhut,* a term defined presently. The other point at which what the one system treated as distinct, the next and connected system chose to address as one and whole is less easily discerned, since to do so we have to ask a question the framers of the Mishnah did not raise in the Mishnah at all. That concerns the character and source of virtue, specifically, the affect, upon the individual, of knowledge, specifically, knowledge of the Torah or Torah-study. To frame the question very simply, if we ask ourselves, what happens to me if I study the Torah, the answer, for the Mishnah, predictably is, my standing and status change. Torah-study and its effects form a principal systemic indicator in matters of hierarchical classification, joining the *mamzer*-disciple of sages in a mixture of opposites, for one example. That is, the mamzer is the child of parents who can never legally wed; he himself is an outcast in an exact sense, being permitted to marry another mamzer or equivalent. And yet if he is also a disciple of sages, he is deemed to stand at the apex of society, above the priesthood, a truly systemic reversal.

But am I changed within? In vain we look in the hundreds of chapters of the Mishnah for an answer to that question. Virtue and learning form distinct categories; I am not changed as to my virtue, my character and conscience, by my mastery of the Torah. And still more strikingly, if we ask, does my Torah-study affect my fate in this world and in the life to come, the Mishnah's authorship is strikingly silent about that matter too. Specifically, we find in the pages of that document no claim that studying the Torah either changes me or assures my salvation. But the separation of knowledge and the human condition is set aside, and studying the Torah is deemed the source of salvation, in the successor-system. The philosophical system, with its interest in *homo hierarchicus*, proved remarkably silent about the effect of the Torah upon the inner man. The upshot is at the critical points of bonding, the received system proved flawed, in its separation of learning from virtue and legitimate power from valued resources. Why virtue joins knowledge (I call this "the gnostic Torah"), politics links to economics, in the religious system but not in the philosophical one is obvious. Philosophy differentiates, seeking the rules that join diverse data; religion integrates, proposing to see the whole all together and all at once, thus (for an anthropology, for example) seeing humanity whole: "in our image, after our likeness." Religion by its nature asks the questions of integration, such as the theory, intended to hold together within a single boundary earth and Heaven, this world and the other, should lead us to anticipate.

The second systemic innovation is the formation of an integrated category of political economy, framed in such a way that at stake in politics and economics alike were value and resource in no way subject to order and rule, but in all ways formed out of the unpredictable resource of *zekhut,* sometimes translated as "merit," but, being a matter of not obligation but supererogatory free will, should be portrayed, I think, as "the heritage of virtue and its consequent entitlements." Between those two conceptions — the Torah as a medium of transformation, the heritage of virtue and its consequent entitlements, which can be gained for oneself and also received from one's ancestors — the received system's this-worldly boundaries were transcended, and the new system encompassed within its framework a supernatural life on earth. And appealing to these two statements of world-view, way of life, and social entity, we may as a matter of fact compose a complete description of the definitive traits and indicative systemic concerns of the successor-Judaism. It remains to observe very simply: the Bavli in no way innovated in the category-formation set forth by the Yerushalmi, and, it follows, no important component of the Bavli's theological statement will have surprised the framers of the Yerushalmi's compositions and compilers of its composites.

V. FROM PHILOSOPHY THROUGH RELIGION TO THEOLOGY

It follows that when we lay out the documents in sequence and follow their course, we characterize the result as three interrelated systems, to be classified as philosophical, then religious, then theological, in character, a taxon to be defined presently. These three systems, autonomous when viewed synchronically in their respective documentary formations but connected when seen diachronically, ultimately, at the end of their formative age, formed a single, wholly and utterly continuous structure, that one we call Judaism. But, as I just said, in their successive stages of autonomy, then autonomy and connection, the three distinct systems may be classified, respectively, as philosophical, religious, and theological. Judaism then took shape in a passage from a philosophical, to a religious, and finally to a theological system, each one taking over and revising the definitive categories of the former and framing its own fresh, generative categories as well. The formative history of Judaism then is the story of the presentations and re-presentations of categorical structures. In method it is the exegesis of taxonomy and taxic systems.

To begin with, then, the classification of types of systems — philosophical, religious, theological — requires explanation. We now know that a philosophical system forms its learning inductively and syllogistically by appeal to the neutral evidence of the rules shown by the observation of the order of universally accessible nature and society. That is the indicative trait of the Mishnah. We further recall that a religious system frames its propositions deductively and exegetically by appeal to the privileged evidence of a corpus of writing deemed revealed by God. That is the dominant trait of the Talmud of the Land of Israel. But what about a theological re-presentation of a religious system?

Symmetrical with the prior religious system in doctrine but imposing its own modes of thought, a theological system imposes upon a religious one systematic modes of thought of philosophy, so in its message regularizing and ordering in a cogent and intellectually rigorous way the materials received from a religious system. The movement from the religious to the theological will involve the systematization and harmonization of the religious categories, their re-formation into a single tight and cogent statement. It is an initiative as radical, in its way, as the passage from the philosophical to religious formation is in its way. For the modes of thought, media of expression, and, as a matter of fact, categorical structure and system are reworked in the enterprise of turning a merely imputed order, imputed within the single heart of the faith, into a wholly-public order, subject to sustained and cogent representation and expression, each component in its place and proper sequence, beginning, middle, and end. Religious conviction differs from theological proposition as do bricks and mortar from a building.

Religious and the theological systems work over the same issues in ways that are common to themselves and that also distinguish them jointly from philosophical ones. But the rigorous task of forming, out of religious attitudes and convictions, a cogent composition, a system and not merely a structure of beliefs, imposes on systems of the theological sort disciplines of mind and perception, modes of thought and media of expression, quite different from those that characterize the work of making a religious system. The connection is intimate, for a theological system succeeding and reshaping a religious one appeals to the same sources of truth in setting forth (often identical) answers to (ordinarily) the same urgent questions. But the theological type of system is different from the religious type in fundamental ways as well, for while there can be a religious system without theological order, there can be no theological system without a religious core. So much for the distinctions among types of systems.

The medium of theological re-presentation was hermeneutics, so that, when we know how the Torah is properly read, we discern the theology of Judaism. Before proceeding, I hasten to give a simple definition of hermeneutics, that of Wilhelm Dilthey, since I claim that in its hermeneutics, the Talmud re-presents the Torah: "The methodological understanding of permanently fixed life-expressions we call explication...explication culminates in the interpretation of the written records of human existence...The science of this art is hermeneutics."[7] When we know the rules of explication that instruct us on how to interpret the Torah, we gain access to the theology that governs the presentation of the religion, Judaism.

Within the diachronic framework, the priority of hermeneutics in the theological venture is not difficult to explain. We deal with a Judaism that affords religious experience — knowledge of God, meeting with God — in particular in books. While that same Judaism, like any other religious system, also meets God in prayer, obedience to the covenant, and right conduct, and expresses the sense of the knowledge of God in music and in art, in pilgrimage and in dance, in rite and in cult, and in most of the ways that religions in general celebrate God, what makes this Judaic system distinctive is its insistence that God is made manifest in, and therefore known through, documents, which preserve and contain the encounter with God that in secular language we call "religious experience." Just as, if the principal medium for meeting God were theater or music, we should search for theology in aesthetics, so since the principal meeting of encounter with God is the Torah, and the Torah is given in writing and oral formulation as well, this Judaism promises knowledge of God through the documents of the Torah, and its theological medium will be hermeneutics (as much as philosophy).

The character of the evidence therefore governs. Because the formation of (this particular) Judaism as a religious system is fully exposed in its successive documents, the history of that Judaism's formative age — the first six centuries of the Common Era — comes to us in the right reading of the Torah. In this Judaism, the Torah comprises the holy documents and persons — written and oral documents, and the person of "our sages of blessed memory;" the deeds and teachings of sages take the form of stories and statements preserved in the same documents. Not only so, but because the medium for theology in this Judaism was a fully-exposed hermeneutics, the message was conveyed through unarticulated but ubiquitous initiatives of a hermeneutical character. Then theological method consisted in

---

[7] Cited by K. M. Newton, *Interpreting the Text,* p. 42.

constantly and ubiquitously showing the same few things through that hermeneutics, worked out in the Talmuds for the Oral Torah, and in the Midrash-compilations for the written Torah.

VI. THEOLOGY IN THE DIACHRONIC, DOCUMENTARY CONTEXT

Theology is the science of the reasoned knowledge of God, in the case of a Judaism made possible by God's self-manifestation in the Torah. Seen in its whole re-presentation in the Talmud of Babylonia, the theology of Judaism sets forth knowledge of God. This is in two ways. The first is to know God through God's self-revelation in the Torah. This requires that we know what the Torah is, or what torah is (in a generic sense, which can pertain to either message or media or modes of thought). Then knowing how to define and understand the Torah affords access to God's self-revelation. The second is to know through that same self-revelation what God wants of Israel and how God responds to Israel and humanity at large.[8] That specific, propositional knowledge comes through reasoned reading of the Torah, oral and written, the Mishnah and Scripture, represented by the Talmuds and Midrash-compilations, respectively.[9] The hermeneutics governing these documents encapsulate that knowledge of reasoned explication.

The schematic classifications of the successive, related Judaic systems as philosophical, religious, and theological, therefore derive from the character of the successive documents, the Mishnah, Yerushalmi, and Bavli.[10] What makes all the difference in the second Talmud's re-presentation of the Judaic religious system therefore is the character of that Talmud itself. Through analysis of the hermeneutics that conveys the intellectual program of that medium, a religion rich in miscellaneous but generally congruent norms of behavior and endowed with a vast store of varied and episodic but occasionally contradictory ideas was turned into a proportioned and harmonious theology.[11]

Having laid heavy emphasis on the priority of the Bavli, I hasten to qualify matters. As a matter of fact, the process of theological re-presentation went forward

---

[8] I paraphrase Ingolf Dalferth, "The Stuff of Revelation: Austin Farrer's Doctrine of Inspired Images," in Ann Loades and Michael McLain, eds., *Hermeneutics, the Bible and literary Criticism* (London, 1992: MacMillan), p. 71.

[9] And that explains why we still will have to undertake a separate account of the theology yielded by the hermeneutics of the Midrash-compilations (not only, or mainly, specific words or phrases or sentences found hither and yon in "The Midrash," as the ignorant conduct the inquiry). The characterization of the hermeneutics of Midrash-compilations, early, middle, and late, will stand side-by-side with the theory set forth here.

[10] That is within the qualification that the Yerushalmi did part of the work of theologizing the Mishnah, the work of showing its proportion, composition, harmony, and coherence. The second Talmud did this work, but it also accomplished the far more sophisticated intellectual tasks.

[11] But I maintain that an important part of the theological work was undertaken by the first of the two Talmuds, which means the differentiation between the two Talmuds provides the key, in literary analysis, to the hermeneutical priority of the second of the two.

in two stages. In the first, in the Talmud of the Land of Israel, the philosophical document that stated that system gained both a vast amplification, in which the categories and methods of the original statement were amplified and instantiated, but also in which took place a remarkable reformulation in counterpart-categories. Of the three traits of "tradition," e.g. as defined in the tractate Abot in its apologia for the Mishnah — harmony, linearity, and unity, — the first of the two Talmuds systematically demonstrated the presence of two: harmony and linearity. The second undertook to demonstrate all three, all together and all at once and everywhere, that is to say, the law behind the laws, meaning, the unity, the integrity of truth. That shown, we know the mind of God, the character of truth.

Viewed as a whole, the result is then to be classified as not philosophical but religious in character and theological in re-presentation. Alongside, earlier Midrash-compilations undertook the task of showing the relationship between the two media of the Torah, the oral and the written, by insisting that the Mishnah rested on Scripture. The goal was to show linearity and harmony. They furthermore began the definition of the Torah — in our terms, the reading of Scripture — by systematizing and generalizing the episodic cases of Scripture. The goal was to demonstrate the comprehensiveness of the Torah: its cases were meant to yield governing rules. The later Midrash-compilations continued that reading of Scripture by formulating syllogistic propositions out of the occasional data of Scripture.

The religious writings that formed the second stage in the unfolding of Judaism — Talmud of the Land of Israel, Sifra and the two Sifrés somewhat before, Genesis Rabbah and Leviticus Rabbah somewhat afterward, finally were succeeded — and replaced — by the Talmud of Babylonia and related Midrash-compilations, particularly Song of Songs Rabbah, Lamentations Rabbah, and Ruth Rabbah. These were documents that restated in rigorous, theological ways the same religious convictions, so providing that Judaism or Judaic system with its theological statement. In these writings, the religious system was restated in a rigorous and philosophical way. The associated midrash-compilations succeeded in making a single, encompassing statement out of the data of the several books of Scripture they presented.

The re-presentation of the religious system in the disciplined thought of theology took the form of rules of reading the Torah — oral and written — and through those rules exposing the character of the intellectual activity of thinking like God, that is, thinking about the world in the way God thinks. The theology of Judaism — reasoned knowledge of God[12] and God's will afforded by God's self-manifestation in the Torah[13] — affords access in particular to the mind of God, revealed in God's words and wording of the Torah. Through the Torah, oral and

---

[12] That is a standard definition of theology.
[13] That is my restatement of the standard definition of theology to state what I mean by, theology of Judaism.

written, we work our way back to the intellect of God who gives the Torah. Thus through learning in the Torah in accord with the lessons of the Talmuds and associated Midrash-compilations, humanity knows what God personally has made manifest about mind, that intellect in particular in which "in our image, after our likeness" we too are made. That defines the theology of the Judaism of the dual Torah and in particular forms the upshot of the Talmud's re-presentation of that theology.

Reading the Mishnah together with one or the other of its Talmudic amplifications, the Talmud of the Land of Israel or the Talmud of Babylonia, or Scripture together with any of the Midrash-compilations, on the surface does not convey such an account. The authoritative writings — the Mishnah and Talmud of the Land of Israel or the Mishnah and Talmud of Babylonia and their associated Midrash-collections — portray not successive stages of the formation of a system but rather a single, continuous Judaism, which everywhere is read as unitary and uniform. Not only so, but in the persons and teachings of sages that same Torah makes part of its statement. But, when examined as single documents, one by one, in the sequence of their closure, to the contrary, matters look otherwise. Each writing then may be characterized on its own, rather than in the continuous context defined by the corpus of which it forms a principal part.

VII. METHOD, MESSAGE, MEDIUM

My account of the formation of Judaism therefore may be stated in these simple stages, involving method, message, and medium:

[1] THE METHOD OF PHILOSOPHY: the initial statement of the Judaism of the dual Torah took the form of a philosophical law code and set forth a philosophical system of monotheism, providing an economics, politics, and philosophy that philosophers in the Aristotelian and Middle- or Neo-Platonic traditions can have understood as philosophical (if they grasped the idiom in which the philosophical system was expressed).

[2] THE MESSAGE OF RELIGION: through the formation of counterpart-categories to economics, politics, and philosophy, the successor-system, which came to expression in the Talmud of the Land of Israel and associated Midrash-compilations, set forth a religious system and statement of the same Judaism of the dual Torah.

[3] THE MEDIUM OF THEOLOGY, MELDING METHOD AND MESSAGE: taking over that system and reviewing its main points, the final Talmud then restated the received body of religion as theology. That then is the point of this book, which explains how Judaism came to completion in its definitive statement when [1] the disciplines of philosophy were used to set forth the message of [2] religion so that Judaism stated [3] its theology. The Talmud that re-presented the Judaism of the dual Torah by joining the method of philosophy to the message of religion. In the context of the historical formation of its principal ideas, that accounts for the formation of normative Judaism.

So much for the documentary history of ideas, theology viewed diachronically. We have completed the historical, diachronic, and analytical reading and now turn to the synchronic and synthetic approach to the same writings, theology viewed synchronically. The diachronic reading produces one approach to the description of the theology of the Oral Torah: the identification of the authoritative statement thereof. And that result conforms to the judgment of the history of Rabbinic Judaism from antiquity to our own day. The Talmud of Babylonia defined the single authoritative statement, the court of final appeal, by the criteria of which all other statements are judged. It is the primary text that is studied, the principal source of authority, the starting point for all else.

Were I to remain within the limits of a diachronic reading of the Oral Torah, I should now set forth the Talmud of Babylonia's theological system.[14] But, as I said in the Preface, that would grossly distort matters by eliminating a vast part of the corpus of evidence. The Talmud of Babylonia's systematization of the whole involved a process of selection and reordering. But an authentic account of the whole, however respectful of that Talmud's work, must find another point of entry altogether, one that permits us to take account of all of the normative writings, seen whole and complete and undistorted by the historical primacy of a single formulation of matters. To that task, the one of synchronic reading of the whole on a single plane of eternity, we now turn.

---

[14] *Judaism States its Theology: The Talmudic Re-Presentation.* Atlanta, 1993: Scholars Press for South Florida Studies in the History of Judaism does just that.

II

The Issue of Theology
in the Description of Rabbinic Judaism

I. WHY THEOLOGY?

Addressing to the writings of the ancient sages of Judaism the theological question framed synchronically — what logic governs in a corpus of religious thought set forth in closely related writings? — to begin with requires an explanation. Why, after all, should anyone assume that writings hold together and make a single statement all at once? Viewing them in an entirely secular context, we should have no reason whatsoever to ask what rationality or conviction — that theological system and structure I propose to identify within the whole — links them all. What objective reason compels us to begin with to investigate the substrate of generative principles that forms their foundation, or to propose to outline the structure of encompassing conceptions that sustains them all?

A variety of simple facts indeed argues against taking up the quest for theology in such diverse writings. Numerous authorities, named sages or rabbis, make their appearance, each with his own opinion and perspective. Why do they all have to concur? The documents deal with different topics. What reason compels us to ask for a coherent structure? They unfolded over long centuries, in different settings and among diverse authorities, and they furthermore drew upon antecedent opinion, going back to Scripture itself. Their authorities lived on the opposite sides of the contested frontier between the Roman and Iranian empires of late antiquity. Why therefore should anyone expect to discover a common corpus of shared convictions based upon a governing rationality? These considerations explain why we must wonder what justifies our investigating the theology — the sustaining logic, the normative statements and the system that they (allegedly) comprise — of the Oral Torah at all.

The entire history of the reception and reading of the documents of the Oral Torah tells the reason why. From the seventh century to our own day those who value these writings have treated them as a continuous statement. In Rabbinic Judaism from antiquity to the present day these writings have functioned all together, without much differentiation, as a source of authoritative teachings, all of them equally valid as parts the Torah, enjoying the status, of generic torah, that is, teachings out of Sinai. That Judaism has appealed indiscriminately to the documents of the Oral Torah, along with Scripture, as a wholly cogent, perfectly coherent and consistent body of doctrine, covering normative behavior and normative belief. The entire history of Judaism from antiquity to the present day therefore testifies to the conviction that the documents are to be read as a single, coherent position. For nearly the whole of their history the documents have impressed with their inner cogency successive generations of sages justly famous for their acumen and perspicacity. The rationality and cogency that countless generations of great sages have found in the discrete documents therefore form the object of this quest: what can sages for centuries have perceived to persuade them that the documents make a single, continuous statement?. That is to say, the Judaism that values and privileges these documents, Rabbinic Judaism, answers the question, why bother? since from the Talmud's time to ours, in all of its varieties, that Judaism has taken for granted the unity and continuity of these particular documents and, but for Scripture, no others.

The facts of the history of the reading of these writings do not prove that sages for thirteen hundred years correctly judged matters, but they do require us to investigate what traits may inhere in the intellectual character of the whole that justify that unanimous judgment. What men of profound learning and sensibility took as self-evident surely demands a serious hearing. In their view, the documents classified as Oral Torah form a corpus of official writings deemed at every point equally to be true, at all points to be harmonious, so that any sentence in one document is supposed to fit together with any sentence of any other document, with the proviso that the rules for making connections and drawing conclusions have been observed.

Not only so, but out of these particular documents of the Oral Torah, sages through all time have found principles that they extended and amplified and applied to new cases and circumstances. Consequently, out of that coherent corpus of official writings, authoritative teachings — Torah — continue to emerge, in this Judaism, from Sinai to this morning's ruling or lesson of a qualified disciple of the sages. This open Torah without limit, accessible to new insight consonant with the received doctrines and rules of right thought and valid interpretation, could and did accommodate new truth because the logic of the Oral Torah served, and continues to serve, to shape intellect and dictate right thinking, and the latest generation finds itself wholly at home within the principles of self-evidence and coherence that inhere from the outset. So much for the challenge to evaluate on the basis of the internal evidence of the writings the often-explicit judgment of the ages.

But what objective evidence shall I adduce to assess matters, and how am I to identify the inner logic, the foundations of cogency, that hold the whole together? And, to extend the framing of the theological question, what are those principles, and how are we to define the modes of logic, the manner of making connections and drawing conclusions? My answer is to inquire into the rationality that animates the entire body of writings, the universal paradigms and models of explanation, the modes of making connections and drawing conclusions, the uniform symbolic speech. It is quite reasonable to search for the foundations for that universal and unanimous premise of all encounter with these writings. The inquiry seeks to identify the building blocks of the entire structure, to account for the dynamism of the entire system. Principles of category-formation having been identified, we may turn to the investigation of the governing categories, their qualities and contents.

An obvious objection to the entire enterprises arises: has this work not already been done many times over in many languages? And is it not true that every book on Rabbinic Judaism — and they are now very many, in Modern Hebrew, English, French, and German — by the nature of its task records the Rabbinic view of God and Man, ethics and history, Israel and the nations, beginnings and endings? And in the context of the faith as it is practiced, do not rabbis' teachings from week to week set forth that one whole Torah that speaks theologically in this week's lesson? Indeed so. Rabbinic theology encompasses a vast labor of paraphrase and recapitulation, to be sure carried out in the primitive mode of hunting and gathering. Whether in theory in the academy or in practice in the pulpit and class room — this work of historical systematic theology has been done merely by collecting sayings on the various topics from the norm-setting documents. These are then assumed to cohere and to make a cogent statement. But that primitive work of hunting and gathering has exhausted the capacities of the generality of those who have done the work. Merely because we can collect two or three sayings on a given topic does not mean we know the position of the Rabbinic sages on that topic; all it means is that we have found two or three pertinent sayings.

What then is wrong with collecting and arranging sayings on a common topic? That commonplace way of describing the theology of the Oral Torah (a.k.a., Rabbinic Judaism) represents a labor-saving device: it assumes we know the answers to questions we have not asked, have validated category-formations that we have not teased out of the sources and shown native to them. Hunting and gathering treats as superfluous what is crucial: the work of deep reflection and close encounter with the character of the documents. Such an encounter will bring us into touch with the category-formation that sages themselves framed, will guide us to the locations at which sages systematically set forth their views, will tell us whether what we think important took so important impressed sages as equally critical. Merely finding sayings pertinent to a given subject yields no insight into these matters of context. But of what interest are sayings out of context, and why should we take as representative of the whole system the position of a single saying assigned to a given named authority in one or another document? Issues of method, prior to substantive inquiry, not having been addressed, the results of the work in hand must be deemed indeterminate, indeed, rather dubious, as I shall show. Merely joining sayings on a given topic hardly solves any urgent problems or indeed answers any questions, for instance, of proportion and coherence.

For whether or not the Oral Torah then yields systematic discussions of God and Man, beginnings and endings, has not been shown, only that sayings on those fabricated topics circulated. How the category-formation defined by those topics and not others proves congruent with the category-formation that governs within, and dictates the character of, the documents of the Oral Torah itself, has not been investigated. Indeed, the category-formations that define the work regularly correspond to the points of interest of Christian theology, e.g., dogmatics or systematics or apologetics, but time and again prove asymmetrical to the category-formations of the Oral Torah itself. So we may concede that, yes, sages had an opinion on that subject, and, indeed, that opinion does register. But whether they deemed the subject as urgent as do their contemporary interlocutors, and whether the isolated saying on the subject represented the governing consensus, remains to be seen. We turn out to ask as important questions that are marginal in context, or to miss critical issues altogether. Always ominous, the historical question of proportion asked differently: whether a rabbi's saying on a topic stands for the opinion of all of the rabbis, and if so, how we are to know that fact — that decisive but inconvenient issue has scarcely been considered. So these questions of system, order, and logic rarely enjoy much systematic attention, and rigorous responses to them prove few and far-between.

Yet collecting and arranging sayings presupposes what in these pages is treated as the critical issue, the hypothesis that demands demonstration. The premise of the hunters and gatherers (always implicit, everywhere deemed self-evident) indeed is that the diverse writings cohere and form that continuous statement, on any given topic, that theology proposes to set forth. So the state of the question, the character of the prevailing method, takes as given what demands demonstration: precisely where and how the documents of the Oral Torah do set forth their systematic discussions, of the issues important to them. The upshot is, available accounts of Rabbinic Judaism seen whole and complete within its normative writings — the documents from the Mishnah through the Talmud of Babylonia — continue the tradition itself (while taking up the pretense of criticism of it) and so take for granted answers to questions that have not yet been asked. Here I propose to raise the fundamental questions of method in the description of the theological system of Rabbinic Judaism in its formative corpus.

II. What Is at Stake in the Study of the Theological System of Rabbinic Judaism in its Formative Writings?

Whether or not in the documents that all together comprise the Oral Torah of Rabbinic Judaism we can locate a cogent foundation of coherent religious ideas — a theology of integrity, not just random sayings or episodic observations on this and that — matters a great deal. It stake is whether Judaism, the religion, speaks with its own voice or registers merely as the echo of what diverse sages say. If among the score or more of documents that all together comprise that corpus of official writings we locate a theological structure, we may speak of — and in the name of — Judaism, whole and complete, as the Oral Torah defines Judaism. If not, we are left with random sayings, but no system, no Judaism at all, only diverse sages' (authoritative) opinions about one thing and another. So at stake in asking about the continuity, from one Rabbinical document to another, of organizing ideas is a considerable question. We ask whether or not we may justify making comprehensive statements of an authoritative and normative character about the theological system and structure of those writings and the Judaism (or "Judaic religious system") that they set forth. For those statements theology alone makes possible.

A few simple questions suffice to show what is at issue. May we speak of "*the* rabbis' position," that is to say, the view on a critical subject set forth in diverse ways by our sages of blessed memory, as the rabbis are called by those who honor them? Or are we limited to atomistic allusion to "Rabbi X's view"? How do we identify the rabbis' position — the topics on which they take positions, the details of their views — and what tests our judgment as to the place and proportionate importance in the whole structure in which that position locates itself? Where are we to look, and what constitute the indicative signals of normativity among diverse opinions? Finally, how do normative views hold together, on the one side, and fit together with the positions that animate the received, written Scripture that sages affirmed to constitute God's revelation to Rabbi Moses at Sinai? This sequence of questions shows what is at issue.

Let me specify what success in the work must yield. If we can identify that substrate of theology — reasoned discourse about God and God's self-manifestation in the Torah — that sustains the structure and show the scriptural foundations thereof, we may reliably describe the whole, the structure at its bed rock and thence upward to its heights — Judaism. But if all we have in hand out of the formative corpus of Judaism is free-standing, episodic sayings, the authority and representative character of which lie beyond all assessment, and if we are able merely to compile and categorize by topic sayings that may or may not come to rest on the ground of Scripture, then we find ourselves unable to speak authoritatively about Judaism in its formative statement: the Torah, oral and written. Instead we shall only be able to cite wise sayings out of all doctrinal context, an anthology like Montefiore and Loewe's *Rabbinic Anthology,* and a scrapbook like Abraham Cohen's *Everyman's Talmud,* not a mature vision of transcendent things. Then we know only what one or another of our sages of blessed memory may have said, but not what the sages as an entire community expressing its consensus really meant.

For, I cannot overemphasize, the books of the Oral Torah encompass a vast range of opinion on subjects of religious interest as commonly construed. Examining the writings, however, shows that that opinion takes nearly every plausible position and its opposite. So how are we to know what the Oral Torah —

a.k.a. Rabbinic Judaism — affirms or denies, what it teaches or rejects? Assembling out of the writings a systematic *sic ut non,* as Abelard did (with unhappy consequences to be sure), would take no very taxing effort and would underscore the confusion that, on the surface, reigns. So while on the basis of manuscript evidence we may allege with confidence that to Rabbi X a given opinion is attributed, and (overcoming what to me are insuperable difficulties) we may even find grounds to suppose that that same Rabbi X actually held such a view, at this time we have not yet learned how to formulate the position of the Oral Torah overall. Indeed, from Rabbi X we may not possess even sufficient evidence to place a saying into the larger context of Rabbi X.'s own thought. We have more atoms than molecules. And yet here we seek a theory of atomic physics, and (to extend the metaphor) one that even coheres with quantum mechanics. In our context what I propose to outline are grounds in the concrete evidence of the documents of the Oral Torah, viewed whole, for speaking in the name of "the rabbis." Here I shall identify the representations of collective opinion such as form the Oral part of the Torah given to Moses our Rabbi at Sinai, such as the documents of the Oral Torah, all together, are supposed to set forth.

If the writings take positions, not merely preserving opinions, as I maintain, I should be able to show that norms of belief do come to expression, not only norms of behavior. Can I then give a single example of what would suffice to prove that theological norms inhere within the discourse of the documents of the Oral Torah? In some few, specific instances, the documents themselves identify a critical building block of a theological structure. Let me give one example. We know full well what some of these norms were (and remain for the faithful), when our sages declare in no uncertain terms what beliefs are essentially for inclusion in the holy Israel to whom they spoke:

A.   All Israelites have a share in the world to come,

B.   as it is said, "your people also shall be all righteous, they shall inherit the land forever; the branch of my planting, the work of my hands, that I may be glorified" (Is. 60:21).

C.   And these are the ones who have no portion in the world to come:

D.   He who says, the resurrection of the dead is a teaching which does not derive from the Torah, and the Torah does not come from Heaven; and an Epicurean.

E.   R. Aqiba says, "Also: He who reads in heretical books,

F.   "and he who whispers over a wound and says, 'I will put none of the diseases upon you which I have put on the Egyptians, for I am the Lord who heals you' (Ex. 15:26)."

> G. Abba Saul says, "Also: He who pronounces the divine
> Name as it is spelled out."
>
> M. SANHEDRIN 11:1

To be "Israel," that is, to have a share in the world to come, one must hold a given view and deny another; that view, then, demands a place high on the list of normative beliefs, alongside the list of normative acts of behavior. Indeed, the line between belief and behavior proves indistinct, reading the wrong books representing an act of conviction, whispering over a wound standing for an attitude and a belief as well, so too pronouncing the divine name as it is spelled out. One does not lose one's standing in Israel for the world to come by an act of sacrilege or blasphemy, as sages assure Achan in Chapter Six of the same tractate, but one does lose one's portion in the world to come by reason of wrong opinion:

> A. [When] he was ten cubits from the place of stoning, they say to him, "Confess," for it is usual for those about to be put to death to confess.
> B. For whoever confesses has a share in the world to come.
> C. For so we find concerning Achan, to whom Joshua said, "My son, I pray you, give glory to the Lord, the God of Israel, and confess to him, [and tell me now what you have done; hide it not from me.] And Achan answered Joshua and said, Truly have I sinned against the Lord, the God of Israel, and thus and thus I have done" (Josh. 7:19). And how do we know that his confession achieved atonement for him? For it is said, "And Joshua said, Why have you troubled us? The Lord will trouble you this day" (Josh. 7:25) — This day you will be troubled, but you will not be troubled in the world to come.
>
> MISHNAH-TRACTATE SANHEDRIN 6:2

What is striking then is the clear evidence that sages fiercely held theological convictions that they deemed authoritative, upon the basis of which they were prepared to take action — and these convictions were many and bore heavy consequence. So they were quite prepared to take positions on norms not only of behavior but also of belief, and they clearly deemed urgent broad public conformity to harmonious norms. In the present instance, moreover, they defined the category — belief in the resurrection of the dead, insistence that the Written Torah set forth that fact — and they imputed to it proportionate importance, and, indeed, they labeled the norm for our convenience, so that we need in no way doubt that we have found a valid case of a theological position, one that constitutes a native category, is defined in a clear way in a generative passage, and is assigned great consequence, all by sages themselves. Extending matters outward to the hypothesis that a coherent logic inheres and that sages knew what it was hardy places a heavy strain on our capacity to reason.

The norms of belief that operate here, as much as the norms of behavior that operate elsewhere, prove blatant: the theology of normative Judaism encompasses belief in resurrection of the dead as a teaching of the Torah and treats sacrilege as a matter of lesser consequence. Any account of the theology of the Oral Torah would include that fundamental conviction; an explanation for how it is identified, that is, the category-formation that encompasses it, for where it is to be located, and for its proportionate importance within the larger system set forth by the Oral Torah. But the simple fact that, at this point, a principal document of the Oral Torah states unambiguously a theological teaching suffices to validate the quest for norms of belief alongside those of behavior. It is therefore reasonable to wonder what other norms the Oral Torah defines for its theological program, how these norms hold together into a coherent structure, much as the norms of behavior, properly realized, define a coherent way of life and fully expose in concrete deed a cogent world-view as well.

III. TORAH, ORAL AND WRITTEN

The first step toward a solution to our problem carries us toward the Written Torah. Any attempt to characterize the whole must begin with the Oral Torah's encounter with the Written Torah.[1] For the Oral Torah regards itself as the other half of the whole Torah, acknowledging throughout the presence of the Written Torah. It must follow that the first charge exacted by the method of hunting and gathering is to cut the Oral off from the Written Torah, to treat the one as essentially autonomous of the other, rather than a sustained response thereto. The Karaites, an early medieval Judaism heretical in the context of Rabbinic Judaism, rebelled against the doctrine of the dual Torah by rejecting the Oral part, and the hunters and gatherers perform an act of reverse-Karaism, treating the Oral Torah as "Judaism" — out of all phase with the Written Torah, diminished as it is to a source of not so much proof-texts as mere pretexts. If, therefore, I can show how to identify the main rules for formulating normative doctrine as the Oral Torah inductively identifies those rules and show how these correlated with the right

---

[1] I look in vain in the various accounts of Rabbinic Judaism, or of "Judaism" in general (e.g., common-denominator Judaism) for a systematic exposition of the way in which the one Torah meets the other. Most discussions limit themselves to the technology of exegesis, rarely asking the basic question of how the one Torah organizes itself around the other. The approach I outline in Chapters Four through Six will show how to proceed with that matter, and the expository shank of the book then works the matter out.

reading of appropriate passages of Scripture, then we may begin to speak of Judaism, the religion that joins the oral to the Written Torah in a single whole and coherent statement.[2] If not, then we shall be left where we now are.

Grounds for hope lie in sages' clear signals concerning the explication of normative rules of behavior; for thirteen centuries, from the closure of the Talmud, Rabbinic learning has found in the Rabbinic literature of the period at hand, particularly the Talmud of Babylonia, ample indication of how to select the right rule among the diverse, even conflicting selection of pertinent rules that are afforded by the written sources and cast by the oral one in concrete terms. Processes of legal learning have uncovered not only laws but the law, not only diverse choices one may make but norms to which one must adhere, and the law and the norms have been shown deeply rooted in the Written Torah. These are matters to which we shall return, but the strategy of exposition that I deem logical requires the position of Scripture in the Torah to take priority over all else. It is the fixed point that on its own holds the whole together. It furthermore validates the position that norms of belief, not only norms of behavior, emerge from the right reading of the Torah, the Written in the prism of the Oral.

Sages conducted an on-going dialogue with Scripture in the formulation of their views. Whenever, in the Talmuds, they ask for the source of a law of the Mishnah, the answer invariably must derive from Scripture: "as it is said...," or "as it is written...." Let me give a single sizable example of how this exegetical work, linking the two parts of the Torah, goes forward, justifying my claim that the starting point for all descriptions of the governing theology of the Oral Torah locates itself within the matrix of the Written part:[3]

> **II.2**   A.   How on the basis of Scripture do we know that [trials of this classification take place before] three judge courts?
>
>   B.   *It is in accord with that which our rabbis have taught on Tannaite authority:*

---

[2] As we shall see in Chapter Six for Ruth Rabbah and in Chapter Eight for the symbolic vocabulary of the Oral Torah, the Written Torah defines every last paradigm and supplies every single symbol. The profound interpenetration of the two parts of the One Whole Torah of Moses, our rabbi, constitutes the definitive trait — not the claim but the trait — of Rabbinic Judaism. Yet I look in vain in accounts of that Judaism for appreciation of that fact, let alone emphasis upon it. In this regard the exegetes who have tried to demonstrate the sources, in the peculiarities of the phrasing of the Written Torah, for midrash-exegeses of the Oral Torah, have worked with a deeper understanding of matters than the historians of religion; but the apologetic intent of the exegetes is blatant, and at face value their work cannot be received as descriptive. They begin with the premise that should define the goal of their demonstration.

[3] Italics indicate that the original is in Aramaic, regular type, in Hebrew; bold face type signifies a passage drawn from the Mishnah or the Tosefta.

C. "'Then the householder shall come near to the judge'
    (Ex. 22:8) — lo, one; 'The case of both parties shall
    come before the judge' (Ex. 22:9) — lo, two; and
    'He whom the judge shall condemn shall pay double
    to his neighbor' (Ex. 22:9) — lo, three, [thus the three
    verses specify that three judges must be involved in
    the case]," the words of R. Josiah.

D. R. Jonathan says, "The first allusion to a judge serves
    to introduce the topic, and further exegetical meaning
    cannot be imputed to the first occurrence of a word
    [which serves simply to supply the facts of the
    matter]. Rather: 'The case of both parties shall come
    before the judge' (Ex. 22:9) — lo, one. 'And he whom
    the judge shall condemn shall pay double to his
    neighbor' (Ex. 22:9) — lo, two. You cannot have a
    court with an even number of judges, so add yet
    another, thus three in all."

In this way the two sages have rooted the law of the Oral Torah in the nourishing
soil of the written part. Now we proceed to generalize on the principles of exegesis
that allow the work to go forward:

E. *May we say at issue is whether or not further
    exegetical meaning may be imputed to the first
    occurrence of a word? Thus? one master takes the
    position that further exegetical meaning may be
    imputed to the first occurrence of a word, and the
    other master maintains that further exegetical
    meaning may not be imputed to the first occurrence
    of a word.*

F. *No, all parties concur that, indeed, one may not
    impute to the first occurrence of a word further
    exegetical meaning. What R. Josiah will say to you
    [in response to Jonathan's criticism of his proof] is
    this: "[If the purpose of the passage at hand were
    merely to specify the need for a judge, and if that
    were its sole meaning,] then the author of the passage
    should have said, 'And the householder shall come
    near to the judge [using the word for judge alone,
    rather than the word which serves to mean both
    'judge' and 'God.'] Why does the verse at hand make
    use of the word that bears the double meaning of both*

'judge' and 'God'? That produces the inference that a secondary issue, the number of judges on the court, also is subject to discussion [with the result as specified above.]"

G. And R. Jonathan?

H. *He takes the view that the framer of the passage used commonplace language [and the choice of the word in question was not to convey yet a secondary sense]. That ordinary usage is illustrated by the saying, "He who has a trial should go to a trial-judge."*

I. *But does R. Josiah not concur that a court must be made up of an odd number of judges? And has it not been taught on Tannaite authority:* R. Eliezer, son of R. Yosé the Galilean, says "What is the meaning of the verse of Scripture, ' ... to incline after many to wrest for yourself a court made up of an uneven number of judges.'"

J. *[Indeed, he does not concur, since] he accords with the view of R. Judah, who holds that there are to be seventy judges. For we have learned in the Mishnah:* **The great sanhedrin was made up of seventy one members. ... R. Judah says, "It is seventy"** [M. 1:6A, F].

K. *But I may propose that R. Judah addresses the composition only of the great sanhedrin, concerning which there are relevant verses of Scripture, but as to other courts, does he take the view [that a court need not be made up of an odd number of judges]? And should you say there is indeed no difference, have we not learned in the Mishnah:* **"The laying of hands on a community sacrifice by elders and the breaking of the heifer's neck are done by three judges,"** the words of R. Simeon. R. Judah says, **"By five"** [M. 1:3A-B]. *In this connection it has been said,* "What is the scriptural basis for the position of R. Judah? '...and they shall lay hands...' (Lev. 4:5) — thus speaking of at least two persons, and further specifies, '...the elders...' (Lev. 4:5), thus speaking of at least two persons. Since there cannot be a court with an even number of judges, they add on one more, thus yielding five." [Hence Judah will not accept a court with an even number of judges, except in the

case of the great sanhedrin. Josiah cannot appeal to
Judah as his precedent.]

L. *The position of R. Josiah goes further than R.*
   Judah's. For R. Judah speaks specifically of
   the great sanhedrin, in maintaining that there
   need not be an odd number of judges, but other
   courts must have an odd number of judges,
   while R. Josiah maintains that for all other
   courts too, there cannot be an even number of
   judges.

M. *Now in Josiah's view, how are we to explain*
   the word, "to incline" (Ex. 23:2) [from which
   we have derived the principle that the court
   must have an odd number of judges]?

N. *One may apply that reference to courts that*
   try capital cases but not to courts that try
   property courses. But lo, we have learned in
   the Mishnah: **[In judging property cases], if**
   two judges say, "He is innocent," and one
   says, "He is guilty," he is innocent. If two
   say, "He is guilty," and one says, "He is
   innocent," he is guilty [M. 3:6I-J].

O. *We may maintain that the cited passage does*
   not accord with the view of R. Josiah [since it
   assumes we have an odd number of judges
   trying a property case].

P. *You may maintain that it accords even with*
   the view of R. Josiah. [Schachter, *Sanhedrin*,
   p. 9: He will agree that the decision of the
   majority is valid even in civil cases] by virtue
   of an argument a fortiori. This argument rests
   on the rule covering capital cases. If in capital
   cases, which deal with more severe penalties,
   the All-Merciful has said, "Follow the
   majority," how much the more so [will we
   follow the majority, and hence require an
   uneven number of judges], in a property case?

The discussion proves elaborate, but amply makes the simple point that one unifying
principle of the Oral Torah affirms the integral character of the whole Torah, Oral
and Written. That affirmation leads to the question, what passages in the Written
Torah take priority, and how does the system of the Oral Torah accomplish its

labor of selection and reformation? These are questions that concern large aggregates of data; by its nature, the method of hunting and gathering cannot raise them. None of those who have practiced the method has done so.

But a simple observation shows what is at stake in the effort to identify recurrent patterns and dominant motifs. When the phrases such as "as it is said" or "as it is written" do occur, as they do on nearly every page of both Talmuds, a single predicate follows: a clause or verse of Scripture. No question, "what is the source?" ever finds its answer outside of the Written Torah — not one. That is why the starting point of any account of the theology of the Oral Torah must always carry us deep into the interplay of the two components of the one whole Torah, the Written and the Oral. I already have made reference to the relationship of the oral to the Written Torah, that is, the besought symmetry of sages' writings with those of Scripture. And that dimension of matters, indeterminate but inviolate, defines the outer limits of our search.

But the issue of identifying native categories recurs at this very point. For by asking about the theology of the Oral Torah in particular, I apparently violate sages' deepest conviction that they set forth the full statement of God's revelation to Moses at Sinai. They did not differentiate their views, which we possess in their documents that all together comprise the Oral Torah, from the views of Scripture, which sages' system calls the written (part of the) Torah. On the contrary, sages made every effort, line by line, to demonstrate that opinions that they set forth simply recapitulate the truths of the Written Torah. The very form that they gave to their theological writings, the commentary to a received text, signals their view of their own work: to amplify, to clarify, to extend and spell out, but never to innovate, let alone to add or to subtract. They privileged Scripture, and, in the end, so must we in trying to understand their thought whole. Our sages of blessed memory, were they to speak in our idiom of thought and expression, would have preferred as the title of this book simply "the theology of the Torah," covering what is oral and written. How, exactly, we shall correlate their normative views with appropriate passages of Scripture will emerge in due course.

Nonetheless, standing later than, and outside of, sages' position, we take as our task the description of their views in their own framework, and not only in relationship to Scripture. In this inquiry into the system of theology that inheres in their sayings and that sustains them, Scripture on its own solves no problems. For two reasons, the Oral Torah must stand on its own. First, we cannot begin an account of Rabbinic theology by recapitulating the theology of Scripture or even those books of Scripture to which they made constant reference and then comparing and contrasting what sages had to say with what the verses of Scripture cited by them said when read in Scripture's own context. Such a procedure, while valid for apologetics and the evaluation of apologetics, would only confuse. For it would raise the issue of comparison and contrast of one theological system with another — sages' with Scripture's — while the first task remains, to describe sages' theological system seen whole.

Second, any claim that Scripture and its teachings provoked the formation of sages' system (if it is a system) and accounts for its character and contents not only would merely recapitulate sages' own apologetics. It also would contain the implicit claim that sages' system forms the logical and authentic development of Scripture's, thus excluding all the other Judaic and Christian systems that equally set forth that same claim in their own behalf. To evaluate such a claim of theological authenticity, of the inevitability of sages' system in consequence of Scripture's, we should have further to mount a sustained critique of all other Judaisms' and Christianities' claims to form the natural next step, the logical and necessary fulfillment, of Scripture. Then, so far as the history of religion is the exegesis of exegesis, we should find ourselves addressing nearly the entire histories of Judaisms and Christianities in the West. That not only would carry us far afield but would also divert attention from our main work.

But if in our inquiry into the systematic, historical theology of the documents of the Oral Torah we avoid issues of theological apologetics ("sages really said what Scripture had said earlier") or the evaluation thereof ("no, they didn't"), we cannot for a single moment turn our backs on Scripture and dismiss sages' vast panoply of proof-texts as mere pretexts. As soon as we examine the basic topical program that the score of documents that all together constitute the written down version of the Oral Torah lay out, we find ourselves deep within the structures of biblical theology. The Deuteronomic theology, prophetic doctrine, the picture of Israel's history set forth in the Authorized History from Genesis through Kings — in the documents of the Oral Torah these dictate the main lines of thought and interpretation. So we find ourselves always poised between a recapitulation of Scripture's account of Israel's existence and an independent and fresh reconsideration of the basic issues of that existence. But in so stating, I have gotten ahead of my story, adumbrating what in fact will ultimately form the solution to our problem. Let us turn back to the problem of theological method.

iv. Framing the Theological Question in the Oral Torah

When to our sages of blessed memory we address the theological question — what normative statements does a given religious system make, and how do those statements cohere into a logical structure of articulated faith concerning God — their answer comes from writings of a very particular character. And that fact governs the problem of identifying the normative position of the Oral Torah, viewed whole or in any important component. These peculiar features now demand attention.

First, the documents that preserve sages' opinions rarely preserve the marks of individual writers but speak for the collectivity of sages. They are public, anonymous, rarely idiosyncratic. That on the face of matters justifies the conviction that sages make coherent statements, all together and all at once. They take positions, they define norms of belief as much as of behavior. But, as I have explained, they also encompass so vast a range of opinion that defining where the weight of opinion takes its position presents considerable difficulty. We do not enjoy the option of dismissing conflicting opinions as idiosyncratic, not when a consensus-statement encompasses them both.

A second trait of sages' writings makes matters still more parlous. In one way or another the documents conduct an exegetical dialogue with a received text, Scripture, on the one side, the Mishnah, on the other. That dialogue makes exceedingly difficult the presentation of well-crafted arguments in behalf of articulated propositions — or any other blatant, syllogistic discourse. Systematic, syllogistic, propositional discourse gives way to occasional and random observations on this and that. The hunters and gatherers carried on as they did for good reason: the very character of the documents required that very work, if indeed they were to accomplish anything at all. Beyond the Mishnah, propositional discourse proves difficult to discern.

If, by contrast, we turn to Aphrahat, representing the Syriac-writing Fathers of Christianity, Augustine for the Latin, and Origen for the Greek, we find systematic essays on a variety of propositions, with the particular Church Father's position clearly stated and rigorously advanced through argument. We therefore encounter little difficulty in stating the position of, e.g., Aphrahat on the theological issues, for instance, the Christian requirement of celibacy, the status of "the people that is of the peoples" that is the Christian community, and the like. Not only so, but Church councils adopted creeds, which set forth normative beliefs. Consequently, those engaged in the counterpart work on Patristic Christianity, of the same time and place, might choose among viable alternatives in composing an account of Christian theology. They could describe the systems of major figures. They could survey the positions, upon a common topic, of a variety of named authorities. They could consult the creeds that Church order produced and that institutional processes delivered as authoritative. But for our part, as I said, we cannot say much about individual sages' systems; we cannot therefore compared and contrast established, articulated positions on the same topic; and we cannot appeal to an institutionally-generated creed for a picture of how things are deemed to emerge at the end, out of diversity.

Thus, by contrast, Aqiba's doctrine of free will comes to us in a single saying, cited earlier, and for sages' doctrine of who and what is Israel (counterpart to the ecclesiological doctrine), we have to assemble a vast variety of sayings and stories. But when we do, all that we produce is a vast variety of sayings and stories. While the documents' traits point to normative as against schismatic judgment, these require careful delineation. We have no evidence of sages' systematically, politically confronting schism and diverse opinion. We find no creeds, beyond those implicit in the liturgy. We rarely even find, in theological discourse, much systematic explication of the choices on a given, shared agenda, such as we find in the presentation of norms of behavior. No wonder then that when scholars have tried to define and describe "Judaism," meaning, the Judaism set forth in the Rabbinic literature, the results have proved wanting.

That is not because pertinent sayings and stories lack. The success, the sheer volume of the results of the hunters and gatherers, demonstrate the contrary. In the corpus of documents that comprise the Oral Torah, ample evidence of opinion on the critical theological issues responds to the standard agenda that dogmatic theology sets forth. If we collect and arrange sayings on God, Torah, Israel, free will, atonement, the meaning of history, and the like, we find ample information on how one or another authority formulated opinion on theological subjects. Three issues remain. First, did sages deem these topics to constitute native categories, or do we find ourselves fabricating categories of our own invention to satisfy curiosity particular to our situation? Then come two further questions, once the category-formation is validated. What we need to find out, second, is the standing of a given opinion within the larger setting of the norms of the faith and the doctrine of the Oral Torah, on the one side, and, third, how normative opinion on one subject cohered with that on some other, e.g., how the doctrine of Israel and the doctrine of history cohered in a single cogent account, which, furthermore, held together with the doctrine of Providence and free will. So ours is a three dimensional inquiry: how to validate our category-formations, how to identify the normative from the idiosyncratic or schismatic, and how to define the principles of rationality and order that made of diverse normative doctrines a single, internally logical doctrine of God, Torah, and Israel, all together.

The work of addressing, asking, and answer the theological question of the Oral Torah therefore carries us, to begin with, to the character of the evidence under discussion. And that is where we commence: what exactly are the topics that the several documents treat? The answer to that question defines the concrete theological agenda of Rabbinic Judaism.

v. Obstacles to Defining the Theology of the ORAL TORAH

The essential character of the documents of the Oral Torah, from the Mishnah through the Talmud of Babylonia, ca. 200-600 C.E., including the Midrash-compilations of the same age, accounts for the difficulty we face in specifying just what these writings say when speaking all together and all at once on any given subject. The obstacles to theological description that the sources set in our path, already alluded to, may be rapidly toted up.

First, the documents record not only decisions but the deliberations that lead to decisions, including schismatic opinion and argument as well as what is normative.

Not only so, but the documents provide only subtle signals to mark what is normative — if they give any at all.

Furthermore, they are not composed as systematic expositions of a given viewpoint or even disquisitions of diverse viewpoints on a given subject. They follow their own plan of organization and exposition, as exegetical compilations often appealing for cogency among sequences of opinions to the order and plan of a prior document.

Fourth, as I have already said, the documents find a place for a wide variety of opinion, on any given topic much of it contradictory. But a text on which comments are collected does not provide the natural setting for systematic expositions of cogent propositions, well-argued, with evidence and analysis. In a literature that invests great effort in preserving sayings of great masters while outside of the context of legal exposition only occasionally comparing these sayings and contrasting them against one another, stating the position of the whole out of the confusion of the parts proves not at all easy.

How then are we to know what "Judaism" or "the Torah" teaches? Let us dwell on the juxtaposition of conflicting opinions, with little or no obvious guidance on which stands for the document and its official statement, its Judaism as to a given topic. In this context I refer not merely to theological paradoxes, such as "R. Aqiba says, 'Everything is foreseen, and free choice is given'" (Mishnah-tractate Abot 3:15A). Contemporary theology has afforded ample experience in dealing with paradox and irony. Nor do I lay emphasis upon the presence of sayings on the same topic that in proposition do not really intersect; these need not conflict, but to show how they contribute to a common system represents a considerable challenge. Rather, I point to side-by-side statements that stand in explicit, direct conflict, statements that jar because both cannot be right at the same time, and, therefore, in the present context, one must be wrong, while the other may be right. Typically, a sequence of opinions on a given theme will set forth a variety of possibilities. On the basis of the following, for instance, we may affirm that "the rabbis" believe that the Messiah will come at some point, under some circumstances — but we should have difficulty in saying precisely what "they" — "the rabbis," or "Judaism" — thought about the details that matter. But the composite before us also shows that a question important in our own time defined a category-formation for the Talmud of Babylonia as well: the Messiah and when he will come. Here we review a bit of that Talmud's thematic composite on the subject, which both proves that the Messiah and his timing defined an organizing category, and also that the materials that are assembled exhibit no system and yield no dogma for further theological analysis.

> **I.88**   A.   *Said R. Qattina, "The world will exist for six thousand years and be destroyed for one thousand..."*
>
>   C.   *Abbayye said, "It will be desolate for two thousand years,* as it is said, 'After two days will he revive us, in the third day, he will raise us up and we shall live in his sight' (Hos. 6:2)."
>
> **I.89**   A.   *A Tannaite authority of the house of Elijah [said],* "For six thousand years the world will exist.
>
>   B.   "For two thousand it will be desolate, two thousand years [will be the time of] Torah, and two thousand years will be the days of the Messiah.

C. **[97B]** but on account of our numerous sins what has been lost [of those years, in which the Messiah should have come but has not come] has been lost.

I.90 A. Said Elijah to R. Sala the Pious, "The world will last for no fewer than eighty-five Jubilees [of fifty years each], and the son of David will come in the last one."

I.91 A. R. Hanan, son of Tahalipa, sent to R. Joseph, "I came across a man who had in hand a scroll, written in Assyrian [block] letters in the holy language.

B. "I said to him, 'Where did you get this?'

C. "He said to me, 'I was employed in the Roman armies, and I found it in the Roman archives.'

D. "In the scroll it is written that after four thousand two hundred ninety-two years from the creation of the world, the world will be an orphan.

E. "[As to the years to follow] in some there will be wars of the great dragons, and in some, wars of Gog and Magog, and the rest will be the days of the Messiah.

F. "And the Holy One, blessed be he, will renew his world only after seven thousand years."

G. R. Aha, son of Raba, said, "'After five thousand years' *is what is said."*

BAVLI SANHEDRIN 97A-B, PASS.

Readers may stipulate that I can have presented a much larger abstract without significantly affecting the outcome. Among the compilations of opinion on various questions that form topical miscellanies in the Talmud of Babylonia and counterparts to those compilations in the Midrash-compilations, numerous counterparts are to be located. Here we address a broad range of opinion, much of it in conflict. The world will exist for six thousand years, or for eighty-five Jubilee cycles (4450 years); it will lie in ruins for a thousand years or two thousand years; the Holy One will renew the world after seven thousand years or five thousand years, and so on. Here we have a minor instance of a major puzzle.

Readers may further allow that I could have presented a formidable array of examples of equivalent confusion. But if in the mouths of sages, all of them honored and authoritative, we find everything and its opposite, then the Oral Torah affords only a compendium of diverse opinions, not a guide to a well-conceived system of coherent ideas framing an orderly world-view. As the upshot of such a result — conceptual chaos — Rabbinic Judaism, defined as it is by the documents of the Oral Torah, loses all claim to possessing a voice and a viewpoint, therefore to a serious hearing from the faithful in quest of a cogent viewpoint and standpoint.

VI. THE ISSUE OF INNER LOGIC: COMPILATIONS OF DIVERSE OPINIONS OR A COHERENT AND SYSTEMATIC STATEMENT?

Now, if all we have before us is a compilation of diverse opinions, the passage at hand serves as well as any other to illustrate what is to be done to form a topical miscellany. But if we ask large scale composites,[4] indeed, the documents all together, to make a coherent statement, to offer a system with a logic and a rationality, then we cannot settle for a scrapbook of odds and ends, frequently in conflict with one another. The great philosopher and historian of Greek science, G. E. R. Lloyd describes this matter in language that serves equally well for the various Judaic systems prior to the Rabbinic one that we consider here:

> The Egyptians...had various beliefs about the way the sky is held up. One idea was that it is supported on posts, another that it is held up by a god, a third that it rests on walls, a fourth that it is a cow or a goddess...But a story-teller recounting anyone such myth need pay no attention to other beliefs about the sky, and he would hardly have been troubled by an y inconsistency between them. Nor, one may assume, did he feel that his own account was in competition with any other in the sense that it might be more or less correct or have better or worse grounds for its support than some other belief.[5]

If we examine the two creation-myths of Genesis, or the two stories of the Flood, we see how readily conflicting stories might be joined together, and how little credence was placed on the possibility that one theory of matters, embodied in one version, might be correct, the other wrong. In search of dispute and debate, articulated and pursued, we simply look in vain through the entire heritage of Israelite Scriptures (with a stated exception given presently) and through all extra-scriptural writings of various Judaic systems. But, like Greek philosophy, Talmudic jurisprudence in due course, by contrast, articulately faced the possibility that differing opinion competed and that the thinker must advocate the claim that his theory was right, the other's wrong. Conflicting principles both cannot be right, and merely announcing an opinion without considering alternatives and proposing to falsify them does not suffice for intellectual endeavor. And with the recognition of that possibility of not only opinion but argument, Greek philosophy engaged in debate:

---

[4] For the distinction between composition and composite, which is critical to my entire analytical system for the documents, see the exposition in *The Rules of Composition of the Talmud of Babylonia. The Cogency of the Bavli's Composite.* Atlanta, 1991: Scholars Press for South Florida Studies in the History of Judaism.

[5] G. E. R.Lloyd, *Early Greek Science. Thales to Aristotle.* New York, 1970: W. W. Norton & Co.,, pp. 11-12. See also G. E. R. Lloyd, *Greek Science after Aristotle.* N.Y., 1973: W. W. Norton Co.and his *Polarity and Analogy. Two Types of Argumentation in Early Greek Thought.* Cambridge, 1966: Cambridge University Press.

> When we turn to the early Greek philosophers, there is a fundamental difference. Many of them tackle the same problems and investigate the same natural phenomena [as Egyptian and other science], but it is tacitly assumed that the various theories and explanations they propose are directly competing with one another. The urge is towards finding the best explanation, the most adequate theory, and they are then forced to consider the grounds for their ideas, the evidence and arguments in their favor, as well as the weak points in their opponents' theories.[6]

Now anyone who has devoted time and effort to Talmud study will find familiar the description of the ethos and method of Greek philosophy, since, in its stress on criticism and analysis, proposition and counter-proposition, evidence and argument, above all, dialectical discourse, the Talmud portrays intellects profoundly engaged in the quest for the logic, the rationality, of all things. The Mishnah and Tosefta and Sifra contain ample arguments that build on the premise, two conflicting views cannot stand. Powerful instruments of analysis compare and contrast governing metaphors, criticizing one party's and validating the other's. The dialectical argument of the Talmud of Babylonia evinces not a shred of tolerance for disharmony and contradictory statements, always insisting one is right, the other wrong; or attempting to show that different results emerge by reason of divergent generative principles.[7] The very character of much of the writing of the Oral Torah testifies against the notion that all we have in hand are random sayings, not formed into propositions and arguments.

It is the simple fact that sages' writings articulate dispute and undertake to select the right opinion and reject the wrong one. The Mishnah finds its simplest definition in the dispute-form, which points up competing views and their principles, rarely then proposing to ignore or harmonize them. The two Talmuds compose systematic, dialectical arguments to articulate difference and negotiate it. In these fundamental ways the writings give ample evidence of conforming to the requirements of philosophical, not mythic, thinking, as Lloyd lays out matters.

That is why I find it implausible to concede at the outset that the same masters who produced the Talmudic argument can have found sufficient for the statement of their views on religious questions — which we have in abundance — a mere collection of random and conflicting opinions. The very nature of the Talmud of Babylonia and the more rigorous Midrash-compilations — Sifra and the two Sifrés, rich as they are in sustained argument, for instance — argues in favor of the hypothesis that the Oral Torah sustains a systematic theology, as much

---

[6] Lloyd, *op. cit.*, p. 12.

[7] See my *Jerusalem and Athens: The Congruity of Talmudic and Classical Philosophy.* Leiden, 1997: E. J. Brill. *Supplements to the Journal for the Study of Judaism.*, and, further, *Talmudic Dialectics: Types and Forms.* Atlanta, 1995: Scholars Press for South Florida Studies in the History of Judaism. I. *Introduction. Tractate Berakhot and the Divisions of Appointed Times and Women.* II. *The Divisions of Damages and Holy Things and Tractate Niddah.*

as it sets forth critical, well- and rigorously examined, systematic law. Not only so, but when, in Chapter Two, readers review the entire topical repertoire of the documents of the Oral Torah, they will find ample reason to concur to begin with in the proposition that a limited and cogent set of ideas animates the whole.

Not only so, but, as we realize, sages insisted on establishing norms of conduct: this is how matters are to be done, this way only. But if we adopt the hypothesis that sages thought about belief as systematically and rigorously as they did about behavior, then what of the result: what were these ideas, and how did they hold together, and where are we to find them, and how shall we know when we do? It is then our task to find out where and how the systematic discourse, yielding cogent and well-construed theology, took shape, alongside the coherent law that at the very surface the free debate and open discussion of politics and law yielded in the Talmud of Babylonia and related writings. For, as a matter of blatant fact, within the world of philosophical rigor, the high appreciation of argument and even dialectics that was exhibited by our sages of blessed memory who produced the documents of the Oral Torah, the same person, within the same logic, cannot maintain that something is be both itself and its opposite, and contradictory facts can claim no equivalence as to accuracy within the same framework of analysis. Two competing theories cannot both be right. So far as the task of theology finds definition in uncovering the logic, order, system, and structure of a corpus of religious statements, identifying the ones that fit and preserving as schismatic the ones that do not, theology nourishes that hunger for order and rationality that the thoughtful among the faithful seek to sate.

VII. THE RELEVANCE, TO THE STUDY OF RABBINIC JUDAISM, OF THE THEOLOGY OF THE ORAL TORAH

The issues now are clearly drawn and the stakes specified. If we can find pretty much anything and its opposite, then the question is, what, among many sayings, is the saying that stands for Judaism, the saying that is authoritative, the one that registers. And the answer to that question proves urgent anytime anyone wishes to use the language, "Judaism teaches...." In the diversity and complexity of contemporary Judaic discourse, in the setting of the world's interest in that religion and of hostile interest at that, the capacity to assess proportion, to say authoritatively, this matters, that does not — these uses of learning in the exercise of taste and judgment in contemporary theological and even political discourse prove more than merely useful. They are critical.

Let me spell this point out. First comes the uses of the documents of the Oral Torah for contemporary Judaic theological discourse. Sages' views circulate throughout contemporary religious discussion in Judaism, forming a vast corpus of probative precedents. People constantly cite "the rabbis said," to prove their point, whether the point concerns theological or social or political and public policy. They therefore engage in a labor of mediation, from then to now. Their premise is that what sages said governs, and further we can understand and invoke sages' statements. The present work promises to work out the requirements of that premise: how to move from then to now? That explains why I propose to ask, how, living by the intellectual rules that govern rationality and logic in our time, how should our sages of blessed memory set forth the theological composition that, within the aesthetics and protocol of cogent discourse that pertained to them in their day, they have laid out in the remarkable writings studied here? Ours is a task of cultural mediation, and the criterion of success emerges in a simple question: this is what they said, but is this in context what they meant? Here is what they meant, and, in the context of shared logic that the theological inquiry presupposes at its foundations, does this make sense?

But, as I have already hinted, matters transcend issues of theoretical inquiry into theology, even thought these predominate. For the challenge of theology to the Oral Torah arises not only out of inquiry into the history and structure of religious ideas. So far as, in our own day, people propose to set forth theological propositions in the name of "Judaism," as in the language, "Judaism teaches...," or "the Torah tells...," they owe themselves answers to the question, on what basis does this "Judaism" or "Torah" take said position? Is it a random opinion, assigned to a named authority in a single document, that you invoke to set forth that Judaic position? Or do you claim to speak in the name of the Torah, written and oral, as the Oral Torah reframes matters for the ages? Not only does the issue of schismatic as against normative opinion demand attention. Even if we can show that a given opinion forms part of a large, perhaps inchoate consensus, we have still to ask ourselves whether said opinion occupies a position of importance relative to other opinions that all together form the corpus of Rabbinic sayings.

As in any system, an opinion may occur, may enjoy standing, but may not make much difference. So the issue of proportion likewise requires close consideration. And, third, our questions do not always correspond to the answers that the documents set forth. We bring to the documents issues vital in our own time, religious questions to which we attach urgency. But even while saying what appears pertinent to our questions, the documents often turn out to take up issues of their own. Anachronism perpetually threatens the authenticity of our account, not only because of disproportion, but also because of sheer incongruity.

To give a practical, if slightly lunatic, example: an anti-Semite here at home in Tampa, Florida, one day discovered in the Talmud what he thought was the statement that Jews should kill gentiles, so he rented a bill board on a busy thoroughfare to announce his discovery. Reporters' calls to me inevitably followed, and I found myself explaining the complexities of dealing with a document that records process, not only proposition, and that preserves, often without signalling a judgment, a wide variety of opinions and sayings in the certainty, sometimes misplaced, that people can differentiate the normative from the schismatic or even disreputable. The little snippet given above shows how difficult it is to determine what, if anything, represents the considered and authoritative position of Judaism on even a simple question of when the Messiah will come.

Not only unlettered idiots but even learned Swedish theology professors find in the Talmud support for imputing to Judaism positions that manifestly contradict the entire heritage of the faith and moral record of the faithful. Finding and (mis)interpreting a saying that seemed apt an Uppsala University Theology Professor discovered a saying that he thought stood for "Judaism" and therefore he too went and announced to the world that in Judaism it is a religious duty for Jews to kill gentiles. He subsequently apologized in public, whereupon his colleague, another Uppsala professor undertook to lecture the international meeting of the Nordic Association for Jewish Studies on why killing a gentile might represent a religious duty such as to transform into a religious action the very character of an auto accident in Stockholm, fatality resulting, if a Jewish driver was at fault. We need not dwell on the convoluted reasoning, the perverse, indeed perverted, mentality, required to produce such ghastly propositions. Critics were reduced to pointing out the diversity of opinion recorded in the Talmud — as though that answered the question. Once more, people faced but could not accomplish the task of explaining the character of the record that was cited, specifically, the proportion and authority of the entire system and structure that the document sustains. So the diffuse and diverse character of the writings of the Oral Torah make the theological question urgent.

The upshot is, theological inquiry into the logic of the whole, its coherence and cogency and modes of making harmonious and balanced statements, presents an immediate and necessary task, not merely an idle inquiry into a long-ago and far-away religion that has passed from the scene. Ours is a problem of theory, but we bear a heavy responsibility to contemporary religious discourse in Judaism: the possibility of conducting such discourse at all.

III

Formulating and Answering the Theological Question: Established Methods

I. FROM DIACHRONIC TO SYNCHRONIC DESCRIPTION

We come, now, to how theological questions have been formulated, ways in which the documents, viewed synchronically, have been asked to produce an account of the entire theology of the Oral Torah. Before laying out the three complementary approaches that I have devised, in Chapters Four through Six, Seven, and Eight, respectively, I turn to an account of the two most important theological studies of Rabbinic Judaism.

Let us begin the review with the basic question: what makes anyone suppose the theological question can be asked at all? My answer, resting on the documentary reading of the Oral Torah, is, because the documents themselves form coherent statements, one by one, it is quite reasonable to inquire whether and how these individually-coherent statements themselves further hold together and where we may identify characteristics of that coherence. These traits will show the patterns that govern the whole. Consequently, they in turn will dictate the task of exegesis of detail taken up by the parts. So in taking the measure of the writings in their dimensions of autonomy, connection, and continuity, we move onward and upward by turning inward.

The quality of the evidence matches the character of the problem, and that fact points toward the solution. As we noted in the Preface and in Chapter One, those who value the books deem them to set forth a public consensus. Consequently (and obviously) in them we find everything that in the judgment of the system and its faithful self-evidently belongs, and nothing that in that same system's judgment that obviously does not belong. And that leads us to the main lines of the solution to the problem of theological description, in the exact language already set forth in the Preface. By the simplest definition of a kindred body of writings of an official character — that is, the written recapitulation of a corporate religious system — *there can be no rationality that governs in one document of a given corpus of kindred, authoritative writings but not in another of the same corpus.*

Details may conflict, governing principles cannot. One sage may hold one opinion, another sage, the opposite. But both must affirm shared premises, or one must be excluded from the textual community and labeled as not schismatic but heretical. The same sense of what is fitting prevails everywhere. That is why, wherever we commence our work, a systematic examination of the corpus seen whole will yield a hypothesis concerning the implicit traits of rationality. In any document we should discern the evidences of the governing logic that pervades the whole. Any piece of evidence serves as well as any other, and all, moreover, stand in judgment upon every result. For what we seek is the paradigm or model that in the end everywhere prevails; what we seek to describe comes to the surface wherever we look, when we know how. These define the conditions that will dictate the solution to the problem of theological description that Chapter Four will set forth.

But that claim of mine — a single rationality governs all documents of the same corpus by reason of the systemic task carried out by the kindred writings — is a matter of theory based on the definition of a body of official writings as recapitulative of a system. Applied theology and practical reason concerning knowledge of God take place, in the documents before us, in the concrete form of doctrines and rulings, norms of belief and behavior, respectively. Practicing philosophical theology and jurisprudence only through cases and examples, sages set forth no abstract inquiry into how we know anything at all about God, let alone into the nature and source of our knowledge or any of the other topics that a theological system shaped within a philosophy of formidable dimensions will address. That explains why established methods of describing the theology of Rabbinic Judaism have addressed questions not of abstract reason or theoretical logic but of practical reason and logic applied to particular questions.[1] When we consider the result, we see why the available models of theological inquiry fail, and therefore understand how a quite fresh approach to the problem of theological description demands formulation.

---

[1] It also accounts for the very odd dogma of nineteenth and earlier twentieth century scholarship on Rabbinic Judaism that "Judaism has no dogmas." From the declaration that God is one to the insistence upon belief in the origin in the Torah for the doctrine of the resurrection of the dead, the liturgy and law of Rabbinic Judaism testify that that Judaism sustains a large corpus of dogmas indeed and is quite prepared to expel those that deny them. Orthopraxy always presents temptation to the faithful of a system that values action as much as attitude. The dogma, "eat kosher but think treif" (that is, unkosher thoughts) that was imparted by the immigrant-generation of professors at the Jewish Theological Seminary of America in the 1940s and 1950s produced Conservative rabbis uncertain of what, if any, convictions they had to teach to their congregations.

II. AVAILABLE MODELS OF SYNCHRONIC DESCRIPTION

We address the two truly formidable and original statements of dogmatic theology that have undertaken to characterize Rabbinic Judaism, those that have rested on a deep knowledge of the Rabbinical writings: George Foot Moore's *Judaism in the First Centuries of the Christian Era. The Age of the Tannaim,*[2] and Ephraim E. Urbach, *The Sages. Their Concepts and Beliefs.*[3] The one concentrated on dogmatic, the other on historical, theology. Both accomplished everything but the main thing. That is, if we wish to review sayings on various topics, Moore and Urbach oblige. If we propose to describe, analyze, and interpret what we find, they do not, substituting paraphrase for rigorous inquiry. Now let me make these judgments stick.

Predictably, historians of Rabbinic theology, here represented by the two best of all time, George F. Moore and Ephraim E. Urbach, one in English and the other in Hebrew, have framed the theological question in concrete rather than in systemic and systematic terms. Moore accomplished a dogmatic theology, Urbach a quasi- (or pseudo-) historical one. Moore's agenda of dogmas came straight out of Protestant Christianity, and Urbach's historical data depended upon accepting as fact, without a trace of criticism, whatever the sources alleged a given authority said or did. The one uninterested in problems of category-formation, the other indifferent to all historical critical method, both produced deeply flawed, and ultimately implausible, accounts of the theology of Rabbinic Judaism. Moore's categories ignored the native categories of the system and consequently paid no attention to vast and critical components of the systemic statement, and Urbach's claim to do any kind of history or history of ideas was utterly fraudulent. In both cases we see a failure of intellect. For what each did, as distinct from what was claimed, was a vast labor of collecting and arranging sayings, which then were paraphrased, elegantly by Moore, clumsily by Urbach (as we shall see). Both defined for themselves a program of concrete questions of dogma and doctrine and, ignoring documentary lines altogether, they then hunted, gathered, and organized the sayings that answered those questions, wherever they found them in the Rabbinic corpus. Their entirely reasonable premise maintained that specific, propositional knowledge comes through reasoned reading of the Torah.

But that then-accepted strategy of inquiry — hunting and gathering sayings on a given subject — erred because questions of detail were addressed too soon, and the logically prior questions of method were not asked at all. Too much was taken for granted, and the givens of their work proved flawed in basic ways. These flaws involved not only an uncritical reading of sources and (in Urbach's case) a vacant intellectual program. Issues that in due course will occupy us — category-

---

[2] Cambridge, 1927: Harvard University Press. I-III.
[3] Translated from the Hebrew by Israel Abrahams. Jerusalem: The Magnes Press, The Hebrew University, 1975. Two volumes. I. Text: pp. xxii and 692. II. Notes: pp. 383.

formation, location, proportion, in the context of the governing system — never came to the fore. Moore's agenda derived from the main lines of Protestant dogmatics. Urbach's improved upon matters only marginally, but the fundamental intellectual incompetence of the work — its incoherence, start to finish — rendered the improvements null. That is why, when it comes to the theology of the Oral Torah, the two outstanding, available models ask questions of detail while missing the main point, telling us the results of modes of thought and rationality that have not been brought to systematic definition.

In fact *how* we know — the intellectual media of God's self-revelation — takes priority over *what* we know, because the how defines the what. The theological method dictates the questions that we to begin with may ask, and once the logic or rationality has registered, then the character of the questions we shall formulate has been determined — or predetermined. However we frame that how — whether we use, for the structure, the terms model, or paradigm, or pattern, and, for the system, rationality, reason, or logic — it is that how of theological thought that requires definition. Only then does propositional knowledge emerges. How we know takes priority over what we know and governs what we know. Much then depends upon how we frame the theological question, the point of entry we define for ourselves taking priority. Urbach's and Moore's indifference to questions of method, their tacit acceptance of what they deemed self-evident rules of theological research, produced the result before us. That is why, to formulate an answer to that question of how we know the theological traits of the documents seen all together, we first take up established models of what has been done and what even now most learning does to define this (or any other) Judaism.

III. WHAT IS WRONG WITH THE DOGMATIC THEOLOGY OF THE ORAL TORAH: MOORE

Morton Smith comments on Moore's work, "Although it too much neglects the mystical, magical and apocalyptic sides of Judaism, its apology for tannaitic teaching as a reasonable, humane, and pious working out of biblical tradition is conclusive..."[4] Putting matters more bluntly, Moore goes down in history as the greatest apologist, gentile or Jewish, in the English language, that Rabbinic Judaism ever produced. And that is why his work enjoyed the remarkable publishing success that it has, being adopted as a text book in Rabbinic schools for the education of generations of rabbis, the only work on Judaism written in a Protestant divinity school to enjoy such extraordinary sponsorship.

His dogmatic theology fails, however, because its category-formation does not match the documents that he described. As a result, what self-evidently played a principal part in sages' religious system found no place in Moore's account, and issues of marginal systemic consequence took priority. Moore's *Judaism*

---

[4] *Encyclopaedia Judaica* 12:293-4; compare *Harvard Library Bulletin* 15, 1967, pp. 169-179.

nonetheless enjoyed immediate success, because it so aptly matched its program with the prevailing sensibility. Telling people what they wanted to know, specifically facing down a century of violently anti-Semitic accounts of Judaism deriving from Christian scholars and setting forth a Judaism that Protestants could respect, the book sold remarkably well from the outset. It made its appearance in May 1927 and was reprinted in November, indicating the publisher had underestimated its market. Then the book had a third printing in 1932, a fourth in 1944, and a seventh in 1954, and remains in print and current. Not only was it an immediate success in the marketplace but the earliest reviews accorded the book a remarkably favorite reception. Among those of 1927 only one, F.C. Porter's, which I shall cite at length below, raised important critical questions alongside entirely appropriate, adulatory comments.

Moore states, "The aim of these volumes is to represent Judaism in the centuries in which it assumed definitive form as it presents itself in the tradition which it has always regarded as authentic. These primary sources come to us as they were compiled and set in order in the second century of the Christian era..." The upshot — an uncomplicated account, covering topics of common interest, placing the system into the century in which Christianity originated and representing that Judaism as a viable alternative to Christianity or at least not as a religion for book keepers, a religion of pots and pans, as German Protestant theology said — was recognized by Jews. Moore became the authoritative account of Judaism for Reform and Conservative seminaries and found its way into synagogue libraries everywhere. But the warmest tribute, of course, is envy and imitation, and the main outlines of Moore's argument and the principal definition of issues and methods came to be imitated in accounts of exactly the same subject, constructed in exactly the same way, yielding exactly the same results, for the following fifty years. So for one set of reasons, Jewish scholars of Judaism and most rabbis, and for another set of reasons, Christian scholars of Judaism, reached the same positive conclusion. Moore had said the last word, which now needed only to be repeated by scholars proposing to say their own last word.

The critical problem of theology is presented by the organizing category, "Judaism" (replaced in this book by "the Oral Torah"). Moore does not think definition is needed. But we now know that it is. Explaining what we propose to define when we speak about "Judaism" is the work of not only theology but also both contemporary philosophy of religion and history of religion. In general historians of religions have tended altogether too rapidly to articulate that phenomenon the history of which they claimed to describe.

Moore fails to tell us also of whom he wishes to speak. So his repertoire of sources for the description of "Judaism" in the "age of the Tannaim" is awry. Not only so, but, as was the way in the study of Judaism (but not of Scripture) in that day, Moore took at face value all attributions. If a saying was assigned to an authority assumed to have lived in the first or second century, Moore took for granted that that sage made that statement at that time, and, moreover, that statement stood for common opinion of the day. He makes use of sources which speak of people assumed to have lived in the early centuries of the Common Era, even when said sources derive from a much later or a much earlier time. And without a shred of evidence, he knew that those sayings described a common Judaism, everywhere normative as a matter of simple fact. In advancing the cause of contemporary religious apologetics for Judaism (and for Protestant Christianity in the Anglo-American framework, eager to take its leave from the blatant anti-Semitism of German Protestant counterparts), Moore set back critical study by a century.

What generates this error is the problem of dealing with a category asymmetrical to the evidence.[5] That is, an essentially philosophical or (for us) theological construct, "Judaism," is imposed upon wildly diverse evidence deriving from many kinds of social groups and testifying to the state of mind and way of life of many sorts of Jews, who in their own day would scarcely have understood one another (for instance, Bar Kokhba and Josephus, or the teacher of righteousness and Aqiba). So for Moore, "Judaism" is a problem of ideas, and the history of Judaism is the history of ideas abstracted from the groups that held them and from the social perspectives of said groups and recombined into an ahistorical, asocial construction of conceptions. This seems to me a fundamental error, making the category "Judaism" a construct of a wholly fantastic realm of thought.

Moore's research is in theology, narrowly construed. It is organized in theological categories. But they are not the categories of the theology of the Oral Torah, principal ones of which Moore simply missed. The relationship of the Oral Torah to the Written one, the theology implicit in the law to which most of the Tannaite sayings are devoted, and the primacy of the sage — the three indicative traits of the theology of the Oral Torah and critical concerns on nearly every page of its documents simply do not play a commensurate role in Moore's picture. Moore therefore not only misses the main points of that theology but also distorts the theology that is set forth. His category-formation presents a mass of blunders; he did not know therefore how to locate and what to make of the most important evidence; and he misconstrued the elementary proportions of the system ("Judaism") as a whole. So what is at stake in these three matters of category-formation, location, and proportion finds definition in Moore's failure.

Moore presents a synthetic account of diverse materials, (deriving from diverse sources) focused upon a given topic of theological interest. What is constructed as a static exercise in dogmatic theology, not an account of the history

---

[5] But his error, on the side of including too much — utilizing sources whenever edited in response to unevaluated attributions — surely is matched by scholars for whom "Judaism" is fully described out of the resources of apocryphal and pseudepigraphic writings of the period before 70, without any attention at all to the social foundations and the historical limitations of the documents adduced in evidence.

of religious ideas and — still more urgent — their unfolding in relationship to the society of the people who held those ideas.[6] Moore in no way describes and interprets the religious world-view and way of life expressed, in part, through the ideas under study. He does not explore the interplay between that world-view and the historical and political context of the community envisioned by that construction of a world. So far as history attends to the material context of ideas and the class structure expressed by ideas and institutions alike, so far as ideas are deemed part of a larger social system and religious systems are held to be pertinent to the given political, social, and economic framework which contains them, Moore's account of dogmatic theology to begin with has nothing to do with religious history, that is the history of Judaism in the first two centuries of the Common Era.

Moore's systematic and dogmatic theology draws upon a vast range of evidence, adducing testimony for the character of the Judaism he describes from documents deriving from diverse groups which, in their own day will not have understood one another, let alone have accepted as part of the same social and cultic community. When "Judaism" is made to refer to the exegetical compilations of the rabbis of the fourth and fifth centuries — and much later — as well as the writings of the "sectaries at Damascus" (as Moore calls them, assuming as he does that he deals with a Judaism that encompasses some non-Rabbinic evidence but excludes much Rabbinic and still more non-Rabbinic!), then the term "Judaism" stretches so far, covers so much diversity, as to lose all definitive use. Evidence from the fifth century of the Common Era and from the first or second century before it — six hundred years — serves no more naturally to describe a single relation (if also no less) than the poetry of the age of Beowulf and that of our own day serves to describe a single language (if also no less).

But from our perspective, Moore's most blatant error, the one that makes his "Judaism" utterly implausible, took place not because of what he included as evidence but what he excluded. He found himself utterly unable to introduce into his "Judaism the evidence of the norms of behavior, or halakhah, with which a massive component of the Rabbinic corpus is concerned. That radical omission attracted attention from the start, but the favorable picture of Judaism that Moore set forth so amazed the Jewish audience for the book that no one took note of the distortion that Moore had committed. One reviewer, right at the outset, took note but was ignored. So I wish to take full account of the important and (in my view)

---

[6] My approach, the documentary history of ideas, systematically proposes to relate the basic ideas and modes of thought to the social world of those who held those ideas, that is, the circumstances of the time in which documents reached closure to the main concerns of those documents, their tensions and points of focus. It is explicitly an effort to pursue the question of the relationship of ideas to the world of those that hold those ideas, and the main results, spread over a variety of books, constitute a systematic theory of the history of not ideas alone but ideas in social (political) context.

ultimately prophetic criticism of Frank C. Porter.[7] I believe that Porter's review should have led to a fruitful debate with Moore and to a fresh approach to the work done by Moore so elegantly, but with such crushing flaws. So far as I know, from the time of Porter's review of Moore to this date, there has been no effort to take seriously the problems pointed out by Porter, even though many independently may have been aware of them.

Indeed, the work's two principal flaws, first, the quite unsubstantiated claim that the "Judaism of the Tannaim" descriptively speaking was normative, and second, the systematic aversion to discussion of the Judaism revealed by the legal texts, were self-evident from that start. Yet everyone who came after Moore — even including Urbach, who knew better — continued the work of dogmatic theology, resorted to precisely the same undefined and undefended, formless canon of topics deemed important to fill in the same categories, and pretended that the Tannaim created everything and anything but the Mishnah. It is time, therefore, for Porter to have that hearing denied him for diverse reasons for so long. I quote the principal paragraphs in which Porter sets forth the problem which has not been solved but has been sidestepped for so long. First let us consider Porter's criticism of the matter of normativity:

> The Judaism which Professor Moore describes with such wealth of learning is that of the end of the second century of our era, and the sources which he uses are those that embody the interpretations and formulations of the law by the rabbis, chiefly from the fall of Jerusalem, 70 A.D., to the promulgation of the Mishnah of the Patriarch Judah, about 200 A.D. When Moore speaks of the sources which Judaism has always regarded as authentic, he means "always" from the third century A.D. onward. It is a proper and needed task to exhibit the religious conceptions and moral principles, the observances, and the piety of the Judaism of the Tannaim. Perhaps it is the things that most needed to be done of all the many labors that must contribute to our knowledge of that age. But Professor Moore calls this Judaism "normative"; and means by this, not only authoritative for Jews after the work of the Tannaim had reached its completion in the Mishnah, but normal or authentic in the sense that it is the only direct and natural outcome of the Old Testament religion. It seems therefore, that the task here undertaken is not only, as it certainly is, a definite, single, and necessary one, but that other things hardly need doing, and do not signify much for the Judaism of the age of Christian beginnings. The book is not called, as it might have been, "The Judaism of the Tannaim," but Judaism in the First Centuries of the Christian Era: The Age of the Tannaim. Was there then no other type of Judaism in the time of Christ that may claim such names as "normative," "normal," "orthodox"? The time of Deuteronomy was also the time of Jeremiah. The religion of revelation in a divinely

---

[7] *Journal of Religion* 1928, 8:30-62.

given written law stood over against the religion of revelation in the heart and living words of a prophet. The conviction was current after Ezra that the age of prophecy had ended; the Spirit of God had withdrawn itself from Israel (I, 237). But if prophecy should live again, could it not claim to be normal in Judaism? Where, in the centuries after Ezra, are we to look for the lines of development that go back, not to Ezra and Deuteronomy, but to Jeremiah and Isaiah? R.H. Charles claims the genuine succession for his Apocalypses. The Pharisees at least had the prophets in their canon, and it is claimed by many, and by Moore, that the rabbis were not less familiar with the prophets than with the Pentateuch, and even that they had "fully assimilated" the teaching of the prophets as to the value of the cultus (II, 13), and that their conception of revealed religion "resulted no less from the teaching of the prophets than from the possession of the Law" (I, 235). Christians see prophecy coming back to Judaism in John the Baptist and in Jesus, and find in Paul the new experience that revelation is giving in a person, not in a book, and inwardly to each one through the in-dwelling Spirit of God, as Jeremiah had hoped (31:31-34). And now, finally, liberal Judaism claims to be authentic and normal Judaism because it takes up the lines that Jeremiah laid down.

It would require more proof than Professor Moore has given in his section on "History" to justify his claim that the only movements that need to be traced as affecting religion are these that lead from Ezra to Hillel and Johanan ben Zakkai and Akiba and Judah the Prince. Great events happened during the three centuries from Antiochus IV to Hadrian, events which deeply affected Judaism as a religion. But of these events and their influence Moore has little to say. It is of course in connection with these events that the Apocalypses were written.

It is to meet Porter's first point that I define the program as I do: Judaism as portrayed within a specific, socially-circumscribed corpus of evidence, the corpus of documents of the Oral Torah in particular.

Porter's second criticism of Moore seems to me still more telling. He points out that Moore almost wholly neglects the Tannaitic legal corpus — the Mishnah itself:

> In [Moore's] actual exposition of the normative, orthodox Judaism of the age of the Tannaim comparatively little place is given to Halakah. One of the seven parts of his exposition is on observances; and here cultus, circumcision, Sabbath, festivals, fasts, taxation, and interdictions are summarily dealt with; but the other six parts deal in detail with the religion and ethics, the piety and hopes, of Judaism, matters about which the Haggada supplies most of the material, and for which authority and finality are not claimed. The tannaite (halakic) Midrash (Mechilta, etc.) contains a good deal of Haggada together with its halakic exegesis, and these books Moore values as the most important of his sources (I, 135ff.; II, 80). The principles of religion and morals do indeed control the interpretation of certain laws, so that Halakah is sometimes a source for such teachings, and "is in many instances of the highest value as evidence of the way and measure in which great ethical principles have been tacitly impressed on whole fields of the traditional

law" (I, 134). This sounds as if the ethical implications constituted the chief value of the Mishnah for Moore's purposes. But these are not its chief contents. It is made up, as a whole, of opinions or decisions about the minutiae of law observance. It constructs a hedge of definitions and restrictions meant to protect the letter of the law from violation, to make its observance possible and practicable under all circumstances, and to bring all of life under its rule.

The Jewish scholar, Perles, in a pamphlet with which Moore is in sympathy, criticized Bousset, in Die Religion des Judentums, for using only books such as Bacher's, on the Haggada, and for expressing a preference for haggadic sources; whereas the Halakah in its unity, in its definitive and systematic form, and its deeper grasp upon life is much better fitted to supply the basis of the structures of a history of the Jewish religion. Moore agrees with Perles' criticism of Bousset's preference for the later, haggadic, Midrashim; but it is not because they are halakic that he gives the first place to the early Midrash. "It is this religious and moral element by the side of the interpretation of the laws, and pervading it as a principle, that gives these works [Mechilta, etc.] their chief value to us" (I, 135). Perles insists on the primary importance of the Halakah, not only because it shows here and there the influence of prophetic ethics, but because throughout as it stands, it is the principal work of the rabbis, and the work which alone has the character of authority, and because, concerned as it is with ritual, cultus, and the law (Recht), it has decisive influence upon the whole of life. This applies peculiarly to the religion of the Tannaim. The Haggada neither begins nor ends with them, so that Bousset ought not, Perles thinks, to have used exclusively Bacher's work on the Haggada of the Tannaim, but also his volumes on the Haggada of the Amoraim, as well as the anonymous Haggada which Bacher did not live to publish. It is only in the region of the Halakah that the Tannaim have a distinctive place and epoch-making significance, since the Mishnah, the fundamental text of the Talmud, was their creation.

Would Perles be satisfied, then, with Moore's procedure? Would he think it enough that Halakah proper, observances, should occupy one part in seven in an exposition of the Judaism of the Tannaim, considering that in their classical and distinctive work Halakah practically fills sixty-two out of sixty-three parts? Moore agrees with Perles that there is no essential distinction between earlier and later Haggada (I, 163), and that the teachings of the Tannaim about God and man, morals and piety, sin, repentance, and forgiveness are not only also the teachings of the later Amoraim, but run backward, too, without essential change into the Old Testament itself. There is no point at which freedom and variety of opinion and belief, within the bounds, to be sure, of certain fundamental principles, came to an end, and a proper orthodoxy of dogma was set up. But orthodoxy of conduct, of observance, did reach this stage of finality and authority in the Mishnah; and the tannaite rabbis were those who brought this about. It is in accordance with Moore's chief interests in haggadic teachings that he does not confine himself to sayings of the Tannaim, but also quotes freely from the Amoraim; how freely may be seen by the list that ends Index IV.

Professor Moore's emphasis upon his purpose to present normative Judaism, definitive, authoritative, orthodox, would lead one to expect that he would give the chief place to those "jurisdic definitions and decisions of the Halakah" to which alone, as he himself sometimes says, these adjectives strictly apply. We should look for more about the Mishnah itself, about its systematic arrangement of the laws, its methods of argument and of bringing custom and tradition into connection with the written law, and more of its actual contents and total character, of those actual rules of life, that "uniformity of observance" which constituted the distinction of the Judaism of the rabbis.

The three-pronged method set forth in Chapters Four through Eight, dealing with the halakhic (Chapter Seven) as much as the aggadic (Chapters Four through Six) sector of the authoritative writings, corrects this enormous flaw in Moore's account. The halakhic sector bears the weight of the construction of society, the formation of a rational, public way of life so that, since dogmatic theology finds itself unable to address fully half of the Rabbinical writings, dogmatic theology pays too heavy a price for ignoring the principal category-formations of the Rabbinic writings themselves, beginning with those very Tannaite sources that Moore claimed to translate into theology.

IV. WHAT IS WRONG WITH THE HISTORICAL THEOLOGY OF THE ORAL TORAH: URBACH

Moore's work, for all its flaws, exhibits keen intelligence. Urbach's does not, but heavy-handedly dismisses what Urbach does not value or even understand; his was not a glistening intellect, as the paragraph given below, chosen more or less at random, indicates. Indeed, Urbach emerges in this long-winded and clumsy account as learned but dull, the archetypal hunter and gatherer of who knows what.

Urbach recognized the problems left unsolved by prior accounts of Rabbinic theology, though he failed to solve those problems. His comments on his predecessors[8] underline the theological bias present in most, though not all, former studies. Wilhelm Bousset and Hugo Gressmann, *Die Religion des Judentums im späthellenistischen Zeitalter* (1926) is wanting because Rabbinic sources are used sparingly and not wholly accurately and because it relies on "external sources," meaning apocryphal literature and Hellenistic Jewish writings. Here Urbach shows himself a theologian of integrationist Orthodox-Judaism, excluded from his "Judaism" as external the writings of other Judaisms besides the one he deemed normative. Here we find the blatant imposition of theological convictions upon historical facts; Urbach simply did not know how to deal with diverse Judaisms, so, without further ado, he simply declared "external" the ones he did not find compatible with his. Would that learning were that easy!

Urbach's own criticism of Moore, that "he did not always go deeply enough into the essence of the problems that he discussed," — a charge that Urbach did not instantiate — certainly cannot be leveled against Urbach himself. His first criticism, then, amounts to the fact that Moore did not possess the learning that

---

[8] I, pp.5-18.

Urbach did. Of that fact there can be no doubt. His further reservation is that Moore "failed to give an account of the origin of the beliefs and concepts, of their struggles and evolution, of their entire chequered course till their crystallization, of the immense dynamism and vitality of the spiritual life of the Second Temple period, of the tension in the relations between the parties and sects and between the various sections of the Sages themselves." That is to say, Urbach rejects dogmatic theology in favor of historical theology, or rather, a history of theology. So Urbach promises to give a historical-theological picture, while Moore presented a merely dogmatic-theological one. Everything depends upon how well Urbach practiced history.

This view underlines the historical ambition of Urbach's approach and emphasizes his view of his own contribution "to elucidate the concepts and beliefs of the Tannaim and Amoraim against the background of their actual life and environment." Since that is Urbach's fundamental claim, the work must be considered not only in the context of what has gone before, but also in the setting of its own definition and understanding of the historical task, its own theory of how talmudic materials are to be used for historical knowledge. In this regard it is not satisfactory. It is pseudo-history: uncritical and paraphrastic. It is uncritical because Urbach accepts at face value every factual allegation in the Rabbinic literature, from attributions of sayings to specific, named sages to stories that are told about them. He treats Rabbinic literature as a mass of wholly valid historical facts, requiring only organization into intelligible patterns of sequence: "against the background of their actual life and environment." It suffices to say, the key word here is "actual," which invokes a process of criticism that Urbach did not even attempt.

It follows that Urbach's historical theology fails because it violates the simplest rules of critical history, on the one side, and turns out merely to paraphrase selected passages of the documents, on the other. Urbach's *The Sages: Their Concepts and Beliefs* presents a compendious work intended "to describe the concepts and beliefs of the Tannaim and Amoraim and to elucidate them against the background of their actual life and environment." When published in Hebrew, in 1969, the work, like Moore's, enjoyed immediate success, going into a second printing within two years and immediately being translated into English. That came about in part because Urbach, an imposing figure in Israeli scholarly and religious-political circles, a major player in the Hebrew University of Jerusalem, president of the Israel Academy of Sciences and Humanities, secured for himself the hearing he wanted.[9]

---

[9] But he was a very good politician; he even ran for the presidency of the State of Israel as candidate of the right-wing and "religious"-Zionist political parties.

Historical reading enjoys a privileged position in the theological method of Urbach's sector of Orthodox Judaism, the sector that took shape in Germany in the mid-nineteenth century, at the height of the historicist-romantic age, and that accounts for his incapacity to conduct genuinely secular and critical research in history. His religious convictions stood in the way of critical historical study; he knew too much a priori, and he rejected too many (negative) propositions, also a priori. Within Orthodox Judaism Urbach derives from the integrationist, German stream, which proposes to combine piety with academic learning. That meant, in practical terms, that critical learning cannot conflict with religious conviction. When it does, critical learning must give way. Historicism for Orthodox Judaism was meant to produce an appealing apologetic, and the homiletics of Urbach's *Sages* leaves no doubt that he intended to do so.

But that position excludes the possibility of historical-critical judgment, because it founds its theology on the veracity of religious convictions treated as historical facts. In Urbach's hands the Judaic sector of historicistic theology provides no imitable model, because his allegations as to history consist of claims of what is early and what is late; there is no sustained narrative, no effort at a continuing, unfolding account, such as the claim of historical investigation would lead us to anticipate. Urbach therefore undertook a project that his deepest convictions prevented his accomplishing. Indeed, as we shall see, he in the end attempted little more than the selection and arrangement of thematically-pertinent materials — not history at all in any conventional sense. His historical theology evades all of the critical issues of historical study by ignoring them and simply telling us, in their words and in his own words, what the sources say: they constitute history. Indeed, they do, but whose history and on what account we are never told.

The work before us has been accurately described by M.D. Heer, the distinguished Israeli specialist in Rabbinic texts: "He [Urbach] outlines the views of the rabbis on the important theological issues such as creation, providence, and the nature of man. In this work Urbach synthesizes the voluminous literature on these subjects and presents the views of the talmudic authorities."[10] The topics are as follows: belief in one God; the presence of God in the world; "nearness and distance — Omnipresent and heaven;" the power of God; magic and miracle; the power of the divine name; the celestial retinue; creation; man; providence; written law and oral law; the commandments; acceptance of the yoke of the kingdom of heaven; sin, reward, punishment, suffering, etc.; the people of Israel and its sages, a chapter which encompasses the election of Israel, the status of the sages in the

---

[10] *Encyclopaedia Judaica* 16:4.

days of the Hasmoneans, Hillel, the regime of the sages after the destruction of the Temple, and so on; and redemption. The second volume contains footnotes, a fairly brief and highly selective — indeed, perfunctory — bibliography, which is of no use for systematic scholarship. Urbach tended to select for citation and even reference only works with which he agreed or with which he felt he could win the argument.

The several chapters are comprised by collections of sayings and stories relevant to the theme under discussion, together with Urbach's episodic observations and comments on them. Lacking energy and evincing the indicative marks of intellectual exhaustion, if not bankruptcy, Urbach does not follow any systematic program I can discern. Predictably, he does not even offer an introduction to the book, beyond his survey of prior work ("a study of the history of the beliefs and concepts of the sages"). He there explains why every prior effort fails, though the net effect is to explain why he has not learned anything from his predecessors. The whole is informative, but merely paraphrastic where it is not altogether dismissive.

This account of the contents reveals a remarkable failure in Urbach's mind: there is no clear logic that governs what comes first and what is discussed then. If we were to reorder the chapters, the book as a whole would neither lose nor gain meaning; the book argues no systematic case and unfolds in accord with no unifying logic. It presents no sustained argument, and that is why any order will have served as well as any other in setting out the topical program. It is less of a book that makes a cumulative case in behalf of a proposition or that offers a solution of a problem than it is an encyclopaedia of free-standing entries. Alas, while we require such an encyclopaedia, Urbach's is not the one we need. The disorganized character of the book finds its match in the odd paragraph we shall consider in a moment.

Let me offer a sample paragraph, which conveys the flavor of the whole and instantiates Urbach's failure of intellect. Here is his opening discussion of Rabbinic anthropology. To show how the passage is put together, I underline the sources that are quoted, as well as the paraphrase thereof. The underlining then highlights the true character of the discussion as a flaccid exercise of citation and paraphrase, together with some random, free association. I also number the entries, to show with great clarity how Urbach does his work; none of these markings appears in the original.

> The views of the Sages concerning man are linked to and hinge upon the Scriptures...But at the same time they result from the contemplation of human existence, with all the contradictions that manifest themselves in man's character and actions, and in particular they flow from a consideration of the paradox in man, in whom there is, on the one hand, existence and being, and, on the other, nothingness and void. Therefore they were very interested in probing into the creation and formation of man. [1] The Sages found a basic principle in the verse, "In the image of God made He man." In his dictum, "Still greater was the love in that it was made known to him that he was created in the image of God..., R.

Aqiba declared that the election of man consists in the fact that it was made known to him that he was created in God's image. His disciple and colleague, Ben Azzai, pointed to the verse, "This is the book of the generations of Adam. In the day that God created man, in the likeness of God made he him" as the great principle of the Torah. The function of man is to know the acts of God. The starting point is God, not man. [2] In the way man was created and in the form that the Creator give him, two principles find expression — that of human unity and that of the individual worth of each man. "Hence man was created a single individual...and for the sake of peace among men, that one should not say to his fellow, My father was greater than yours...and to declare the greatness of the Holy One, blessed be He, for a man stamps many coins with one seal, and they are all identical, but the King of the kings of kings stamped every man with the seal of the first man, and none is identical with his fellow. Therefore it is the duty of every one to say: for my sake the world was created." This Mishna states, on the one hand, that no man is identical with his fellow, but is a separate personality, possessing his own worth and bearing responsibility for the existence of the world, but at the same time all men are stamped with the one seal, and no one can say to his fellow that he is unique. The Baraita, which elaborates the theme of the Mishna, also adds the question why "man was born last." The first answer, "that the sectarians should not say that he was a partner with Him in his work," seeks to contradict dualistic conceptions. The second answer, "Another explanation is: Why was he created last? So that if he becomes overweening, one can say to him, A gnat preceded you in the work of creation," comes to emphasize the antithesis in man. On the one hand he is stamped with the seal of the Holy One...and on the other a gnat came before him. The awareness of man's greatness and nothingness, which the poet expressed in the verses, "What is man that thou art mindful of him...," the Tannaim discovered even before Philo's time, in the section of Creation in Genesis. The fact that death deprives man of the faculty of speech and of the ability to move but leaves the body with all its organs, strengthened the sense of duality.[11]

Urbach clearly loses his way rather easily; the concluding sentences stand quite out of phase with the rest, and why they were required for the exposition I cannot say.

In fact, the paragraph, in lifeless, adolescent prose, is made up of two sources that are first given more or less verbatim, then paraphrased, as marked. The opening sentences set forth little more than banalities, and, as I said, the concluding sentence bears no obvious relationship to the prior materials. Clearly, then, Urbach comes with no organizing question, no encompassing problem that he wishes to work out; he presents no proposition, proves no point, argues no case. He has simply selected and arranged and then paraphrased two Rabbinic teachings

---

[11] pp. 217-218.

pertinent to the subject at hand — and that is all. That is why, from start to finish, we find in Urbach no model of theological analysis, only a compendium of sayings that, properly analyzed, may contribute to such analysis.

In the context of earlier work on Talmudic theology and religion, nonetheless, Urbach's contribution marks a distinct improvement. Compared to a similar, earlier compendium of talmudic sayings on theological subjects, A. Hyman's *Osar divré hakhamin ufitgamehem* (1934), a collection of sayings laid out alphabetically, according to catchword, Urbach's volumes have the advantage of supplying not merely sayings but (sometimes) cogent discussions of the various sayings and a more fluent, coherent presentation of them in essay form Urbach has asked more of himself than Hyman, but, on the other hand, he claimed more in his own behalf as well. Solomon Schechter's *Some Aspects of Rabbinic Theology*[12] covers exactly what it says, *some aspects,* by contrast to the much more ambitious dimension of the present work. Schechter had the advantage of a more fluent writing style and his presentations engage interest. Urbach, doing things pretty much the way Schechter did, however, evinced more ambition in sheer research. He was less eloquent but more industrious than Schechter. But the evidence of Schechter's superiority writing marks him as the more intelligent of the two.

The comparison to George Foot Moore's *Judaism in the First Centuries of the Christian Era* is somewhat more complex. Moore certainly has the advantage of elegant presentation. Urbach's prose, not only in the original Hebrew but also in I. Abraham's English translation, comes through as turgid and stodgy, while Moore's is the opposite. By contrast to Moore, Urbach introduces sayings of Amoraim into the discussion of each category, and since both Urbach and Moore aim to present a large selection of sayings on the several topics, Urbach's work is on the face of it a more comprehensive collection. As we have noted, Urbach thought that he was doing history by ordering sayings on a topic in the sequence of authorities, therefore Tannaite ones before Amoraic ones. But it is very rare indeed in his presentation that he draws any conclusions from the alleged temporal order of opinions that he claims to adduce.

But seen on its own, Urbach's book reveals some fairly obvious problems, on which we need not dwell at length. Urbach's selection of sources for analysis is both narrowly canonical and somewhat confusing. We often hear from Philo, but seldom from the Essene Library of Qumran, still more rarely from the diverse works assembled by R.H. Charles as the apocrypha and pseudepigrapha of the Old Testament, and the like. True, Urbach promises to tell us only about "the sages." But then, if we seek to describe the talmudic rabbis, surely we cannot ask Philo to testify to their opinions. If we listen to Philo, who lived outside of the Holy Land, surely we ought to hear — at least for the purpose of comparison and contrast —

---

[12] 1909, based on essays in the *Jewish Quarterly Review* printed in 1894-1896.

from books written by Palestinian Jews of various kinds. The Targumim are allowed no place at all because they are deemed "late." But the Talmuds are not late. So documents which came to redaction much later than the several Targumim (by any estimate of the date of the latter) make rich and constant contributions to the discussion.

Indeed, the promiscuous union of sources that occur in documents spread out over many centuries generates enormous confusion. Within a given chapter, the portrayal of the sources will move rapidly from biblical to Tannaitic to Amoraic sources, as though the line of development were single, unitary, and harmonious, and as though there were no intervening developments which shaped later conceptions. Differentiation among the stages of Tannaitic and Amoraic sayings tends to be episodic. Commonly, slight sustained effort is made to treat them in their several sequences, let alone to differentiate among schools and circles within a given period. What difference the temporal ordering of sayings makes, what we are supposed to learn from this allegedly-historical account, we are not told; no argument encompasses the whole, and conclusions only very rarely are drawn from the parts. Urbach takes with utmost seriousness his title, the sages, their concepts and beliefs, and his "history," topic by topic, reveals remarkably little variation, development, or even movement. It would not be fair to Urbach to suggest that all he has done is publish his card-files. But I think his skill at organization and arrangement of materials tends to outrun his interest in differentiation and comparison within and among them, let alone in the larger, sequential history of major ideas and their growth and coherent development over the centuries. One looks in vain for Urbach's effort to justify treating "the sages" as essentially a coherent and timeless group.

Let us turn, rather, now to the more fundamental difficulties presented by the work, because, as I said, it is to be received as the definitive and (probably) final product of a long-established approach to the study of talmudic religion and history. Urbach has certainly brought to their ultimate realization the methods and concepts of his predecessors. The step forward that I propose to take has then to identify the errors of past approaches and correct them. What errors do I deem require correction in Urbach's unfortunate work?

First, let us ask, does the world-view of the talmudic sages emerge in a way which the ancient sages themselves would have recognized? That is to say, do native categories, revealed in the topical organization of the documents, register? From the viewpoint of their organization and description of reality, their world-view, it is certain that the sages would have organized their card-files quite differently. We know that is the case because we do not have, among the chapters before us, a single one which focuses upon the theme of one of the Mishnah's orders, let alone the tractates, within which the rabbis divided and presented their various statements on reality, e.g., Seeds, the material basis of life; Seasons, the organization and differentiation of time; Women, the status of the individual;

Damages, the conduct of civil life including government; Holy Things, the material service of God; and Purities, the immaterial base of divine reality in this world. The matter concerns not merely the superficial problem of organizing vast quantities of data. The talmudic rabbis left a large and exceedingly complex, well-integrated legacy of law. Clearly, it is through that legacy that they intended to make their fundamental statements upon the organization and meaning of reality. An account of their concepts and beliefs which ignores nearly the whole of the halakhah surely is slightly awry. Urbach, an Orthodox Jew of impeccable pedigree, makes exactly the same fundamental mistake as did Moore, on whom he presumed to improve.

In fairness to Urbach, I must stress that he shows himself well-aware of the centrality of halakhah in the expression of the world-view of the talmudic rabbis. He correctly criticizes his predecessors for neglecting the subject and observes, "The Halakha does not openly concern itself with beliefs and concepts; it determines, in practice, the way in which one should walk... Nevertheless beliefs and concepts lie at the core of many Halakhot; only their detection requires exhaustive study of the history of the Halakha combined with care to avoid fanciful conjectures and unfounded explanations." But only rarely, then, does Urbach act upon that valid perception. Urbach occasionally does introduce halakhic materials. But, as is clear, the fundamental structure — the category-formation — of his account of talmudic theology is formed in accord not with the equivalent structure of the Talmud — the halakhah — but with the topics and organizing rubrics treated by all nineteenth- and twentieth-century Protestant historical studies of theology: God, ethics, revelation, and the like. That those studies are never far from mind is illustrated by Urbach's extensive discussion of whether talmudic ethics was theonomous or autonomous (I, pp. 320ff.), an issue important only from the viewpoint of nineteenth-century Jewish ethical thought and its response to Kant.[13] Integrationist German Orthodox Judaism had every reason to enter into an *Auseinandersetzung* — a mutually-critical dialogue — with Kant. "Our sages of blessed memory" did not. So much for historical-critical method in the encounter with pure anachronism!

Second, has Urbach taken account of methodological issues important in the study of the literary and historical character of the sources? In particular, does he deal with the fundamental questions of how these particular sources are to be used for historical purposes? The answer, as I have already indicated, is simply negative. On many specific points, he contributes episodic philological observations, interesting opinions and judgments as to the lateness of one saying as against the antiquity of another, subjective opinions on what is more representative or reliable than something else. If these opinions are disorganized, incoherent, and not

---

[13] But Urbach's discussion on that matter is completely persuasive, stating what is certainly the last word on the subject. He can hardly be blamed for criticizing widely-held and wrong opinions.

systematic and if they reveal no uniform criterion, sustainedly applied to all sources, they nonetheless derive from a mind of immense learning. But learning alone never suffices.

Yet we must now articulate the basic historical flaw that ruins Urbach's history and validates its being classified as pseudo-history: if a saying is assigned to an ancient authority, how do we know that he really said it? If a story is told, how do we know that the events the story purports to describe actually took place? And if not, just what are we to make of said story and saying for historical purposes? Further, if we have a saying attributed to a first-century authority in a document generally believed to have been redacted five hundred or a thousand years later, how do we know that the attribution of the saying is valid, and that the saying informs us of the state of opinion in the first century, not only in the sixth or eleventh in which it was written down and obviously believed true and authoritative? Do we still hold, as an axiom of historical scholarship, *ein muqdam umeuhar* ["temporal considerations do not apply"] — in the Talmud! And again, do not the sayings assigned to a first-century authority, redacted in documents deriving from the early third century, possess greater credibility than those first appearing in documents redacted in the fifth, tenth, or even fifteenth centuries? Should we not, on the face of it, distinguish between more and less reliable materials? The well-known tendency of medieval writers to put their opinions into the mouths of the ancients, as in the case of the Zohar, surely warns us to be cautious about using documents redacted, even formulated, five hundred or a thousand or more years after the events of which they speak. Urbach ignores all of these questions and the work of those who ask them.

There is yet a further, equally simple problem. The corpus of evidence is simply huge. Selectivity characterizes even the most thorough and compendious accounts, and I cannot imagine one more comprehensive than Urbach's. But should we not devise means for the filtering downward of some fundamental, widely- and well-attested opinions, out of the mass of evidence, rather than capriciously selecting what we like and find interesting?[14] We have few really comprehensive accounts of the phenomenology and the history of a single idea or concept. Urbach himself has produced some of the better studies that we do have. In earlier, and far superior research, he even matched aggadah and corresponding halakhah, showing how the latter embodied the former. But that work produced no succession and was not even very systematic. It seems somewhat premature to describe so vast a world in the absence of a far more substantial corpus of Vorstudien of specific ideas and the men who held them than is available. Inevitably, one must characterize Urbach's treatment of one topic after another as unhistorical and superficial, and this is despite the author's impressive efforts to do history and to do it thoroughly and in depth. He is not merely selective. He is downright capricious.

---

[14] The formulation of the notion of the paradigm, set forth in Chapter Four, is meant to solve this fundamental problem.

So while Urbach dismisses all of his predecessors, sometimes with sound reason, sometimes with no reason, he himself has corrected none of their errors except those of ignorance and incompleteness — which the later generations always contribute to the improvement of the work of their predecessors. But Urbach then has done this ambitious work without the advantage of studies of the history of the traditions assigned over the centuries to one authority or another. He had at hand scarcely any critical work comparing various versions of a story appearing in successive compilations. He had no possibility of recourse to comprehensive inquiries into the Talmud's forms and literary traits, redactional tendencies, even definitive accounts of the date of the redaction of most of the literature used for historical purposes. He could not consult work on the thought of any of the individual Amoraim or on the traits of schools and circles among them, for there was none of critical substance. Most collections which passed as biographies even of Tannaim effect no differentiation among layers and strata of the stories and sayings, let alone attempting to describe the history of the traditions on the basis of which historical biography is be recovered. The laws assigned, even in Mishnah-Tosefta, to a given Tannaite authority had not been investigated as to their underlying presuppositions and unifying convictions, even their gross thematic agendum. All of that work would commence after the appearance of Urbach's *Sages,* and when it began to appear, Urbach did not choose to confront it but did what he could to suppress it. If Urbach speaks of "the rabbis" and differentiates only episodically among the layers and divisions of sayings, in accord either with differing opinions on a given question or with the historical development of evidently uniformly-held opinions, he was no better than anyone else of his time.

Nor — coming close to the project at hand — have I alluded to the intractable problems of internal, philosophico-theological analysis of ideas and their inner structures, once their evident historical, or sequential, development, among various circles and schools of a given generation and over a period of hundreds of years, has been elucidated. That quite separate investigation and analysis of the logic and meaning of the concepts and beliefs of the sages requires definition in its own terms, not in accord with the limited and simple criteria of historians. If Urbach did not attempt it, no one else entirely succeeded either. In this regard, Urbach's cavalier dismissal of the work of Marmorstein, Heschel, and Kadushin, among others, bespeaks pure quackery. He simply did not understand the problems they tried to solve, problems that Kadushin in fact did solve. While the others may not have "persuaded" Urbach of the correctness of their theses,[15]

---

[15] Urbach deemed the intensely subject judgment, "I am not persuaded," to settle all questions, a trait of mind more congruent to politician than professor. The truly great figures in Judaic learning have always relied upon reasoned argument, not mere personal opinion or political Diktat. It is the simple fact that, at the Hebrew University from Urbach's time forward, no further research on the problems of Urbach's *Sages,* no further effort to portray Rabbinic Judaism in a systematic work, ever was undertaken, nor have systematic efforts to reconsider

while they may have been wrong in some of their conclusions, and while their methods may have been unrefined, they at least have attempted the task which Urbach refuses even to undertake. Since the whole opinion on works of considerable scholarship is the single word "worthless" or "unpersuasive," it may be observed that there is certain subjectivity which seems to preclude Urbach's reasoned discussion of what he likes and does not like in the work of many others and to prevent any sort of rational exchange of ideas. That is what I mean by quackery, the price to be paid for an excess of success in academic politics joined to a considerable deficit in academic acumen.

Urbach's work, as I said, in the balance brings to their full realization the methods and suppositions of the past hundred years. I cannot imagine that anyone again will want, from these perspectives, to approach the task of describing all of "the concepts and beliefs of the Tannaim and Amoraim," of elucidating all of them "against the background of their actual life and environment." So far as the work can be done in accord with established methods, here it has been done very competently indeed. Accordingly, we may well forgive the learned author for the sustained homiletical character of his inquiry and its blatantly apologetic purposes:

> The aim of our work is to give an epitome of the beliefs and concepts of the Sages as the history of a struggle to instill religious and ethical ideals into the everyday life of the community and the individual, while preserving at the same time the integrity and unity of the nation and directing its way in this world as a preparation for another world that is wholly perfect... Their eyes and their hearts were turned Heavenward, yet one type was not to be found among them... namely the mystic who seeks to liberate himself from his ego and in doing so is preoccupied with himself alone. They saw their mission in work here in the world below. There were Sages who inclined to extremism in their thoughts and deeds, and there were those who preached the way of compromise, which they did not, however, determine on the basis of convenience. Some were severe and exacting, while others demonstrated an extreme love of humanity and altruism. The vast majority of them recognized the complexities of life with its travail and joy, its happiness and tragedy, and this life served them also as a touchstone for their beliefs and concepts.

All of this may well be so, but it remains to be demonstrated as historical fact in the way in which contemporary critical historians generally demonstrate matters of

---

Urbach's results and improve upon them ever reached scholarly discussion. So Urbach closed many doors and, in his own setting, managed to lock them all. His disciples and successors would turn away from his entire project and never refer to it again as a starting point of further learning. That forms the judgment of history.

fact. It requires analysis and argument in the undogmatic and unapologetic spirit characteristic of contemporary studies in the history of ideas and of religions. But in the context in which these words of Urbach are written, among the people who will read them, this statement of purpose puts forth a noble ideal, one which might well be emulated by the "sages" — exemplars and politicians of Orthodox Judaism — to whom, I believe, Urbach speaks most directly and persuasively, and by whom (alone) his results certainly will be taken as historical fact. It is by no means a reduction of learning to its sociological and political relevance to say that, if it were only for his advocacy, in circles not characterized by rich appreciation of humane and enlightened learning, of the constructive position just now quoted. Urbach has made a truly formidable contribution to the contemporary theological life of Orthodox Judaism in the State of Israel.

v.   THE ISSUE OF PROPORTION AND BALANCE: SEEING THE WHOLE ALL TO-
GETHER AND ALL AT ONCE

Moore's failed to address the critical formulation of norms of behavior, and his account of norms of belief suffered accordingly. Urbach's historical theology is neither historical nor theological; it is rather an exercise in anachronistic category-formation and systematic only at Orthodox apologetics.   Knowing how matters unfolded in documents that took shape and reached closure over determinate time answers one set of questions. Still, for the sake of argument, let us grant that Urbach accomplished his goals. But then, these are historical ones of diachrony. Discovering the inner logic that holds the entire corpus together poses a different set of problems. These require asking the analytical questions of synchrony: coherence, balance, proportion, harmonious relationship. Theology after all speaks not of what came first and what happened then, but rather of how all truth coheres, without regard to the time or circumstance of its initial manifestation. That is why, to answer the logically next, and urgent, question of theological description, the documentary history of ideas has now to give way to the documentary foundations of the theology of those same ideas.

Why not simply record what (we think) came first and what (we suppose) happened then? For what reason do I hold that diachrony must give way to synchrony? Because to take up the outcome of intellectual work, wherever, whenever carried on, we must address the result of the work whole and complete. For a theological system — a governing rationality, a sustaining logic — the temporal sequence in which components of the whole emerged makes slight difference in making sense of the whole. The character of theology explains why: God is made known here in this way, there on that occasion. The task of synchronic description requires us to put forth a theory of the whole, the logic, rationality, and system, to use three dimensions of the same construction. For at stake is not details of doctrine but how doctrine coheres. If we can describe the entire repertoire of important ideas but cannot say how we think they hold together in a single sound structure, then while we define some doctrines, we still cannot claim to have carried out the work of synchronic description of the theological system viewed in all its parts and in proportion. For, to revert to the definition given in the preceding chapter, theology is the science of the reasoned knowledge of God, in the case of a Judaism made possible by God's self-manifestation in the Torah. It is only from the whole that we may proceed to the parts, for it is always that One God who dwells in the details. Then for theology the details stand for the Whole.

IV

Theological Paradigms of the Oral Torah

I. FROM KINDRED WRITINGS TO COGENT SYSTEM: THE WAY FORWARD

Out of the resources of a corpus of kindred writings I seek to describe whole and complete that theological system and structure that the authoritative writings adumbrate. The structure then holds the whole together, the system completely encompasses the details and forms of them a single coherent statement, one that, in all simplicity, speaks in a single way about many matters. But how are we to discern system in diverse documents, each with its topical program, and where shall we identify the marks of a sustaining structure, bearing the weight of detail? To begin with, it is by identifying the governing paradigms, patterns, or models (here I use the words interchangeably) to which in detail the documents make reference.[1] A paradigm signals a native category-formation, a medium for the formation of data into a consequential statement of a principle that governs now and for all time and so can account for the future as well. It is to models that, time and again, diverse propositional compositions appeal to explain and then to prove a point.

Paradigms impose regularity and order upon data, show how to make connections among, and draw conclusions from, raw facts. They represent therefore

---

[1] As is clear from the Preface, two other approaches will be suggested, to deal with other kinds of evidence besides that on which I focus in the matter of paradigms. These other approaches are easier to set forth. The one deals with the documents' own systematic statements on given categories of their own formation, explained in Chapter Seven, the other with the matter of verbal symbolism on which all documents draw equally, set forth in Chapter Eight. Nor do I mean to exclude the possibility of yet other approaches to the solution of the problem of describing the whole, of reading the documents as a continuous statement. But the three laid out here, and particularly the way of the paradigm, strike me as the most promising; they will, at any rate, generate facts, which we do not now have, for reliable identification of category-formations, designation of the pertinent evidence in its documentary location and presentation, and estimation of the proportionate importance of the parts and balance and cohesion of the whole.

modes of organizing and explaining the world. When we can define those modes by locating the recurrent patterns of imputing consequence and meaning, then we can state what we conceive a given system to comprise, the main lines of order and sense of which a given system is composed. The theology of the Oral Torah is comprised by the few and simple paradigms that impose regularity and transform what is indeterminate into what can be explained and understood. Theology in the Oral Torah then forms the exercise in systematic reflection, through the medium of paradigms of structure and systematization of properly classified data, upon life that is lived by holy Israel.

Before proceeding, let me give a concrete case of what I have in mind when I speak of model, pattern, or paradigm.. Here is an instance of that paradigmatic thinking that defines and sustains argument about the meaning of events, about the formation of the social order. Before proceeding, let me give two instances of how a paradigm comes to concrete expression, without losing its power to explain concrete events in abstract generalizations. What we shall see is a situation that stands for a question — why gentiles prosper, Israel suffers. The paradigm comes to expression in narrative discourse. The point emerges in the particular case — and yet the possibility of generalizing to all cases that the paradigm realizes proves blatant.

7.   A.   Rabban Gamaliel, R. Joshua, R. Eleazar b. Azariah, and R. Aqiba were going toward Rome. They heard the sound of the city's traffic from as far away as Puteoli, a hundred and twenty *mil* away. They began to cry, while R. Aqiba laughed.

         B.   They said to him, "Aqiba, why are we crying while you are laughing?"

         C.   He said to them, "Why are you crying?"

         D.   They said to him, "Should we not cry, since gentiles, idolators, sacrifice to their idols and bow down to icons, but dwell securely in prosperity, serenely, while the house of the footstool of our God has been put to the torch and left a lair for beasts of the field?"

         E.   He said to them, "That is precisely why I was laughing. If this is how he has rewarded those who anger him, all the more so [will he reward] those who do his will."

8.   A.   Another time they went up to Jerusalem and go to Mount Scopus. They tore their garments.

         B.   They came to the mountain of the house [of the temple] and saw a fox go forth from the house of the holy of holies. They began to cry, while R. Aqiba laughed.

C. They said to him, "You are always giving surprises. We are crying when you laugh!"

D. He said to them, "But why are you crying?"

E. They said to him, "Should we not cry over the place concerning which it is written, ''And the common person who draws near shall be put to death' (Num. 1:51)? Now lo, a fox comes out of it.

F. "In our connection the following verse of Scripture has been carried out: 'For this our heart is faint, for these things our eyes are dim, for the mountain of Zion which is desolate, the foxes walk upon it' (Lam. 5:17-18)."

G. He said to them, "That is the very reason I have laughed. For lo, it is written, 'And I will take for me faithful witnesses to record, Uriah the priest and Zechariah the son of Jeberechiah' (Is. 8:2).

H. "And what has Uriah got to do with Zechariah? What is it that Uriah said? 'Zion shall be plowed as a field and Jerusalem shall become heaps and the mountain of the Lord's house as the high places of a forest' (Jer. 26:18).

I. "What is it that Zechariah said? 'Thus says the Lord of hosts, "Old men and women shall yet sit in the broad places of Jerusalem'" (Zech. 8:4).

J. "Said the Omnipresent, 'Lo, I have these two witnesses. If the words of Uriah have been carried out, then the words of Zechariah will be carried out. If the words of Uriah are nullified, then the words of Zechariah will be nullified.

K. "'Therefore I was happy that the words of Uriah have been carried out, so that in the end the words of Zechariah will come about.'"

L. In this language they replied to him: "Aqiba, you have given us comfort."

SIFRÉ TO DEUTERONOMY TO EQEB XLIII:III

Here we see how paradigmatic thought appeals to an established pattern. So parties to a debate, for instance about the meaning of an event or the interpretation of a social fact, will frame their arguments within the limits of the pattern: that event corresponds to this component of the paradigm shared among all parties to debate. Sorting out the revealed facts of the Torah, paradigms derive from human invention and human imagination, imposed on nature and on history alike. But, we recognize

immediately, the reason that prophecy serves has little bearing on the possibility of
divine revelation in the here and now of Aqiba's time. Aqiba finds a solution in
prophecy because prophecy has identified the paradigmatic data and so defined a
pattern, a mode through which the present is to be interpreted and the future made
known. So prophecy is converted into that rule-making, generalization-framing,
logical mode of thought and inquiry that sages proposed to form out of the Torah
of Moses itself.

Here the paradigm that Aqiba finds in Scripture tells him what data require
attention, and what do not. The prosperity of the idolaters matters only because
the paradigm explains why to begin with we may take account of their situation.
The destruction of the Temple matters also because it conforms to an intelligible
paradigm. In both cases, we both select and also understand events by appeal to
the pattern of defined by the working of God's will. The data at hand then yield
inferences of a particular order — the prosperity of idolaters, the disgrace of Israel
in its very cult. We notice both facts because they both complement one another
and illustrate the workings of the model: validating prophecy, interpreting experience
in light of its message. Here the generative paradigm is the exile and return, the
destruction and rebuilding of the Temple. Referred to that paradigm, an
indeterminate number of specific cases and problems may be worked out.

Let me now generalize on the case we have examined. In paradigmatic
thinking existence takes shape and acquires structure in accord with a paradigm
that is independent of nature and the givens of the social order: God's structure,
God's paradigm, our sages of blessed memory would call it; but in secular terms, a
model or a pattern that in no way responds to the givens of nature or the social
order. Take the case of time, for example, and how we divide and keep time. In the
paradigmatic thinking of Rabbinic Judaism, time is comprised of components that
themselves dictate the character of events: what in particular — by appeal to the
governing model — is noteworthy, chosen out of the variety of things that merely
happen. And what is remarkable conforms to the conventions of the paradigm.

Paradigmatic thinking presents a mode of making connections and drawing
conclusions and is captured in its essence by two statements of Augustine:

> We live only in the present, but this present has several dimensions: the present
> of past things, the present of present things, and the present of future things...
> Your years are like a single day...and this today does not give way to a
> tomorrow, any more than it follows a yesterday. Your today is Eternity...
> Augustine, confessions 10:13

I cannot imagine a more accurate précis of sages' conception of time: the past is
ever present, the present takes place on the same plane of existence as the past, the
whole forming an eternal paradigm, altogether beyond time. For our sages of
blessed memory, the Torah, the written part of the Torah in particular, defined a set
of paradigms that served without regard to circumstance, context, or, for that matter,

dimension and scale of happening. A very small number of models emerged from Scripture, as I shall explain presently. Like models for mathematicians, these paradigms serve a vast variety of particular cases and solved a broad range of problems.

Paradigms of explanation, structure, and order may sort out concrete data of worldly events, politics, wars, calamities, for instance, or they may describe the virtuous man, or they may dictate conduct that will yield one result and prevent another. They may also explain the classification of beasts and of nations, flora and fauna. The governing paradigm takes over data and selects what it requires, making connections particular to the paradigm, drawing conclusions inexorable within the paradigm.[2] Like social science, which seeks the rules that social transactions reveal, and like mathematics, "the abstract science which investigates deductively the conclusions implicit in the elementary conceptions of spatial and numerical relations,"[3] theology described through its paradigms proposes to state the rule, identify the law revealed in, and governing, a variety of concrete situations. Social science, mathematics, paradigmatic theology bear in common the power to describe the concrete in abstract terms, the details of the world in symbolic language. To state matters simply, it is through the paradigm that Rabbinic thought finds its logos, transforms itself into theology, and makes statements within the rules of natural history that, for antiquity, framed science.

Now for a more encompassing example of how paradigmatic theology takes over events and transforms them into patterns, the whole emerging as a model of Israel's existence. Here is a reading of Scripture that encompasses the entirety of Israel's being (its "history" in conventional language) within the conversation that is portrayed between Boaz and Ruth; I abbreviate the passage to highlight only the critical components:

> XL:i.1.A. "And at mealtime Boaz said to her, 'Come here and eat some bread, and dip your morsel in the wine.' So she sat beside the reapers, and he passed to her parched grain; and she ate until she was satisfied, and she had some left over":
> B. R. Yohanan interested the phrase "come here" in six ways:
> C. "The first speaks of David.
> D. "'Come here': means, to the throne: 'That you have brought me here' (2 Sam. 7:18).

---

[2] Chapter Seven shows how this works in a different context altogether, and Chapter Eight moves to the outer limits of abstraction with its attention to symbolic discourse.
[3] *The Compact Edition of the Oxford English Dictionary* (Oxford, 1971: Oxford University Press), 1:1743.

E. "'...and eat some bread': the bread of the throne.

F. "'...and dip your morsel in vinegar': this speaks of his sufferings: 'O Lord, do not rebuke me in your anger' (Ps. 6:2).

G. "'So she sat beside the reapers': for the throne was taken from him for a time."

I. [Resuming from G:] "'and he passed to her parched grain': he was restored to the throne: 'Now I know that the Lord saves his anointed' (Ps. 20:7).

J. "'...and she ate and was satisfied and left some over': this indicates that he would eat in this world, in the days of the messiah, and in the age to come.

2. A. "The second interpretation refers to Solomon: 'Come here': means, to the throne.

B. "'...and eat some bread': this is the bread of the throne: "And Solomon's provision for one day was thirty measures of fine flour and three score measures of meal' (1 Kgs. 5:2).

C. "'...and dip your morsel in vinegar': this refers to the dirty of the deeds [that he did].

D. "'So she sat beside the reapers': for the throne was taken from him for a time."

G. [Reverting to D:] "'and he passed to her parched grain': for he was restored to the throne.

H. "'...and she ate and was satisfied and left some over': this indicates that he would eat in this world, in the days of the messiah, and in the age to come.

3. A. "The third interpretation speaks of Hezekiah: 'Come here': means, to the throne.

B. "'...and eat some bread': this is the bread of the throne.

C. "'...and dip your morsel in vinegar': this refers to sufferings [Is. 5:1]: 'And Isaiah said, Let them take a cake of figs' (Is. 38:21).

D. "'So she sat beside the reapers': for the throne was taken from him for a time: 'Thus says Hezekiah, This day is a day of trouble and rebuke' (Is. 37:3).

E. "'...and he passed to her parched grain': for he was restored to the throne: 'So that he was exalted in the sight of all nations from then on' (2 Chr. 32:23).

F. "'...and she ate and was satisfied and left some over': this indicates that he would eat in this world, in the days of the messiah, and in the age to come.

4.   A.   "The fourth interpretation refers to Manasseh: 'Come here': means, to the throne.

B.   "'...and eat some bread': this is the bread of the throne.

C.   "'...and dip your morsel in vinegar': for his dirty deeds were like vinegar, on account of wicked actions.

D.   "'So she sat beside the reapers': for the throne was taken from him for a time: 'And the Lord spoke to Manasseh and to his people, but they did not listen. So the Lord brought them the captains of the host of the king of Assyria, who took Manasseh with hooks' (2 Chr. 33:10-11)."

K.   [Reverting to D:] "'and he passed to her parched grain': for he was restored to the throne: 'And brought him back to Jerusalem to his kingdom' (2 Chr. 33:13).

N.   "'...and she ate and was satisfied and left some over': this indicates that he would eat in this world, in the days of the messiah, and in the age to come.

5.   A.   "The fifth interpretation refers to the Messiah: 'Come here': means, to the throne.

B.   "'...and eat some bread': this is the bread of the throne.

C.   "'...and dip your morsel in vinegar': this refers to suffering: 'But he was wounded because of our transgressions' (Is. 53:5).

D.   "'So she sat beside the reapers': for the throne is destined to be taken from him for a time: For I will gather all nations against Jerusalem to battle and the city shall be taken' (Zech. 14:2).

E.   "'...and he passed to her parched grain': for he will be restored to the throne: 'And he shall smite the land with the rod of his mouth' (Is. 11:4)."

I.   [reverting to G:] "so the last redeemer will be revealed to them and then hidden from them."

RUTH RABBAH PARASHAH FIVE

The paradigm here may be formed of six units: [1] David's monarchy; [2] Solomon's reign; [3] Hezekiah's reign; [4] Manasseh's reign; [5] the Messiah's reign. So paradigmatic time compresses events to the dimensions of its model. All things happen on a single plane of time. Past, present, future are undifferentiated, and that is why a single action contains within itself an entire account of Israel's social order under the aspect of eternity. What we have is a list of "things" held, all together, to make a statement, to form a logical sentence for parsing.

The foundations of the paradigm, of course, rest on the fact that David, Solomon, Hezekiah, Manasseh, and therefore also, the Messiah, all descend from Ruth's and Boaz's union. Then, within the framework of the paradigm, the event that is described here — "And at mealtime Boaz said to her, 'Come here and eat some bread, and dip your morsel in the wine.' So she sat beside the reapers, and he passed to her parched grain; and she ate until she was satisfied, and she had some left over" — forms not an event but a pattern. The pattern transcends time; or more accurately, aggregates of time, the passage of time, the course of events — these are all simply irrelevant to what is in play in Scripture. Rather we have a tableau,[4] joining persons who lived at widely separated moments, linking them all as presences at this simple exchange between Boaz and Ruth; imputing to them all, whenever they came into existence, the shape and structure of that simple moment: the presence of the past, for David, Solomon, Hezekiah,and so on, but the pastness of the present in which David or Solomon — or the Messiah for that matter — lived or would live (it hardly matters, verb tenses prove hopelessly irrelevant to paradigmatic thinking).

These paradigms served severally and jointly, e.g., the paradigm built upon Eden and Adam on its own but also superimposed upon the Land of Israel and Israel, the loss experienced by Adam compared to the loss experienced by Israel; Sinai and the Torah on its own but also superimposed upon the Land and Israel,. The Temple, embodying natural creation and its intersection with national and social history, could stand entirely on its own or be superimposed upon any and all of the other paradigms. In many ways, then, we have the symbolic equivalent of a set of two- and three- or even four-dimensional grids, e.g., Adam and Eden, Israel and the Land of Israel, for two dimensions. Add to that the Temple (for Eden) and sin and we have a third, and each will then impart meaning to all others.

A given pattern forms a grid on its own, one set of lines being set forth in terms of, e.g., Eden, timeless perfection, in contrast against the other set of lines, Adam, temporal disobedience; but upon that grid, a comparable grid can be superimposed, the Land and Israel being an obvious one; and upon the two, yet a third and fourth, Sinai and Torah, Temple and the confluence of nature and history. By reference to these grids, severally or jointly, the critical issues of existence, whether historical, whether contemporary, played themselves out in the system and structure of Rabbinic Judaism. In particular, we identify four models by which, out of happenings of various sorts, consequential or meaningful events would be selected, and by reference to which these selected events would be shown connected ("meaningful") and explicable in terms of that available logic of paradigm that governed both the making of connections and the drawing of conclusions.

---

[4] For the notion of the representation of Israel's existence as an ahistorical tableau, see my *Judaism. The Evidence of the Mishnah.* Chicago, 1981: University of Chicago Press.

Paradigmatic thinking is not static, merely making lists of things that all together teach lessons, but dynamic. That is to say, as in the case of Aqiba's reading of the future considered at the outset, it is a medium for making sense of what happens, identifying consequential events and interpreting their meaning, and a mode of pointing out of the present toward what is going to happen. Once, after all, we know to what pattern a given event adheres, we also can say what will happen next, in line with the familiar lines that said pattern adumbrates. To understand paradigmatic thinking, we have then to address the kinds of problems it chooses for solution, the tasks it undertakes.

Now let me generalize. Discerning a pattern in events treats events not as one-time, historical moments of the past but as all-time facts susceptible to analysis yielding rules. The paradigm then states the rules that cases produce, bringing them to a high level of abstraction. The power of the paradigm lies in its capacity both to identify pattern and also to explain what is happening when a pattern is replicated. Issues of time, circumstance, and dimension scarcely register. Rabbis hear traffic, see a fox — and invoke eternity. Here the metaphor of mathematics enters in in the form of fractal thinking (in mathematics), which isolates points of regularity or recurrence and describes, analyzes, and even in the face of chaos and disorder, permit us to interpret them. Proportionality as much as context gives way; the cosmic and the humble conform to the same paradigm (much as is the case mutatis mutandis in fractal mathematics).

At stake in the paradigm is discerning order and regularity not everywhere but in some few sets of happenings. The scale revised both upward and downward the range of concern: these are not all happenings, but they are the ones that matter — and they matter very much. Realizing or replicating the paradigm, they uniquely constitute events, and, that is why by definition, these are the only events that matter. Paradigmatic thinking about past, present, and future ignores issues of linear order and temporal sequence because it recognizes another logic all together, besides the one of priority and posteriority and causation formulated in historical terms. That mode of thinking, as its name states, appeals to the logic of models or patterns that serve without regard to time and circumstance, on the one side, or scale, on the other. The sense for order unfolds, first of all, through that logic of selection that dictates what matters and what does not. And, out of the things that matter, that same logic defines the connections of things, so forming a system of description, analysis, and explanation that consists in the making of connections between this and that, but not the other thing, and the drawing of conclusions from those ineluctable, self-evident connections. At stake now is the definition of self-evidence: how did our sages know the difference between event and mere happening?

Paradigmatic thinking contrasts with historical thinking.[5] As a medium of organizing and accounting for experience, history — the linear narrative of singular events intended through the narrative of one came first and what happened then to explain how things got to their present state and therefore why — does not enjoy the status of a given. A way of thinking about the experience of humanity, whether past or contemporary, that makes other distinctions than the historical ones between past and present and that eschews linear narrative and so takes account of the chaos that ultimately prevails, in the Oral Torah competes with historical thinking. Paradigmatic thinking, a different medium for organizing and explaining things that happen, deals with the same data that occupy historical thinking, and that is why when we refer to paradigmatic thinking, the word "history" gains its quotation marks: it is not a datum of thought, merely a choice; contradicting to its core the character of paradigmatic thinking.

In Chapter Two I laid heavy emphasis upon the problem of correlating the two Torahs, Oral and Written. What, concretely, does the written Torah contribute to the theology of the Oral Torah? The answer is, nearly the entirety of the paradigmatic structure to be discerned in the documents of the Oral Torah finds its definition in the ordering of the events and persons and actions portrayed in the Written Torah. The Oral Torah at its foundations constitutes a profound and encompassing reflection upon the patterns of the Written Torah, the models that are represented by its persons and incidents. This mode of thinking reads as a paradigm what in Scripture is set forth as (mere) narrative, bearing deep meaning to be sure. So paradigmatic thinking represents at its core a hermeneutics devised for the transformation of Scripture into Torah — revealed truth for eternity:

[1] Scripture set forth certain patterns which, applied to the chaos of the moment, selected out of a broad range of candidates some things and omitted reference to others.

[2] The selected things then are given their structure and order by appeal to the paradigm, or described without regard to scale by the fractal, indifference to scale forming the counterpart to the paradigm's indifference to context, time, circumstance.

[3] That explains how some events narrated by Scripture emerged as patterns, imposing their lines of order and structure upon happenings of other times.

These events of Israel's life (we cannot now refer to Israel's "history") — or, rather, the models or patterns that they yielded — served as the criteria for selection, among happenings of any time, past, present, or future, of the things that mattered out of the things that did not matter: a way of keeping track, a mode of marking time. The model or paradigm that set forth the measure of meaning then applied whether to events of vast consequence or to the trivialities of everyday

---

[5] I spell out these matters at length in my *The Presence of the Past, the Pastness of the Present. History, Time, and Paradigm in Rabbinic Judaism*. Bethesda, 1996: CDL Press.

concern alone. Sense was where sense was found by the measure of the paradigm; everything else lost consequence. Connections were then to be made between this and that, and the other thing did not count. Conclusions then were to be drawn between the connection of this and that, and no consequences were to be imputed into the thing that did not count.

While mathematics finds its models in the here and now, translated, then, into abstract symbol, and social science discovers regularities in social behavior, whence the paradigms that define the theology of Rabbinic Judaism? The Oral Torah naturally discovers its paradigms in the written Torah. What the Oral Torah contributes to the one whole Torah, written and oral, that enjoys the status of the revelation by God to Rabbi Moses at Mount Sinai is the recognition of those paradigms and the utilization thereof. What Scripture ("written Torah," "Old Testament") yields for Rabbinic Judaism therefore is not one-time events, arranged in sequence to dictate meaning, but models or patterns of conduct and consequence. These models are defined by the written Torah or the Old Testament (read in light of the perspective of the Oral Torah or the New Testament). No component of the paradigm we shall consider emerges from other than the selected experience set forth by Scripture. But the paradigms are at the same time pertinent without regard to considerations of scale and formulated without interest in matters of singular context. Forthrightly selective — this matters, that is ignored — the principle of selection is not framed in terms of sequence; order of a different sort is found.

II. THE PLAUSIBILITY OF PARADIGMS

Thinking through models or paradigms (the words refer to the same mode of organizing thought) proves entirely plausible when we consider a contemporary counterpart to the paradigmatic thought of the sages. Can I offer an accessible and quite contemporary example of that same mode of thought, so that the way in which our sages of blessed memory organized and explained experience will prove accessible and reasonable to the world of historical explanation that retains plausibility, even self-evidence, to us? Having introduced the metaphor of mathematics (in the use of the word "model," for instance, and in the allusion to fractals), let me proceed by turning once more to mathematics for help in explaining the present approach to the theology of the Oral Torah.

So I turn to a brief reference to the use of model in mathematics, since that is the source for my resort to the same word and that mode of description, analysis, and interpretation of data for which it stands. For it would be difficult to find a more substantial, a more concrete and immediate mode of addressing events and explaining the concrete here and now than the paradigmatic: ahistorical, yes, and from one angle of vision atemporal too, but far from insubstantial, and, in the context of natural time, profoundly time-oriented. The paradigm forms a medium for the description, analysis, and interpretation of selected data: existence, rightly construed. In this, paradigmatic thinking forms a counterpart to that of the mathematics that produces models.

Specifically, mathematicians compose models that, in the language and symbols of mathematics, set forth a structure of knowledge that forms a "surrogate for reality."[6] These models state in quantitative terms the results of controlled observations of data, and among them, the one that generates plausible analytical generalizations will serve. Seeking not so much the regularities of the data as a medium for taking account of a variety of variables among a vast corpus of data, the framer of a model needs more than observations of fact, e.g., regularities or patterns. What is essential is a structure of thought, which mathematicians call "a philosophy:"

> As a philosophy it has a center from which everything flows, and the center is a definition,...[7]

What is needed for a model is not data alone, however voluminous, but some idea of what you are trying to compose: a model of the model:

> Unless you have some good idea of what you are looking for and how to find it, you can approach infinity with nothing more than a mishmash of little things you know about a lot of little things.[8]

So, in order to frame a model of explanation, we start with a model in the computer, and then test data to assess the facility of the model; we may test several models, with the same outcome: the formation of a philosophy in the mathematical sense. Comparably, Aqiba worked with a model quite different from that of the other sages. The latter saw matters as at the outset, Aqiba's model as at the end. To understand the relevance of this brief glimpse at model-making in mathematics, let me cite the context in which the matter comes to me, the use of mathematics to give guidance on how to fight forest fires:

> If mathematics can be used to predict the intensity and rate of spread of wildfires of the future (either hypothetical fires or fires actually burning but whose outcome is not yet known), why can't the direction of the analysis be reversed in order to reconstruct the characteristics of important fires of the past? Or why can't the direction be reversed from prophecy to history?[9]

---

[6] Norman Maclean, *Young Men and Fire* (Chicago, 1992: University of Chicago Press), p. 257.
[7] Maclean, p. 261.
[8] Maclean, p. 262.
[9] Maclean, p. 267.

Here the reversibility of events, their paradigmatic character, their capacity to yield a model unlimited by context or considerations of scale, — the principal traits of paradigmatic thinking turn out to enjoy a compelling rationality of their own. Reading those words, we can immediately grasp what service models or patterns or paradigms served for our sages of blessed memory, even though the framing of mathematical models began long after the birth of this writer, and even though our sages lived many centuries before the creation of the mathematics that would yield models in that sense in which, sages' paradigms correspond in kind and function to model-explanation in contemporary mathematics. Before us is a mode of thought that is entirely rational and the very opposite of "insubstantial."

What is at stake in the appeal to "paradigm" or "model" to explain how sages answered the same questions that, elsewhere, historical thinking admirably addresses is now clear. To use the term in the precise sense just now stated, philosophy now took the place of history in the examination of the meaning of human events and experience. Forming a philosophical model to hold together such data as made a difference, sages found ready at hand the pattern of the destruction of the Temple, alongside explanations of the event and formulations of how the consequences were to be worked out. The Temple for sages constituted the mother of all models. It represented the focus and realization of the abstractions of nature — from the movement of sun and moon to the concrete rhythm of the offerings celebrating these events, from the abundance of nature, the natural selection, by chance, and presentation of God's share on the altar.

III. THE PARADIGMATIC PERSON

Of what, exactly, does the Oral Torah's paradigmatic theology consist? To lend concreteness to the conception of the theological paradigm, let me take up, first, the case of virtue or ethics, then turn to the case of history and the quest for sound social morality. Narrative, on the one side, and biography, on the other, find their counterparts in the paradigmatic conception that governs in Rabbinic documents. Narrative in a paradigm serves the purpose of the paradigm, selecting a topic and expounding that topic within the model's rules; and the same is so for biography.

Rabbinic literature contains numerous sayings about right action, Torah-study, the virtuous man. But when we collect and arrange such settings, we find — as I showed in the case of Urbach's vapid discussion of theological anthropology — mere paraphrase. That is to say, when we know pertinent sayings, what more we know than those sayings is not self-evident. But discerning the pattern that the sayings adumbrate allows us to broaden our inquiry, to generalize and to test our generalization, concerning the large theory of matters that we should anticipate discerning throughout the kindred writings.

How do the authoritative writings express their theological anthropology? It is through the description of persons, mostly men, who exemplify the pattern of virtue. The kindred corpus contains no biographies (equivalent to gospels, for example) but only stories about deeds and sayings of sages.[10] Paradigmatic episodes in place of distinctive and individual biography yielded the model of the life framed by the Torah: a life lived within the rules of nature, but facing outward toward supernature, a life transcending the natural world, measured by moments of transcendence: advent into the Torah, the active and complex realm of negotiation within the Torah, virtue measured by the Torah and responding to the special vices that the Torah can nurture, and death in the supernatural setting that overcomes nature: not dirt to dirt, but soul to Heaven, along with the Torah. To make that statement, narrative yielding an account of the realization of nature in the cult cannot have served; only anecdotes about persons convey the message of how Israel through the Torah transcends nature. The question asked at Eden for Adam, restated in the Land of Israel for Israel, finds its answer in the Torah, and its resolution in the person of the sage. Exemplary pattern was the only way to say so.

Why no biography (all the more so, no gospels!) in the authoritative books? For the same reason that — as we shall see — the same corpus excludes narrative history. Linear and sustained narrative of the events of the social entity ("nation," in general, "Israel" in particular) corresponds to biography, in the present context, lives of sages. Just as the historical mode of thought generates the composition of sustained narratives, so practitioners of history also will write lives of persons, e.g., Moses, or at least continuous tales of a biographical character, with some sort of connected narrative, real or contrived, to give the impression of personal history. Not only so, but practitioners of the historical sciences — Josephus for instance — give us not only biography but autobiography, just as much as philosophers or theologians of history, Augustine being the best example, will supply a biographical counterpart to a history. It obviously follows that where history leads, biography follows close behind.

What place can we define for the counterpart to biography? The answer is, exemplary anecdotes, the counterpart to singular events, but no "lives" or biographies, the counterpart to sustained historical narrative. That answer is obvious. The real question is the character of those exemplary, one-time anecdotes, for knowing that they are going to exemplify paradigmatic concerns or realize the model through the medium of persons, rather than public events does not guide us to a theory of the particular character of the personal anecdotes that the model generates. And yet, given our theory of the character of the Rabbinic paradigm, we also should be able to formulate a clear definition of the particular traits of its account of particular persons.

---

[10] In this context, see my *Why No Gospels in Talmudic Judaism?* Atlanta, 1988: Scholars Press for Brown Judaic Studies

Paradigmatic thinking about the social order yields anecdotes instead of continuous history (such as Josephus wrote). It also attends to the representation of persons, but solely for paradigmatic purposes and in a manner calculated to yield not continuous narrative but that which is here deemed of definitive consequence: a restatement, in individual terms, of the paradigm. And that is to be expected. For once time loses its quality of continuity and sequentiality, marking time calls upon other indicators of order and division than those demanded by the interplay of nature's telling time and humanity's interposing its rhythms. Lives of persons, beginning to end, need not be told; indeed, cannot be told, for the same reason that sequential, continuous narrative, which by its nature obliterates paradigms, also cannot be constructed.

The paradigm will identify, out of the moments presented by a human life, those that gain importance by appeal to the paradigm itself; the natural course of a human life, from death to birth, bears no more meaning in the amplification of the paradigm than the passage of empires, viewed as singular, or the story of a reign or a dynasty, viewed in its own terms. These matter, for paradigmatic thinking, when the pattern or model determines; otherwise, they do not register at all. Of the many empires of antiquity, four counted to the paradigm of Rabbinic Judaism, Babylonia, Media, Greece, and Rome. What of Parthians, what of Sasanians, certainly as weighty as Greece and Rome and for long centuries quite able to hold their own (with their huge Jewish populations) against Greece and Rome? They did not count, so were not counted. We know why they did not matter: they never intersected with the natural life of the holy people, Israel, in the holy land, the Land of Israel; they never threatened Jerusalem, in the way in which Babylonia, Greece (in Seleucid times), and Rome did. That principal part of the paradigm points to one main principle of selection in the range of events. Working back from events to the principle of selection that operates within the model governing Rabbinic Judaism's disposition of time (past, present, future), we are able to define out of what is selected the operative criterion: the congruence of the selected model to nature's time, not its contrast in conjunction therewith. Then what is to be said about the paradigm's points of interest in human lives? Since, we must anticipate, the paradigm will not elicit interest in a continuous life and so will not produce biography let alone autobiography, at what points will the model encompass episodes in human lives? To state the question more simply: where, when, and why, will individual persons make a difference, so as to warrant the writing down of details of personal lives?

Asked in this way, the question produces a ready answer, in three parts, two of which take but a moment for their exposition. First, does the paradigm before us take an interest in the lives of persons? It does. Second, if it does, then at what point in a human life will anecdotes preserve the model for exemplary conduct, defining, then, the principle of selection, out of a human life as much as out of the happenings of the social world, of what counts? The principle of selection, at each point, somehow relates to the Torah. And, third, how does the paradigm emerge, having received a richer and more nuanced definition, out of the encounter with individual lives?

The answer is that the model that governs the formation of the Rabbinic writings certainly does narrate episodes in personal lives, not only events in the social order. Second, the points of special interest are [1] how an individual studies the Torah, with special attention to beginnings; [2] remarkable deeds of virtue in the individual's life; [3] how the individual dies. The beginning of life, meaning or learning in the Torah, the middle of life, meaning, virtue, and a dignified death — these form the paradigmatic points of interest. This survey leaves no reasonable doubt that the function of — not biography but — episodes individual's lives is to show the union of the nature and the social order through the person of the sage. That union takes place within the medium of the Torah, which corresponds to nature and lays out the governing rules thereof, but also encompasses the social order and defines its laws as well. Anecdotes about the master of the Torah then serve to convey principles of the Torah, with the clear proviso that anecdotes about events may equally set forth precisely those same principles. So as I said the paradigm describes regularities without regard to considerations of scale, whether social or private, any more than matters of earlier or later, past or present or future, make any difference at all.

That fact, by the way, also explains why the paradigm in play really excludes not only biography but personality in any form. Individuals make a difference, so as to warrant the writing down of components of personal lives, at that point at which they lose all individuality and serve in some way or other to embody and exemplify a detail of the paradigm best set forth in the dimensions of private life. We then identify no difference between the social entity and the private person, because the paradigm works out indifferent to matters of scale or context; says what it says wherever it says it .

How does the paradigm emerge? A paradigm that proposes to present a single, coherent, and cogent picture of the life of Israel under the aspect of the timeless Torah has to make its statement about not only the social order viewed whole, but also the individuals who comprise that order. The paradigm requires the counterpart to biography, as much as the counterpart to history, for its own reasons; it cares about individuals for the same reason that it cares about the social entity, Israel. Biography does for history what personal anecdotes do for the paradigm at hand. Just as the one renders the large conclusions of its companion manageable and in human scale, so the other expresses the statements of the paradigm in a form accessible of human imitation and identification. But anecdotes about people also deepen our perception of the paradigm. For the issue of time is recast, now, as the span of a human life enters consideration. Paradigm in place of history yielded the narrative of the cult and the story of the Temple.

IV. THE PARADIGMATIC EVENT

For our sages of blessed memory, the Torah, the written part of the Torah in particular, defined a set of paradigms that served without regard to circumstance, context, or, for that matter, dimension and scale of happening. As I said, very small number of models emerged from Scripture, such as [1] Eden and Adam, [2] Sinai and the Torah, [3] the land and Israel, and [4] the Temple and its building, destruction, rebuilding. By reference to these grids, severally or jointly, the critical issues of existence, whether historical, whether contemporary, played themselves out in the system and structure of Rabbinic Judaism. In particular, I identify four models by which, out of happenings of various sorts, consequential or meaningful events would be selected, and by reference to which these selected events would be shown connected ("meaningful") and explicable in terms of that available logic of paradigm that governed both the making of connections and the drawing of conclusions.

THE PARADIGM OF ISRAEL'S PAST, PRESENT, AND FUTURE (="HISTORY"): how shall we organize happenings into events? On the largest scale the question concerns the division into periods of not sequences but mere sets of happenings. Periodization involves explanation, of course, since even in a paradigmatic structure, once matters are set forth as periods, then an element of sequence is admitted into the processes of description and therefore analysis and explanation.

ISRAEL AND THE NATIONS (=WORLD ORDER): moving from large aggregates, bordering on abstraction, we turn to the very concrete question of how Israel relates to the rest of the world. This involves explaining not what happened this morning in particular, but what always happens, that is, defining the structure of Israel's life in the politics of this world, explaining the order of things in both the social, political structure of the world and also the sequence of actions that may occur and recur over time (the difference, paradigmatically, hardly matters).

EXPLAINING THE PATTERN OF EVENTS: MAKING CONNECTIONS, DRAWING CONCLUSIONS (PHILOSOPHY AND SCIENCE): paradigmatic thinking, no less than historical, explains matters; but the explanation derives from the character of the pattern, rather than the order of events, which governs historical explanation. Connections then are drawn between one thing and something else serve to define a paradigm, rather than to convey a temporal explanation based on sequences, first this, then that, therefore this explains why that happened. The paradigm bears a different explanation altogether, one that derives from its principle of selection, and therefore the kinds of explanations paradigmatic thinking sets forth, expressed through its principles of selection in making connections and drawing conclusions, will demand rich instantiation.

THE FUTURE HISTORY OF ISRAEL (TELEOLOGY): just as studying the past is supposed to explain the present and point to the future — surely the rationale for historical thinking and writing — so paradigmatic thinking bears the same responsibility. That concerns not so much explaining the present as permitting informed speculation about what will happen in the future. And that speculation will appeal to those principles of order, structure, and explanation that the paradigm to begin with sets forth. So future history in historical thinking and writing projects out of past and present a trajectory over time to come, and future history in paradigmatic thinking forms projects along other lines altogether.

These paradigms serve to form and inform events large and small, now and then, here and there, without regard to dimensions or considerations of past, present, or future. Whatever happens that bears consequence and demands explanation is accommodated within these patterns, which serve equally well for past and present, public and private, small and large occasions. To refer once more to the analogy drawn from mathematics, fractal thinking, paradigmatic thinking in place of the historical kind finds sameness without regard to scale, from small to large and so makes possible the quest for a few specific patterns, which, controlling for chaos by claiming only a proportionate order, isolate points of regularity or recurrence and describe, analyze, and permit us to interpret them.

Let me then specify some particular types of paradigms and the sort of events that they encompass. First is the paradigm of Israel's past, present, and future (="History" in the counterpart structure of historical thinking): how shall we organize happenings into events? On the largest scale the question concerns the division into periods of not sequences but mere sets of happenings. Periodization involves explanation, of course, since even in a paradigmatic structure, once matters are set forth as periods, then an element of sequence is admitted into the processes of description and therefore analysis and explanation.

Second and equally critical is the paradigm that organizes events concerning Israel and its experience among the nations. Moving from large aggregates, bordering on abstraction, we turn to the very concrete question of how Israel relates to the rest of the world. This involves explaining not what happened this morning in particular, but what always happens, that is, defining the structure of Israel's life in the politics of this world, explaining the order of things in both the social, political structure of the world and also the sequence of actions that may occur and recur over time (the difference, paradigmatically, hardly matters). Paradigmatic thinking, no less than historical, explains matters; but the explanation derives from the character of the pattern, rather than the order of events, which governs historical explanation. Connections then are drawn between one thing and something else serve to define a paradigm, rather than to convey a temporal explanation based on sequences, first this, then that, therefore this explains why that happened. The paradigm bears a different explanation altogether, one that derives from its principle of selection, and therefore the kinds of explanations paradigmatic thinking sets forth, expressed through its principles of selection in making connections and drawing conclusions, will demand rich instantiation.

And this brings us to how paradigmatic thinking moves from the past that is present to the future that — in the theory at hand — is going to recapitulate past and present. The single most important task of paradigmatic thinking about events pertains to the analysis of what happens in line with what has happened so as to delineate the future history of Israel. Just as studying the past is supposed to explain the present and point to the future, so paradigmatic thinking bears the same responsibility. That concerns not so much explaining the present as permitting informed speculation about what will happen in the future. And that speculation will appeal to those principles of order, structure, and explanation that the paradigm to begin with sets forth. So future history in historical thinking and writing projects out of past and present a trajectory over time to come, and future history in paradigmatic thinking forms projects along other lines altogether.

The paradigm does its work on all data, without regard to scale or context or circumstance, What this means is that any paradigmatic case — personality, event, idea — imposes structure and order on all data; and the structure will be the same for the small and the large, the now and the then. By that criterion of paradigmatic structuring of "history," we should be able to tell the story of Israel's past, present, and future, by appeal to any identified model, and what we need not predict is which model will yield what pattern, for the patterns are always the same, whatever the choice of the model. In the following, for a striking example, we are able to define the paradigm of Israel's history out of the lives of the founders of the Israelite tribes. That is not a matter of mere generalities. The tribal progenitors moreover correspond to the kingdoms that will rule over Israel, so there is a correspondence of opposites. In the following, as the single best formulation of paradigmatic thinking in the Rabbinic corpus, Israel's history is taken over into the structure of Israel's life of sanctification, and all that happens to Israel forms part of the structure of holiness built around cult, Torah, synagogue, sages, Zion, and the like; I give only a small part:

> 2. A. "As he looked, he saw a well in the field:"
>   B. R. Hama bar Hanina interpreted the verse in six ways [that is, he divides the verse into six clauses and systematically reads each of the clauses in light of the others and in line with an overriding theme:
>   C. "'As he looked, he saw a well in the field:' this refers to the well [of water in the wilderness, Num. 21:17].
>   D. "'...and lo, three flocks of sheep lying beside it:' specifically, Moses, Aaron, and Miriam.
>   E. "'...for out of that well the flocks were watered:' from from there each one drew water for his standard, tribe, and family."
>   F. "And the stone upon the well's mouth was great:"
>   G. Said R. Hanina, "It was only the size of a little sieve."
>   H. [Reverting to Hama's statement:] "'...and put the stone

back in its place upon the mouth of the well:' for the coming journeys. [Thus the first interpretation applies the passage at hand to the life of Israel in the wilderness.]

3.   A. "'As he looked, he saw a well in the field:' refers to Zion.

      B. "'...and lo, three flocks of sheep lying beside it:' refers to the three festivals.

      C. "'....for out of that well the flocks were watered:' from there they drank of the holy spirit.

      D. "'...The stone on the well's mouth was large:' this refers to the rejoicing of the house of the water-drawing."

      E. Said R. Hoshaiah, "Why is it called 'the house of the water drawing'? Because from there they drink of the Holy Spirit."

      F. [Resuming Hama b. Hanina's discourse:] "'...and when all the flocks were gathered there:' coming from 'the entrance of Hamath to the brook of Egypt' (1 Kgs. 8:66).

      G. "'...the shepherds would roll the stone from the mouth of the well and water the sheep:' for from there they would drink of the Holy Spirit.

      H. "'...and put the stone back in its place upon the mouth of the well:' leaving it in place until the coming festival. [Thus the second interpretation reads the verse in light of the Temple celebration of the Festival of Tabernacles.]

5.   A. "'As he looked, he saw a well in the field:' this refers to Zion.

      B. "'...and lo, three flocks of sheep lying beside it:' this refers to the first three kingdoms [Babylonia, Media, Greece].

      C. "'...for out of that well the flocks were watered:' for they enriched the treasures that were laid upon up in the chambers of the Temple.

      D. "'...The stone on the well's mouth was large:' this refers to the merit attained by the patriarchs.

      E. "'...and when all the flocks were gathered there:' this refers to the wicked kingdom, which collects troops through levies over all the nations of the world.

      F. "'...the shepherds would roll the stone from the mouth

of the well and water the sheep:' for they enriched the treasures that were laid upon up in the chambers of the Temple.

G. "'...and put the stone back in its place upon the mouth of the well:' in the age to come the merit attained by the patriarchs will stand [in defense of Israel].' [So the fourth interpretation interweaves the themes of the Temple cult and the domination of the four monarchies.]

7. A. "'As he looked, he saw a well in the field:' this refers to the synagogue.

B. "'...and lo, three flocks of sheep lying beside it:' this refers to the three who are called to the reading of the Torah on weekdays.

C. "'...for out of that well the flocks were watered:' for from there they hear the reading of the Torah.

D. "'...The stone on the well's mouth was large:' this refers to the impulse to do evil.

E. "'...and when all the flocks were gathered there:' this refers to the congregation.

F. "'...the shepherds would roll the stone from the mouth of the well and water the sheep:' for from there they hear the reading of the Torah.

G. "'...and put the stone back in its place upon the mouth of the well:' for once they go forth [from the hearing of the reading of the Torah] the impulse to do evil reverts to its place." [The sixth and last interpretation turns to the twin themes of the reading of the Torah in the synagogue and the evil impulse, temporarily driven off through the hearing of the Torah.]

GENESIS RABBAH LXX:VIII[11]

So much for the correlation of the structures of the social and cosmic order with the condition of Israel. In the passage just reviewed, paradigms take over the organization of events. Time is no longer sequential and linear. What endures are the structures of cosmos and society: prophets, Zion, the Sanhedrin, holy seasons, and on and on. Clearly, the one thing that plays no role whatsoever in this tableau and frieze is Israel's linear history; past and future take place in an eternal present.

---

[11] J. Neusner, trans., *Genesis Rabbah. The Judaic Commentary on Genesis. A New American Translation.* Atlanta, 1985: Scholars Press for Brown Judaic Studies. III. *Genesis Rabbah. The Judaic Commentary on Genesis. A New American Translation. Parashiyyot Sixty-Eight through One Hundred. Genesis 28:10-50:26.*

That formulation, however, cannot complete the picture, since Israel's experience encompasses the nations, on the one side, Rome, on the other. Any claim to classify spells of time has to take account of the worldly political experience of Israel; that, after all, is what sets the agenda of thought to begin with. The periodization of history can be worked out in terms of Rome's rule now, Israel's dominance in the age to come. The comparability of the two is expressed in various ways, e.g.:

> 2.   A.   "Two nations are in your womb, [and two peoples, born of you, shall be divided; the one shall be stronger than the other, and the elder shall serve the younger]" (Gen. 25:23):
>
> B.   There are two proud nations in your womb, this one takes pride in his world, and that one takes pride in his world.
>
> C.   This one takes pride in his monarchy, and that one takes pride in his monarchy.
>
> D.   There are two proud nations in your womb.
>
> E.   Hadrian represents the nations, Solomon, Israel.
>
> F.   There are two who are hated by the nations in your womb. All the nations hate Esau, and all the nations hate Israel.
>
> G.   The one whom your creator hates is in your womb: "And Esau I hated" (Mal. 1:3).
>
> GENESIS RABBAH LXIII:VII[12]

Thus far, paradigmatic thinking has come to expression in the transformation of actions or traits of the patriarchs into markers of time, modes of the characterization of what history treats as historical. But any conception that thinking about social experience by appeal to patterns or models, rather than sequences in teleological order, requires attention to data of a narrowly historical character, e.g., persons or events "paradigmatized," misconstrues the character of the mode of thinking that is before us. We may indeed make sense of Israel's social world by appeal to the deeds or traits of the patriarchs or tribal progenitors. But other statements of the Torah serve equally well as sources for paradigmatic interpretation: models of how things are to be organized and made sensible, against which how things actually are is to be measured.

As a medium of organizing and accounting for experience, history — the linear narrative of singular events intended to explain how things got to their present state and therefore why — does not enjoy the status of a given. Nor does historical

---

[12] ibid.

thinking concerning the social order self-evidently lay claim on plausibility. It is one possibility among many. Historical thinking — sequential narrative of one-time events — presupposes order, linearity, distinction between time past and time present, and teleology, among data that do not self-evidently sustain such presuppositions. Questions of chaos intervene; the very possibility of historical narrative meets a challenge in the diversity of story-lines, the complexity of events, the bias of the principle of selection of what is eventful, of historical interest, among a broad choice of happenings: why this, not that. Narrative history first posits a gap between past and present, but then bridges the gap; why not entertain the possibility that to begin with there is none? These and similar considerations invite a different way of thinking about how things have been and now are, a different tense structure altogether.

I have stressed that the purpose of paradigmatic thinking, as much as historical, points toward the future. History is important to explain the present, also to help peer into the future; and paradigms serve precisely the same purpose. The choice between the one model and the other, then, rests upon which appeals to the more authentic data. In that competition Scripture, treated as paradigm, met no competition in linear history, and it was paradigmatic, not historical, thinking that proved compelling for a thousand years or more. The future history of Israel is written in Scripture, and what happened in the beginning is what is going to happen at the end of time. That sense of order and balance prevailed. It comes to expression in a variety of passages, of which a severely truncated selection will have to suffice:

> **2.** A. Said R. Abin, "Just as [Israel's history] began with the encounter with four kingdoms, so [Israel's history] will conclude with the encounter with the four kingdoms.
>
> B. "'Chedorlaomer, king of Elam, Tidal, king of Goiim, Amraphel, king of Shinar, and Arioch, king of Ellasar, four kings against five' (Gen. 14:9).
>
> C. "So [Israel's history] will conclude with the encounter with the four kingdoms: the kingdom of Babylonia, the kingdom of Medea, the kingdom of Greece, and the kingdom of Edom."
>
> GENESIS RABBAH XLII:II.[13]

---

[13] J. Neusner, trans., *Genesis Rabbah. The Judaic Commentary on Genesis. A New American Translation.* Atlanta, 1985: Scholars Press for Brown Judaic Studies. II. *Genesis Rabbah. The Judaic Commentary on Genesis. A New American Translation. Parashiyyot Thirty-Four through Sixty-Seven. Genesis 8:15-28:9.*

Another pattern serves as well, resting as it does on the foundations of the former. It is the familiar one that appeals to the deeds of the founders. The lives of the patriarchs stand for the history of Israel; the deeds of the patriarchs cover the future historical periods in Israel's destiny.

A single formulation of matters suffices to show how the entire history of Israel was foreseen at the outset:

> **1.**   A.   R. Hiyya taught on Tannaite authority, "At the beginning of the creation of the world the Holy One, blessed be He, foresaw that the Temple would be built, destroyed, and rebuilt.
>
>   B.   *"In the beginning God created the heaven and the earth* (Gen. 1:1) [refers to the Temple] when it was built, in line with the following verse: *That I may plant the heavens and lay the foundations of the earth and say to Zion, You are my people* (Is. 51:16).
>
>   C.   *"And the earth was unformed* – lo, this refers to the destruction, in line with this verse: *I saw the earth, and lo, it was unformed* (Jer. 4:23).
>
>   D.   *"And God said, Let there be light* – lo, it was built and well constructed in the age to come."
>
>   PESIQTA DERAB KAHANA XXI:V[14]

A single specific example of the foregoing proposition suffices. It is drawn from that same mode of paradigmatic thinking that imposes the model of the beginning upon the end. In the present case the yield is consequential: we know what God is going to do to Rome. What God did to the Egyptians foreshadows what God will do to the Romans at the end of time. What we have here is the opposite of cyclical history; here history conforms to a pattern, end-time recapitulated creation's events and complementing them; here we see a good example of how paradigmatic thinking addresses the possibility of cyclicality and insists instead upon closure:

> A. R. Levi in the name of R. Hama bar Hanina: "He who exacted vengeance from the former [oppressor] will exact vengeance from the latter.

---

[14] J. Neusner, trans., *The Components of the Rabbinic Documents: From the Whole to the Parts.* XI. *Pesiqta deRab Kahana.* Atlanta, 1997: Scholars Press for South Florida Studies in the History of Judaism.. Part i. *Pesiqta deRab Kahana Pisqaot Twelve through Twenty-Eight*

B. "Just as, in Egypt, it was with blood, so with Edom it will be the same: *I will show wonders in the heavens and in the earth, blood, and fire, and pillars of smoke* (Job 3:3).

C. "Just as, in Egypt, it was with frogs, so with Edom it will be the same: *The sound of an uproar from the city, an uproar because of the palace, an uproar of the Lord who renders recompense to his enemies* (Is. 66:6).

D. "Just as, in Egypt, it was with lice, so with Edom it will be the same: *The streams of Bosrah will be turned into pitch, and the dust thereof into brimstone, and the land thereof shall become burning pitch* (Is. 34:9). *Smite the dust of the earth that it may become lice* (Ex. 8:12).

E. "Just as, in Egypt, it was with swarms of wild beasts, so with Edom it will be the same: *The pelican and the bittern shall possess it* (Is. 34:11).

F. "Just as, in Egypt, it was with pestilence, so with Edom it will be the same: *I will plead against Gog with pestilence and with blood* (Ez. 38:22).

G. "Just as, in Egypt, it was with boils, so with Edom it will be the same: *This shall be the plague wherewith the Lord will smite all the peoples that have warred against Jerusalem: their flesh shall consume away while they stand upon their feet* (Zech. 14:12).

H. "Just as, in Egypt, it was with great stones, so with Edom it will be the same: *I will cause to rain upon Gog...an overflowing shower and great hailstones* (Ez. 38:22).

I. "Just as, in Egypt, it was with locusts, so with Edom it will be the same: *And you, son of man, thus says the Lord God: Speak to birds of every sort...the flesh of the mighty shall you eat...blood shall you drink...you shall eat fat until you are full and drink blood until you are drunk* (Ez. 39:17-19).

J. "Just as, in Egypt, it was with darkness, so with Edom it will be the same: *He shall stretch over Edom the line of chaos and the plummet of emptiness* (Is. 34:11).

K.   "Just as, in Egypt, he took out their greatest figure
and killed him, so with Edom it will be the same: *A
great slaughter in the land of Edom, among them to
come down shall be the wild oxen* (Is. 34:6-7).

PESIQTA DERAB KAHANA VII:XI.3[15]

The exposition of matters through the small sample given here leaves no doubt on precisely how paradigmatic thinking recast Israel's recorded experience ("history") into a set of models that pertained everywhere and all the time.

Seeking models subject to recapitulation in place of singular events, paradigmatic thinking about the experience of humanity, whether past or contemporary, makes other distinctions than the historical ones between past and present. It eschews linear narrative and so takes account of the chaos that ultimately prevails, now competes with historical thinking. Rabbinic literature contains no sustained historical or biographical narrative, only anecdotes, makes no distinction between past and present but melds them. But that writing, resting as it does on the Hebrew Scriptures, then presents a paradox. A set of writings of a one-sidedly historical character, the Hebrew Scripture deriving from ancient Israel finds itself expounded in an utterly ahistorical way by its heirs, both Judaic and Christian. Paradigmatic thinking, a different medium for organizing and explaining things that happen, deals with the same data that occupy historical thinking.

So what Scripture ("written Torah," "Old Testament") yields for Rabbinic Judaism is not one-time events, arranged in sequence to dictate meaning, but models or patterns of conduct and consequence. These models are defined by the written Torah or the Old Testament (read in light of the perspective of the Oral Torah or the New Testament). No component of the paradigms emerges from other than the selected experience set forth by Scripture. But the paradigms are at the same time pertinent without regard to considerations of scale and formulated without interest in matters of singular context. Forthrightly selective — this matters, that is ignored — the principle of selection is not framed in terms of sequence; order of a different sort is found.

The models or paradigms that are discerned out of, and instead of, history, then pertain not to one time alone — past time — but to all times equally — past, present and future. Then "time" no longer forms an organizing category of understanding and interpretation. The spells marked out by moon and sun and

---

[15] J. Neusner, trans., *The Components of the Rabbinic Documents: From the Whole to the Parts.* XI. *Pesiqta deRab Kahana.* Atlanta, 1997: Scholars Press for South Florida Studies in the History of Judaism. Part i. *Introduction. Pesiqta deRab Kahana Pisqaot One through Eleven*

fixed stars bear meaning, to be sure. But that meaning has no bearing upon the designation of one year as past, another as present. The meaning imputed to the lunar and solar marking of time derives from the cult, on the one side, and the calendar of holy time, on the other: seven solar days, a Sabbath; a lunar cycle, a new month to be celebrated, the first new moon after the vernal equinox, the Passover, and after the autumnal, Tabernacles. Rabbinic Judaism tells time the way nature does and only in that way; events in Rabbinic Judaism deemed worth recording in time take place the way events in nature do. What accounts for the difference, between history's time and paradigmatic time as set forth here, I maintain, is a conception of time quite different from the definition of historical time that operates in Scripture: the confluence of the nature's time and history's way of telling time: two distinct chronographies brought together, the human one then imposed upon the natural one.

We cannot take for granted that the range of events chosen for paradigms struck everyone concerned as urgent or even deserving of high priority, and we also must assume that other Israelites, besides those responsible for the corpus of writings of the Oral Torah, will have identified other paradigms altogether. But — for those who accorded to these books authority and self-evidence — the paradigm encompassing the things that did conform to the pattern and did replicate its structure excluded what it did not explain. So it left the sense that while chaos characterized the realm beyond consciousness, the things of which people took cognizance also made sense — a self-fulfilling system of enormously compelling logic. For the system could explain what it regarded as important, and also dismiss what it regarded as inconsequential or meaningless, therefore defining the data that fit and dismissing those that did not.

V. WHY THE THEOLOGY OF PARADIGMS AND MODELS?

Stated in simple language, the search for the model or paradigm stands for chaotic history in quest of orderly philosophy. In the Rabbinic documents we have sustained and systematic thought that shows an alternative to history as a mode of accounting for how things are; that treats as null the most fundamental datum of the historical thinking to which we are accustomed; and that served Judaism (and Christianity) for nearly the whole of its history. If I had to explain why paradigmatic rather than historical thinking predominated, for the beginning of the answer I should have to revert to that very mode of explanation, the historical and contextual, that Scripture set forth but our sages abandoned. Precisely where and when, in the context of Israel's life, did historical thinking emerge? With the answer to that question in hand, we proceed to take up the issue that confronts us.

First, whence the source of the sense of separation of present from past characteristic of historical but not paradigmatic thinking? To answer that question (which is a historical one), we turn to the setting in which, in Israel, history first was set down in a sustained narrative about times past. The Official History of ancient Israel set forth by Genesis through Kings recognizes the pastness of the past and explains how the past has led to the present. That document, called variously Official, Authorized, or Primary History, came to literary formulation (whatever the state of the facts contained therein) in the aftermath of the destruction of the first Temple of Jerusalem, in 586. Faced with decisive closure, looking backward from the perspective of a radically different present, the thinkers who put together the Primary History took up two complementary premises, the definitive pastness of the past, its utter closure and separation from the present, and, alongside, the power of the past to explain the present and of its lessons, properly learned, to shape the future.

The historical thinking that produced the Authorized History took place at a very specific time and responded to an acute and urgent question by taking account of the facts of the moment. An age had come to a conclusion; the present drastically differed from the now-closed past. History might begin, the sense of closure having taken hold. Since, all scholarship concurs, the Official or Primary History represented by Genesis through Kings came to closure at just this time, the allegation that historical thinking in Israel in particular reaches literary expression in the aftermath of the catastrophe of 586 rests upon solid foundations. Here is when people wrote history-books; here is why they wrote them; here, therefore, is the circumstance in which, for Israel, historical thinking took place.

The advent of historical thinking and writing became possible precisely when great events from the past receded over the last horizon, and those responsible for the books at hand recognized a separation from those events and so produced a history of how things had reached their present pass. Our sages of blessed memory, however, evinced no sense of separation that precipitates the quest for reconciliation, restoration, renewal of relationship between now and then; therefore they thought in a different manner about the same events. That is the starting point of matters, and it also brings us to a conclusion: why did they think in a different way, what, in particular, led them to this other mode of thought?

Our sages of blessed memory recognized no barrier between present and past. To them, the present and past formed a single unit of time, encompassing a single span of experience. Why was that so? It is because, to them, times past took place in the present too, on which account, the present not only encompassed the past (which historical thinking concedes) but took place in the same plane of time as the past (which, to repeat, historical thinking rejects). How come? It is because our sages of blessed memory experienced the past in the present. What happened that mattered had already happened; an event then was transformed into a series; events themselves defined paradigms, yielded rules. A simple formulation of this mode of thought is as follows:

> A. Five events took place for our fathers on the seventeenth of Tammuz, and five on the ninth of Ab.
> B. On the seventeenth of Tammuz

    (1) the tablets [of the Torah] were broken,
    (2) the daily whole offering was cancelled,
    (3) the city wall was breached,
    (4) Apostemos burned the Torah, and
    (5) he set up an idol in the Temple.

C.   On the ninth of Ab
    (1) the decree was made against our forefathers that they should not enter the land,
    (2) the first Temple and
    (3) the second [Temple] were destroyed,
    (4) Betar was taken, and
    (5) the city was ploughed up [after the war of Hadrian].

D.   When Ab comes, rejoicing diminishes.

MISHNAH-TRACTATE TAANIT 4:6

We mark time by appeal to the phases of the moon; these then may be characterized by traits shared in common — and so the paradigm, from marking time, moves outward to the formation of rules concerning the regularity and order of events.

    In the formulation just now given, we see the movement from event to rule. What is important about events is not their singularity but their capacity to generate a pattern, a concrete rule for the here and now. That is the conclusion drawn from the very passage at hand:

A.   In the week in which the ninth of Ab occurs it is prohibited to get a haircut and to wash one's clothes.

B.   But on Thursday of that week these are permitted,

C.   because of the honor owing to the Sabbath.

D.   On the eve of the ninth of Ab a person should not eat two prepared dishes, nor should one eat meat or drink wine.

E.   Rabban Simeon b. Gamaliel says, "He should make some change from ordinary procedures."

F.   R. Judah declares people liable to turn over beds.

G.   But sages did not concur with him.

MISHNAH-TRACTATE TAANIT 4:7

Events serve to define paradigms and therefore, also, to yield rules governing the here and now: what we do to recapitulate. All of this comes to concrete expression in the life of the everyday world.

    That brings us to the workings of theology into the fabric of the everyday. By what people do, we may reconstruct what is in their minds, the governing paradigm that accounts for random actions or omissions. Observing holy Israel's conduct some time after the summer solstice, no longer eating everyday meals but diminished ones, going about in a subdued manner, one would know that something has happened. What has happened is then signified by the season: the city wall has been breached, the Temple has fallen — the past forms an integral part of the present, and what I do not eat for supper testifies to a world-historical caesura in nature. So paradigmatic thinking, norms of belief, finds its counterpart and fulfillment in paradigmatic action, norms of behavior — and so throughout the system of Rabbinic Judaism, as we shall see when the work that commences here comes to fruition. What makes the present case accessible is that we are told the meaning of concrete activities of everyday life in consequential moments of the governing paradigm. So every year the Temple falls.

The transformation of a one-time event into a moment that forms an intangible model of meaning for the every day then brings us to the question: how is an event turned into a series, what happened once into something that happens in general? The answer lies in the correspondence (real or imagined) of the two generative events sages found definitive: the destruction of the Temple, the destruction of the Temple. The singular event that framed their consciousness recapitulated what had already occurred, exile and return recur. For they confronted a Temple in ruins, and, in the defining event of the age just preceding the composition of most of the documents surveyed here, they found quite plausible the notion that the past was a formidable presence in the contemporary world. And having lived through events that they could plausibly discover in Scripture — Lamentations for one example, Jeremiah another — they also found entirely natural the notion that the past took place in the present as well.

Since, then, sages did not see themselves as removed in time and space from the generative events to which they referred the experience of the here and now, they also had no need to make the past contemporary. They neither relived nor transformed one-time historical events, for they found another way to overcome the barrier of chronological separation. Specifically, if history began when the gap between present and past shaped consciousness, then we naturally ask ourselves whether the point at which historical modes of thought concluded and a different mode of thought took over produced an opposite consciousness from the historical one: not cycle but paradigm. For, it seems to me clear, the premise that time and space separated our sages of the Rabbinic writings from the great events of the past simply did not win attention. The opposite premise defined matters: barriers of space and time in no way separated sages from great events, the great events of the past enduring for all time. How then are we to account for this remarkably different way of encounter, experience, and, consequently, explanation? The answer has already been adumbrated.

Sages assembled in the documents of Rabbinic Judaism, from the Mishnah forward, all recognized the destruction of the Second Temple and all took for granted that that event was to be understood by reference to the model of the destruction of the first.[16] A variety of sources reviewed here maintain precisely that position and express it in so many words, e.g., the colloquy between Aqiba and sages about the comfort to be derived from the ephemeral glory of Rome and the temporary ruin of Jerusalem. It follows that for our sages of blessed memory, the destruction of the Temple in 70 did not mark a break with the past, such as it had for their predecessors some five hundred years earlier, but rather a recapitulation of the past. Paradigmatic thinking then began in that very event that precipitated thought about history to begin with, the end of the old order. But paradigm replaced history because what had taken place the first time as unique and unprecedented took place the second time in precisely the same pattern and therefore formed of an episode a series. Paradigmatic thinking replaced historical when history as an account of one-time, irreversible, unique events, arranged in linear sequence and pointing toward a teleological conclusion, lost all plausibility. If the first time around, history — with the past marked off from the present, events arranged in linear sequence, narrative of a sustained character serving as the medium of thought — provided the medium for making sense of matters, then the second time around, history lost all currency.

The real choice facing our sages was not linear history as against paradigmatic thinking, but rather, paradigm as against cycle. For the conclusion to be drawn from the destruction of the Temple once again, once history, its premises disallowed, yielded no explanation, can have taken the form of a theory of the cyclicality of events. As nature yielded its spring, summer, fall and winter, so the events of humanity or of Israel in particular can have been asked to conform to a cyclical pattern, in line, for example, with Qohelet's view that what has been is what will be. But our sages obviously did not take that position at all.

---

[16] We have then to account for those who read the same Scriptures but did not formulate the same paradigms — that is, all Judaisms other than the Judaism of the Dual Torah. That is simple enough. Heirs to the same Scriptures who did not attach to the Temple any consequence at all, and did not assign to its destruction a central place in their consciousness, also would not look in Scripture for a paradigm to interpret that particular event. Their modes of paradigmatic thinking — and among Christianities the paradigmatic, not the historical, hermeneutic would reach full articulation — would continue to compete with historical ones, so that biographies — Gospels concerning Jesus, lives of the later sayings — and sustained histories, beginning with that of Eusebius, would come forth, right alongside writings of a paradigmatic kind. What mattered to one set of heirs did not make much difference to many among the other. One could, after all, draw the conclusion that the destruction of the second Temple represented the penalty for "the Jews" rejection of Jesus as Christ and not then abandon all manner of historical modes of thought. The origin of paradigmatic, as against historical, thinking in among Christianities requires an explanation in its own terms and context, but, I should claim, the explanation will conform to the model of explanation that is offered here.

They rejected cyclicality in favor of a different ordering of events altogether. They did not believe the Temple would be rebuilt and destroyed again, rebuilt and destroyed, and so on into endless time. They stated the very opposite: the Temple would be rebuilt but never against destroyed. And that represented a view of the second destruction that rejected cyclicality altogether. Sages instead opted for patterns of history and against cycles because they retained that notion for the specific and concrete meaning of events that characterized Scripture's history, even while rejecting the historicism of Scripture. What they maintained, as we have seen, is that a pattern governed, and the pattern was not a cyclical one. Here, Scripture itself imposed its structures, its order, its system — its paradigm. And the Official History left no room for the conception of cyclicality. If matters do not repeat themselves but do conform to a pattern, then the pattern itself must be identified.

Paradigmatic thinking formed the alternative to cyclical thinking because Scripture, its history subverted, nonetheless defined in its linear account exactly how matters were to be understood. Viewed whole, the Official History indeed defined the paradigm of Israel's existence, formed out of the components of Eden and the Land, Adam and Israel, Sinai, then given movement through Israel's responsibility to the covenant and Israel's adherence to, or violation, of God's will, fully exposed in the Torah that marked the covenant of Sinai. Scripture laid matters out, and our sages then drew conclusions from that lay-out that conformed to their experience. So the second destruction precipitated thinking about paradigms of Israel's life, such as came to full exposure in the thinking behind the Midrash-compilations we have surveyed. The episode made into a series, sages' paradigmatic thinking asked of Scripture different questions from the historical ones of 586 because our sages brought to Scripture different premises; drew from Scripture different conclusions. But in point of fact, not a single paradigm set forth by sages can be distinguished in any important component from the counterpart in Scripture, not Eden and Adam in comparison to the land of Israel and Israel, and not the tale of Israel's experience in the spinning out of the tension between the word of God and the will of Israel.

To conclude: in accord with the theology of the Oral Torah existence takes on sense and meaning not by reason of sequence and order, as history maintains in its response to nature's time. Rather, existence takes shape and acquires structure in accord with a paradigm or model that is independent of nature and the givens of the social order: God's structure, God's paradigm, our sages of blessed memory would call it; but in secular terms, a model or a pattern that in no way responds to the givens of nature or the social order. It is a conception of time that is undifferentiated by event, because time is comprised of components that themselves dictate the character of events: what is noteworthy, chosen out of the variety of things that merely happen. And what is remarkable conforms to the conventions of the paradigm.

V

The Paradigmatic Reading of a Document

I. The Critical Issues: Category-formation, Location, and Proportion

Uncovering within or behind the chaotic evidence exactly the main lines of the theology of the Oral Torah — the dominant paradigmatic structures, whether mythic or propositional, whether having to do with Adam and Israel or sin and atonement — demands that we solve three interrelated problems. These are, first, how do we identify the system's native categories, hence the problem of category-formation; second, where to find the system's authoritative expositions of its native categories, hence the quest for the correct location, and, finally, how to assess the balance and proportion of the system as a whole and in its principal parts. Once we have formed a theory of how to proceed, we have to test the theory against sample evidence, conducting a probe. We have then to make use of the solution to those problems in defining the rules that will govern theological study of the Oral Torah. A solid program of well-founded theological inquiry — description of native categories, analysis of primary and secondary statements on those categories, and interpretation of the parts in the setting of the whole — will emerge, and this first word will have been spoken to good effect.

For the purpose of a probe, then, these three fundamental, and rather simple questions demand definition. First, we have to define for ourselves the categories appropriate for the classification of theological data: what questions do we wish to answer that our sages ask and deem critical? Second, we have to determine where to find the data for said categories. Third, we have to devise a way of determining the relative importance, the proportionality, of the categories once defined and fully instantiated. All three represent issues of method in the inquiry into a historical theological system set forth by a set of books deemed by a given religious community to form an authoritative statement and therefore to cohere in some very profound way. Let me spell out the issues at hand.

Category-Formation: by category-formation people refer to the organizing rubrics into which random data will find their place, e.g., the category-formation of dogmatic theology, God, Man, Sin, Atonement, theological and applied ethics, and the like. But if we are to correct the errors of Moore and (to the degree that he thought about such matters at all) Urbach, we have to identify the native category-formations of our documents. As in natural history, so in examining the diverse data of theology, the first task is to determine the taxonomic traits of the data, which tell us which data hold together and form a genus, and which do not belong in said genus. That is the starting point of all logical inquiry into order, structure, and system. Then when a saying or story pertains to Sin and Atonement, divine grace and love, having defined categories of Sin and Atonement that accommodate such a saying or story, we know where it belongs. That forms the initial, the descriptive, process. Collecting all data that belong and omitting all data that do not, we set for ourselves the field of analysis and interpretation: how the pertinent data compare and contrast, form species of the genus, or turn out to challenge the very viability of the defined genus. In our context, out of all appropriate data we should be able to make statements of generalization: Judaism on atonement takes the following position.... Of that systematic inquiry into the character of the evidence, in the work of sorting and sifting evidence, all learning takes place.

But what is our starting point and whence the organizing categories to begin with? The question bears both a negative and a positive answer. We cannot commence with the categories of religious thought familiar in the West, whether the secular or the Christian or the Jewish-ethnic West. Then we have to start within the documents, now many times recognized as the system's building blocks: what are the principal categories that the several documents utilize?

On the one side, the documents of the Oral Torah do not define a theological category-formation at all, though they do compose composites of topical sayings on given theological categories. The documents are organized, as I indicated, mainly around received books of Scripture. These by nature do not form propositional or even topical statements. But the case given at the beginning shows how we may identify the character of sages' own organizing categories: a subject, which will then hold together topically relevant sayings. But how said subject pertains to, works with, other subjects and sayings pertinent thereto hardly proves self-evident. One task I shall carry out is a full account of sages' own category-formation for issues of theological conviction and doctrine. For that purpose, in Chapter Six, we examine the topical program of Ruth Rabbah, its discrete propositional statements, and its principal, recurrent points of tension and conflict. These will indicate for us that document's categories and define a starting point in that larger quest for the main cognitive components — once more, whether mythic, whether propositional and philosophical — of the theology of the Oral Torah.

But why ask sages to define their categories and neglect the categories we may readily fabricate out of modern and contemporary theological reflection, whether the classical problem of evil, whether the acutely current feminist issues? Merely giving these examples in a casual reference shows the dilemma of the misplaced metaphor: their theology is like our theology. But we do not know that unless we can show it. If we bring to the documents of the Oral Torah a contemporary category-formation, the account that we present of what the Oral Torah has to say on the categories at hand may, and often is, entirely awry. As in the case of Moore and the vast halakhic components of the corpus, we may simply miss what is there. We may also seek what is not there to begin with, as blindly as if we pressed our sages of blessed memory to define their Christology, on the one side, or their theory of other religions, besides the Torah, on the other — topics on which to begin with sages prove remarkably reticent, and understandably so. Our categories would then correspond to the lunatic set cited in the preface for Chinese zoology — "(i) frenzied, (j) innumerable, (k) drawn with a very fine camel hair brush, (l) et cetera, (m) having just broken the water pitcher, (n) that from a long way off look like flies" — and we should not even know it.

And, still more to the point, this brings us to the matter of balance and proportion, which must take up a permanent presence in our consciousness as we do our work. If we take over an urgent, contemporary category-formation, one that to our way of thinking seems natural to all religious systems, we may assign far greater consequence to a given category than sages evidently would accord to that same category. To give a silly example: for very good reason Lutheran theology deems the doctrine of salvation by faith an absolutely central category in its category-formation for the apostle Paul. While made urgent by the central issues of the Reformation, the issue of salvation by faith by any and all measures certainly finds a place at the very heart of Paul's system. But what if, animated by another set of issues altogether, people wrote large and learned tomes on Paul's doctrine of the dietary laws, for instance, does he approve eating chicken and cheese together (as some authorities in the age did)? That would hardly fit. But how should we ever know, absent the insistence of the native categories themselves?

That self-evident obstacle — the possibility of a category-formation asymmetrical to the data — hardly exhausts the list of problems confronting us when we formulate our category-formation anywhere but within the documentary framework. Equally obtusely, we may identify a category that does pertain but still turn out to lay excessive emphasis upon matters of little consequence in the documents, while missing categories of enormous importance in the documents themselves. For instance, if the main thing we wished to know is Paul's doctrine of the dietary laws as these govern food of pagan origin, e.g., food that has been offered to a pagan god, a subject on which Paul does make comments here and there, our category-formation would fit but would distort the writings of Paul. For while, it is clear, Paul does deal with the topic, it is not critical and scarcely animates his system. My perspective, as a historian of Judaism, would turn out to distort what I wanted to find out in Paul's writings.

To take an example closer to home, the issue of the legalism of Rabbinic Judaism leads liberal Christian apologists for that Judaism to insist upon the covenantal character of the "nomism" (a.k.a., legalism) of the Rabbinic system.

No one can doubt that, within the logic of the system and its sources in Scripture, covenantal nomism finds an honorable place. But it is not a critical category. That is to say, no doubt the sources will conform to the principles of covenantal nomism and yield appropriate sayings to that effect. But whether or not covenantal nomism defines an active or an inert category, one that defines a considerable program of exegesis or one that makes very little difference in the active discourse of the system and its statements, would hardly register. So too the intense Christian interest in Messianism in Judaism ,— often a category-formation constituted by little more than a clumsy paraphrase, in historical language, of Gospels' narratives and one of their category-formations for Jesus Christ, and little more than that — tends to obscure the character of the evidence on the matter. It is the simple fact that in some Judaic systems, or in some phases of a single unfolding system, Messianism (rather: the Messiah-theme) takes a modest role, while in others, it comes to the forefront.[1] So a given category may enjoy excessive prominence by reason of contemporary interest. Category-formation may drastically understate, or overstate, the importance of a given set of categories in the Oral Torah's theological system as a whole.

Anachronistic disproportion brought about by imposing our, not the documents' own native, category-formations presents only one considerable problem. Out-and-out misrepresentation presents another. Not only may we ask the wrong questions, we also may fail to ask the right ones, and our categories may simply omit reference to rubrics or issues that prove critical to the documents themselves. The already familiar example, the failure to deal with halakhah in Moore's picture of the structure of Rabbinic theology, brings us to a counterpart in the working of the theological system. That is, critical in any examination of Rabbinic Judaism as a cogent, working system of thought, makes the point. Any account of Rabbinic Judaism has to pursue the interrelationship of the native categories, *halakhah,* law, and *aggadah,* lore (inclusive of theology). In theory, the categories should correspond, with the result that what is stated in one way, a concrete way of action, in the one, should find its corresponding category in what is expressed in another way, one of myth or symbol or exegesis of Scripture, in the other. When, however, we find accounts of the theology of Rabbinic Judaism that simply omit all reference to what is primary in the principal documents of the Oral

---

[1] This is spelled out in my *Judaisms and their Messiahs in the beginning of Christianity.* New York, 1987: Cambridge University Press. [Edited with William Scott Green] places on display the entire range of data, set forth by experts. It is to be noted that when half a decade after this book was published, James Charlesworth at Princeton Theological Seminary organized a conference and published a volume on this same issue, to formulate a single "Jewish Messianism," in opposition to my view that various Judaisms made diverse use of the Messiah-theme (not an -ism at all), he simply declined to invite any of those whose scholarly work was published in *Judaisms and their Messiahs* and ignored the existence of the book and the evidence it amassed in behalf of its proposition.

Torah, which is law, the exegesis of the legal texts of Scripture and the Mishnah, and the sifting and sorting out of sayings ("traditions") of a legal character. Here is a case that illustrates how a category-formation may take shape out of all dialogue with the data that are to be classified within said category-formation. So one fundamental task turns our attention to defining categories of inquiry that both encompass the evidence and also form of it a cogent, balanced structure for analysis, exposing the inner rationality that makes the documents cohere all together, all at once. Every step we take has then to find its direction in an explicit confrontation with the challenge: is this their native, or our anachronistic, category-formation?

LOCATION: the question here concerns precisely where, with our categories formed, we are to look for our authoritative data, and, in consequence, how we are to identify the normative from the schismatic. Do we collect sayings hither and yon and allow them to dictate what counts, or can we identify the starting point, the critical center of the issue? Here context is everything. When we know what we wish to find out, where do we turn for reliable data on what the rabbis as a whole can be said to have maintained? The answer characteristic of all prior accounts of Rabbinic theology is simple: find sayings or stories that pertain. Organize them by their topics, then fabricate them into paragraphs through a combination of quotation and paraphrase — and lo, we have our chapter and our book. But these then are ripped out of context; they are cited as singletons, and we do not know how, in the authoritative documents themselves, they fit together and made sense.

But ordinarily — except in tractate Abot — the sayings to begin with come to us in an elaborate context of exposition, sometimes also argument and analysis. Ignoring the given document's own utilization of a saying for a concrete purpose denies that saying the consequence originally imparted to it by the sages who selected that saying and put it together with others to make a statement that, for them, cohered within their frame of reference. The Rabbinic writings are comprised by elaborate composites, themselves made up of well-crafted compositions. With the stated exception, sayings do not float about hither and yon. They take their position within paragraphs, the paragraphs within chapters, the chapters within topical compositions and even still larger composites. Then taken out of that mediating context, the sayings are asked to speak not to those with which they are redacted and for and by those who did the redacting, but to us, directly and without mediation. It is as though we may take for granted that the sayings out of their own context bear any message at all. That act of cultural vandalism involving the utter destruction of context and traits of intellectual setting and composition clearly will not do. No saying can testify outside of its probative setting, for even if we know what a text says, out of context we still do not know what it means.

But then, if finding topically-pertinent sayings on their own does not suffice, what is to be done? The answer is: find the location, within the Oral Torah, in which a given category-formation is not only defined but systematically set forth, so that sayings in context, even within a framework of dialectical argument and inquiry, may make their statement. Only then may we inspect free-standing, discrete sayings on the same topic, having established the context in which all of them are to be read. In context sayings form part of an account of a topic. We have then to ask whether the presentation of the topic is systematic, and, if so, what system is conveyed therein? The structure and system of that context afford guidance to the direction of thought of the framers thereof: the ones who originally chose or made up discrete free-standing sayings and wove them together and so transformed them into a coherent and systematic exchange on a given problem (as in the snippet given above on what will happen when the Messiah comes). Since a mind or a set of minds has intervened, mediating between what it is alleged Rabbi X said on topic Y, and what it is alleged Rabbi B said on topic Y, and forming of both sayings a statement in one order, rather than another, and with one implicit result, rather than another, context is everything.

Raising the question of location yields the further issue, how are we to identify not merely relevant sayings but also the authoritative, norm-imparting contexts: locations for discussions of an orderly and comprehensive, even dialectical character? In due course I shall spell out the answer. Here it suffices to say, the documents of the Oral Torah do present systematic and orderly disquisitions on topics, not merely random, free-standing sayings on said topics, and these disquisitions — topical appendices in the Talmud of Babylonia, entire units of proposition and argument on a given subject in the Midrash-compilations — define the locations for initial inquiry, at any given point, into what our sages of blessed memory wish to say about a given subject. I stress, not what Rabbi X says, but what "our sages of blessed memory," or the rabbis, a.k.a., the Oral Torah or Judaism, wish to say. I have already explained why finding the correct way of identifying what "the Oral Torah teaches," or what "the rabbis say," defines what is ultimately at stake in descriptive, historical theology, such as I propose to design.

PROPORTION: we have already noticed many times over how critical an issue assessing the proportionate importance and centrality of a given category presents. But the matters of proportion, balance, perspective — these vastly transcend the problem of category-formation. The principles that dictate balance and proportion in the end define the character of the theological structure and system. That is because they govern the very representation of the theological system of the Oral Torah, not only what is to be said on a given subject, but the prominence to be accorded to the subject, the emphasis to be laid upon what is said. These matters of critical judgment pertain beginning to end: the sequence of topics, from most important to most peripheral, the place of topics within the structure as a whole, the structure seen all together and all at once. Even if our category-formation exactly corresponds, so far as we can discern, to the category-formation of the documents of the Oral Torah, even if it can be validated point by point with the operative rubrics of the Rabbinic theology, the problem of assessing the relative importance of one category over another, the appropriate position, in the narrative of the whole, of one proposition over another — these considerations of proportion demand much reflection.

For even though our sages of blessed memory indeed maintained a given position, and even though they accorded to that position a rigorous exposition, that does not mean that that given position mattered a great deal. Within the system as a whole that encompassed all of the propositions and positions that sages maintained, that position may have occupied a subordinated position, constituting a mere detail in some other construction altogether. The issue of proportion may be restated in terms of immediacy and urgency, and, once more, what is urgent to an apologist for Judaism before its Christian critics — covenantal nomism — may in the nature of things have required, therefore received, far less attention in its own context. The upshot is, we have to see the parts not only in their context — in the context of the rigorous exposition of a given proposition — but also in the context of the whole, the structure seen in its totality. Here again, it suffices to say, I shall set forth an answer to the question of how we are to gain perspective on the whole. Here the character of the documents, the matters upon which they lay their heaviest stress, their points of emphasis — these are the indicative data that will dictate answers to questions of proportions. Now to the concrete task of reading a document to identify its precipitating paradigm: how is this to be done?

II. THE STARTING POINT

Let us start with the formalities: the Oral Torah in response to the Written Torah, the categories of the one shaped out of the reading of the other. Principal documents of the Oral Torah match those of the Written Torah in the most formal sense. Within the vast Oral Torah, in substantive terms too, it is the document (or its chapters' counterparts in the Talmud of Babylonia, the large-scale topical composite) that frames our analysis of patterns, start to finish.[2] Why so? To recapitulate the critical point, the reason is that, if the system governs the organization of (the oral part of the) the whole Torah, the documents of the Oral Torah comprise the building blocks of the system, defined and shaped by its theological program. That system then comes to concrete expression only in the details of those completed statements. Read one by one, whole and complete, documents constitute the medium that sages chose for their work of systemic exegesis.

---

[2]This statement will require, and receive, qualification in due course. Within the Talmud of Babylonia, we also find systematic expositions of themes, sometimes even of principles and propositions, in large-scale topical composites. I have catalogued these in my *Rationality and Structure: The Bavli's Anomalous Juxtapositions.* Atlanta, 1997: Scholars Press for South Florida Studies in the History of Judaism. So the document or its large-scale components does not constitute the sole medium for the description of paradigms, though it is the center of our interest in this Prolegomenon. Chapter Seven deals with the topical composites as media of category-formation and locations of doctrinal expositions as well.

So now begins the quest for the system's paradigms, document by document. The search carries us to the very organizing principle of the Oral Torah, which finds its location principally, though not solely, within the framework of the Written Torah.[3] That is to say, sages made their own the map of the Written Torah, so that as I explained in Chapter Four they organized a large part of their thought within the framework of the documentary structure of the books of the Written Torah. These are, specifically, the ones of liturgical importance, read in synagogue worship. While comments, even systematic compositions, address passages of other scriptural books, only the liturgical ones — the Pentateuch, the Five Scrolls — define the documentary lines of the Oral Torah. In joining to the Written Torah the complement of the Oral part, sages tended to select entire scriptural books for their medium.[4] But, as I shall explain through the cases dealt with in this and the following chapters, they turned the work of exegesis into the occasion for systematic study of a problem or presentation of a proposition, in some documents explicitly, at in Leviticus Rabbah, in others by indirection, as in Genesis Rabbah. In the several documents, they emerge with large and simple patterns, models of explaining a circumstance or answering a fundamental question. One way or the other, the paradigm emerges, not to be missed. That, sum and substance, is why we commence the description of the theology of the Oral Torah with the reading of documents in quest of the paradigms that shape the critical mass of those documents, that hold the documents together, severally, into sets of entirely coherent statements.

---

[3] Neither Moore nor Urbach seems to me to appreciate the power of the Written Torah over the Oral Torah, because both undertook a work of historical description, the one systematic (but merely categorical) the other historical (but utterly uncritical). But what is needed, as I hardly need repeat, is a view of the whole yielding perspective on the parts. And we simply start with the established title of the whole, which is Oral Torah. That leads beginning, middle, and end, back to the Written Torah, as sages themselves signal incessantly. In this regard Urbach did not fully grasp his own theological position within integrationist-Orthodoxy, because he thought of Scripture as a problem of historical fact, not theological principle.

[4] I make provision for Pesiqta deRab Kahana, which takes as its organizing medium the special occasions of the sacred calendar, and then, in the manner of the exegesis of Scripture and its stories, then systematically presents a proposition through the exegesis of pertinent verses, selected from lections associated with those special occasions. That book therefore represents an exception that proves the rule. All other Midrash-compilations of late antiquity take shape around specific books of Scripture. So too, while the Mishnah is free-standing, the documents of Mishnah-exegesis take shape around specific tractates of the Mishnah. So the sole anomaly, the one to which we are used, is the Mishnah. The theological reading of the Mishnah must come at the very end of the matter, after we have formulated the main lines of the Oral Torah's theological structure in relationship to that of the Written Torah. Any other strategy of analysis will introduce variables before we have identified our norms.

Then the character of that exegesis defines our problem of description. In most exegetical documents the work of explanation and amplification requires reading successive verses; few of the documents form those ad hoc readings into patterns aimed at proving points. Sages' statement emerges as rich and dense, because they speak mostly in details. These set forth in terms of the here and now — the exegesis of specific verses of Scripture, the definition of rules governing concrete cases — that entire conception and vision that the Oral Torah conveyed as its contribution to the one whole Torah of Sinai. They severally take up specific problems and jointly constitute those whole and complete exegeses of data that, all together, form expositions of formidable proportions. The surface, studded like the moon, with rocks and boulders widely separated from each other, lacking all clear markings of direction, impedes all progress toward a single goal, a uniform pattern.

But we should not miss the point of what sages meant to accomplish. It was to treat Scripture as a corpus of facts to be sorted out for the principles contained by the facts, properly organized, correctly construed. Whether whether accounts of the rules of the social order, whether the laws of history conveyed by particular incidents or trajectories of events, sages set forth in the details that they selected a large and highly orderly conception of what they deemed Scripture to portray. It becomes our task to find a way of tracing those trajectories. When we speak of paradigms, that is specifically what we mean, namely, the patterns or principles, the models of organization and (consequent) explanation, that sages discerned in Scripture and conveyed in their own language and voice. So to state matters simply, sages took the details of Scripture and ordered them in the way they chose. They then set forth the pattern they discerned in their own recapitulation, within their models and patterns, expressed equally through acute details. The mass of details of the Written Torah then defined a paradigmatic structure that sages restated in the mass of details that all together comprise the Oral Torah — a quite remarkable progress, a restructuring of the same atoms yielding molecules into other molecules.

Since sages' entire mode of discourse favored speaking about great and abstract matters of mind through small and concrete things both impedes and facilitates the work of recovering these expositions, we must ask, why did they choose the way of exegesis rather than the path of hermeneutics,. Further, why identify patterns in cases but then restate the patterns only in cases once more? On the one hand, preferring to repeat through a mass of exemplary detail a single main point requires us to identify the generative conception that inheres. That forms a considerable impediment. The writers and compilers of documents pay us the compliment of knowing we shall see their main point. But their mode of discourse empowers us to join in the quest for paradigms by requiring us to take the part of active participants.[5] Imparting to the documents a cogent character, repeating the main point again and again through a given document, sages provide not only ample guidance as to their intent but an articulated model for us to follow in dealing with the data that latter-days sages may have to face in the indeterminate future.[6] Learning through inductive reasoning in their time and circumstance, sages afforded the same occasion to the ages.

These preferences on modes for expressing their views in the medium of endless detail match sages' own mode of receiving Scripture's lessons as well. In reading Scripture sages worked inductively, sorting out data to discover governing rules, setting forth those rules through the examination of concrete data. In setting forth the result of their process of thought and reflection, then, and in doing so in what they held represented another component of the Torah, sages spoke as they deemed Scripture to speak, that is, through sets of cases that [1] formed a series and [2] yielded a rule. That mode of discourse characterizes the Mishnah and constitutes the hermeneutical precipitant of the Talmud. And, as a matter of fact, it frames the manner of demonstration of the pertinent Midrash-compilations.[7] That is why, if we hope to identify the governing paradigms of their comprehensive theological structure and system, we too have to read in the manner of sages' reading Scripture, which is to say, to identify the correct data, properly proportioned, that in painstaking detail, with unforgiving repetition, convey the paradigms of the Oral Torah. That is why the quest for paradigms can only be accomplished through the paradigmatic reading of documents — the identification, within documents, of governing patterns or models, first of exegesis, then of hermeneutics, finally of theology, in ascending order of abstraction. And this brings us back to the work at hand.

III. DOCUMENTARY DETERMINATES FOR CATEGORY-FORMATION, LOCATION, AND PROPORTION

No reader to this point will find surprising the direction that the argument now takes: that the documents dictate the character of our hypotheses concerning

---

[5] I have spelled this out at some length in *A History of the Mishnaic Law of Purities*. Leiden, 1977: Brill. XXI. *The Redaction and Formulation of the Order of Purities in the Mishnah and Tosefta.*

[6] This forms the counterpart to my argument of empowerment of generations to come in connection with Talmudic dialectic in my *Jerusalem and Athens: The Congruity of Talmudic and Classical Philosophy.* Leiden, 1997: E. J. Brill. *Supplements to the Journal for the Study of Judaism.* Here there is no reason to amplify the matter. I have already spelled out what I conceive to be the constructive theological result in *Judaism's Theological Voice: The Melody of the Talmud.* Chicago, 1995: The University of Chicago Press. The ultimate hope of renewing the discourse when its language has been deciphered forms the concluding statement of this account.

[7] I originally made this point for Leviticus Rabbah in *Judaism and Scripture: The Evidence of Leviticus Rabbah.* Chicago, 1986: The University of Chicago Press.

category-formation, location, and proportion. That is to say, we will ask the documents to tell us their principal category-formations, with which we shall work; we shall ask them to direct us to the locations at which these categories come under most dense definition; and, to the degree that without a picture of the whole we are able to form a theory on the balance of the parts, the documents will also help us take the measure of our findings.

CATEGORY-FORMATION THROUGH DOCUMENTARY CONSTRUCTS: I have already set forth what I deem to define the first task of theological description within the Oral Torah: the identification of pertinent category-formations, the definition of where and how these category-formations find their contents in the specific discourses of the documents, and the estimation of the proportionate importance of one category-formation in comparison to another, first in the document of favored venue, then in the statement of the system as a whole. Why do I propose as the source of information on category-formation, location, and proportion, the documentary framework? The reason is that it is the documents mediate between compositions and composites, on the one side, and the entire corpus of sayings and stories and analytical discussions, start to finish, on the other side. They in particular initially define category-formations. This they do by the items on which they repeatedly focus, the issues to which they return, the points of tension they find it necessary to solve time and again.

As I have explained, they not only present the discrete data but they do so in a repetitive way. A systematic reading of a document shows time and again the main foci of discourse, the points of generative tension, the recurrent issues of weight. We then determine what we wish to know, what questions we may answer, out of those definitive and organizing categories. These set forth the generative problematic that sages bring to a particular book of Scripture or other set of data. The result, the propositions set forth in a large and systematic way in the several documents, then yields the patterns of organization, the models of explanation, the paradigms and their structure and system. Our inquiry into the paradigms of the system therefore carries us to an examination of the propositions set forth not in bits and pieces of free-floating sayings but through the systematic exegesis of entire sets of data implicitly deemed to cohere. Ours is the task to make explicit that principle of coherence — the comprehensive message of the whole, buried in the deep structure of a given set of bits and pieces of surface-data.

LOCATION WITHIN DOCUMENTARY BOUNDARIES, PROPORTION WITHIN DOCUMENTARY DIMENSIONS: The matter of location — where we should begin our work of describing a given paradigm, out of which data, and how we establish a control to tell us where we may err in our estimate of paramount category-formations and their propositions — directs us again to the documentary building blocks of the entire framework of the Oral Torah. That is because, as I shall show in the exemplary case dealt with in Chapter Six for Ruth Rabbah a given document turns out to center its reading of a given work of Scripture upon a limited agenda of problems, then repeatedly to impose those concerns or raise those issues in the reading of the verses of Scripture that are set forth. So the document itself tells us what to expect, its character dictates that for which we should go in search, within its pages. The counterpart, for the Talmuds, is the enormous topical composite, which draws together compositions on a single theme and, properly construed, turns out to set forth a systematic treatment of a large and important problem. This we shall see in Chapter Seven for the theology of Israel's history in Bavli-tractate Abodah Zarah. These represent two separate cases in which documents' topical traits and even propositional concerns dictate the direction of our inquiry.

That hardly surprises, for it is the document that, in its own context, organizes and sets forth the data that all together embody a generative pattern, a model of explanation, a paradigm of meaning. At the present stage in the work, we cannot hope to form an estimate of the proportionate structure of the system as a whole; the individual document does not define the correct venue for such a judgment. It is, by definition, precisely the wrong one, since, if my claim is valid, the document will lay disproportionate emphasis upon a given paradigm and will not promiscuously appeal to a range of models or patterns. Only at the end of the paradigmatic reading of the entire corpus of writings of the Oral Torah will the proportions of the several paradigms reveal themselves. But even now we are able within a given document to identify what takes a prominent place and what does not.

The documents, therefore, mark the boundaries of sets of data — these belong, those do not. There, at some one place, we must address our questions concerning the native category-formations. Where [1] a clear formation of a category comes into view, we also ought to find [2] the correct location for systematic presentation of a pattern of facts, a model that affords an explanation of other sets of facts, a paradigm. And, it goes without saying, it is within the confines of a documentary presentation that we may hope to find guidance in assessing [3] the proportionate importance, to the system as a whole, of a given component — and, at this elementary stage of matters, even instruction in how to sort out the important from the less important.

IV. A SINGLE, WHOLE TORAH, A UNIFORM MODE OF THOUGHT: FROM EX-
AMPLES TO THE MODEL THAT IS EXEMPLIFIED

Sages insisted that their re-presentation of the Torah formed a single, whole Torah, received in two distinct media, writing and memory. That explains why theological description of the Oral Torah can be carried out only through a thorough and patient sifting of the details of the documents one by one, always beginning, always ending, in the same place: in the context of the written Torah that is subjected to amplification. It is because, as I argued in Chapter Four, sages' presentation of the Oral Torah took the detailed statements of the Written Torah as a set of facts yielding through proper analysis deep meaning and consequence. They undertook to articulate the meaning and consequence implicit in the discrete facts in hand, to take data they deemed to form a coherent category-formation and to identify their deep structure and order and articulate their meaning.

The exegesis then realized in a tangible way the hermeneutics of a theological reading of Scripture that the Oral Torah undertook. It was this work of generalization resting on concrete data, a synthesizing and reconstructive process of thought set forth through the exegesis of detail in a principled manner that gave immediate expression to the component within a given document of that large system that I have called "the theology of the Oral Torah." The way sages read Scripture defines, also, the manner in which they set forth the Mishnah, as a mass of exemplary cases, formed into lists of like data (counterpart to the category-formations identified by sages in Scripture) that implicitly set forth rules. As I have explained, it becomes our task to retrace their steps, from the parts to the whole.

If as I have argued, the theology of the Oral Torah is comprised by a limited and simple repertoire of paradigms, we further must wonder why it is that in the Oral Torah we find no systematic statement of the entire system — only the one that is for us to compose! — but only the documents that all together recapitulate the system. Not only so, but we have to ask ourselves why (beyond the pages of tractate Abot, The Fathers) we find so paltry a selection of generalizations at all, but mostly examples of a principle rarely articulated and cases that illustrate a rule we are not told. In line with the hypothesis already set forth — sages construct a system through the presentation of comprehensive paradigms which organize and explain data in a rational way — we must wonder why sages have chosen the way of hermeneutics, itself indicated only in paths — trajectories, really — of exegesis. My answer, stated briefly (if prematurely) is that that is how Scripture too set forth its lessons, wholly in concrete details. The Torah teaches jurisprudence through law and theology inductively as well — both parts of the Torah.

A suitable explanation for the mode of discourse that requires us to work in the way I have explained must account for the Oral Torah and its character. It cannot account only for the Scripture-exegetical part of the Oral Torah but must encompass also the Mishnah-exegetical part of that same part of the Torah. So let us turn to the manner of setting forth generalizations and rules that characterizes the Mishnah and the Talmuds, particularly the Talmud of Babylonia. In these documents as in the Midrash-compilations sages rarely formulated ideas as generalizations but ordinarily favored making their points through specific cases, the more mundane the better. The Talmud of Babylonia — that is, the Mishnah with its commentary, the Gemara — translates the principal mode of Western intellectual inquiry into the analysis of the rules of rationality governing concrete, this-worldly realities.[8]

---

[8] I build upon the results of my *Jerusalem and Athens.*

In their study of philosophy and science — dialectical argument out of philosophy, hierarchical classification out of natural history, the one associated with the name of Socrates via Plato, the other of Aristotle — sages found their data not in biology or physics but in the facts of everyday life. They defined and set forth their problematics not in abstract analysis of how language works in expressing abstraction but in workaday affairs and ordinary relationships. Specifically, I identify with the natural history of Aristotle the Mishnah's modes of making connections between and among data. I regard as comparable to the dialectics of Plato's Socrates and Aristotle the Gemara's media of analytical argument, appeal to accepted accounts of Classical philosophy in the English language. To understand the writings that convey the system to us, then, we have to grasp the basic trait of mind of those behind the writings, specifically asking, how did they choose to convey their message?

The answer is clear on every page of the Talmud of Babylonia itself. The authors of the compositions and compilers of the composites of the Talmud of Babylonia proposed to make sense of the law, to discover the correspondence between everyday life and the rationality of what we should call the facts of nature and society and of what they deemed the repository of those facts, namely, the Torah. The sages recapitulated principal ideas of science and philosophy within the setting of ordinary affairs ought to account for the enduring capacity of the Talmud to define the holy life of Israel, the people. The Talmud formed in concrete terms an infinitely detailed and concrete statement of the abstract rationality that the West in general deemed self-evident — that is, the matching rationalities of science and philosophy. So the Talmud served as the medium of inductive instruction in the universal modes of right thinking about workaday matters. The Talmud works through modes of thought and argument that for the West in general form the foundations of science and philosophy, which are (in this context) natural history and analytical dialectics. What makes the Talmud special, the power of the Talmud in particular, lies in its translation into concrete and everyday matters of the two most powerful intellectual components of Western civilization from its roots to our own time, science and philosophy: [1] Aristotle's principles of knowledge and [2] Socrates' (Plato's) principles of rational inquiry and argument.

The modes of scientific inquiry of the one and of reasoned analysis of the other are translated by the Talmud into everyday terms, so that the experience of the everyday is turned into the academy for reasoned explanation of how things are: a book that turns concrete facts of the home and street into propositions of scientific interest and problems of philosophical inquiry. The Talmud turns the world into a class room, the holy people into disciples, and culture into a concrete exemplification of abstract and reliable truth. Here is the source of the Talmud's power: its capacity to hold together its two components, a philosophical law code, the Mishnah, which, in concrete ways, inculcates the principles of natural history, those of rational classification that Aristotle stated in abstract form; and a commentary to the Mishnah, called the Gemara which, through the utilization of applied reason and practical logic, forms a moving ("dialectical") and analytical argument about the working of those principles in concrete cases. Therein lies the continuing importance of the moving or dialectical argument. Its open-endedness made it possible for successive generations to find themselves not merely invited, but empowered, to join in the argument. So from age to coming age, Israel was to assume the disciplines of rational argument that the Talmud exemplifies — all sorted out in terms of pots and pans. The inductive mode of thought that I claim characterizes the Midrash-compilations, the Mishnah, and the Talmud, the counterpart to the presentation of truth through truths, generalizations only through exemplary cases, forms the intellectual structure of the entire Torah, Oral and Written, as sages teach us to receive the Torah. And that is because what we learn through cases and a consequent process of reasoning and generalization we retain, and the process through which we learn prepares us to take up new cases and reckon their implications for what is general and routine once again.

v. What Is to be Done?

The theoretical Prolegomenon having been completed and illustrated, it is now time to set forth its counterpart, a practical and concrete exemplification of what is to be done. Our ultimate task is to follow is to describe the documentary theologies of all of the components of the Oral Torah in such a way as to identify the governing paradigms that comprise that theology. The sum of these paradigms will form our initial hypothesis on the governing theology of the Oral Torah. With that hypothesis in hand, the Oral Torah will have once more to be reread, start to finish, to refine, extend, and complete the hypothesis, to ascertain that the preponderance of data fit.[9] But our proximate task is to do so for only a single document. This I do, for the matter of documents and their category-formations (thus: category-formation, location) in Chapter Six. Chapters Seven and Eight then introduce other methods and instantiate them as well.

The quest for the governing paradigms in documents must go forward along two distinct tracks, just as the writings of the sages divide into two. These

---

[9] Clearly, a rather considerable work of documentary description awaits. Readers will now understand my view that Moore and Urbach, all the more so their rather common successors and imitators, worked much too rapidly and superficially. They sought results before they did the bulk of the work, drew conclusions without analysis, and, it becomes clear, neither of them — and certainly none of their imitators — knew the documents very well at all or can be said to have understood them in their basic traits. They published too much and too quickly. If Moore wrote any *Vorstudien* at all, I have not found them. Urbach did some first rate articles on specific problems of *halakhah* and *aggadah* and their interplay — the relationship of norms of behavior and norms of belief — but these did not then influence his design of his large research, and after *The Sages* appeared, he published nothing that extended or refined that work in any considerable way. But I should not mean to suggest either scholar lacked patience or respect for the complexity of the sources.

native categories into which all the writing divides find definition in the terms *halakhah,* law, yielding norms of behavior, and *aggadah,* exegesis of scriptural narrative lore, yielding norms of belief. The halakhic sector is comprised by the Mishnah and the works of exegesis thereof, the aggadic sector by works of exegesis of certain books of Scripture.[10] When it comes to the aggadic sector of the Oral Torah, formulating the correct, native category-formation(s) poses no problem. Scripture's books constitute the primary formal category-formation of the Oral Torah. For the sages of the Oral Torah liturgical components of Scripture, the Written Torah, defined those sets: Genesis or Leviticus, Ruth or Lamentations. To specified books of the Written Torah most, though not all, of the Oral Torah's documents corresponded. (The remainder of those documents respond to the Mishnah, to be dealt with in due course.) These books of Scripture they read systematically, and, I shall now have to show, systemically as well. Once the formal category-formation, the scriptural book, came into view, a particular problem would dictate what sages wished to investigate in that book, therefore the large-scale inquiry they would undertake in that context, whether the meaning of Israel's history, in Lamentations, worked out in Lamentations Rabbati, or the relationship of God and Israel, in Song of Songs, described in Song of Songs Rabbah, and so throughout.

Take the case of the book of Lamentations, for instance, From the details of Lamentations a paradigm emerged, and through the detailed exegesis of Lamentations, in Lamentations Rabbati, sages spelled out and described that paradigm. The reading, in the book of Lamentations, on the part of the sages of Lamentations Rabbati, of the destruction of the First Temple in 586 B.C.E. then takes up details and finds in them the governing rules, and the rules are reshaped into a universal paradigm transcending the case at hand and its limitations. From why this event, the loss of Jerusalem and the Temple, to why events of this kind, future catastrophes, to the still broader questions, individual suffering, the defeat of a whole society — these steps of thought (in ideal terms at least) define the stages and form the progression of thought. More concretely: why suffering, defeat, and exile? Scripture set forth the facts that nourished and then sustained sages' model of explanation and yielded the paradigm that in their view would govern for all time. Then, to reach our point of entry into the process, their theology inhered in that paradigm. Those steps in theory define the progress from case to rule, rule to pattern, pattern to recapitulation in alien contexts of the familiar and inherent paradigm that (from sages' view, and probably Scripture's as well) inhered for all eternity in the exemplary moment of 586, type producing typology (so to speak). And so throughout: nothing defies the power of the system to order, regularize, and explain.

---

[10] Other systematic exegetical work on Scripture finds its way into compositions and composites of the halakhic documents as well.

So to give a concrete example, the occasion of reading Lamentations precipitated an inquiry into the principal point of interest that sages defined for that book. Their exegesis then turned into a n exposition, through detail, of a large-scale pattern, a model of explanation or interpretation of detailed data to demonstrate the large and general proposition that a paradigm conveys. But in consequence, with the model or paradigm established, sages found it possible to organize the chaos of the everyday world they then confronted and also formulate a picture of the future they could realize. How so? By investigating the traits of the social and world order that Scripture conveyed, they could discern the rules that governed: if this, then that, if not this, then not that.

What then does documentary description require? Two — alas, tedious! — tasks await, document by document. We have first to review the entire contents of each document in detail, so to characterize the parts, e.g., a brief reconsideration of the whole in the form of a systematic and complete outline. Second, we have to analyze the outline and find the principal points of repetition, the recurrent propositions, the principles of identifying the details to be highlighted. These critical tensions then define the hermeneutics of the document, the point at which the document becomes accessible to us, the issue that we may legitimately address in taking up the detailed exegesis of the document. When we know the basic hermeneutics of a document as sages read it, we also know the point(s) they make through the detailed exegesis of that document. And in the result we discern the governing paradigm, which the document yields for generalization and extension and amplification in an on-going process of renewal. Now to undertake a concrete experiment, a probe of a specific document, so to transform this rather abstract presentation of method in theory to the concrete execution of the proposed method.

VI

Ruth Rabbah:
The Messiah Out of Moab,
the Transforming Power of the Torah

I. AN INITIAL PROBE: THE CASE OF RUTH RABBAH

Ruth Rabbah, a short document, illustrates the main traits of an entire class of documents, those Midrash-compilations that form exegesis into a purpose, hermeneutical exercise, so affording us a perspective on categories that are native to the documents and the system that they represent. Our task is now to discern the category-formations that serve through reviewing, then recapitulating, a complete outline of the document, looking for principal points of emphasis and recurrent points of tension. My outline, drawn from my systematic outline of nearly the entire corpus of Midrash-compilations,[1] contains the marks of primary discourse

---

[1] I refer to my *Components of the Rabbinic Documents*. I did this work as a preparation for the form-history of Rabbinic literature, which is complete in its initial statement as *The Documentary Form-History of Rabbinic Literature*. But the outline serves perfectly well to allow us to survey the contents of the Midrash-compilation as well. The bibliographical details are as follows: *The Components of the Rabbinic Documents: From the Whole to the Parts.* Volume I. *Sifra.* Atlanta, 1997: Scholars Press for South Florida Studies in the History of Judaism. Part i. *Introduction. And Parts One through Three, Chapters One through Ninety-Eight.* Part ii. *Parts Four through Nine. Chapters Ninety-Nine through One Hundred Ninety-Four* Part iii. *Parts Ten through Thirteen. Chapters One Hundred Ninety-Five through Two Hundred Seventy-Seven.* Part iv. *A Topical and Methodical Outline of Sifra. The Components of the Rabbinic Documents: From the Whole to the Parts.* Volume II. *Esther Rabbah I.* Atlanta, 1997: Scholars Press for South Florida Studies in the History of Judaism. *The Components of the Rabbinic Documents: From the Whole to the Parts.* Volume III. *Ruth Rabbah.* Atlanta, 1997: Scholars Press for South Florida Studies in the History of Judaism. *The Components of the Rabbinic Documents: From the Whole to the Parts.* Volume IV.

and secondary interpolation; what I find principal extends to the left-hand margin. What I deem to constitute a gloss, secondary expansion, or sheer interpolation I then indent. This allows us to identify the main lines of argument that characterize the document throughout.[2]

Lamentations Rabbati. Atlanta, 1997: Scholars Press for South Florida Studies in the History of Judaism. *The Components of the Rabbinic Documents: From the Whole to the Parts.* Volume V. *Song of Songs Rabbah.* Atlanta, 1997: Scholars Press for South Florida Studies in the History of Judaism. Part i. *Introduction. And Parashiyyot One through Four* Part ii. *Parashiyyot Five through Eight. And a Topical and Methodical Outline of Song of Songs Rabbah. The Components of the Rabbinic Documents: From the Whole to the Parts.* VI. *The Fathers Attributed to Rabbi Nathan.* Atlanta, 1997: Scholars Press for South Florida Studies in the History of Judaism. *The Components of the Rabbinic Documents: From the Whole to the Parts.* VII. *Sifré to Deuteronomy.* Atlanta, 1997: Scholars Press for South Florida Studies in the History of Judaism. Part i. *Introduction. And Parts One through Four.* Part ii. *Parts Five through Ten* Part iii. *A Topical and Methodical Outline of Sifré to Deuteronomy. The Components of the Rabbinic Documents: From the Whole to the Parts.* VIII. *Mekhilta Attributed to R. Ishmael.* Atlanta, 1997: Scholars Press for South Florida Studies in the History of Judaism. Part i. *Introduction. Pisha, Beshallah and Shirata* Part ii *Vayassa, Amalek, Bahodesh, Neziqin, Kaspa and Shabbata* Part iii. *A Topical and Methodical Outline of Mekhilta Attributed to R. Ishmael. The Components of the Rabbinic Documents: From the Whole to the Parts.* IX. *Genesis Rabbah.* Atlanta, 1997: Scholars Press for South Florida Studies in the History of Judaism. Part i. *Introduction. Genesis Rabbah Chapters One through Twenty-One* Part ii. *Genesis Rabbah Chapters Twenty-Two through Forty-Eight* Part iii. *Genesis Rabbah Chapters Forty-Nine through Seventy-Three* Part iv. *Genesis Rabbah Chapters Seventy-Four through One Hundred* Part v. *A Topical and Methodical Outline of Genesis Rabbah. Bereshit through Vaere, Chapters One through Fifty-Seven* Part vi. *A Topical and Methodical Outline of Genesis Rabbah. Hayye Sarah through Miqqes. Chapters Fifty-Eight through One Hundred The Components of the Rabbinic Documents: From the Whole to the Parts.* X. *Leviticus Rabbah.* Atlanta, 1997: Scholars Press for South Florida Studies in the History of Judaism. Part i. *Introduction. Leviticus Rabbah Parashiyyot One through Seventeen* Part ii. *Leviticus Rabbah Parashiyyot Eighteen through Thirty-Seven* Part iii. *Leviticus Rabbah. A Topical and Methodical Outline The Components of the Rabbinic Documents: From the Whole to the Parts.* XI. *Pesiqta deRab Kahana.* Atlanta, 1997: Scholars Press for South Florida Studies in the History of Judaism. Part i. *Introduction. Pesiqta deRab Kahana Pisqaot One through Eleven* Part ii. *Pesiqta deRab Kahana Pisqaot Twelve through Twenty-Eight* Part iii. *Pesiqta deRab Kahana. A Topical and Methodical Outline The Components of the Rabbinic Documents: From the Whole to the Parts.* XII. *Sifré to Numbers.* Atlanta, 1997: Scholars Press for South Florida Studies in the History of Judaism. Part i. *Introduction. Pisqaot One through Eighty-Four* Part ii *Pisqaot Eighty-Five through One Hundred Twenty-Two* Part ii *Pisqaot One Hundred Twenty-Three through One Hundred Sixty-One* Part i *Sifré to Numbers. A Topical and Methodical Outline.*

[2] I considered abbreviating the outline, leaving out the subordinate entries, but this would not convey an accurate picture of the character of the document, which is superficially diffuse but fundamentally cogent, as my discussion in part iii of this chapter will indicate and as the further analysis of part iv will make explicit. But readers will have to invest a bit

The document is divided into two parts, a set of complex forms called *petihtaot*, starting points, and a set of simple ones that I call, simple exegetical form. The first type involves the juxtaposition of a verse from some passage of Scripture other than the book of Ruth with a verse of the book of Ruth. The verse that is cited to clarify a passage of the book of Ruth is first of all amplified in its own terms, for instance, in its theme. The cited verse only then sheds new light upon the the passage of Ruth selected for discussion, ordinarily by highlighting the theme or the deeper proposition of that passage.

The intersecting-verse/base-verse form links the details of this book of Scripture to those of some others, with the effect of setting the passage at hand into a larger framework. If I choose to speak through detailed exegesis of small matters, as sages always do, then I can think of no better way of making the statement of a governing paradigm than through this form.[3] The second type — simple exegetical form — requires the citation of a verse of the book of Ruth, which is then subjected to a comment, ordinarily a few words of clarification. This latter form contributes data to the amplification of paradigms and often, though not always, carries within the exegesis a deep hermeneutical principle, but it hardly compares, as the medium of paradigmatic analysis, to the monumental intersecting-verse/base-verse form. The two distinct sets are clearly marked, the former comprising Part One, the latter, the other parts of the work.

II. AN OUTLINE OF RUTH RABBAH
PART ONE
THE PETIHTAOT

I:i.   1.   "And it came to pass in the days when the judges ruled [judged]": R. Yohanan commenced discourse by citing [the following verse of Scripture: "Hear, O my people, and I will speak; O Israel, and I will testify against you. [God, your God, I am.]" (Ps. 50:7). Said R. Yohanan, "People give evidence only in the hearing [of the accused]."

2.   R. Yudan b. R. Simon said, "In the past, Israel was called by a name just like every other nation, e.g., 'And Sabta and Raamah and Sabteca' (Gen. 10:7). But from now on, 'my people,' as in the verse, 'Hear, O my people, and I will speak; O Israel, and I will testify against you.'

---

of patience into the detailed review of the data or all the claims that I make upon the basis of those data will rest on no more than my word for the facts. My main point is that the exegesis embodies a cogent hermeneutics, and that the hermeneutics takes shape in a systemic concern, so we work from the details to the large structures to the working system, just as readers, by this point, have come to anticipate.

[3] When I first made the form my own — it has been recognized for a century and its workings carefully delineated in entirely acceptable work — I did not grasp the notion of paradigmatic reading of Scripture, so I did not have a clear idea of how the form accomplished a theological goal.

3. Said R. Yohanan, "'Hear, O my people': concerning the past. 'and I will speak': concerning the age to come. Hear, O my people': in this world. and I will speak': in the world to come.

    4. And is there a session [of the court] that is held in heaven?

5. [Continuing 3.F:] "Said to him the Holy One, blessed be He, 'Do you stand silent and not defend my children? By your life, I shall speak in righteousness and save my children.'"

    6. And in virtue of what righteousness?

7. "God, your God, I am": R. Yohanan said, "'It's enough for you that I am your patron.'" R. Simeon b. Laqish said, "'Even though I am your patron, what good does my patronage do for you in judgment?'"

8. Taught R. Simeon by. Yohanan [concerning the verse, "God, your God, I am"], "I am God for everybody in the world, but I have assigned my name in particular only to my people, Israel. "'I am called not 'the God of all nations' but 'the God of Israel.'"

9. "God, your God, I am": R. Yudan interpreted the verse to speak of Moses: "Said the Holy One, blessed be He, to Moses, 'Even though I called you 'God' as to Pharaoh, ' 'God, your God, I am' over you."

10. ["God, your God, I am":] R. Abba bar Yudan interpreted the verse to speak of Israel: "'Even though I called you 'gods,' as it is said, "I said, You are gods" (Ps. 82:6), nonetheless, "God, your God, I am" over you.'"

11. ["God, your God, I am":] Rabbis interpreted the verse to speak of the judges: "'Even though I called you gods, "You shall not revile gods" [that is, judges] (Ex. 22:27), "God, your God, I am" over you.'" "He further said to the Israelites, 'I have given a share of glory to the judges and I have called them gods, and they humiliate them. "Woe to a generation that judges its judges." [Supply: "And it came to pass in the days when the judges were judged."]

The intersecting verse reaches the base verse at No. 11, contrasting the honor God accords to judges with the judgment of the judges inflicted by Israel. This then accounts for the misfortune of Israel at that time. We note that the composite works out its own interests and only at the end draws us back to the passage of special interest, the reading of Ruth. In this way the passage of Ruth is removed from its particular setting and placed into the larger framework of other passages of Scripture that are deemed to deal with the same phenomenon.

II:i. 1. "And it came to pass in the days when the judges ruled": "Slothfulness casts into a deep sleep, and an idle person will suffer hunger. [He who keeps the commandment keeps his life; he who despises the word will die]" (Prov. 19:15-16): ["Slothfulness casts into a deep sleep"] because the Israelites were slothful about burying Joshua: "And they buried him in the border of his inheritance...on the north of the mountain of Gaash" (Josh. 24:30).

2.   "...and an idle person will suffer hunger": It is because they were deceiving the Holy One, blessed be He. Some of them were worshipping idols. Therefore he starved them of the Holy Spirit [as in the continuation of the intersecting-verse, "He who keeps the commandment keeps his life; he who despises the word will die"]: "And the word of the Lord was precious in those days."

3.   Another interpretation of the verse, "Slothfulness casts into a deep sleep, and an idle person will suffer hunger. [He who keeps the commandment keeps his life; he who despises the word will die]" (Prov. 19:15-16): ["Slothfulness casts into a deep sleep"] because the Israelites were slothful about repenting in the time of Elijah. "...casts into a deep sleep": — prophecy increased.

   4.   For R. Derusa said, "Sixty myriads of prophets arose for the Israelites in the time of Elijah."

      5.   How come their prophecy was not publicized?

6.   "...and an idle person will suffer hunger": It is because they were deceiving the Holy One, blessed be He. Some of them were worshipping idols, and some of them were worshipping the Holy One, blessed be He. That is in line with what Elijah said to them, "How long will you halt between two opinions" (1 Kgs. 18:21).

7.   "...will suffer hunger": a famine in the days of Elijah: "As the Lord of hosts lives, before whom I stand" (1 Kgs. 18:15).

8.   Another interpretation of the verse, "Slothfulness casts into a deep sleep, [and an idle person will suffer hunger]": ["Slothfulness casts into a deep sleep"] because the Israelites were slothful about repentance in the time of the Judges, they were "cast into a deep sleep."

9.   "...and an idle person will suffer hunger": Because they were deceiving the Holy One, blessed be He: some of them were worshipping idols, and some of them were worshipping the Holy One, blessed be He, the Holy One, blessed be He, brought a famine in the days of their judges: [Supply: "And it came to pass in the days when the judges ruled, there was a famine in the land."]

What accounts for the famine that afflicted Israel at this time was deceit of God. Once more, Israel's conduct governs Israel's fate.

III:i. 1.   "And it came to pass in the days when the judges ruled, there was a famine in the land": "The way of the guilty man is crooked and strange, but the conduct of the pure is right" (Prov. 21:8): This speaks of Esau, who comes crookedly against Israel with harsh decrees: "You have stolen!" "We have not stolen." "You have murdered!" "We have not murdered." "You have not stolen? Then who stole with you?" "You have not murdered? Then who was your accomplice?" He fines them on false charges: "Produce your share of the crop, produce your poll tax, produce your state tax."

        2.   "Man": this speaks of Esau: "And Esau was a man, a cunning hunter" (Gen. 25:27) "Strange": for he estranged himself from circumcision and from the obligations of religious duties "The pure": this refers to the Holy One, blessed be He, who behaves toward him in a fair measure and gives him his reward in this world, like a worker who in good faith carries out work for a householder.

        3.   Another interpretation of the verse, "The way of the guilty man is crooked and strange, but the conduct of the pure is right" (Prov. 21:8): "The way of the guilty man is crooked": this speaks of the nations of the world, who come crookedly against Israel with harsh decrees. "Man": for they derive from Noah, who is called a man. "Strange": for they worship alien gods. "The pure": this refers to the to the Holy One, blessed be He, who behaves toward him in a fair measure [supply: and gives him his reward in this world, like a worker who in good faith carries out work for a householder].

        4.   R. Aha said, "'the way...is crooked' refers to the Israelites: 'For they are a crooked generation' (Dt. 32:20). "'man': 'Now the men of Israel had sworn' (Judges 21:1). "'strange': they alienated themselves from the Holy One, blessed be He: 'They have dealt treacherously against the Lord for they have produced strange children' (Hos. 5:7). "'...but the conduct of the pure is right': this speaks of the Holy One, blessed be He, who behaves toward him in a fair measure in this world, but gives them the full reward that is coming to them in the world to come, "like a worker who in good faith carries out work for a householder. "At that time said the Holy One, blessed be He, 'My children are rebellion. But as to exterminating them, that is not possible, and to bring them back to Egypt is not possible, and to trade them for some other nation is something I cannot do. But this shall I do for them: lo, I shall torment them with suffering and afflict them with famine in the days when the judges judge.' "That is in line with this verse: 'And it came to pass in the days when the judges ruled, there was a famine in the land.'"

The same point recurs: God will not exterminate Israel, but God will bring famine on them when they sin.

III:ii.1 R. Nehemiah commenced discourse by citing the following verse: "'Your prophets have been like foxes among ruins, O Israel. You have not gone up into the breaches or built up a wall for the house of Israel, that it might stand in battle in the day of the Lord' (Ez. 13:4-5): "Just as a fox spies out in the ruins for a place to flee when it sees people coming, so 'Your prophets have been like foxes among ruins, O Israel. You have not gone up into the breaches,' "like Moses. "To whom may our lord Moses be compared? "To a faithful shepherd, whose fence collapsed at twilight. "He went and repaired it on three sides, but a breach remained on the fourth. "Since he had no time to repair it before dark, he himself stood in the breach. "Came a lion, and he stood against it. "Came a wolf, and he stood against it. "But as for you, 'You have not gone up into the breaches,' like Moses. "For had you thrust yourselves into the breach like Moses, you would have been able to stand in war on the day of the wrath of the Lord." [Supply: "And it came to pass in the days when the judges ruled, there was a famine in the land."]

    IV:i.1 "The name of the man was Elimelech": Because trouble has come, you forsake them? [Supply: "and a certain man of Bethlehem in Judah went."]

2. "...and a certain man of Bethlehem in Judah went": This is in line with the following verse of Scripture: "[Whose leaders are borne with. There is no breach and no going forth [and no outcry]" (Ps. 144:14). R. Yohanan said, "What is written here is not 'bear' but 'borne with.' "When the young bear with the old, 'there is no breach [and no going forth and no outcry].' "That is, there is no breaking forth of plague: 'And the plague broke in upon them' (Ps. 106:29). "'...and no going forth': there is no going forth of plague: 'And there came forth fire from before the Lord' (Lev. 10:2). "'...and no outcry': there is no outcry on account of plague: 'And all Israel that were round about them fled at the cry of them' (Num. 16:34)."

3. [As to the verse, "Whose leaders are borne with. There is no breach and no going forth and no outcry" (Ps. 144:14)], R. Simeon b. Laqish would transpose the elements as follows: "When the elders bear with the youngers, 'there is no breach' into exile: 'And you shall go out at the breaches' (Amos 4:3). "'...and no going forth': into exile: 'Cast them out of my sight and let them go forth' (Jer. 15:1). "'...and no outcry': of exile: 'Behold, the voice of the cry of the daughter of my people' (Jer. 8:19). 'And the cry of Jerusalem went up.'"

4. [As to the verse, "Whose leaders are borne with. There is no breach and no going forth and no outcry" (Ps. 144:14)], R. Luliani [Julius]

said, "When the young listen to the old, but the old do not bear with
the young, then 'The Lord will enter into judgment' (Is. 3:14). "'The
name of the man was Elimelech': 'Because trouble has come, do you
forsake them?' "'...and a certain man of Bethlehem in Judah went.'"

The reversion to our base-verse places Elimelech into the framework of other great
leaders of Israel, who stood in the breach and defended them. The next pericope is
inserted whole and makes a point of general interest, which encompasses, also,
our verse. It makes the point that the language "and it came to pass" signals a tale
of woe, and that point is demonstrated by reference to a variety of probative cases.

IV:ii. 1   [Genesis Rabbah XLII:III.1-6=Lev. R. XI:VII=Ruth Rabbah
IV:ii]. 1. R. Tanhuma and R. Hiyya the Elder state the
following matter, as does R. Berekhiah in the name of R.
Eleazar [the Modite], "The following exegetical principle
we brought up from the exile. Any passage in which the
words, 'And it came to pass' appear is a passage that relates
misfortune." [Ruth Rabbah adds here: "R. Hiyya the Elder
said, "Where it is said, 'and it came to pass,' it may denote
either trouble of rejoicing; if trouble, then unprecedented
trouble; if rejoicing, then unprecedented rejoicing."]

2.   "And it came to pass in the days of Ahaz" (Is. 7:1):
What was the trouble in that case? "The Aramaeans
on the east and the Philistines on the west devour
Israel with open mouth" (Is. 9:12): The matter [of
Israel's position] may be compared to the case of a
king who handed over his son to a tutor, who hated
the son. The tutor thought, "If I kill him now, I
shall turn out to be liable to the death penalty before
the king. So what I'll do is take away his wet-nurse,
and he will die on his own." So thought Ahaz, "If
there are no kids, there will be no he-goats. If there
are no he-goats, there will be no flock. If there is
no flock, there will be no Shepherd, if there is no
Shepherd, there will be no world."

3.   "And it came to pass in the days of Jehoiakim, son
of Josiah" (Jer. 1:3). What was the trouble in that
case? "I look on the earth and lo, it was waste and
void" (Jer. 4:23). The matter may be compared to
the case of royal edicts which came into a province.
What did the people do? They took the document,

tore it up and burned the bits in fire. That is in line with the following verse of Scripture: "And it came to pass, as Jehudi read three or four columns, that is, three or four verses, the king would cut them off with a penknife and throw them into the fire in the brazier until the entire scroll was consumed in the fire that was in the brazier" (Jer. 36:23).

4.   "And it came to pass in the days of Ahasuerus" (Est. 1:1). What was the trouble in that case? "Haman undertook to destroy, to slay, and to annihilate all the Jews, young and old, women and children, in one day" (Est. 3:13). The matter may be compared to the case of a king who had a vineyard, and three of his enemies attacked it. One of them began to clip off the small branches, the next began to take the pendants off the grape clusters, and the last of them began to uproot the vines altogether. Pharaoh [began by clipping off the small branches]: "Every son that is born will you throw into the river" (Ex. 1:22). Nebuchadnezzar [began to clip off the pendants of the grape clusters,] deporting the people: "And he carried away captive the craftsmen and smiths, a thousand" (2 Kgs. 24:16). The wicked Haman began to uproot the vines altogether. "To destroy, to slay, and to annihilate all the Jews" (Est. 3:13). When everybody saw that [Ahasuerus had sold and Haman had bought the Jews], they began to cry, "Woe, woe." "And it came to pass in the days of Ahasuerus" (Est. 1:1).

5.   "And it came to pass in the days in which the judges ruled" (Ruth 1:1). What was the trouble in that case? "There was a famine in the land" (Ruth 1:1). The matter may be compared to a province which owed taxes in arrears to the king, so the king sent a revenuer to collect. What did the inhabitants of the province do? They went and hung him, hit him, and robbed him. They said, "Woe is us, when the king gets word of these things. What the king's representative wanted to do to us, we have done to him."

6.   R. Simeon b. Abba in the name of R.
Yohanan: "Any context in which the
words, 'And it came to pass...,' appear
serves to signify either misfortune or good
fortune. If it is a case of misfortune, it is
misfortune without parallel. If it is a case
of good fortune, it is good fortune without
parallel." R. Samuel b. Nahman came and
introduced this distinction: "Any context
in which the words, 'And it came to pass...'
occur signifies misfortune, and any
context in which the words, 'And it shall
come to pass...' are used signifies good
fortune."

The petihtaot have come to an end, and from the now-concluded work of theological
contextualization, we proceed to the systematic exegesis of the book. We have
been told that one principal point of interest will concern theodicy: explaining
God's treatment of Israel, Israel's fate in terms of Israel's faith. But that is only set
forth, so far, in generalities. Everything will take place in the details.

PARASHAH ONE
V:i.   1.   "And it came to pass in the days when the judges were judged": Woe
to the generation that has judged its judges, and woe to the generation
the judges of which need to be judged: as it is said, "And yet they did
not obey their judges" (Judges 2:17).
   2.   "And yet they did not obey their judges" (Judges 2:17)": And who were
they? Rab said, "They were Barak and Deborah." R. Joshua b. Levi said,
"They were Shamgar and Ehud." R. Huna said, "They were Deborah, Barak,
and Jael. "[In the verse, 'when the judges were judged,'] 'judge' refers to
one judge, 'judges' to two, 'the judges' to three."
            3.   Rabbi asked R. Besallel, "What is the meaning of this verse
of Scripture: 'For their mother has played the harlot' (Hos.
2:7)? Is it possible that our matriarch, Sarah, was a whore?!"
He said to him, "God forbid! When are the words of Torah
despised before the ordinary folk? It is when those who have
mastered them despise them."
            4.   R. Yohanan proved the same proposition from the
following verse: 'The poor man's wisdom is
despised' (Qoh. 9:16).
            5.   R. Hiyya taught on Tannaite authority, "'You shall
do no unrighteousness in judgment' (Lev. 19:15):

This teaches that a judge who perverts justice is called by five names:

6. R. Hiyya taught on Tannaite authority, "'You shall do no unrighteousness in judgment' (Lev. 19:15) — that is, in law. Now if the reference is to law, this has already been specified [at Lev. 19:15]. If so, why does Scripture refer to 'judgment'?

7. Woe to the generation that has false measures.

8. Said R. Berekhiah in the name of R. Abba, "It is written: 'Shall I be pure with wicked balances?' (Micah 6:11).

9. Said R. Levi, "Also Moses in the Torah indicated the same to the Israelites: 'You shall not have in your bag diverse weights...you shall not have in your house diverse measures' (Dt. 25:13-14). And if you have done so, in the end the government will come and exact a penalty from that generation.

10. Said Rabbi, "Blessings bless those who possess them, and curses curse those who possess them. Blessings bless those who possess them': 'A perfect and just weight there shall be,' and if so, 'there shall be to you....'

We now return to the exposition of the verses in sequence.

V:ii.1   "...there was a famine in the land, and a certain man of Bethlehem in Judah went to sojourn in the country of Moab, he and his wife and his two sons" [=Genesis Rabbah XXV:III.1:]Ten famines came into the world.

V:iii. 1.   And lo, it has been taught, in a time of pestilence and war, sit on your feet [and stay home], but in a time of famine, stretch forth your feet [and move]. So why was Elimelech punished? It is because he broke the Israelites' heart. He may be compared to a councillor who lived in a town, and the people of the town relied on him, saying, "If years of famine should come, he can provide for the whole town with ten years of food." When the years of drought came, his maid went out into the marketplace, with her basket in her hand. So the people of the town said, "Is this the one on whom we depended, that he can provide for the whole town with ten years of food? Lo, his maid is standing in the marketplace with her basket in her hand!" So Elimelech was one of the great men of the town and one of those who sustained the generation. But when the years of famine came, he said, "Now all the Israelites are going to come knocking on my door, each with his basket." He went and fled from them. That is in line with this verse: "there was a famine in the land, and a certain man of Bethlehem in Judah went to sojourn in the country of Moab, he and his wife and his two sons."

2.   "...and a certain man...went": like a stump [empty-handed]? What did he take with him?] Come and see how the Holy One, blessed be He, values coming into the land of Israel more than going out of the land! Elsewhere it is written, "Their horses...their mules...their camels" (Ezra 2:66). But here: "and a certain man...went" — like a stump. In this case, since they were leaving the land for abroad, Scripture does not allude to their property: "and a certain man...went" — like a stump.

3.   "...to sojourn in the country of Moab": Said R. Levi, "In any passage in which you find the word 'field,' it means, town; 'town' means province; 'province' means 'district.' "'...field as town': 'Go to Anatot, to your own fields' (1 Kgs. 2:26). "'...town as province': Go through the midst of the town, through the midst of Jerusalem' (Ezek. 9:4). "'...province as district': 'Over a hundred and twenty-seven provinces' (Est. 1:1)."

5.   "...he and his wife and his two sons": he was the principal, his wife was secondary, and the sons contingent.

From the treatment of Israel in general we turn to the penalties exacted of Elimelech in particular. He did the right thing in leaving his come, so why was he punished. The reason is as given, "Because he broke the Israelites' heart." He should not have abandoned the community.

The next parashah begins with its own petihta, that is, an exercise in generalization through juxtaposing a verse that calls to mind some other event in Scripture with a verse of the book of Ruth. We proceed to read our verse in the context of events in the life of Rahab, David, Elimelech, and thence to Ruth. So the events of the book of Ruth are reworked into an account of critical interest, the formation of the Davidic house, the Messianic family.

Parashah Two

VI:i. 1   R. Simon in the name of R. Joshua b. Levi and R. Hama, father of R. Joshua, in the name of Rabbi: "The purpose of the book of Chronicles is only for interpretation [and not for a literal reading, as we shall now see in the following verse [which will be read not literally but as an account of the encounter of the spies and Rahab, leading to the priest-prophets of

Israel]: "'The sons of Shelah son of Judah: Er father of Lecah, [Laadah father of Mareshah, and the families of the linen factory at Beth-ashbea; and Jokim, and the men of Cozeba and Joash, and Saraph, who married into Moab and Jashubi Lehem (the records are ancient). These are the potters who dwelt at Netaim and Gederah; they dwelt there in the king's service]' (1 Chr. 4:21-23). "'...father of Lecah': head of the court of Lecah. "'...Laadah father of Mareshah': head of the court of Mareshah. "'...and the families of the linen factory': this speaks of Rahab the whore, who hid the spies in linen: 'And she hid them with stalks of flax' (Josh. 2:6)."

2. R. Samuel b. Nahman interpreted the passage to speak of David: "'The sons of Shelah son of Judah: Er father of Lecah, [Laadah father of Mareshah, and the families of the linen factory at Beth-ashbea; and Jokim, and the men of Cozeba and Joash, and Saraph, who married into Moab and Jashubi Lehem (the records are ancient). These are the potters who dwelt at Netaim and Gederah; they dwelt there in the king's service]' (1 Chr. 4:21-23). "'...father of Lecah': head of the court of Lecah. "'...Laadah father of Mareshah': head of the court of Mareshah. "'...and the families of the linen factory': this speaks of David, who took care of the curtain [of the ark (2 Sam. 6)]." [Reverting now to E:] "'at Beth-ashbea': since the Holy One, blessed be He, took an oath to him: 'I have made a covenant with my chosen one' (Ps. 89:4). "'...and Jokim': since he kept the oath: 'The Lord swore to David in truth; he will not renege' (Ps. 132:11)." "'Joash': he despaired of life [the words for despair and Joash sharing the same consonants]: 'Let your hand, I pray you, O Lord be against me' (1 Chr. 21:17). "'...and Saraph': for he called to mind the deed of those who were to be burned to death: 'O Lord, the god of Abraham, of Isaac, and of Israel, our fathers' (1 Chr. 29:18). "'...who married into Moab': who came from Ruth the Moabite. "'...and Jashubi Lehem': who came from Beth Lehem in Judah." "'These are the potters': this refers to Ruth and Boaz [reading 'potter' as 'creator,' which shares the same consonants]. "'...who dwelt at Netaim and Gederah [plantations and hedges]': plantations refers to Solomon, who in his monarchy was like a planting. "'...hedges': this speaks of the Sanhedrin, who hedged him with teachings of the Torah." "...they dwelt there in the king's service": on this basis they said, "Ruth the Moabite did not die before she saw Solomon, son of her son, in session and trying the case involving the whores. "That is in line with this verse: 'And caused a throne to be set for the king's mother' (1 Kgs. 2:19) — Bath Sheba. "'And she sat at his right hand' (1 Kgs. 2:19) — that is Ruth the Moabitess."

3. R. Menahem b. Abin interpreted the verse to speak of Moses: "'[The sons of Shelah son of Judah: Er father of Lecah, [Laadah father of Mareshah, and the families of the linen factory at Beth-ashbea;] and Jokim, [and the

men of Cozeba and Joash, and Saraph, who married into Moab and Jashubi Lehem (the records are ancient). These are the potters who dwelt at Netaim and Gederah; they dwelt there in the king's service]' (1 Chr. 4:21-23). "'...and Jokim':in line with the verse, 'Rise up, O Lord, and let your enemies be scattered' (Num. 10:35). [The word for 'rise up' uses the letters that serve Jokim.] "'...and the men of Cozeba': for he belied the word of the Holy One, blessed be He: 'Lord, why do you lose your temple against your people' (Ex. 32:11). "'...and Joash': since he despaired for his life: 'And if not, blot me, I pray you, out of your book which you have written' (Ex. 32:32). '...and Saraph': for he called to mind the deed of those who were to be burned to death: 'Remember Abraham, Isaac, and Israel your servants' (Ex. 32:13). "'...who married into Moab': whose pleasant deeds came and went up before his father in heaven. "'...and Jashubi Lehem': who ascended on high and captured the Torah: 'You have ascended on high, you have led an exile into captivity' (Ps. 68:19). [The word for 'capture' and Jashubi use the same letters.] "...the records are ancient":

4.	Another interpretation of "and Jokim": this refers to Elimelech. "...and the men of Cozeba": this speaks of his sons, who were lost [the words for lost and Cozeba use the same consonants]. "...and Joash": they despaired of the land of Israel. "...and Saraph": they burned the Torah. R. Menahema in the name of R. Aha: "Did they really burn it? But this serves to teach you that whoever abandons the Torah even in a single matter is as though he had burned it." "who married into Moab": they married Moabite women and left [the people of] Israel and joined in the fields of Moab. "...and Jashubi Lehem": this refers to Naomi: "So Naomi returned, and Ruth the Moabitess her daughter-in-law with her, who returned out of the field of Moab; they came to Bethlehem" (Ruth 1:22).

The pattern of turning from the general to the particular and taking up verses in sequence now repeats itself.

VI:ii.1.	"The name of the man was Elimelech": R. Meir would interpret the meaning of names. R. Joshua b. Qorhah would interpret the meaning of names. "The name of the man was Elimelech": For he would say, "To me the throne is coming [through David]." "...and the name of his wife Naomi": for her actions were all lovely and pleasant. "...and the names of his two sons were Mahlon and Chilion": "Mahlon": for they were blotted out from the world [blot out and Mahlon use the same consonants[. "Chilion": they perished from the world [perish and Chilion use the same letters].

2.	"...they were Ephrathites from Bethlehem in Judah": R. Joshua b. Levi says, "Courtiers." Rabbi b. R. Nehemiah says, "Aristocrats."

3.   Another interpretation of the name, "Ephrathites": R. Phineas said, "[They held] the entire crown that Ephraim was given by our father, Jacob, when he was dying. "He said to him, 'Ephraim, head of the tribe, head of the session, the beast and most praiseworthy of my sons will be called by your name.' "Thus: 'The son of Tohu, son of Zuph, an Ephraimite' (1 Sam. 1:1); 'And Jeroboam, son of Nebat, an Ephraimite' (1 Kgs. 11:26); 'Now David was the son of an Ephrathite' (1 Sam. 17:12); 'his two sons were Mahlon and Chilion; they were Ephrathites.'"

4. "They went into the country of Moab and remained there": To begin with they came to the towns and found them unrestrained in transgression. Then they went into the cities and found them short of water. So they went back to the towns: "They went into the country of Moab and remained there."

VII:i.1 "But Elimelech, the husband of Naomi, died, and she was left with her two sons":

2. When a man dies, who feels the loss but his wife: "But Elimelech, the husband of Naomi, died"? When a woman dies, who feels the loss but her husband: "And as for me, when I came from Paddan, Rachel died to me" (Gen. 48:7).

      3.   [Supply: "And as for me, when I came from Paddan, Rachel died to me" (Gen. 48:7).] Said R. Yohanan, "'The death of Rachel is upon me.'

      4.   Said R. Yohanan in the name of R. Simeon b. Yehosedeq, "Cohorts in numbers, fellowships in numbers, does the Holy One, blessed be He, bring to the world. If one of the members of a cohort dies, let the whole cohort worry, if one associate of the association dies, let the whole association worry."

      5.   Said R. Yosé b. Halafta, "In my whole Life I never called my wife 'my wife,' or my house, 'my house,' but I called my wife 'my house,' and my house 'my wife.' Nor did I call my ox 'my ox,' or my field 'my field,' but I called my ox 'my field,' and my field 'my ox.'

6. "...and she was left with her two sons": Said R. Hanina son of R. Abbahu, "She was equivalent to the residue of meal-offerings."

VIII:i.1 "These took Moabite wives": It was taught on Tannaite authority in the name of R. Meir, "They did not convert them nor baptize them nor had the law been taught: 'Amonite male,' but not female, 'Moabite male,' but not female. [Since such a law had not been taught, permitting marriage to a formerly prohibited ethnic group,] they did not escape punishment on that account.

2. "...the name of the one was Orpah": [The name Orpah and the word back share the same consonants, so] it was because she turned her back on her mother-in-law. "...and the name of the other Ruth": for she paid attention to the words of her mother-in-law [and the word for see or pay attention and Ruth share the same consonants].

3. R. Bibi in the name of R. Reuben said, "Ruth and Orpah were the daughters of Eglon: 'I have a secret errand for you, O King. And he said, Keep silence' (Judges 3:19). 'And Ehud came to him...and Ehud said, "I have a message from God for you. And he arose out of his seat' (Judges 3:20). Said the Holy One, blessed be He, to him, 'You have arisen form your throne in my honor. By your life, I shall raise up from you a son who will sit on the throne of the Lord.'"

4. "They lived there about ten years": ["about"] as in about thirty, about forty, either less or more.

We commence with a new generalization, noting that punishment is first exacted from one's property, and only then from one's person. This generalization is sustained with a variety of probative cases.

IX:i. 1   "...and both Mahlon and Chilion died": R. Huniah in the name of R. Joshua b. R. Abin and R. Zechariah son-in-law of R. Levi in the name of R. Levi: "The merciful Lord does not do injury to human beings first. [First he exacts a penalty from property, aiming at the sinner's repentance.] From whom do you derive that lesson? From the case of Job: 'The oxen were plowing and the asses feeding beside them [and the Sabeans fell upon them and took them and slew the servants with the edge of the sword; and I alone have escaped to tell you' (Job 1:14). Afterward: 'Your sons and daughters were eating and drinking wine in their eldest brother's house, and behold, a great wind came across the wilderness and struck the four corners of the house, and it fell upon the young people, and they are dead' (Job 1:19).]"

2.   So too it was in Egypt [that God punished the Egyptians herds before he punished the people themselves: "He gave over their cattle to the hail and their flocks to thunderbolts" (Ps. 78:48). And then: "He smote their vines and fig trees and shattered the trees of their country" (Ps. 105:33). And finally: "He smote all the firstborn in their land, the first issue of all their strength" (Ps. 105:36).

3. So when leprous plagues afflict a person, first they afflict his house. If he repents the house requires only the dismantling of the affected stones. If not, the whole house requires demolishing. Lo, when they hit his clothing, if he repents, the clothing has only to be torn. If he did not repent, the clothing has to be burned. Lo, if one's body is affected, if he repents, he may be purified. If the affliction comes back, and if he does not repent, "He shall dwell alone in a habitation outside the camp."

4. So too in the case of Mahlon and Chilion: first their horses and asses and camels died, and then: Elimelech, and finally the two sons.

5. "...so that the woman was bereft of her two sons and her husband": Said R. Hanina [son of R. Abbahu], "She was equivalent to the residue of meal-offerings."

X:i. 1 "Then she started with her daughters-in-law to return from the country of Moab, for she had heard in the country of Moab": She heard it from the peddlers who were making the rounds of the towns.

2. What had she heard? "...that the Lord had visited his people and given them food":

        3.   One verse of Scripture says, "For the Lord will not cast off his people, nor will he forsake his inheritance" (Ps. 94:14), and another verse of Scripture says, "For the Lord will not forsake his people for his great name's sake" (1 Sam. 12:22).

XI:i. 1. "So she set out from the place where she was": And was she the only one who left that day? Is it not the fact that any number of camels went forth, any number of asses, and yet Scripture says, "So she set out"? R. Azariah in the name of R. Judah b. R. Simon: "The great man of a town — he is its splendor, he is its glory, he is its praise. When he has turned from there, so too have turned its splendor, glory, and praise. And so you find in the case of Jacob, our father, when he left Beer Sheba [Gen. 28:10: 'And he went forth']. Is it not the fact that any number of camels went forth, any number of asses, and yet Scripture says, 'And he went forth' (Gen. 28:10)? But when a righteous man is in a town, he is its splendor, he is its glory, he is its praise. When he has gone forth from there, so too have left its splendor, glory, and praise." That explains the case [involving Naomi], for there she was the only righteous person. But in this case [of Jacob], is it not the fact that Isaac remained there? Said R. Azariah in the name of R. Azariah b. R. Simon, "The merit that accrues to a single righteous person is not the same as the merit that accrues to two righteous persons."

2. "...and they went on the way to return to the land of Judah": Said R. Judah said R. Yohanan, "They violated the standard of the law and traveled on a festival day."

3. Another interpretation of the clause, "and they went on the way to return to the land of Judah": The way was tough for them, because they went barefoot.

4. "...and they went on the way [to return to the land of Judah]": they were occupied with the laws governing converts.

XII:i.1 "But Naomi said to her two daughters-in-law, 'Go, return each of you to her mother's house'": "...to her people's house."

        2. Abnimos of Gadara's mother died, and R. Meir went up to greet him and found them sitting in mourning.

3. "'May the Lord deal kindly with you'": R. Hanina b. R. Adda said, "What is written is 'he will deal.' "He assuredly will deal...."

4. "...as you have dealt with the dead": "for you have occupied yourself with their burial shrouds."

5. "...and with me": For they had given up on their rights to a marriage-settlement.

        6. Said R. Zeira, "This scroll contains nothing of uncleanness or cleanness, nothing of prohibition or remission, so why has it been written? It is to tell you how great a reward of goodness is coming to those who do deeds of mercy [by burying the dead, which is a kindness that the deceased cannot repay]."

XIII:i.1 "'The Lord grant that you": Said R. Yosé, "'All of those acts of goodness and consolation that the Holy One, blessed be He, is destined to give to Solomon, in line with this verse, "And God gave Solomon wisdom and understanding" (1 Kgs. 5:9), shall come on your account.'"

2. "...may find a home": What is written is in the singular, meaning, one of you will find a home, but not both of you.

3. "...each of you in the house of her husband!'" This verse proves that a woman has satisfaction only in the house of her husband.

XIV:i.1 "Then she kissed them and they lifted up their voices and wept." "And they said to her, 'No, we will return with you to your people.'"

XV:i.1 "But Naomi said, 'Turn back, my daughters, why will you go with me? Have I yet sons in my womb that may become your husbands?'" And does a man [who was not conceived prior to the death of the childless brother] take in levirate marriage the wife of his brother? [Of course not.]

XVI:i.1. "Turn back, my daughters, go your way": R. Samuel bar Nahmani in the name of R. Yudan bar Hanina: "In three passages it is written here, 'turn back.' "These correspond to the three times that people are to turn a proselyte away. "But if he is insistent beyond that point, he is accepted."

        2. Said R. Isaac, "'The stranger did not lodge in the street' (Job 31:32). A person should always push away with the left hand while offering encouragement with the right."

3. "...for I am too old to have a husband. If I should say I have hope, even if I should have a husband this night and should bear sons, would you therefore wait till they were grown?" Said R. Yohanan, "The Torah thus teaches you proper conduct. Sexual relations are to take place not by day but by night: 'In the evening she went in, and on the morrow she returned' (Est. 2:14). Here too: 'even if I should have a husband this night.'"

4. "...even if I should have a husband this night and should bear sons, would you therefore wait till they were grown?" But if I had had a husband tonight, I should have borne sons." Even so 'would you therefore wait till they were grown?' Could you wait until they grow up?"

XVII:i.1 ["...for I am too old to have a husband. If I should say I have hope, even if I should have a husband this night and should bear sons, would you therefore wait till they were grown?] Would you therefore refrain from marrying?" "Can you then sit as abandoned wives, without marrying?"

2. "No, my daughters": "Woe is me, my daughters."

3. "...for it is exceedingly bitter to me for your sake": "on your account."

4. "...that the hand of the Lord has gone forth against me": "Against me, my sons, my husband."

XVII:ii. 1   R. Hanina, son of R. Abbahu interpreted the verse to speak of Moses.

2.   Said R. Levi, "In every passage in which Scripture says, 'the hand of the Lord,' the reference is to pestilence.

3.   [Supply: "Behold, the hand of the Lord is upon your cattle" (Ex. 9:3): Bar Qappara said, "They asked for 'hand' ['Would that we had died by the hand of the Lord' (Ex. 16:3)] and they got 'hand' with pestilence."

4.   Said R. Simon, "It was those who went out of their houses that the pestilence smote, but those who stayed home were not subject to it." The disciples of R. Nehemiah derived the same fact from the following verse: 'Wherever they went out, the hand of the Lord was against them for evil' (Judges 2:15).

5.   Said R. Reuben, "Even their children were troublesome to them, saying, 'When will these die, so that we can enter the land?'"

XVIII:i.1 "Then they lifted up their voices and wept again": The word [lifted up] lacks one of its letters. [This means that] they were growing weak as they went along and wept.

2. R. Berekiah in the name of R. Isaac: "Forty steps did Orpah take with her mother-in-law, and [consequently] her son['s] punishment was suspended

for forty days: 'And the Philistine drew near morning and evening and presented himself for forty days' (1 Sam. 17:16)." R. Yudan in the name of R. Isaac: "Four miles did Orpah take with her mother-in-law, and [consequently] four heroes were born to Orpah: 'These four were born to the giant' (2 Sam. 21:22)."

3. Said R. Isaac, "For that entire night that she departed from her mother in law, the gentile semen of a hundred men was mixed up in her: 'And as he talked with them, behold, there came up the champion out of the ranks of the Philistines' (1 Sam. 17:23). What is written for 'ranks' is so spelled as to suggest a sexual relationship, that is, the semen of a hundred uncircumcised men that was mixed up in her."

4. "...and Orpah kissed her mother-in-law": Every act of kissing is frivolous except for three:

XIX:i.1 "And she said, 'See your, sister-in-law has gone back'": "Because she has gone back to her people, she has gone back also to her gods."

XX:i.1 "But Ruth said, 'Entreat me not to leave you or to return from following you'": What is the meaning of "entreat me not to leave you"? This is what she said to her, "Do not sin against me. Do not take your troubles from me." [The words for "entreat" and "troubles" share the same consonants.]

2. "...to leave you or to return from following you, for where you go I will go, and where you lodge I will lodge; your people shall be my people, and your God my God": "Under all circumstances I intend to convert, but it is better that it be through your action and not through that of another."

3. When Naomi heard her say this, she began laying out for her the laws that govern proselytes. She said to her, "My daughter, it is not the way of Israelite women to go to theaters and circuses put on by idolators." She said to her, "Where you go I will go." She said to her, "My daughter, it is not the way of Israelite women to live in a house that lacks a mezuzah." She said to her, "Where you lodge I will lodge." "...your people shall be my people": This refers to the penalties and admonitions against sinning. "...and your God my God": This refers to the other religious duties.

4. Another interpretation of the statement, "for where you go I will go": to the tent of meeting, Gilgal, Shiloh, Nob, Gibeon, and the eternal house. and where you lodge I will lodge": "I shall spend the night concerned about the offerings." "...your people shall be my people": "so nullifying my idol." "...and your God my God": "to pay a full recompense for my action."

XXI:i.1. "...where you die I will die": this refers to the four modes of inflicting the death penalty that a court uses: stoning, burning, slaying, and strangulation.

2. "...and there will I be buried": this refers to the two burial grounds that are provided for the use of the court, one for those who are stoned and burned, the other for the use of those who are slain or strangled.

3 May the Lord do so to me and more also [if even death parts me from you]": She said to her, "My daughter, whatever you can accomplish in the way of religious duties and acts of righteousness in this world, accomplish. "Truly in the age to come, 'death parts me from you.'"

4.   This [proposition that after death one cannot repent] is in line with the following verse: "The small and great are there alike, and the servant is free from his master" (Job 3:19).

5.   R. Miaha son of the son of R. Joshua fell unconscious from illness from three days, and then three days later he regained consciousness. His father said to him, "What did you see?" He said to him, "In a world that was mixed up I found myself." He said to him, "And what did you see there?" He said to him, "Many people I saw who here are held in honor and there in contempt."

6.   R. Huna the exilarch asked R. Hisdai, "What is the meaning of this verse: 'Thus says the Lord God, the miter shall be removed, and the crown taken off; this shall be no more the same; that which is low shall be exalted, and that which is high abased' (Ez. 21:31)?" He said to him, "The miter shall be taken away from our rabbis, and the crown shall be taken away from the gentile nations."

7.   It is written, "For to him who is joined to all living there is hope; for a living dog is better than a dead lion" (Qoh. 9:4): It has been taught on Tannaite authority there: **One who sees an idol — what should he say? Blessed is he who is patient with those who violate his will. [One who sees a place in which miracles were performed for Israel says, "Blessed is he who performed miracles for our fathers in this place.] One who sees a place from which idolatry has been uprooted says, "Blessed is he who uprooted idolatry from our land" [M. Ber. 9:1A-B].**

8.   It has been taught on Tannaite authority: Minor gentiles and the armies of Nebuchadnezzar are not going to be either resurrected or punished. To them the following verse refers: "They shall sleep a perpetual sleep and not awake" (Jer. 51:39).

9. "For to him who is joined to all living there is hope; for a living dog is better than a dead lion" (Qoh. 9:4): In this world one who is a dog can be made into a lion, and he who is a lion can be made into a dog. But in the world to come, a lion cannot become a dog, nor a dog a lion.

10. Hadrian — may his bones rot! — asked R. Joshua b. Hananiah, saying to him, "I am better off than your lord, Moses." He said to him, "Why?" "Because I am alive and he is died, and it is written, 'For to him who is joined to all living there is hope; for a living dog is better than a dead lion' (Qoh. 9:4)."

11. "Tell me, O Lord, what my term is, what is the measure of my days; I would know how fleeting my life is. [You have made my life just handbreadths long; its span is as nothing in your sight; no man endures longer than a breath. Man walks about as a mere shadow; mere futility is his hustle and bustle, amassing and not knowing who will gather in]" (Ps. 39:5-7): Said David before the Holy One, blessed be He, "Lord of the world, tell me when I shall die."

12. He died on a Pentecost that coincided with the Sabbath. The Sanhedrin went in to greet Solomon. He said to them, "Move him from one place to another."

13. It is said, "A twisted thing cannot be made straight, a lack cannot be made good" (Qoh. 1:15): In this world

one who is twisted can be straightened out, and one who is straight can become a crook. But in the world to come, one who is twisted cannot be straightened out, and one who is straight cannot become a crook.

14. "...a lack cannot be made good" (Qoh. 1:15) There are among the wicked those who were partners with one another in this world. But one of them repented before his death and the other did not.

15. There is the following story. On the eve of Passover (and some say it was on the eve of the Great Fast [of the day of atonement]), R. Hiyya the Elder and R. Simeon b. Halafta were in session and studying the Torah in the major school house of Tiberias. They heard the noise of the crowd murmuring One said to the other, "As to these people, what are they doing?" He said to him,l "The one who has is buying, the one who doesn't have is going to his master to make him give to him." He said to him, "If so, I too will go to my lord to make him give me."

PARASHAH THREE

XXII:i.1 "And when Naomi saw that she was determined to go with her, [she said no more]": Said R. Judah b. R. Simon, "Notice how precious are proselytes before the Omnipresent. Once she had decided to convert, the Scripture treats her as equivalent to Naomi."

XXIII:i.1 "So the two of them went on": Said R. Samuel b. R. Simon, "That day was the day for reaping the sheaf of first barley for offering in the temple." Thus have we learned there: All the villages nearby assembled there so that it might be cut with great ceremony. Others say, "It was the day on which Ibzan [Judges 12:8, the judge of Bethlehem, who had thirty daughters] married off his daughter. R. Tanhuma in the name of R. Azariah, R. Menahema in the name of R. Joshua b. Abin: "It is written, 'The Lord, God of hosts, — who is the might one, like to you, O Lord' (Ps. 89:9): "who brings things to come about when they should. "The wife of Boaz died that day, and all the Israelites had gathered to pay their respects [this is repeated in Aramaic]. "Then Ruth came in with Naomi, and so this one left as that one entered." "And when they came to Bethlehem, the whole town was stirred because of them; and the women said, 'Is this Naomi'": "Is this the one whose deeds are so pleasant and right? "In times passed she would be carried in a palanquin, and now she is walking barefoot, and yet you say, 'This is Naomi'! "In times passed she would cloth herself in fine wool and now she is clothed in rags, and yet you say, 'This is Naomi'? "In times passed her face was ruddy with good nourishment and drink, and now her face is pale with hunger, and yet you say, 'This is Naomi'?" [Supply: "She said to them, 'Do not call me Naomi, call me Mara, for the Almighty has dealt very bitterly with me.'"]

XXIV:i.1 "She said to them, 'Do not call me Naomi, call me Mara [bitter], for the Almighty has dealt very bitterly with me'": Bar Qappara said, "This is to be compared to the case of an ordinary ox that the owner has put into the market for sale. "He said, 'It is good for ploughing and drives straight furrows.' "They say, 'If it is good for ploughing, then what are these stripes doing on its back [and why did you have to beat it]?' "So did Naomi say, 'Do not call me Naomi, call me Mara, for the Almighty has dealt very bitterly with me.'"

XXV:i.1 "I went away full, and the Lord has brought me back empty. Why call me Naomi, when the Lord has afflicted me, and the Almighty has brought calamity upon me?" "I went away full" of sons and "full" of daughters. Another interpretation of "I went away full": "for I was pregnant." "Why call me Naomi, when the Lord has afflicted me, and the Almighty has brought calamity upon me": ["He has brought calamity upon me"] in accord with the attribute of justice: "If you afflict him in any way" (Ex. 22:22). Another interpretation of the word "afflict" [in the verse, "I went away full, and the Lord has brought me back empty. Why call me Naomi, when the Lord has afflicted me, and the Almighty has brought calamity upon me"]: He has brought testimony against me: "He has testified falsely against his brother" (Dt. 19:18). Another interpretation of the word "afflict" [in the verse, "I went away full, and the Lord has brought me back empty. Why call me Naomi, when the Lord has afflicted me, and the Almighty has brought calamity upon me"]: All of his concern is for me, for in this world, "the Lord has afflicted me, and the Almighty has brought calamity upon me," but in the world to come: "Yes, I will rejoice over them to do good for them" (Jer. 32:41).

PARASHAH FOUR

Once more we introduce a verse taken from another context to broaden the meaning of the one at hand. At issue is the pattern of events involving Moab, linking Boaz and Ruth to other moments and occasions, which is what the intersecting-verse/ basic-verse form accomplishes.

XXVI:i.1   [Supply: "So Naomi returned, and Ruth the Moabitess her daughter-in-law with her, who returned from the country of Moab. And they came to Bethlehem at the beginning of barley harvest:"] This is in line with the following verse: "And Shaharaim had sons in the country of Moab after he had sent away Hushim and Baara his wives. He had sons by Hodesh his wife: Jobab, Zibia, Mesha, Malcam, Jeuz, Sachia, and Mirmah. These were his sons, heads of fathers' houses" (1 Chr. 8:8-9): Elijah of blessed memory asked R. Nehorai, saying to him, "What is the meaning of the verse, 'And Shaharaim had sons in the country of Moab'?" He said to him, "A great man has had sons in the country of Moab. "'...after he had sent away': for they were from the tribe of Benjamin: 'And the tribes of Israel sent men through all the tribe of Benjamin, saying' (Judges 20:12) "begot children...of those to whom man had been sent" i.e., the tribe of Benjamin."]

2.   Another interpretation of the verse, "And Shaharaim had sons in the country of Moab after he had sent away Hushim and Baara his wives": "Shaharaim" is Boaz. Why is he called Shaharaim? Because he was free of sins. [The word "free of" uses the same consonants as the name Shaharim.] "...had sons in the country of Moab": he produced sons from Ruth the Moabitess. "...after he had sent away": for he was of the tribe of Judah: "And he sent Judah before him to Joseph" (Gen. 46:28). "...Hushim and Baara his wives": can someone father his own wives? It means that he was swift as a leopard [the word swift uses the same consonants as Hushim]. And he explained the rule "Ammonite but not Ammonitess, Moabite but not Moabitess" [the word for explain uses the consonants that are in Baara].

3.   "He had sons by Hodesh his wife: [Jobab, Zibia, Mesha, Malcam, Jeuz, Sachia, and Mirmah]": Should it not also say, "he had sons by Baara his wife."

4.   One verse of Scripture says, "Itra the Israelite" (2 Sam. 17:25), and another verse of Scripture says, "Jether the Ishmaelite" (1 Chr. 2:17) [and both are recorded as the father of Amasa]. [How is this possible?] R. Joshua b. Levi said, "Itra the Israelite is the same as Jether the Ishmaelite." R. Samuel b. Nahman and rabbis:

Now we revert to the exegesis of details.

5.   "So Naomi returned, and Ruth the Moabitess her daughter-in-law with her, who returned from the country of Moab": This is the one who has returned from the country of Moab."

6.   "And they came to Bethlehem at the beginning of barley harvest": Said R. Samuel b. R. Nahman, "Any passage in which it is said, 'harvest of barley' refers to the cutting of the first sheaf of barley for the offering in the temple of the new barley-crop. "If it speaks of 'harvest of grain,' it refers to the two loaves of bread. "If it says simply, 'harvest,' it may refer to the one or the other."

XXVII:i.1   "Now Naomi had a moda [kinsman] of her husband's, a man of wealth, of the family of Elimelech, whose name was Boaz": The word moda means kinsman.

2.   ["A man of wealth" translates what is literally "a mighty man of valor, so:] said R. Abbahu, "If a giant marries a giantess? What do they produce? Mighty men of valor. "Boaz married Ruth, and whom did they produce? David: 'Skillful in playing, and a mighty man of valor, and a man of war, prudent in affairs, good-looking, and the Lord is with him' (1 Sam. 16:18)."

3.   [Supply: "Skillful in playing, and a mighty man of war, prudent in affairs, good-looking, and the Lord is with him" (1 Sam. 16:18)":] "Skillful in playing": in Scripture. "...and a mighty man of valor": in Mishnah. "...a man of war": who knows the give and take of the war of the Torah. "...prudent in affairs": in good deeds. "...good-looking": in Talmud.

4.   Another interpretation of ""Skillful in playing, and a mighty man of war, prudent in affairs, good-looking, and the Lord is with him":] "prudent in affairs": able to reason deductively. "...good-looking": enlightened in law. "...and the Lord is with him": the law accords with his opinions.

5. "...of the family of Elimelech, whose name was Boaz" As to the wicked, the name is given before Scripture says, "his name"

XXVIII:i.1 "And Ruth the Moabitess said to Naomi, 'Let me go to the field and glean among the ears of grain after him in whose sight I shall find favor.' And she said to her, 'Go, my daughter'": R. Yannai said, "She was forty years old, but she is called only daughter? "But she looked like a girl of fourteen."

XXIX:i.1 "So she set forth and went": Up to now she did not go, and yet you say, "she came"? R. Judah b. R. Simon say, "She began to mark the ways before her."

2. "[...and gleaned in the field after the reapers;] and she happened": Said R. Yohanan, "Whoever saw her was aroused." [The word for "happened" and the word for "sexual arousal" use the same consonants.]

3. "...to come to the part of the field belonging to Boaz, who was of the family of Elimelech": What was given to her came from what was suitable to fall into her share [later on].

XXX:i.1 "And behold, Boaz came from Bethlehem; and he said to the reapers, 'The Lord be with you!' And they answered, 'The Lord bless you'": R. Tanhuma in the name of Rabbis said, "There were three decrees that the earthly court issued, and the heavenly court concurred in their decision. "And these are the ones: [1] to give greetings using the name of God; [2] the scroll of Esther; [3] and tithing."

2. ["...to give greetings using the name of God":] How on the basis of Scripture do we know the matter of giving greetings using the name of God?

3. ["...the scroll of Esther":] How on the basis of Scripture do we know the matter of the scroll of Esther?

4. R. Helbo in the name of R. Samuel bar Nahman: "Eighty-five elders, and among them were thirty and some odd prophets, found anguish in this verse: 'These are the commandments which the Lord commanded Moses' (Lev. 27:34). "[They understood as follows:] '"these" — one may not add or take away [from them].

5. Rab, R. Hanina, R. Jonathan, Bar Qappara, and R. Joshua b. Levi said, "This scroll [of Esther] was not stated on the authority of a court.

6. [Reverting to 3.F:] And how do we know that the Holy One, blessed be He, signalled that he concurred with them? Rab said, "What is written is not 'the Jews took upon themselves' but 'he

took upon himself.' "[And who was this? It was] the Lord of the Jews who accepted it."

7.   [and tithing:] How on the basis of Scripture do we know the matter of tithing?

      8.   One verse of Scripture says, "upon what is sealed" (Neh. 10:1), and another, "upon what are sealed" (Neh. 10:2). How are the two [to be fit together]?

9.   And some say, also the prohibition of using the spoil of Jericho [was made by the earthly court and confirmed by the heavenly one].

XXXI:i.1   "Then Boaz said to his servant who was in charge of the reapers": Over how many was he in charge? Said R. Eliezer b. R. Miriam, "He was in charge of forty-two. It is shown by this verse: 'And Solomon counted all the strangers that were in the land of Israel...and he set three score and ten thousand of them to bear burdens, and fourscore thousands to be hewers in the mountains, and three thousand six hundred overseers to set the people at work' (12 Chr. 2:16). One who does things this way can go and know what he is doing."

2.   "'Whose maiden is this'": Didn't he know her?

      3.   Along these same lines: "And when Saul saw David go forth against the Philistine, he said to Abner,...whose son is this youth" (1 Sam. 17:55). Didn't he know him?

XXXII:i.1   "And the servant who was in charge of the reapers answered, 'It is the Moabite maiden who came back with Naomi from the country of Moab'": And you say that her deeds were all that proper? But her mother-in-law had instructed her.

XXXIII:i.1   "She said, 'Pray, let me glean and gather among the sheaves after the reapers'" She gathered only a small quantity for her who was in the house, since she was waiting for it.

XXXIV:i.1   " Then Boaz said to Ruth, 'Now listen, my daughter, do not go to glean in another field": This is on the strength of the verse, "You shall have no other gods before me" (Ex. 20:3). "'...or leave this one'": This is on the strength of the verse, "This is my God and I will glorify him" (Ex. 15:2). "but keep close to my maidens": This speaks of the righteous, who are called maidens: "Will you play with him as with a bird, or will you bind him for your maidens" (Job 40:29).

XXXV:i.1   "Let your eyes be upon the field which they are reaping and go after them. Have I not charged the young men not to molest you? And when you are thirsty, go to the vessels and drink what the young men have drawn": "...your eyes": this is the Sanhedrin.

2.   There are two hundred forty eight limbs in a human being, but people follow only their eyes:

3.   "Have I not charged the young men not to molest you": That they not distance you [from being a Jew].

4.   "And when you are thirsty, go to the vessels": These are the righteous, who are called vessels:

5.   "...and drink what the young men have drawn": this refers to the Festival of Drawing the Water.

The secondary development of the exegesis of the base-verse now requires a sizable link to another incident in the life of David, now the event at Pas-dammim.

> XXXVI:i.1 "He was with David at Pas-dammim, and there the Philistines were gathered together to battle, where there was a plot of ground full of barley...but they...defended it" (1 Chr. 11:13-14): R. Yohanan said, "'Pas-dammim' means 'red field.'" R. Samuel b. Nahman said, "It means that there bloodshed ceased."
>
> > 2.   "He was with David at Pas-dammim, and there the Philistines were gathered together to battle, where there was a plot of ground full of barley": One verse of Scripture says it was full of barley, while another [2 Sam. 23:11: "The Philistines had gathered in force where there was a plot of ground full of lentils, and the troops fled from the Philistines"] says it was full of lentils.
> >
> > 3.   "But they stood in the midst of the plot and defended it": The parallel says, "He defended it." This indicates that they restored the field to its original owner, who held it as precious as a field full of saffron.
> >
> > 4.   R. Samuel b. Nahman said, "It was a one year but two fields. It was clear to David that it was allowed to destroy the field [to cut a road through it] and pay compensation. What he needed was a ruling on this question: Is it permitted to destroy it without paying compensation?
> >
> > 5.   "David felt a craving and said, 'If only I could get a drink of water from the cistern which is by the gate of Bethlehem.' [So three warriors got through the Philistine camp and drew water from the cistern which is by the gate of Bethlehem, and they carried it back. But

when they brought it to David, he would not drink it, and he poured it out as a libation to the Lord. For he said, 'The Lord forbid that I should do this! Can I drink the blood of men who went at the risk of their lives?' So he would not drink it. Such were the exploits of the three warriors" (2 Sam. 23:15-17)]:

6. "So three warriors got through the Philistine camp": Why were they three?

7. "...and drew water from the cistern which is by the gate of Bethlehem, and they carried it back. But when they brought it to David, he would not drink it": He did not want the law to be decided in their name [which would portray the decision as schismatic].

   8. Bar Qappara said, "It was the Festival [of Tabernacles], and it was the occasion of the libation of water, during the age in which high places were permitted. "'So three warriors got through the Philistine camp':

9. Hunia in the name of R. Joseph said, "He required rulings on the laws governing kidnapped women."

10. R. Simeon b. Rabbi said, "He sought to build the house of the sanctuary."

PARASHAH FIVE

XXXVI:ii.1 "Then she fell on her face, bowing to the ground, and said to him, 'Why have I found favor in your eyes, that you should take notice of me, [when I am a foreigner]'": This [reference to "take notice of me"] teaches that she prophesied that he was destined to know her in the way of all the world [carnally].

XXXVII:i.1 "But Boaz answered her, 'All that you have done for your mother-in-law since the death of your husband has been fully told me": [Since the phrase "has been fully told me" translated the repetition of the verb "told" two times,] why is the verse "told" repeated twice? "It has been told me in the house, it has been told me in the field."

2. "All that you have done for your mother-in-law since the death of your husband": For Scripture does not say merely, "in the lifetime of your husband," [but since the death].

3. "...and how you left your father and mother": this refers to your district.

4. "...and how you left your father and mother": your idol: "Who say to a piece of wood, You are my father, and to a stone, You have brought us forth" (Jer. 2:27).

5. "...and your native land": her surroundings.

6. "...and came to a people that you did not know before": for had you been here before, you would not have been [accepted].

XXXVIII:i.1 "The Lord recompense you for what you have done, and a full reward be given you by the Lord, the God of Israel": Said R. Hasa, "Solomon shall be your reward."

2. "under whose wings you have come to take refuge":
Said R. Abun, "We derive from Scripture that the earth has wings:
"So notice the power of the righteous and the power of righteousness the the power of those who do deeds of grace. For they take shelter not in the shadow of the dawn, nor in the shadow of the wings of the earth, not in the shadow of the wings of the sun, nor in the shadow of the wings of the hayyot, nor in the shadow of the wings of the cherubim or the seraphim.

XXIX:i.1 1. "Then she said, 'You are most gracious to me, my lord, for you have comforted me and spoken kindly to your maidservant, though I am not one of your maidservants'": He said to her, "God forbid! You are not as one of the handmaidens, but as one of the matriarchs" [amahot, imahot].

2. Along these same lines: "And Nobah went and took Kenat and the villages thereof and called it Nobah" (Num. 32:42).

3. Along these same lines: "And he said to me, To build her a house in the land of Shinar" (Zech. 5:11).

The next exegesis links the occasion to David, Solomon, Hezekiah, Manasseh, the throne, and finally Boaz, so transforming the incident into a Messianic moment.

XL:i. 1 "And at mealtime Boaz said to her, 'Come here and eat some bread, and dip your morsel in the wine.' So she sat beside the reapers, and he passed to her parched grain; and she ate until she was satisfied, and she had some left over": R. Yohanan interested the phrase "come here" in six ways: "The first speaks of David. "'Come here': means, to the throne: 'That you have brought me here' (2 Sam. 7:18). "'...and eat some bread': the bread of the throne. "'...and dip your morsel in vinegar': this speaks of his sufferings: 'O Lord, do not rebuke me in your anger' (Ps. 2. "The second interpretation refers to Solomon: 'Come here': means, to the throne. "'...and eat some bread': this is the bread of the throne: "And Solomon's provision for one day was thirty measures of fine flour and three score measures of meal' (1 Kgs. 5:2). "'...and dip your morsel in vinegar': this refers to the dirty of the deeds [that he did]. "'So she sat beside the reapers': for the throne was taken from him for a time."

3.   "The third interpretation speaks of Hezekiah: 'Come here': means, to the throne. "'...and eat some bread': this is the bread of the throne. "'...and dip your morsel in vinegar': this refers to sufferings [Is. 5:1]: 'And Isaiah said, Let them take a cake of figs' (Is. 38:21). "'So she sat beside the reapers': for the throne was taken from him for a time: 'Thus says Hezekiah, This day is a day of trouble and rebuke' (Is. 37:3). "'...and he passed to her parched grain': for he was restored to the throne: 'So that he was exalted in the sight of all nations from then on' (2 Chr. 32:23). "'...and she ate and was satisfied and left some over': this indicates that he would eat in this world, in the days of the messiah, and in the age to come.

4.   "The fourth interpretation refers to Manasseh: 'Come here': means, to the throne. "'...and eat some bread': this is the bread of the throne. "'...and dip your morsel in vinegar': for his dirty deeds were like vinegar, on account of wicked actions. "'So she sat beside the reapers': for the throne was taken from him for a time: 'And the Lord spoke to Manasseh and to his people, but they did not listen. So the Lord brought them the captains of the host of the king of Assyria, who took Manasseh with hooks' (2 Chr. 33:10-11)."

5.   "The fifth interpretation refers to the Messiah: 'Come here': means, to the throne.

"'...and eat some bread': this is the bread of the throne. "'...and dip your morsel in vinegar': this refers to suffering: 'But he was wounded because of our transgressions' (Is. 53:5). 'So she sat beside the reapers': for the throne is destined to be taken from him for a time: For I will gather all nations against Jerusalem to battle and the city shall be taken' (Zech. 14:2). "'...and he passed to her parched grain': for he will be restored to the throne: 'And he shall smite the land with the rod of his mouth' (Is. 11:4)."

6.   "The sixth interpretation refers to Boaz: 'Come here': [supply:] means, to the throne.

"'...and eat some bread': this refers to the bread of the reapers. "'...and dip your morsel in vinegar': it is the practice of reapers to dip their bread in vinegar."

7.   R. Isaac b. Merion said, "The verse ['and he passed to her parched grain; and she ate until she was satisfied, and she had some left over'] teaches you

that if one carries out a religious duty, he should do it with a whole heart.

8.   R. Kohen and R. Joshua of Sikhnin in the name of R. Levi: "In the past a person would do a religious duty and a prophet would inscribe it, but now when a person does a religious duty, who writes it down?

XLII:i.1 "And also pull out some from the bundles for her and leave it for her to glean and do not rebuke her": R. Yohanan would scatter coins so that R. Simeon b. R. Abba could take possession of them. R. Judah would scatter lentils about so that R. Simeon b. R. Halafta could take possession of them.

XLIII:i.1 "So she gleaned in the field until evening; then she beat out what she had gleaned, and it was about an ephah of barley": How much is an ephah?

XLV:i.1   "And her mother-in-law said to her, 'Where did you glean today'": It has been taught on Tannaite authority in the name of R. Joshua, "More than the householder does for the poor, the poor does for the householder. For so did Ruth say to Naomi, 'The man's name with whom I worked today,' but she did not say, 'who worked for me,' but rather, 'for whom I worked.' Many acts and many deeds of goodness I did with him because he fed me a piece of bread.'"

Now comes a composite on the theme just now introduced, that is, an assembly of topical entries that rework the same basic proposition; this kind of topical miscellany is a common way of setting forth a theological or moral rule, as we shall see presently.

2.   Said R. Yosé, "'Because, even because [they spurned my ordinances and their soul abhorred my statutes]' (Lev. 26:43): [since the word for 'because' and the word for 'poor' uses the same consonants,] because of the poor man [all these things have come about]."

3.   Said R. Shiloh of Noveh, "As to the impoverished person, your wealth is on his account."

4.   Said R. Nahman, "It is written, 'Because that for this thing the Lord your God will bless you in all your work' (Dt; 15:10: [poverty] is a wheel that turns through the world over everybody, like the wheel of a waterwheel, which empties what is full and fills what is empty."

5.   Bar Qappara said, "No person fails to fall into this measure [of poverty], for if the person himself does not, then it will be his son, and if not his son, then his grandson."

6. It was taught on Tannaite authority: R. Eliezer b. Jacob says, "The vengeance that is coming upon the nations of the world is on account of Israel, and the vengeance that is coming upon Israel is on account of the poor.

7. Said R. Abin, "When the poor man is standing at your door, the Holy One, blessed be He, is standing at his right hand. And if you give him, this one who is standing at his right hand will bless you. But if not, then he is going to exact punishment from that men: 'For he stands at the right hand of the needy' (Ps. 109:31)."

8. Said R. Abbahu, "We have to be grateful to the fakers among the [poor]."

   9. There is this story: R. Yohanan and R. Simeon b. Laqish went down to bathe in the public bath in Tiberias. A miserable person met them. He said to them, "Acquire merit by [giving] me [something]."

XLVI:i.1 1. "And Naomi said to her daughter-in-law, 'Blessed be he by the Lord, whose kindness has not forsaken the living'": for he sustains and feeds the living. "...or the dead": for he concerns himself with their shrouds.

   2. "Naomi also said to her, 'The man is a relative of ours, one of our nearest kin'": Said R. Samuel b. R. Nahman, "Boaz was a great man of that generation, but the woman treated him as a relative: 'The man is a relative of ours.'"

XLVII:i.1 "And Ruth the Moabitess said, 'Besides, he said to me, "You shall keep close by my servants till they have finished all my harvest"'": Said R. Hanin b. Levi, "She most certainly was a Moabite woman [in having desire for the young men], for while Boaz had said to her, 'but keep close to my maidens,' she said to Naomi, 'by my [male] servants.'"

XLIX:i.1 "So she kept close to the maidens of Boaz, gleaning until the end of the barley and wheat harvests": Said R. Samuel b. R. Nahman, "From the beginning of the harvest of barley to the end of the harvest of wheat is three months."

LII:i. 1. "Wash therefore and anoint yourself": "Wash yourself": from the filth of idolatry that is yours. "...and anoint yourself": this refers to the religious deeds and acts of righteousness [that are required of an Israelite].

   2. and put on your best clothes": Was she naked?

   3. "...and go down to the threshing floor": She said to her, "My merit will go down there with you."

   4. Another teaching concerning the phrase, "and go down to the threshing floor": On the strength of this passage we learn that people make the threshing floor only in the lowest spot in town.

5.   There was the following case:

LIII:i.1   "But when he lies down, observe the place where he lies; then go and uncover his feet and lie down; and he will tell you what to do": "The word to me" is what is read but not what is written. She said to her, "But perhaps one of the dogs will come and mate with me? Still, it is my task to carry out the instructions."

LV:i.1   "I know his conception, says the Lord, that it was not so" (Jer. 48:30): R. Hinena bar Pappa and R. Simon: R. Hinena bar Pappa said, "In the beginning of the conception of Moab, it was not for the sake of fornication but for the sake of heaven. 'But his scions did not act thus' (Jer. 48:30), but rather for the sake of fornication, and so it says, 'And Israel abode in Shittim and the people began to commit harlotry with the daughters of Moab' (Num. 25:1). [What Lot's daughters did they did for an honorable motive, but what the descendants did at Shittim they did not do for an honorable motive.]" R. Simon said, "In the beginning of the conception of Moab, it was not for the sake of heaven but for the sake of fornication. 'But his scions did not act thus' (Jer. 48:30), but rather for the sake of heaven, and so it says, 'And she went down to the threshing floor and did according to all that her mother-in-law had commanded her' (Ruth 3:6). [Reversing matters, we point to Ruth as the descendant.]"

LVI:i.1   "And when Boaz had eaten and drunk and his heart was merry": Why was "his heart merry"?

2.   Another explanation of the phrase, "And when Boaz had eaten and drunk and his heart was merry": for he had eaten various sorts of sweets after the meal, since they make the tongue used to Torah.

3.   Another explanation of the phrase, "And when Boaz had eaten and drunk and his heart was merry": For he had occupied himself with teachings of the Torah: "The Torah of your mouth is good to me" (Ps. 119:72).

4.   Another explanation of the phrase, "And when Boaz had eaten and drunk and his heart was merry": He was seeking a wife: "Who finds a wife finds a good thing" (Prov. 18:22).

5.   "...he went to lie down at the end of the heap of grain": R. Judah the Patriarch raised the question before R. Phineas b. R. Hama: "Boaz was a leading figure in his generation, and you say, 'at the end of the heap of grain'! He said to him, "It is because that generation was drunk with fornication, and they were paying wages of whores from the harvest of the threshing floors: 'Do not rejoice, O Israel, like the

peoples...you have loved a harlot's hire on every threshing floor' (Hos. 9:1). "But the righteous do not act in that way. "Not only so, but the righteous are far from thievery, so their capital is valuable to them" [since they do not want it used for immoral purposes].

Parashah Six

LVII:i.1 "The fear of man brings a snare, but whoever puts his trust in the Lord shall be exalted" (Prov. 29:25): R. Aqiba went to Rome. He said to someone of his entourage, "Go, buy me something from the marketplace that is acceptable to all." He went and brought him fowl. He said to him, "How come it took so long? Did you have to trap them?" He said to him, "It is because they frighten people." He recited in his regard the following verse: 'The fear of man brings a snare.'"

2. [Supply: "The fear of man brings a snare, but whoever puts his trust in the Lord shall be exalted" (Prov. 29:25):] [This refers to] the fear that Jacob caused to Isaac: "And Isaac trembled very much" (Gen. 27:33). It would have been reasonable for him to curse him, but, "whoever puts his trust in the Lord shall be exalted," so God put in his heart the desire to bless him: "Yes, he shall be blessed" (Gen. 27:33).

3. [Supply: "The fear of man brings a snare, but whoever puts his trust in the Lord shall be exalted" (Prov. 29:25):] [This refers to] the fear that Ruth caused to Boaz: "At midnight the man was startled." It would have been reasonable for him to curse her, but, "whoever puts his trust in the Lord shall be exalted," so God put in his heart the desire to bless her: "And he said, 'May you be blessed by the Lord, my daughter."

4. "...and turned over": She clung to him like ivy, and he began to feel her hair. He said, "Spirits don't have hair."

LVIII:i.1 "He said, 'Who are you'": "Are you a spirit or a woman?" She said, "A woman." "Are you unmarried or married?" She said to him, "Unmarried." "Unclean [in your menstrual period] or clean?" She said to him, "Clean."

2. "...and behold, a woman [lay at his feet!]" She was the cleanest of all women.

3. "...lay at his feet. He said, "Who are you?" And she answered, "I am Ruth, your maidservant; spread your skirt over your maidservant":

The intersecting verse that follows is taken to speak for David and to review his virtue.

LIX:i.1   "At midnight I will rise to give thanks to you because of your righteous judgments" (Ps. 119:62): [In the version of Lamentations Rabbah LXXV:i.4:] R. Phineas in the name of R. Eleazar b. Menaham said, "There was a harp placed under his pillow, and he would get up and play it at night. R. Levi said, "There was a harp suspended above David's bed, and when midnight came, the north wind would blow upon it, and it made a melody on its own 'When the instrument played' (2 Kgs. 3:15): what is written is not 'when he played on the instrument' but 'when the instrument played' on its own. Now when David would hear the sound, he would get up and study the Torah. When the Israelites heard that David was studying the Torah, they would say, 'If David, King of Israel, is studying the Torah, how much more should we!' They immediately got up and studied the Torah."

2.   "[At midnight I will rise to give thanks to you] because of your righteous judgments" (Ps. 119:62): The judgments that you brought on Pharaoh: "And the Lord plagued Pharaoh and his house with great plagues" (Gen. 12:17). And the righteous judgments that you carried out with Abraham and Sarah.

4.   Another interpretation of the verse, "[At midnight I will rise to give thanks to you] because of your righteous judgments" (Ps. 119:62): The judgments that you carried out upon the Egyptians, and the acts of righteousness that you did for our ancestors in Egypt. For they had in hand no religious deeds to carry out so that they might be redeemed, but you gave them two religious deeds to carry out so that they would be saved.

5.   Another interpretation of the verse, "[At midnight I will rise to give thanks to you] because of your righteous judgments" (Ps. 119:62): [David speaks,] "The acts of judgment that you brought upon the Ammonites and Moabites. "And the righteous deeds that you carried out for my grandfather and my grandmother [Boaz, Ruth, of whom David speaks here]. "For had he hastily cursed her but once, where should I have come from? "But you put in his heart the will to bless her: 'And he said, "May you be blessed by the Lord."'"

LIX:ii.1   "And he said, 'May you be blessed by the Lord, my daughter; you have made this last kindness greater than the first, [in that you have not gone after young men, whether poor or rich]'": R. Yohanan, R. Simeon b. Laqish, and rabbis: R. Yohanan said, "A person should never refrain from going to an elder for his blessing. Boaz was eighty years old and had not been visited [with a child]. But because that righteous woman praised for him, forthwith he was visited with a child, as it is said, 'And Naomi said to her daughter-in-law, "Blessed be he by the Lord, whose kindness has not forsaken the living or the dead'" (Ruth 2:20)." R. Simeon b. Laqish said, "Ruth was then forty years old and had not yet been visited with a child for she was married to Mahlon. But because that righteous man prayed for her, she was visited with a child: 'May you be blessed by the Lord, my daughter.'" And rabbis said, "Both of them were visited with a child only on account of the blessings of the righteous: 'Then all the people who were at the gate and the elders said, "We are witnesses. May the Lord make the woman, who is coming into your house, like Rachel and Leah, who together built up the house of Israel. My you prosper in Ephrathah and be renowned in Bethlehem; and may your house be like the house of Perez, whom Tamar bore to Judah, because of the children that the Lord will give you by this young woman' (Ruth 4:11-12)."

2. "...you have made this last kindness greater than the first, in that you have not gone after young men, whether poor or rich": Said R. Samuel bar R. Isaac, "A woman loves a poor young man more than a rich old man."

LXI:i.1 ["And now it is true that I am a near kinsman, yet there is a kinsman near than I":] Rabbis and R. Joshua b. Levi: Rabbis take the view that Tob, Elimelech, and Boaz were brothers. R. Joshua said, "Salmon, Elimelech, and Tob were brothers." They objected, "It is written, 'which was our brother Elimelech's' (Ruth 4:3)." He said to them, "A person does not hesitate to call his uncle 'brother.'"

LXII:i.1 "Remain this night": "This night you will spend without a husband, but you will not spend another night without a husband."

LXII:ii.1 On the Sabbath R. Meir was in session and expounding in the school of Tiberias, and Elisha, his master, was passing in the market riding a horse. They said to R. Meir, "Lo, Elisha your master is passing by in the market." He went out to him. He [Elisha] said to him [Meir], "With what were you engaged?"

Now comes a systematic exposition of the rule that, to strengthen oneself against doing evil, one may take an oath; three probative examples make the point stick.

LXII:iii.1 Said R. Yosé, "There were three who were tempted by their inclination to do evil, but who strengthened themselves against it in each case by taking an oath: Joseph, David, and Boaz. "Joseph: 'How then can I do this great wickedness and sin against God' (Gen. 39:9). [Yosé continues, citing] R. Hunia in the name of R. Idi: 'Does Scripture exhibit defects? What Scripture here says is not, "and sin against the Lord," but "and sin against God." "For he had sworn [in the language of an oath] to his evil inclination, saying,

'By God, I will not sin or do this evil.'" "David: 'And David said, "As the Lord lives, no, but the Lord shall smite him" (1 Sam. 26:10).' "To whom did he take the oath? "R. Eleazar and R. Samuel b. Nahman: "R. Eleazar said, 'It was to his impulse to do evil.' "R. Samuel b. Nahman said, 'It was to Abishai b. Zeruiah. He said to him, "As the Lord lives, if you touch him, I swear that I will mix your blood with his."'" "Boaz: 'As the Lord lives, I will do the part of the next of kin for you. Lie down until the morning.' "R. Judah and R. Hunia: "R. Judah said, 'All that night his impulse to do evil was besieging him and saying to him, "You are a free agent and on the make, and she is a free agent and on the make. Go, have sexual relations with her, and let her be your wife!" "'And so he took an oath against his inclination to do evil, saying, "'as the Lord lives.'" "'And to the woman he said, "Remain this night and in the morning, if he will do the part of the next of kin for you, well; let him do it; but if he is not willing to do the part of the next of kin for you, then...I will do the part of the next of kin for you. Lie down until the morning." "And R. Hunia said, 'It is written, "A wise man is strong [beoz]. Yes, a man of knowledge increases strength" (Prov. 24:5). "'Read the word for strong [beoz] as Boaz: "'A wise man is Boaz. "''and a man of knowledge increases strength," because he strengthened himself with an oath.'"

<h3 style="text-align:center">PARASHAH SEVEN</h3>

LXIII:i.1 "So she lay at his feet until the morning, but arose before one could recognize another": Said R. Berekhiah, "The phrase, 'before one could recognize another' is written with an extra vav [which stands for six]. This teaches that she remained there for six hours, the numerical value of that letter."

2. "...and he said, 'Let it not be known that the woman came to the threshing floor'": To whom did he make that statement?

3. R. Hunia and R. Jeremiah in the name of R. Samuel b. R. Isaac: "That entire night Boaz lay stretched out prostrate, saying, 'Lord of the ages, it is perfectly obvious to you that I never laid a hand on her. "'May it be your will that it not be known that the woman has come to the threshing floor, so that the Name of Heaven not be profaned through me."

LXIV:i.1 "And he said, 'Bring the mantle you are wearing'": What is written is "bring" in the masculine.

2. "...and hold it out": This teaches that she girded her loins like a male.

3. "[So she held it,] and he measured out six measures of barley and laid it upon her": Said R. Simeon, "Bar Qappara expounded this matter in Sepphoris: 'And is it the way of a king to marry a woman for six measures of barley! Or is it the way for a woman to be married for six seahs?'"

4.   [Supply: "So she held it, and he measured out six measures of barley and laid it upon her":] Said R. Judah b. R. Simon, "It is on the merit of 'and he measured out six measures of barley and laid it upon her' that six righteous persons came forth from him, and each one of them had six virtues. "[These are] David, Hezekiah, Josiah, Hananiah, Mishael, Azariah, Daniel, and the royal Messiah:

5.   "...then he went into the city": Should it not have said, "and she went into the city"?

LXV:i.1 "And when she came to her mother-in-law, she said, 'Who are you, my daughter?'" Did she not know her? But she said to her, "What are you, a free agent or a married woman?" She said to her, "Still a free agent." "Then she told her all that the man had done for her."

LXVI:i.1 "Said R. Alexandri, "In every place in which the Israelites came, they did not go forth empty-handed. "From the spoil of Egypt they did not go forth empty-handed. "From the spoil of Sihon and Og they did not go forth empty-handed. "From the spoil of the thirty-one kings they did not go forth empty-handed. "The word 'empty-handed' occurs in connection with Egypt: 'And it shall come to pass that when you go, you shall not go empty-handed' (Ex. 3:21). "The word 'empty-handed' occurs in connection with those who go up for the festivals: 'You will not appear before me empty-handed' (Ex. 23:15). ""The word 'empty-handed' occurs in connection with the righteous: 'for he said, 'You must not go back empty-handed to your mother-in-law.' "The appearance of the word 'empty-handed' in connection with the righteous is to be related not to that in connection with Egypt but to that in connection with those who go up for the festivals.

LXVII:i.1 "She replied, 'Wait, my daughter, until you learn how the matter turns out, for the man will not rest, but will settle the matter today'": R. Huna in the name of R. Samuel b. R. Isaac: "The yes said by a righteous person is yes, their no is a no: 'for the man will not rest, but will settle the matter today.'"

LXVIII:i.1 "And Boaz went up to the gate and sat down there; and behold, the next of kin, of whom Boaz had spoken, came by": Now was the man waiting behind the gate [to produce such a coincidence]?

2.   Said R. Berekhiah, "So did the two great men of the age, R. Eliezer and R. Joshua, expound: "[Supply: "And Boaz went up to the gate and sat down there; and behold, the next of kin, of whom Boaz had spoken, came by":] R. Eliezer says, 'Boaz did his part, Ruth did her part, Naomi did her part, so said the Holy One, blessed be He, 'I too shall do my part.' 'So Boaz said, "Turn aside, friend, sit down here." And he turned aside and sat down': R. Joshua says, '[The word translated "friend," Peloni-almoni,] is a proper name.'"

3.   ["So Boaz said, 'Turn aside, friend, sit down here.' And he turned aside and sat down":] [As to the name Peloni-Almoni,] R. Samuel b.

R. Nahman said, "He was dumb as to words of the Torah. [For the word for dumb and the name Almoni share the same consonants.]" "[The reason I think so is as follows:] He thought, 'The ancients [Mahlon and Chilion] died only because they took them as wives. Shall I go and take her as a wife? God forbid that I take her for a wife! I am not going to disqualify my seed, I will not disqualify my children.' But he did not know that the law had been innovated: 'A male Ammonite' but not a female Ammonite,' 'a male Moabite' but not a female Moabite' [is subject to prohibition. Hence it was now legal to marry Ruth.]"

LXIX:i.1.   "And he took ten men of the elders of the city and said, 'Sit down here,' so they sat down": Said R. Alexandri, "On the basis of this passage we derive the rule that an unimportant person has not got the right to take his seat before the more important person invites him to do so."

2.   [Supply: "And he took ten men of the elders of the city and said, 'Sit down here,' so they sat down":] Said R. Phineas, "On the basis of this passage we derive the rule that this ruling house [David's, hence the patriarch's at this time] appoints elders [to the governing body, even] in their banquet halls!"]

3.   [Supply: "And he took ten men of the elders of the city and said, 'Sit down here,' so they sat down": Said R. Eleazar b. R. Yosé, "On the basis of this passage we derive the rule that the blessing of the bridegroom requires a quorum of ten."

LXXI:i.1 "So I thought I would tell you of it and say, Buy it in the presence of those sitting here and in the presence of the elders of my people. If you will redeem it, redeem it": This he said to the redeemer. "...but if you will not": This he said to the court. "...tell me, that I may know": "so that you may not say, 'I have a wife and children, lo, I shall take her into my house on condition that I not be obligated to her [as a husband]." When the redeemer heard this, he said, "Certainly, 'I will redeem it,'" and Boaz said, "There goes Ruth."

LXXII:i.1 "Buying Ruth the Moabitess, the widow of the dead, in order to restore the name of the dead to his inheritance'": What is written is [not you buy but] 'I have bought." This is in line with what R. Samuel b. R. Nahman said: "He was dumb as to words of the Torah. He thought, 'The ancients [Mahlon and Chilion] died only because they took them as wives. Shall I go and take her as a wife? God forbid that I take her for a wife! I am not going to disqualify my seed, I will not disqualify my children.' "But he did not know that the law had been innovated: 'A male Ammonite' but not 'a female Ammonite,' 'a male Moabite' but not 'a female Moabite' [is subject to prohibition. Hence it was now legal to marry Ruth.]"

LXXIV:i.1   "Now this was the custom in former times in Israel concerning redeeming and exchanging: to confirm a transaction, the one drew off his sandal and gave it to the other, and this was the manner of attesting in Israel R. Hanina interpreted the passage to speak of Israel "Just as in the beginning, Israel gave praise for the redemption: 'This is my God and I will glorify him' (Ex. 15:2 "now it is for the substitution [of false gods for God]: 'Thus they exchanged their glory for the likeness of an ox that eats grass' (Ps. 106:20 "You have nothing so repulsive and disgusting and strange as an ox when it is eating grass "In the beginning they would effect acquisition through the removal of the sandal, as it is said, 'Now this was the custom in former times in Israel concerning redeeming and exchanging: to confirm a transaction, the one drew off his sandal and gave it to the other, and this was the manner of attesting in Israel. "But now it is by means of the rite of cutting off."

2.   What is the rite of cutting off?

3.   [Reverting to the point broken off at 1.G:] "Then they would effect acquisition through a shoe or sandal: 'the one drew off his sandal and gave it to the other, and this was the manner of attesting in Israel.' "Then they would effect acquisition through an exchange of money or a document or through usufruct."

4.   All three [effecting acquisition through an exchange of money or a document or through usufruct] are written in the same verse of Scripture:

5.   R. Yosé in the name of R. Yohanan: "Money is not acquired through an exchange of less than what is worth a perutah, "and real estate is not acquired through an exchange of less than what is worth a perutah."

LXXV:i.1   "So when the next of kin said to Boaz, 'Buy it for yourself,' he drew off his sandal": Whose sandal?

2.   Along these same lines: "And Ahijah laid hold onto the new garment" (1 Kgs. 11:30): whose garment?

3.   Along these same lines: "And as Samuel turned about to go away, he laid hold of the skirt of his robe, and it was torn" (1 Sam. 15:27): whose skirt?

4.   Along these same lines: "Neither did Jeroboam recover strength again in the days of Ahijah, and the Lord smote him and he died" (2 Chr. 13:20):

5.   And why was he smitten?

6.   [Answering the same question:] R. Yohanan and R. Simeon b. Laqish [supply: and rabbis]:

LXXVIII:i.1 "Then all the people who were at the gate and the elders said, 'We are witnesses. May the Lord make the woman, who is coming into your house, like Rachel and Leah, who together built up the house of Israel. My you prosper in Ephrathah and be renowned in Bethlehem'": Said R. Berekhiah, "Most of the people present were of the line of Leah, therefore the statement treats Rachel as principal."

LXXIX:i.1 "...and may your house be like the house of Perez, whom Tamar bore to Judah, because of the children that the Lord will give you by this young woman": They said, "May all the children whom the Holy One, blessed be He, is destined to give you come from this righteous woman."

2. Along these same lines: "And Isaac prayed [to (or: entreated) the Lord for his wife, because she was barren, and the Lord granted his prayer, and Rebeccah his wife conceived]" (Gen. 25:21):

3. Along these same lines: "And Eli would bless Elkanah and his wife" (1 Sam. 2:20):

LXXX:i.1 So Boaz took Ruth and she became his wife; and he went in to her, and the Lord gave her conception, and she bore a son": R. Simeon b. Laqish: "She had no ovary, so the Holy One, blessed be He, formed an ovary for her."

LXXXI:i.1 "Then the women said to Naomi, 'Blessed be the Lord, who has not left you this day without next of kin; and may his name be renowned in Israel'": Just as "this day" rules dominion in the firmament, so will your descendants rule and govern Israel forever. Said R. Hunia, "On account of the blessings of the women, the line of David was not wholly exterminated in the time of Athaliah." R. Tanhuma in the name of R. Samuel said, "There is is written, 'That we may preserve seed of our father' (Gen. 19:32). "What is written is not 'a son' but 'seed,' "and that is 'seed' that comes from another source. "Who is meant? The messiah."

LXXXII:i.1 He shall be to you a restorer of life and a nourisher of your old age; for your daughter-in-law who loves you, who is more to you than seven sons, has borne him": R. Judah and R. Nehemiah: R. Judah said, "'more to you then seven sons' — the seven heads of fathers' households recorded later: 'Ozem, the sixth, David the seventh' (1 Chr. 2:115)." R. Nehemiah said, "'more to you then seven sons' — the seven noted here in the following verses: 'Now these are the descendants of Perez: Perez was the father of Hezron, Hezron of Ram, Ram of Amminadab, Amminadab of Nahshon, Nahshon of Salmon, Salmon of Boaz, Boaz of Obed, Obed of Jesse, and Jesse of David' (Ruth 4:19-22)."

PARASHAH EIGHT

The intersecting verse again introduces the figure of David and identifies a statement of his that illuminates the context of the present text.

LXXXV:i.1 1. ["Now these are the descendants of Perez: Perez was the father of Hezron":] R. Abba b. Kahana commenced by citing the following verse: "'Rage and do not sin; [commune with your own heart upon your bed and shut up]' (Ps. 4:5). Said David before the Holy One, blessed be He, 'How long will they rage against me and say, "Is his family not invalid [for marriage into Israel]? Is he not descended from Ruth the Moabitess?"' "'...commune with your own heart upon your bed': [David continues,] 'You too have you not descended from two sisters? "'You look at your own origins "and shut up." "'So Tamar who married your ancestor Judah — is she not of an invalid family? "'But she was only a descendant of Shem, son of Noah. So do you come from such impressive genealogy?'"

2. [Supply: "Rage and do not sin; [commune with your own heart upon your bed and shut up":] R. Jacob b. R. Abijah said, "Fight against your inclination to do evil and do not sin." Rabbis say, "Anger your inclination to do evil and do not sin."

LXXXVI:i.1 "Hezron of Ram, Ram of Amminadab": But was not Jerahmeel the elder son: "The sons also of Hezron, there were born to him: Jerahmeel and Ram and Chelubai" (1 Chr. 2:9)

LXXXVII:i.1 "Amminadab of Nahshon, Nahshon of Salmon": [Why is he called Salmon?] Because up to him they formed ladders [sulamot] of princes.

The same process introduces another pertinent discussion, now the way in which the Torah makes provision for the descendant of the Moabite to enter the congregation of the Lord.

LXXXIX:i.1 R. Isaac commenced discourse by citing this verse: "Then I said, Lo, I have come [in the roll of the book it is written of me]' (Ps. 40:8). [David says,] 'Then I had to recite a song when I came, for the word "then" refers only to a song, as it is said, "Then sang Moses" (Ex. 15:1). "'I was covered by the verse, "An Ammonite and a Moabite shall not come into the assembly of the Lord" (Dt. 23:4), but I have come "in the roll of the book it is written of me" (Ps. 40:8). "'"...in the roll": this refers to the verse, [David continues], "concerning whom you commanded that they should not enter into your congregation" (Lam. 1:10). "'"...of the book it is written of me": "An Ammonite and a Moabite shall not enter into the assembly of the Lord" (Dt.

23:4). "'It is not enough that I have come, but in the roll and the book it is written concerning me: ""...in the roll": Perez, Hezron, Ram, Amminadab, Nahshon, Salmon, Boaz, Obed, Jesse, David. ""...in the book": "And the Lord said, Arise, anoint him, for this is he" (1 Sam. 16:12)."

2. R. Huna says, "It is written, 'For God has appointed me another seed' (Gen. 4:25) — seed from another place, meaning the Messiah."

3. R. Berekhiah b. R. Simon in the name of R. Nehemiah: "The matter may be compared to the case of a king who was traveling from place to place, and a pearl fell out of his crown. The king stopped there and held up his retinue there, collected sand in heaps and brought sieves. He had the first pile sifted and did not find the pearl. So he did with the second and did not find it. But in the third heap he found it. People said, 'The king has found his pearl.' So said the Holy One, blessed be He, to Abraham, 'Why did I have to spell out the descent of Shem, Arpachshad, Shelah, Eber, Peleg, Reu, Serug, Nahor, and Terah (1 Chr. 1:24)? Was it not entirely for you?' 'Abram, the same is Abraham' (1 Chr. 1:24). And he found his heart faithful before you' (Neh. 9:8). [Freedman, p. 319, n. 2: He was the pearl that God found.] So said the Holy One, blessed be He, to David, 'Why did I have to spell out the descent of Perez, Hezron, Ram, Amminadab, Nachshon, Salmon, Boaz, Obed, and Jesse? Was it not entirely for you?' Thus: 'I have found David my servant, with my holy oil have I anointed him' (Ps. 89:21)."

So much for the details. Now how shall we see matters whole and complete? It is by a two part process of moving from exegesis, now surveyed, to hermeneutics, and then from hermeneutics to category-formation, inclusive of doctrine.

III. THE PROPOSITIONS OF RUTH RABBAH

To compose the Oral Torah, sages wrote with Scripture. It is not so much by writing fresh discourses as by compiling and arranging materials that the framers of the document accomplished that writing. It would be difficult to find a less promising mode of writing than merely collecting and arranging available compositions and turning them into a composite. But that in the aggregate is the predominant trait of this writing. That the compilers were equally interested in the exposition of the book of Ruth as in the execution of their paramount proposition through their compilation is clear. A large number of entries just now reviewed contain no more elaborate proposition than the exposition through paraphrase of the sense of a given clause or verse. To me that signals that sages found evidence for their hermeneutics in low-level exegesis of simple matters: everything served to say the same thing, however simple the detail.

Indeed, Ruth Rabbah proves nearly as much a commentary in the narrowest sense — verse by verse amplification, paraphrase, exposition — as it is a compilation in the working definition of this inquiry of mine. Not only so, but the compilation contains its share of propositional demonstrations to which the book of Ruth makes a contribution, but which do not take shape around the exposition of that or any other book. Both types of composition impart to the document a rather diffuse quality. What holds the document together and gives it, if not coherence, then at least flow and movement are the successive passages of (mere) exposition. All the more stunning, therefore, is the simple fact that, when all has been set forth and completed, there really is that simple message that the Torah (as exemplified by the sage) makes the outsider into an insider, the Moabite into an Israelite, the offspring of the outsider into the Messiah: all on the condition, the only condition, that the Torah governs. This is a document about one thing, and it makes a single statement, and that statement is coherent.

The outline now makes possible the identification of the principal propositions that the compilation sets forth. Like the other Midrash-compilations of its class, the late Rabbah-documents, Ruth Rabbah makes one paramount point through numerous exegetical details. Ruth Rabbah has only one message, expressed in a variety of components but single and cogent. It concerns the outsider who becomes the principal, the Messiah out of Moab, and this miracle is accomplished through mastery of the Torah. The main points of the document are these:

[1]   Israel's fate depends upon its proper conduct toward its leaders.

[2]   The leaders must not be arrogant.

[3]   The admission of the outsider depends upon the rules of the Torah. These differentiate among outsiders. Those who know the rules are able to apply them accurately and mercifully.

[4]   The proselyte is accepted because the Torah makes it possible to do so, and the condition of acceptance is complete and total submission to the Torah. Boaz taught Ruth the rules of the Torah, and she obeyed them carefully.

[5]   Those proselytes who are accepted are respected by God and are completely equal to all other Israelites. Those who marry them are masters of the Torah, and their descendants are masters of the Torah, typified by David. Boaz in his day and David in his day were the same in this regard.

[6]   What the proselyte therefore accomplishes is to take shelter under the wings of God's presence, and the proselyte who does so stands in the royal line of David, Solomon, and the Messiah. Over and over again, we see, the point is made that Ruth the Moabitess, perceived by the ignorant as an outsider, enjoyed complete equality with all other Israelites, because she had accepted the yoke of the Torah, married a great sage, and through her descendants produced the Messiah-sage, David, himself vindicated from his very public sin through his devotion to the Torah.

Scripture has provided everything but the main point, which demands heavy emphasis: *the Moabite ancestry of the Messiah is validated through the Torah.* That is how sages imposed upon the whole their distinctive message, which is the priority of the Torah, the extraordinary power of the Torah to join the opposites — Messiah, utter outsider — into a single figure, and to accomplish this union of opposites through the systemic anomaly, the woman.[4] The femininity of Ruth proves as critical to the whole as the Moabite origin: the two modes of the (from the Israelite perspective) abnormal, [1] outsider as against Israelite, [2] woman as against man, therefore are invoked, and both for the same purpose, to show how, through the Torah, all things are susceptible of transformation and can become one. That is the message of the document, and, seen whole, the principal message, to which all other messages prove peripheral.

The authorship decided to compose a document concerning the book of Ruth in order to make a single point. Everything else was subordinated to that definitive intention. Once the work got underway, the task was not one of exposition so much as repetition, not unpacking and exploring a complex conception, but restating the point, on the one side, and eliciting or evoking the proper attitude that was congruent with that point, on the other. The decision, viewed after the fact, was to make one statement in an enormous number of ways. It is that the Torah dictates Israel's fate, if you want to know what that fate will be, study the Torah, and if you want to control that fate, follow the model of the sage-Messiah. As usual, therefore, what we find is a recasting of the Deuteronomic-prophetic theology, recapitulated within the framework of sages' convictions about the two-part composition of the Torah and their unique mastery thereof.

IV. AN INITIAL SCAN OF THE WHOLE: ISRAEL AND GOD, ISRAEL AND THE NA-TIONS, ISRAEL ON ITS OWN

I have insisted on the priority of native categories. To test that point of insistence, I introduce and test against the data of Ruth Rabbah three autonomous categories of fundamental theological interest — not teased out of the sources at all. These categories of relationship now require attention: Israel and God, Israel and the nations, and Israel on its own. In theory the fundamental building-blocks of the world of our document consist of the categories, Israel (and the nations), God (and Israel, God and the nations), and the life of Israel on its own account, not in relationship to outside elements. The document repeatedly works out discourses on all three matters, treating our story as an occasion for generalization and large-scale investigation of governing rules. But, as we shall now see, only one of these categories acquires central importance, Israel on its own. This is not a document

---

[4] I spell this matter out in *A History of the Mishnaic Law of Women.* Leiden, 1980: Brill. V. *The Mishnaic System of Women,* and expand on the matter in *Androgynous Judaism. Masculine and Feminine in the Dual Torah.* Macon, 1993: Mercer University Press.

that reflects on the fate of Israel among the nations or on Israel's relationship with God, though both matters make an appearance. The sole native category validated by the document concerns the inner life of the community of Israel; that means we shall have to look elsewhere — as Chapter Seven is going to show us — for an account of how Israel's relationships with the nations are formed into a categorical paradigm. Let us now consider how our document delivers data for each of these categories, which take the measure of the dimensions of Israel's supernatural being.

ISRAEL AND GOD: Israel's relationship with God encompasses the matter of the covenant, the Torah, and the Land of Israel, all of which bring to concrete and material expression the nature and standing of that relationship. This is a topic treated only casually by our compilers. They make a perfectly standard point. It is that Israel suffers because of sin (I:i). The famine in the time of the judges was because of Israel's rebellion: "My children are rebellious. But as to exterminating them, that is not possible, and to bring them back to Egypt is not possible, and to trade them for some other nation is something I cannot do. But this shall I do for them: lo, I shall torment them with suffering and afflict them with famine in the days when the judges judge" (III:i). This was because they got overconfident (III:ii).

Sometimes God saves Israel on account of its merit, sometimes for his own name's sake (X:i). God's punishment of Israel is always proportionate and appropriate, so LXXIV:i: "Just as in the beginning, Israel gave praise for the redemption: 'This is my God and I will glorify him' (Ex. 15:2), now it is for the substitution [of false gods for God]: 'Thus they exchanged their glory for the likeness of an ox that eats grass' (Ps. 106:20). You have nothing so repulsive and disgusting and strange as an ox when it is eating grass. In the beginning they would effect acquisition through the removal of the sandal, as it is said, 'Now this was the custom in former times in Israel concerning redeeming and exchanging: to confirm a transaction, the one drew off his sandal and gave it to the other, and this was the manner of attesting in Israel.' But now it is by means of the rite of cutting off." None of this forms a centerpiece of interest, and all of it complements the principal points of the writing.

ISRAEL AND THE NATIONS: Israel's relationship with the nations is treated with interest in Israel's history, past, present, and future, and how that cyclical pattern is to be known. This topic is not addressed at all. Only one nation figures in a consequential way, and that is Moab. Under these circumstances we can hardly generalize and say that Moab stands for everybody outside of Israel. That is precisely the opposite of the fact. Moab stands for a problem within Israel, the Messiah from the periphery; and the solution to the problem lies within Israel and not in its relationships to the other, the nations. These are not points critical to our document; the category serves only peripherally.

ISRAEL ON ITS OWN: Israel on its own concerns the holy nation's understanding of itself: who is Israel, who is not? Within the same rubric we find consideration of Israel's capacity to naturalize the outsider, so to define itself as to extend its own limits, and other questions of self-definition. And, finally, when Israel considers itself, a principal concern is the nature of leadership, for the leader stands for and embodies the people. Therein lies the paradox of the base-document and the Midrash-compilation alike: how can the leader most wanted, the Messiah, come, as a matter of fact, from the excluded people and not from the holy people? And, more to the point (for ours is not an accusatory document), how is the excluded included? And in what way do peripheral figures find their way to the center? Phrased in this way, the question yields the obvious answer: through the Torah as embodied by the sage, anybody can become Israel, and any Israelite can find his way to the center. Even more — since it is through Ruth that the Moabite becomes the Israelite, and since (for sages) the mother's status dictates the child's, we may go so far as to say that it is through the Torah that the woman may become a man (at least, in theory).

The topical and propositional program may be rapidly summarized in the following terms: The sin of Israel, which caused the famine, was that it was judging its own judges. "He further said to the Israelites, 'So God says to Israel, "I have given a share of glory to the judges and I have called them gods, and the Israelites nonetheless humiliate them. Woe to a generation that judges its judges" (I:i). The Israelites were slothful in burying Joshua, and that showed disrespect to their leader (II:i). They were slothful about repentance in the time of the judges, and that is what caused the famine; excess of commitment to one's own affairs leads to sin. The Israelites did not honor the prophets (III:iii). The old have to bear with the young, and the young with the old, or Israel will go into exile (IV:i). The generation that judges its leadership ("judges") will be penalized (V:i).

Arrogance to the authority of the Torah is penalized (V:i). Elimelech was punished because he broke the peoples' heart; everyone depended upon him, and he proved undependable (V:iii); so bad leadership will destroy Israel. Why was Elimelech punished? It is because he broke the Israelites' heart. When the years of drought came, his maid went out into the market place, with her basket in her hand. So the people of the town said, "Is this the one on whom we depended, that he can provide for the whole town with ten years of food? Lo, his maid is standing in the marketplace with her basket in her hand!" So Elimelech was one of the great men of the town and one of those who sustained the generation. But when the years of famine came, he said, "Now all the Israelites are going to come knocking on my door, each with his basket." The leadership of a community is its glory: "The great man of a town — he is its splendor, he is its glory, he is its praise. When he has turned from there, so too have turned its splendor, glory, and praise":(XI:i.1C).

A distinct but fundamental component of the theory of Israel concerns who is Israel and how one becomes a part of Israel. That theme proves fundamental to our document, so much of which is preoccupied with how Ruth can be the progenitor of the Messiah, deriving as she does not only from gentile but from

Moabite stock. Israel's history follows rules that are to be learned in Scripture; nothing is random and all things are connected (IV:ii). The fact that the king of Moab honored God explains why God raised up from Moab "a son who will sit on the throne of the Lord" (VIII:i.3). The proselyte is discouraged but then accepted. Thus XVI:i..2B: "People are to turn a proselyte away. But if he is insistent beyond that point, he is accepted. A person should always push away with the left hand while offering encouragement with the right." Orpah, who left Naomi, was rewarded for the little that she did for her, but she was raped when she left her (XVIII:i.1-3). When Orpah went back to her people, she went back to her gods (XIX:i).

Ruth's intention to convert was absolutely firm, and Naomi laid out all the problems for her, but she acceded to every condition (XX:i). Thus she said, "Under all circumstances I intend to convert, but it is better that it be through your action and not through that of another." When Naomi heard her say this, she began laying out for her the laws that govern proselytes. She said to her, "My daughter, it is not the way of Israelite women to go to theaters and circuses put on by idolators." She said to her, "Where you go I will go." She said to her, "My daughter, it is not the way of Israelite women to live in a house that lacks a mezuzah." She said to her, "Where you lodge I will lodge." "your people shall be my people:" This refers to the penalties and admonitions against sinning. "and your God my God:" This refers to the other religious duties. And so onward: "for where you go I will go:" to the tent of meeting, Gilgal, Shiloh, Nob, Gibeon, and the eternal house. "and where you lodge I will lodge:" "I shall spend the night concerned about the offerings." "your people shall be my people:" "so nullifying my idol." "and your God my God:" "to pay a full recompense for my action." I find here the centerpiece of the compilation and its principal purpose. The same message is at XXI:i.1-3.

Proselytes are respected by God, so XXII:i: "And when Naomi saw that she was determined to go with her, [she said no more]:" Said R. Judah b. R. Simon, "Notice how precious are proselytes before the Omnipresent. Once she had decided to convert, the Scripture treats her as equivalent to Naomi." Boaz, for his part, was equally virtuous and free of sins (XXVI:i). The law provided for the conversion of Ammonite and Moabite women, but not Ammonite and Moabite men, so the acceptance of Ruth the Moabite was fully in accord with the law, and anyone who did not know that fact was an ignoramus (XXVI:i.4, among many passages). An Israelite hero who came from Ruth and Boaz was David, who was a great master of the Torah, thus: "he was "Skillful in playing, and a mighty man of war, prudent in affairs, good-looking, and the Lord is with him" (1 Sam. 16:18):" "Skillful in playing:" in Scripture. "and a mighty man of valor:" in Mishnah. "A man of war:" who knows the give and take of the war of the Torah. "prudent in affairs:" in good deeds. "good-looking:" in Talmud. prudent in affairs:" able to reason deductively. "good-looking:" enlightened in law. "and the Lord is with him:" the law accords with his opinions.

Ruth truly accepted Judaism upon the instruction, also, of Boaz (XXXIV:i), thus: "Then Boaz said to Ruth, 'Now listen, my daughter, do not go to glean in another field:'" This is on the strength of the verse, "You shall have no other gods before me" (Ex. 20:3). "'or leave this one:'" This is on the strength of the verse, "This is my God and I will glorify him" (Ex. 15:2). "But keep close to my maidens:" This speaks of the righteous, who are called maidens: "Will you play with him as with a bird, or will you bind him for your maidens" (Job 40:29). The glosses invest the statement with a vast tapestry of meaning. Boaz speaks to Ruth as a Jew by choice, and the entire exchange is now typological. Note also the typological meanings imputed at XXXV:i.1-5. Ruth had prophetic power (XXXVI:ii). Ruth was rewarded for her sincere conversion by Solomon (XXXVIII:i.1).

The language that Boaz used to Ruth, "Come here," bore with it deeper reference to six: David, Solomon, the throne as held by the Davidic monarchy, and ultimately, the Messiah, e.g., in the following instance: "The fifth interpretation refers to the Messiah: 'Come here:' means, to the throne. "'and eat some bread:' this is the bread of the throne. "'and dip your morsel in vinegar:' this refers to suffering: 'But he was wounded because of our transgressions' (Is. 53:5). "'So she sat beside the reapers:' for the throne is destined to be taken from him for a time: For I will gather all nations against Jerusalem to battle and the city shall be taken' (Zech. 14:2). "'and he passed to her parched grain:' for he will be restored to the throne: 'And he shall smite the land with the rod of his mouth' (Is. 11:4)." R. Berekhiah in the name of R. Levi: "As was the first redeemer, so is the last redeemer: "Just as the first redeemer was revealed and then hidden from them, so the last redeemer will be revealed to them and then hidden from them" (XL:i.1ff.).

Boaz instructed Ruth on how to be a proper Israelite woman, so LIII:i: "Wash yourself:" from the filth of idolatry that is yours. "and anoint yourself:" this refers to the religious deeds and acts of righteousness [that are required of an Israelite]. and put on your best clothes:" this refers to her Sabbath clothing. So did Naomi encompass Ruth within Israel: "and go down to the threshing floor:" She said to her, "My merit will go down there with you." Moab, whence Ruth came, was conceived not for the sake of fornication but for the sake of Heaven (LV:i.1B). Boaz, for his part, was a master of the Torah and when he ate and drank, that formed a typology for his study of the Torah (LVI:i). His was a life of grace, Torah study, and marriage for holy purposes. Whoever trusts in God is exalted, and that refers to Ruth and Boaz; God put it in his heart to bless her (LVII:i). David sang Psalms to thank God for his great-grandmother, Ruth, so LIX:i.5, "[At midnight I will rise to give thanks to you] because of your righteous judgments" (Ps. 119:62): [David speaks,] "The acts of judgment that you brought upon the Ammonites and Moabites. "And the righteous deeds that you carried out for my great-grandfather and my great-grandmother [Boaz, Ruth, of whom David speaks here]. "For had he hastily cursed her but once, where should I have come from? But you put in his heart the will to bless her: 'And he said, "May you be blessed by the Lord." Because of the merit of the six measures that Boaz gave Ruth, six righteous persons came forth from him, each with six virtues: David, Hezekiah, Josiah, Hananiah-Mishael-Azariah (counted as one), Daniel and the royal Messiah.

God facilitated the union of Ruth and Boaz (LXVIII:i). Boaz's relative was ignorant for not knowing that while a male Moabite was excluded, a female one was acceptable for marriage. The blessing of Boaz was, "May all the children you have come from this righteous woman" (LXXIX:i), and that is precisely the blessing accorded to Isaac and to Elkanah. God made Ruth an ovary, which she had lacked (LXXX:i). Naomi was blessed with messianic blessings (LXXXI:i), thus: "Then the women said to Naomi, 'Blessed be the Lord, who has not left you this day without next of kin; and may his name be renowned in Israel:'" Just as "this day" has dominion in the firmament, so will your descendants rule and govern Israel forever. On account of the blessings of the women, the line of David was not wholly exterminated in the time of Athaliah.

David was ridiculed because he was descended from Ruth, the Moabitess, so LXXXV:i. But many other distinguished families derived from humble origins: "Said David before the Holy One, blessed be he, 'How long will they rage against me and say, "Is his family not invalid [for marriage into Israel]? Is he not descended from Ruth the Moabitess?"' "'commune with your own heart upon your bed:' [David continues,] 'You too have you not descended from two sisters? You look at your own origins "and shut up." "'So Tamar who married your ancestor Judah — is she not of an invalid family? 'But she was only a descendant of Shem, son of Noah. So do you come from such impressive genealogy?'" David referred to and defended his Moabite origins, so LXXXIX:i: "Then I said, Lo, I have come [in the roll of the book it is written of me]' (Ps. 40:8). "[David says,] 'Then I had to recite a song when I came, for the word "then" refers to a song, as it is said, "Then sang Moses" (Ex. 15:1). "'I was covered by the verse, 'An Ammonite and a Moabite shall not come into the assembly of the Lord' (Dt. 23:4),, but I have come "in the roll of the book it is written of me" (Ps. 40:8). "in the roll:" this refers to the verse, [David continues], "concerning whom you commanded that they should not enter into your congregation" (Lam. 1:10). """of the book it is written of me:" "An Ammonite and a Moabite shall not enter into the assembly of the Lord" (Dt. 23:4). "'It is not enough that I have come, but in the roll and the book it is written concerning me: """In the roll:" Perez, Hezron, Ram, Amminadab, Nahshon, Salmon, Boaz, Obed, Jesse, David. """in the book:" "And the Lord said, Arise, anoint him, for this is he"' (1 Sam. 16:12)." Just as David's descent from Ruth was questioned, so his descent from Judah via Tamar could be questioned too, and that would compromise the whole tribe of Judah. Before us is an inner-facing, inward-looking document, reflecting on the way in which the Torah dictates Israel's fate, both public and individual — for it all comes down to that.

v. Category-Formation, Location, Proportion

The paramount categories of Ruth Rabbah draw together contributions from both Torahs. The Written Torah defines the category of the Messiah from beyond the borders — the descendant of a Moabite woman. The Oral Torah accounts for the remarkable origins of Israel's savior: the Torah brings about the possibility of transformation. And, directly to the point of the book of Ruth itself, adherence to the Torah so transforms the outsider as to make her and her descendants equal to all native-born Israelites back to Sinai. The governing categories of the document — the Messiah, the Torah — form a single category, which collects the facts that pertain to the salvation of Israel. A theology of the Oral Torah (encompassing, we see, the Written Torah as well) then will identify as a principal category the Torah, its disciplines and requirements and their consequences, and a major chapter will organize data on how and why the Torah defines the condition of redemption, and the only condition. Then the category-formation of redemption will move from the outer limits — the outsider, the woman — to the very center of matters — the sage, the Messiah, and above all, the Messiah who is qualified by sagacity, master of the Torah. The details then fall into place easily: sin is forgiven through Torah-study, virtue is embodied in Torah-study, authentic love of man and woman is realized in accord with the rules of the Torah, and so on throughout.

What about the location of the doctrine of salvation? The Written Torah sets forth more than a single candidate, but given the clear intent of the writing, the book of Ruth is an obvious starting point, and, given its blatant points of stress, Ruth Rabbah makes a fine match. But only a comprehensive survey of the components of the Oral Torah can confirm the hypothesis that, for a systematic and authoritative statement of the Rabbinic doctrine of salvation, we turn first to Ruth Rabbah. That survey will undertake both positive and negative tests of the hypothesis, the former as here exemplified, the latter through attention to other documents. There we should want to find out whether the doctrine of salvation through the Torah defines the principal focus and message of a document, or whether other category-formations altogether take over. It suffices at this point to point to the other late-Rabbah compilations, Lamentations Rabbati and Song of Songs Rabbah, to uncover initial evidence to sustain the hypothesis. Lamentations Rabbati forms a vast exercise on the twin-problems, the meaning of history (Israel's exile and the conditions of redemption) and the mystery of sin and atonement. Song of Songs Rabbah for its part takes up the category-formations, Israel's relationship with God, and God's relationship with Israel, and in neither document is the doctrine of salvation through Torah an articulated and organizing category-formation, though in both the conviction that Torah governs forms the foundation of all else.

What category-formations do we miss? Two immediately come to mind. The first emerges when we notice that the Oral Torah's reading of a book of the Written Torah devoted to virtuous woman at the same time celebrates the woman's virtues and subordinates her femininity. In Ruth Rabbah Ruth exemplifies the virtues of a disciple of sages, a master of the Torah; that she is a woman, not a man, is treated as adventitious, not critical to matters. The story works only because she is a woman — by definition. But the movement of the story and its critical turnings, the moments at which salvation emerges and the consideration of redemption comes to the fore — at all these points what the woman does in no way differs from what a man is supposed to do: not practice idolatry, not go to circuses and theaters, not to live in a house lacking a mezuzah, and the like. One may claim that the narrative in the Written Torah builds upon opposites — Moab/Israel, woman/man — to reach its climax with the paradox of the Messiah descended from a Moabite woman, who is the hero of the tale, whose remarkable loyalty to her (Israelite) mother-in-law marks her as a vessel overflowing with virtue. The Oral Torah, we must assume, takes these noteworthy details into account, but its stress is elsewhere.

The second missing category-formation hardly requires attention: the gentile. In the version of the Written Torah, Moabite origin, residence outside of the Land, and equivalent matters ignite the tension that moves the tale. In the Oral Torah these matters, taken for granted as necessary to the story, do not advance the narrative, which moves along lines required by the exposition of the centrality of the Torah and what it requires. We have therefore to form the hypothesis that among the principal category-formations of the theology of the Oral Torah we should not anticipate finding either the gentile or the woman; both self-evidently will play subordinated roles, finding no place in the category-formation, but certainly marking contrast and igniting tension in the workings of the theological system of the Oral Torah. That is to say, the principal category-formations define the structure, the contrastive category-formations — the important players that do not define matters at all — transform the stable structure into a working system.

Clearly, the documentary approach to the definition of the category-formations of the Oral Torah leads to promising possibilities. Some documents, those devoted to the exposition of norms of belief, as exemplified by Ruth Rabbah, do define for themselves, out of diverse data, in dialogue with the Written Torah, a category-formation so fundamental and so blatantly systemic as to demand considerable investigation. Here we have a statement that serves as touchstone and criterion when other formulations of the doctrine of salvation come to the fore, both singleton-sayings and even topical composites. The reason is that Ruth Rabbah not only sets forth a category-formation but dictates the doctrine conveyed therein, identifies itself as a principal location for the presentation of the category and the doctrine thereof, and at least at this preliminary stage also marks the category as proportionately consequential, defining as it does the critical center of a systematic exposition carried out through massive detail. Many, though not all, of the Midrash-compilations exhibit the same qualities as this one, allowing the movement from exegesis to hermeneutics to theological category-formation fully exposed and in detail expounded as well.

Now the question arises, what of those documents of the Oral Torah that deal with norms of behavior, not belief, and how, for an initial survey of theological norms, are we to read them? To that question we now turn, as the most important document of all, the Talmud of Babylonia, makes theological statements in its way. What we want to know is how to identify organizing categories, topics systematically expounded, where to find the authoritative presentations of those categories and the propositions that are contained therein, and ways in which to assess the proportionate importance accorded to the category within the larger perspective of the entire Oral part of the Torah.

VII

Another Kind of Paradigm:
The Model for Making Connections
and Drawing Conclusions

I. THE HALAKHIC SECTOR AND THE THEOLOGY OF THE ORAL TORAH

When in the halakhic sector of the Oral Torah we know the answer to the
question of connection and even propose a theory of the self-evident conclusion
we are supposed to draw, we have in hand the counterpart to the governing
paradigms, the presence and systematic exposition of which forms the principle of
coherence — hermeneutic shading over to theology — in the massive array of
exegetical detail of a Midrash-compilation such as Ruth Rabbah. Here we take up
two striking traits of the halakhic sector. First, the writings, particularly the Talmud
of Babylonia, contain compositions and composites devoted to theological topics.
Second, those topics rarely intersect with the Mishnah's rule that otherwise, in a
given passage, forms the organizing program but disrupts discourse. So here I
explain [1] what is to be learned about the governing theology of the Oral Torah
from the topical composites that the halakhic writings set forth, and [2] how topics
that on the surface do not intersect in fact fit together very nicely and by their
juxtaposition convey a message in tandem that on their own the respective parts do
not deliver or even adumbrate. Let me explain these terms and the thesis they
convey.

While important Midrash-compilations focus upon theological topics
expounded in detail in accord with a governing hermeneutic, by its nature the
halakhic sector of the Oral Torah cannot do so. For the principal parts of the
halakhic sector of the Oral Torah — the Tosefta, both Talmuds — organize
themselves around the Mishnah and take the form of a commentary and exposition
of the Mishnah's statements and of the law implicit therein. And while the Mishnah
participates in the theological enterprise of the Oral Torah and indeed precipitates

that enterprise,[1] the document contains only a few statements of an obviously theological classification, e.g., M. San. 10:1: "All Israelites have a share in the world to come." More to the point, the Mishnah concerns itself with systematic investigation of this worldly data and has little writing that corresponds to the study of the implicit regularities present in the Written Torah such as we have just noted. In that kind of philosophical law code, we may hardly expect to find systematic expositions of propositions standing on their own, such as might yield those paradigms of theology that we seek.

If, however, we open the pages of the largest and most important document of the Oral Torah, the Talmud of Babylonia, we find important evidence of the workings of the theological system, the ubiquitous rationality, the modes of thought guided by a deep structure of self-evident truths, that sustain equally all documents of the Oral Torah and hold the whole together. Specifically, alongside paradigms, such as entire documents set forth, I shall now point to a different sort of evidence of the rationality that governs throughout. That other evidence derives from two facts.

First, the Bavli encompasses numerous systematic expositions of theological themes. Right on the surface, therefore, systematic topical compositions define a theological category-formation and tell us what we should know about its contents. The organization of data within such a theological category by the framers of composites constitutes irrefutable evidence of a category-formation native to the system as a whole. Chapter Two has already set forth one such topical composite, on the Messiah, so the type of writing is familiar to us.

Second, and still more important, these topical composites are located in a way that is jarring to the flow of the Talmud's exposition of the law. The very placement of these topical composites on theological themes time and again proves not fortuitous but significant, since the topic of the composite turns out to make a statement upon the legal subjects round about.

So the question, what has this to do with that, arises when the subject takes an unexpected turn. Juxtapositions that jar and disrupt turn out to bear an

---

[1] But how the Mishnah yields systematic, as distinct from episodic, theological data remains to be spelled out. I do not deal with that problem in *Judaism. The Evidence of the Mishnah*. Chicago, 1981: University of Chicago Press. The Mishnah's generative problematics derive from philosophy — natural history, hierarchical classification, list-making, generalizing out of cases — and not from theology. Its theological goal, the demonstration out of the rules of this world, of how the One relates to the many, and the many to the One (so *Judaism as Philosophy. The Method and Message of the Mishnah*. Columbia, 1991: University of South Carolina Press), is accomplished through other-than-theological demonstrations out of the resources of the Written Torah. So how to identify the theological issue out of the philosophical structure set forth in the Mishnah remains to be seen. Systematic work on other documents will prepare the way.

entirely pertinent, even urgent, message for the larger discourse in which they take their place. Indeed, these topical composites themselves commonly constitute a comment upon the paramount subject of the Mishnah-tractate at the very point at which they find their position — if only by highlighting what belongs but has been omitted. Properly understood, the topical miscellanies do not jar and do not violate the document's prevailing rationality.[2] Rather, they alert us to cases that all together contain that inner, structural (theo-)logic, the halakhic counterpart to the paradigm of the aggadic compilations.

As I shall show in some detail in cases spelled out in this chapter, the juxtaposition of a legal analysis and a theological exposition matches the one with the other — another kind of theological paradigm — and opens new perspectives upon both. And, granting the assertion of self-evidence and entering into its inner logic, as soon as we ask, what has this to do with that, we penetrate into the world of what turns out to be theological reflection that the framers and compilers of the Talmud of Babylonia wished to precipitate — from this surprising connection, draw that inexorable conclusion.

And this brings us back to the matter of the self-evidence of making connections of a certain, specific sort, yielding conclusions that stand beyond all doubt. We may find surprising the logic that provokes connecting one thing with another, but to the compilers of the Talmud, linking the one with the other responded to the connection that, within the theological system at hand, they perceived made that linkage an act of self-evidence. When we can define the self-evident logic that imposed connections of one sort but not another and yielded conclusions of an inexorable character, then we may claim to have found our way into the deepest foundations of the sense for the self-evident, the most profound layers of the system's rational mode of thought and analysis. Then we shall have penetrated into the heart of the theology of the Oral Torah, so we may assess even the proportionate balance and coherence of the whole. What is needed, first of all, is a systematic account of the connections the principal halakhic documents seek, their modes of juxtaposition and intersection. The data are spread out for all to see; here no speculation is required, little more than patient description is necessary. Let me now spell out the kind of data that are to be collected, their traits and uses.

---

[2] I summarize *Rationality and Structure: The Bavli's Anomalous Juxtapositions.* Atlanta, 1997: Scholars Press for South Florida Studies in the History of Judaism.

II. THE BAVLI'S COMPOSITES AND THEIR JARRING JUXTAPOSITIONS

While the Talmud of Babylonia, a.k.a., the Bavli, through better than 90% of its completed units of thought,[3] takes shape as a commentary to the Mishnah, the document in most tractates also encompasses sizable composites of materials that do not organize themselves around the Mishnah or its law but focus on their own free-standing topics, collecting sayings and stories about said topics. And not uncommonly, these topics define theological category-formations, blending verses of Scripture with a program of questions that concern systematic reflection on questions involving God and holy Israel. Sometimes the thematic composite not only assembles topically-coherent data but also uses the data to demonstrate a theological proposition, sometimes not. But in all cases these composites stand on their own and scarcely pretend to serve the document's principal purpose, which is the exegesis of the Mishnah and analysis of the law. When these topical composites are inserted, they therefore create a jarring interruption in the steady course of Mishnah-exegesis and legal exposition and analysis, and they also constitute anomalies in the exegetical and analytical large-scale program of the document. Clearly, someone compiled these composites[4] to serve a purpose and even make a point, and equally obviously, some of them address those issues that, in the aggadic sector of the Oral Torah, concern theology, practical or theoretical.

And that fact brings us to the relevance of topical composites to our study of the theology of the Oral Torah. As a matter of fact at every point that draws our attention, to the compilers of the Bavli a clear rationality, which we can discern, guided the inclusion of the exposition a topic. And when we ask and answer the question, what has one thing to do with the other — this law with that other-than-legal topic that is expounded, or two superficially-unrelated theological topics — we identify and define the governing rationality that, at the foundations of the system, imparts self-evidence throughout. For in the cases of the jarring juxtapositions, what appears to impede the work in fact enriches it. When a highly orderly exposition is disrupted, time and again the disruption turns out to recast our perspective on the exposition itself, its topic, its problematic. That explains why an account of the structure of the Talmud, its sequence of exegetical problems and its palpable requirement of supplementary topical information, shows the rationality of inserting discussions of topics not required by the labor of Mishnah-exposition. One important way of identifying the rationalities that sustain the

---

[3] See *The Bavli's Primary Discourse. Mishnah Commentary, its Rhetorical Paradigms and their Theological Implications in the Talmud of Babylonia Tractate Moed Qatan.* Atlanta, 1992: Scholars Press for South Florida Studies in the History of Judaism, and *The Bavli's Massive Miscellanies. The Problem of Agglutinative Discourse in the Talmud of Babylonia.* Atlanta, 1992: Scholars Press for South Florida Studies in the History of Judaism.

[4] For the distinction between composition and composite, see *The Rules of Composition of the Talmud of Babylonia. The Cogency of the Bavli's Composite.* Atlanta, 1991: Scholars Press for South Florida Studies in the History of Judaism.

writings of the Oral Torah then is examining these composites and assessing the self-evidence — the rationality — that accounts for juxtaposing them with the legal topics with which they find their placement.

When we know the principles of association, of making connections and drawing conclusions, then we can define the logic, the rationality, that governs throughout. That takes shape in the (to the compilers of the document) self-evident principle of coherence that holds the whole together, even (or especially) where the sequence of completed cogent discourses appears to disintegrate into a haphazard and incoherent collection of unrelated sayings and stories about nothing in particular.

Two issues intersect, the structure of the document, on the one side, the rationality of those inserted discourses that seem to violate the rules of structure and order that otherwise govern throughout, on the other. Questions of structure pertain to how the document is put together and is so framed as to convey its framers' messages in consistent forms. These privileged forms define the document. Questions of system encompass the matters of rationality, principles of self-evidence, yielding the governing laws of list-making. These then concern the points of emphasis and current stress, the agenda that comes to expression in whatever topic is subject to analysis.

The framers of the composites that comprise the document pursue a uniform analytical program throughout. Here too, they never leave us in doubt as to what they wish to discover or demonstrate. By explaining the coherence of the whole through the identification of the parts and the systematic specification of what links one part to another, I mean to show the Talmud's rationality for what it is. And that is that monotonous voice says the same thing about many things and changes the subject only to re-present the original subject itself. Since, by axiom, there can be no rationality that governs in one document of a given corpus of kindred writings privileged by a determinate religious system but not in another component of the same authoritative corpus, the rest follows. How to set forth the evidence and argument that sustains my proposition? Through my already-completed analytical outlines of the Talmud's thirty-seven tractates I claim to have penetrated into that rationality that made this fit very well with that, and that rationality that at the same time excluded the other thing.[5] I work not through a

---

[5] *The Talmud of Babylonia. A Complete Outline.* Atlanta, 1995-6: Scholars Press for *USF Academic Commentary Series.* In eight parts.

handful of examples but through a complete survey of all data. The work is complete, and through the sample set forth here I present the principles pertinent to this Prolegomenon.[6]

III. AN INITIAL PROBE: THE RATIONALITY THAT EXPLAINS THE PLACEMENT OF COMPOSITES IN BAVLI ABODAH ZARAH

The initial probe is detailed and works stage by stage from Scripture through the Mishnah to the Talmud of Babylonia. The other units more briefly instantiate the same phenomenon as is fully exposed here. Our question is, How do the topical composites fit into the Talmud-tractate Abodah Zarah and what do they contribute that the Mishnah-tractate of the same name would lack without them? I first survey those large-scale composites that accomplish a task other than

---

[6] I do not offer general arguments but detailed treatments of every piece of data in all thirty-seven tractates of the Bavli. This I systematically carried out in my *Academic Commentary* to the Bavli (and the Yerushalmi), where at each point I systematically addressed issues of coherence. There I defined the Talmud's definitive character as a commentary, through visual signals portraying the whole in a process of large-scale description, analysis, and interpretation. I further identified and defined the components, beyond Mishnah-commentary. The path I took carried me through a detailed, line by line rereading of the document, with a uniform program of questions always guiding our progress. Since Mishnah-exegesis defines the Talmud's purpose, though not its character, I identified, then frame my discussion around, the Talmud's definitive units of discourse, which are those organized around Mishnah-paragraphs. These are, in general, to be divided into two types, sources and traditions, as I have defined the basic taxonomy of types of compositions of the Bavli in my *Sources and Traditions. Types of Composition in the Talmud of Babylonia.* Atlanta, 1992: Scholars Press for South Florida Studies in the History of Judaism; and note also the following: *The Bavli's One Voice: Types and Forms of Analytical Discourse and their Fixed Order of Appearance.* Atlanta, 1991: Scholars Press for South Florida Studies in the History of Judaism.*The Bavli's Massive Miscellanies. The Problem of Agglutinative Discourse in the Talmud of Babylonia.* Atlanta, 1992: Scholars Press for South Florida Studies in the History of Judaism.*The Bavli's Primary Discourse. Mishnah Commentary, its Rhetorical Paradigms and their Theological Implications in the Talmud of Babylonia Tractate Moed Qatan.* Atlanta, 1992: Scholars Press for South Florida Studies in the History of Judaism. I have provided a systematic and detailed account of the other theories, both earlier and contemporary, of the same matter in *The Modern Study of the Mishnah.* Leiden, 1973: Brill, and *The Formation of the Babylonian Talmud. Studies on the Achievements of Late Nineteenth and Twentieth Century Historical and Literary-Critical Research.* Leiden, 1970: Brill. In addition, my discussion of the literary-historical and exegetical theories of David W. Halivni, in addition to the treatment of his work in those two volumes, is presented in *Sources and Traditions.* Note also the section edited by me concerning Halivni's ideas in comparison to those of Shamma Friedman in *Law as Literature,* Chico, 1983: Scholars Press. = *Semeia. An Experimental Journal for Biblical Criticism* Volume 27.

that of Mishnah-exegesis. I omit reference to those items that are mere compilations of sayings in the name of an authority who figures in a Mishnah-comment. The remainder are as follows:[7]

I.B: A Theology of Gentile Idolatry: Its Origins and its Implications for Holy Israel: Why the gentiles rejected the Torah. It was offered to each of them, but they were too much absorbed by their own matters to accept God's will. They did not even carry out the seven commandments of the children of Noah.

I.C: The Critical Importance of Torah-Study for the Salvation of Israel, Individually and Collectively: Why are human beings compared to fish of the sea? To tell you, just as fish in the sea, when they come up on dry land, forthwith begin to die, so with human beings, when they take their leave of teachings of the Torah and religious deeds, forthwith they begin to die.

I.D: God Favors Holy Israel over the Gentiles, Because the Former Accept, Study, and Carry Out the Torah and the Latter Do Not. Therefore at the End of Days God Will Save Israel and Destroy Idolatry: R. Hinena bar Pappa contrasted verses of Scripture: "It is written, 'As to the almighty, we do not find him exercising plenteous power' (Job 37:23), but by contrast, 'Great is our Lord and of abundant power' (Ps. 147:5), and further, 'Your right hand, Lord, is glorious in power' (Ex. 15:6). But there is no contradiction between the first and second and third statements, for the former speaks of the time of judgment when justice is tempered with mercy, so God does not do what he could and the latter two statements refer to a time of war of God against his enemies."

I.E: God's Judgment and Wrath, God's Mercy and Forgiveness for Israel: "It is written, 'You only have I known among all the families of the earth; therefore I will visit upon you all your iniquities' (Amos 3:2). If one is angry, does he vent it on someone he loves?" He said to them, "I shall tell you a parable. To what is the matter comparable? To the case of a man who lent money to two people, one a friend, the other an enemy. From the friend he collects the money little by little, from the enemy he collects all at once."

---

[7] I preserve the enumeration-system that I have created for the Bavli and sustained both in my *Academic Commentary* and in my *Complete Outline*.

I.F: BALAAM, THE PROPHET OF THE GENTILES, AND ISRAEL; GOD'S ANGER WITH THE
           GENTILES BUT NOT WITH ISRAEL: The prophet of the gentiles was a fool, but
           he did have the power to curse; Israel was saved by God. Said R. Eleazar,
           "Said the Holy One, blessed be He, to Israel, 'My people, see how many
           acts of righteousness I carried out with you, for I did not grow angry with
           you during all those perilous days, for if I had grown angry with you,
           there would not have remained from Israel a remnant or a survivor.'"

I.G: THE TIME OF GOD'S ANGER IN RELATIONSHIP TO THE GENTILES AND TO ISRAEL;
           THE ROLE OF IDOLATRY IN GOD'S WRATH AGAINST THE NATIONS: That time at
           which God gets angry comes when the kings put on their crowns on their
           heads and prostrate themselves to the sun. Forthwith the Holy One, blessed
           be He, grows angry.

I.H: THE SINFUL ANCESTOR OF THE MESSIAH AND GOD'S FORGIVENESS OF HIM AND
           OF ISRAEL: God's forgiveness of David is the archetype of God's forgive-
           ness of Israel. If an individual has sinned, they say to him, 'Go to the
           individual such as David, and follow his example, and if the community
           as a whole has sinned, they say to them, 'Go to the community such as
           Israel. TORAH-STUDY IS THE ANTIDOTE TO SIN: "What is the meaning of the
           verse of Scripture, 'Happy are you who sow beside all waters, that send
           forth the feet of the ox and the ass' (Isa. 32:20)? 'Happy are you, O
           Israel, when you are devoted to the Torah and to doing deeds of grace,
           then their inclination to do evil is handed over to them, and they are not
           handed over into the power of their inclination to do evil."

III.C: THE DIVISIONS OF ISRAEL'S HISTORY; THE HISTORY OF THE WORLD IN ITS PERI-
           ODS: here we deal with the history of Israel by its periods, with special
           attention to Israel's relationships with Rome, on the one side, and the
           point at which the Messiah will come, on the other, ca. 468: When four
           hundred years have passed from the destruction of the Temple, if some-
           one says to you, 'Buy this field that is worth a thousand denars for a
           single denar, don't buy it.

III.E: COLLECTION OF STORIES ABOUT RABBI AND ANTIGONUS: Rabbi maintained
           cordial relationships with the Emperor, in which Rabbi gave the sage
           advice, and the emperor took it.

VIII.C: THE TRIAL OF ELIEZER B. HYRCANUS. IN THE MATTER OF MINUT: Reference
           to the idolators' judges' tribunal, scaffold, and stadium, calls to mind the
           trial of the sage by reason of the charge of Minut, or, in context, Chris-
           tianity. It is no different in its workings from the state: "the two daugh-
           ters who cry out from Gehenna, saying to this world, 'Bring, bring.' And
           who are they? They are Minut and the government."

VIII.D: IDOLATRY AND LEWDNESS: the antidote is Torah-study.

VIII.E: ROMAN JUSTICE, JEWISH MARTYRDOM: Hanina, my brother, don't you know
           that from Heaven have they endowed this nation Rome with dominion?

> For Rome has destroyed his house, burned his Temple, slain his pious ones, and annihilated his very best — and yet endures! And yet I have heard about you that you go into session and devote yourself to the Torah and even call assemblies in public, with a scroll lying before you in your bosom.

VIII.F: THE STADIUM, THE CIRCUS, THE THEATER: He who goes to a stadium or to a camp to see the performances of sorcerers and enchanters or of various kinds of clowns, mimics, buffoons, and the like — lo, this is a seat of the scoffers, as it is said, "Happy is the man who has not walked in the counsel of the wicked...nor sat in the seat of the scoffers. But his delight is in the Torah of the Lord" (Ps. 1:12). Lo, you thereby learn that these things cause a man to neglect the study of the Torah.

VIII.G: HAPPY IS THE MAN WHO HAS NOT WALKED IN THE COUNSEL OF THE WICKED, NOR STOOD IN THE WAY OF SINNERS, NOR SAT IN THE SEAT OF THE SCORNFUL. "'Happy is the man who has not walked' — to theaters and circuses of gentiles; 'nor stood in the way of sinners' — he does not attend contests of wild beasts..."

IX.B: COMPOSITE ON THE PROHIBITION OF STARING IN A LASCIVIOUS OR OTHERWISE IMPROPER MANNER

Can we state what the compilers of this document propose to accomplish in producing this complete, organized piece of writing? Clearly, sages have made a massive and governing transformation of the tractate. We know that is the fact because the topic, idolatry, that emerges from the Bavli is presented in a quite different way from the manner in which the Mishnah has portrayed it. And the shift takes place in the extraneous composites. In this tractate, strikingly, the real re-presentation of the topic takes place in the opening pages, as though the framers wished to make certain we would address the subject of idolatry in the proper context. Specifically, the large and fundamental composites that accomplish other than the exegesis of the Mishnah, many of them standing at the very head of the tractate, place the subject, idolatry, into an entirely new framework, a historical one. Everything is recast in light of our sages' perception of matters, their definition of the context in which we are to discuss this particular subject. Consequently, I doubt that any other tractate has been so thoroughly or profoundly recast into the image, after the likeness, of sages' Judaic system than this one. These strong judgments require ample demonstration, which I shall now provide.

A full grasp of what our sages have accomplished in this Talmud-tractate requires that we compare the foregoing outline with the outline of the topic as it is set forth in the Mishnah-tractate. The first point to note is that the Mishnah-tractate restates the Written Torah's theology of idolatry and imparts to it a practical and concrete character. We have therefore to examine the three principal stages in the unfolding of the Torah's teachings on idolatry, the Written one, the oral one, and the authoritative re-presentation of the oral one, for Scripture, the Mishnah, and the Talmud, respectively. First comes the relationship of the Mishnah to Scripture.

A. SCRIPTURE

The tractate devoted to idolatry illustrates that relationship between the Oral Torah embodied in the Mishnah and Scripture in which Mishnah makes concrete and everyday the general conceptions of Scripture. Specifically, what our tractate does is to supply rules and regulations to carry out the fundamental Scriptural commandments about the destruction of idols and all things having to do with idolatry. It follows that while our tractate deals with facts and relies upon suppositions which Scripture has not supplied, its basic viewpoint and the problem it seeks to solve in fact derive from the Mosaic code. Before proceeding, we had best review those general statements which Scripture does make:

> *Ex. 23:13:* Take heed to all that I have said to you; and make no mention of the names of other gods, nor let such be heard out of your mouth."
>
> *Ex. 23:24*: "When my angel goes before you, and brings you in to the Amorites, and the Hittites, and the Perizzites, and the Canaanites, the Hivites, and the Jebusites, and I blot them out, you shall not bow down into their gods, nor serve them, nor do according to their work, but you shall utterly overthrow them and break their pillars in pieces."
>
> *Ex. 23:32-33*: "You shall make no covenant with them or with their gods. They shall not dwell in your land, lest they make you sin against me; for if you serve their gods, it will surely be a snare to you."
>
> *Ex. 34:12-16*: The Lord said to Moses, "Come up to me on the mountain, and wait there; and I will give you the tables of stone, with the law and the commandment, which I have written for their instruction." So Moses rose with his servant Joshua, and Moses went up into the mountain of God. And he said to the elders, "Tarry here for us, until we come to you again; and, behold Aaron and Hur are with you; whoever has a cause, let him go to them."
>
> Then Moses went up on the mountain, and the cloud covered the mountain. The glory of the Lord settled on Mount Sinai, and the cloud covered it six days; and on the seventh day he called to Moses out of the midst of the cloud.
>
> *Deut. 7:1-5*: "When the Lord your God brings you into the land which you are entering to take possession of it, and clears away many nations before you, the Hittites, the Girgashites, the Amorites, the Canaanites, the Perizzites, the Hivites, and the Jebusites, seven nations greater and mightier than yourselves, and when the Lord

your God gives them over to you, and you defeat them; then you must utterly destroy them; show no mercy to them. You shall not make marriages with them, giving your daughters to their sons or taking their daughters for your sons. For they would turn away your sons from following me, to serve other gods; then the anger of the Lord would be kindled against you, and he would destroy you quickly. But thus shall you deal with them: you shall break down their altars, and dash in pieces their pillars, and hew down their Asherim, and burn their graven images with fire."

Deut. 7:25-26: "The graven images of their gods you shall burn with fire; you shall not covet the silver or the gold that is on them, or take it for yourselves, lest you be ensnared by it; for it is an abomination to the Lord your God. And you shall not bring an abominable thing into your house, and become accursed like it; you shall utterly detest and abhor it; for it is an accursed thing."

Deut. 12:2-3: "You shall surely destroy all the places where the nations whom you shall dispossess served their gods, upon the high mountains and upon the hills and under every green tree; you shall tear down their altars, and dash in pieces their pillars, and burn their Asherim with fire; you shall hew down the graven images of their gods, and destroy their name out of that place."

B. FROM SCRIPTURE TO THE MISHNAH

The tractate which proposes to realize these commandments in ordinary life is in three parts, moving form the general to the specific. It turns, first, to commercial relationships, second, to matters pertaining to idols, and, finally, to the very urgent issue of the prohibition of wine, part of which has served as a libation to an idol. There are a number of unstated principles before us. What a gentile is not likely to use for the worship of an idol is not going to be prohibited. What may serve not as part of idolatry but as an appurtenance thereto is prohibited for Israelite use but permitted for Israelite commerce. What serves for idolatry is prohibited for use and for benefit. Certain further assumptions about gentiles, not pertinent specifically to idolatry, are expressed. Gentiles are assumed routinely to practice bestiality, bloodshed, and fornication, without limit or restriction. This negative image of the gentile finds expression in the laws before us. The outline of the tractate follows.

I. Commercial relationships with gentiles. 1:1-2:7
    A. Festivals and fairs. 1:1-4
        1:1   For three days before gentile festivals it is forbidden to do business with them.
        1:2   Ishmael: Three days afterward also.

1:3   These are the festivals of gentiles.

1:4   A city in which there is an idol – in the area outside of it, it is permitted to do business.

B.   Objects prohibited even in commerce. 1:5-2:2

1:5   These are things which it is forbidden to sell to gentiles.

1:6   In a place in which they are accustomed to sell small cattle to gentiles, they sell them (the consideration being use of the beasts for sacrifices to idols).

1:7   They do not sell them bears, lions, or anything which is a public danger. They do not help build with them a basilica, scaffold, stadium, or judges' tribunal.

1:8-9 They do not make ornaments for an idol, sell them produce which is not yet harvested, sell them land in the Holy Land.

2:1   They do not leave cattle in gentiles' inns, because they are suspect in regard to bestiality.

2:2   They accept healing for property (e.g., animals) but not for a person.

C.   Objects prohibited for use but permitted in trade. 2:3-7

2:3   These things belonging to gentiles are prohibited, and the prohibition concerning them extends to deriving any benefit from them at all: wine, vinegar, earthenware which absorbs wine, and hides pierced at the heart.

2:4   Skins of gentiles and their jars, with Israelite wine collected in them – they are prohibited, the prohibition extends to deriving benefit, so Meir. Sages: Not to deriving benefit.

2:5   On what account did they prohibit cheese made by gentiles?

2:6-7 These are things of gentiles which are prohibited, but the prohibition does not extend to deriving benefit from them. Milk, bread, oil, etc.

2:7   These are things which to begin with are permitted for Israelite consumption.

II.   Idols. 3:1-4:7

A.   General Principles. 3:1-7

3:1   All images are prohibited, because they are worshipped once a year, so Meir, Sages: Prohibited is only one which has an emblem of authority.

3:2-3 He who finds the shreds of images – lo, these are permitted.

5:3-4   A gentile who with an Israelite was moving jars of wine from place to place – if the wine is assumed to be watched, it is permitted. If the Israelite told the gentile he was going away for any length of time, the wine is prohibited.

5:5   The same point, now in the context of eating at the same table.

5:6   A band of gentile raiders which entered a town peacefully – open jars are forbidden, closed ones permitted.

5:7   Israelite craftsmen, to whom a gentile sent a jar of libation-wine as salary, may ask him to pay in money instead, only if this is before the wine has entered their possession. Afterward it is forbidden.

5:8-9   Libation-wine is forbidden and imparts a prohibition on wine with which it is mixed in any measure at all. If it is wine poured into water, it is forbidden only if it imparts a flavor.

5:10   Libation-wine which fell into a vat – the whole of the vat is forbidden for benefit. Simeon b. Gamaliel: All of it may be sold except the value of the volume of libation-wine which is in it.

5:11-12   A stone winepress which a gentile covered with pitch – one dries it off, and it is clean. One of wood, one of earthenware.

The opening unit unfolds in a fairly orderly way, from a prologue on the special problems of fairs, to the general matter of things Israelites may not even buy or sell, as against things they may not use but may trade, I.B, C. The second unit lays down some general principles about images, then presents special ones on two specific kinds of idols, II.B, C, and at the end asks the logical necessary question about how one nullifies an idol entirely. The third unit is a very long essay about libation-wine and its effect upon Israelite-gentile commerce. I do not see any coherent subdivisions of this sizable discussion, which goes over the same ground time and again.

C. From the Mishnah to the Talmud

From its initial insertion of a massive account of gentile idolatry, the Talmud reframes issues. The Mishnah asks not a single question of history or theology. It deals only with 1 commercial relationships with gentiles, so far as these are affected by idolatry, 2 idols, and 3 libation wine. So the topic at hand is treated in a routine and commonplace manner. The Talmud transforms and transcends the topic. It transforms it by re-framing the issue of idolatry so that at stake is no longer relationships between Israel and idolatrous nations but rather, those between idolatrous nations and God. It then transcends the topic by introducing the antidote to idolatry, which is the Torah. So Israel differs from idolatrous nations by reason of the Torah, and that imparts a special character to all of Israel's everyday conduct, not only its abstinence from idol-worship. In fact, the Talmud makes this tractate into an occasion for reflection on the problem of Israel and the nations.

Predictably, our sages of blessed memory invoke the one matter that they deem critical to all else: the Torah. Israel differs from the gentiles not for the merely negative reason that it does not worship idols but only an invisible God. It differs from them for the positive reason that the Torah that defines Israel's life was explicitly rejected by the gentiles. Every one of them had its chance at the Torah, and all of them rejected it. When the gentiles try to justify themselves to God by appealing to their forthcoming relationships to Israel, that is dismissed as self-serving. The gentiles could not even observe the seven commandments assigned to the Noahides. From that point, the composite that stands at the head of the tractate and imparts its sense to all that will follow proceeds to the next question, that is, from the downfall of the gentiles by reason of their idolatry and rejection of the Torah to the salvation of Israel through the Torah.

Lest we miss the point, the reason for God's favor is made explicit: God favors Israel because Israel keeps the Torah. God therefore is strict with the gentiles but merciful to Israel. This is forthwith assigned a specific illustration: Balaam, the gentiles' prophet, presents the occasion to underscore God's anger toward the gentiles and his mercy to Israel. Bringing us back to the beginning, we then are shown how God's anger for the gentiles comes to the fore when the gentiles worship idols: when the kings who rule the world worship nature rather than nature's Creator. How God forgives Israel is then shown in respect to David's sin, and Torah-study as the antidote to sin once more is introduced. It is difficult to conclude other than that the framers of the Talmud have added to the presentation of the topic the results of profound thought on idolatry as a force in the history of humanity and of Israel. They thus have re-presented the Mishnah's topic in a far more profound framework of reflection than the Mishnah, with its rather petty interests in details of this and that, would have lead us to anticipate.

The next set of free-standing composites present episodic portraits of the matters introduced at the outset. The first involves world history and its periods, divided, it goes without saying, in relationship to the history of Israel, which stands at the center of world history. Rome defines the counterpart, and Israel's and Rome's relationships, culminating in the coming of the Messiah, are introduced. The next two collections form a point and counterpoint. On the one side, we have the tale of how Rabbi and the Roman Emperor formed a close relationship, with Rabbi the wise counsellor, the ruler behind the throne. So whatever good happens in Rome happens by reason of our sages' wisdom, deriving as it does from the Torah, on which the stories predictably are going to harp. Then comes as explicit a judgment upon Christianity in the framework of world-history as I think we are likely to find in the Talmud. The set of stories involves Eliezer b. Hyrcanus and how he was tried for Minut, which the story leaves no doubt stands for Christianity. Now "Minut" and the Roman government are treated as twin-sources of condemnation. And it is in that very context that the stories of Roman justice and Jewish martyrdom, by reason of Torah-study, are introduced. Not only so, but — should we miss the contrast the compilers wish to draw — the very same setting sets forth the counterpart and opposite: the stadium, circus, and theater, place for scoffers and buffoons, as against the sages' study-center, where people avoid the seat of the scornful but instead study the Torah.

D. THE THEOLOGY OF HISTORY SET FORTH BY THE TORAH, WRITTEN, THEN ORAL

The Talmud's associations with idolatry then compare and contrast these opposites: Israel and Rome; martyrdom and wantonness; Torah and lewdness and other forms of sin; probity and dignity and buffoonery; and on and on. The Mishnah finds no reason to introduce into the consideration of idolatry either the matter of the Torah or the issue of world history. The Talmud for its part cannot deal with the details of conduct with gentiles without asking the profound questions of divine intentionality and human culpability that idolatry in the world provokes. And yet, if we revert to the Mishnah's fabricated debates with the philosophers, we see the issue introduced and explored. What the Mishnah lacks is not a philosophy of monotheism in contrast with polytheism and its idols, but a theology of history and a theodicy of Israel's destiny, a salvific theory. These the Talmud of Babylonia introduces, with enormous effect.[8] And, we note, once these propositions have been inserted, the Talmud allows the systematic exposition of the Mishnah to go forward without theological intrusion of any kind. The point has been made.

Now, we wonder, where have our sages learned to interpret the issue of idolatry in a historical and theological framework, rather than in a merely practical and reasonable one, such as the Mishnah's authorship provides? A glance at the verses of Scripture given earlier answers the question. Idolatry explains the fate of the nations, Israel's covenant through the Torah, Israel's. But the verses of Scripture cited earlier hardly serve as source for the reflections on Israel and Rome, the ages of human history, the power of God to forgive, and, above all, the glory of the Torah as the mediating source of God's love and forgiveness. All of this our sages of blessed memory themselves formulated and contributed. Scripture provided important data, the Mishnah, the occasion, but for the theology of history formed around the center of the Torah, we look to our sages for the occasion and the source. And sages' success in meeting the challenge of the topic at hand explains why no tractate more successfully demonstrates how the Talmud's framers' massive

---

[8] In *Transformation of Judaism,* Chapter Nine, I introduce the question of theology of history in the comparison of the Talmud of the Land of Israel's formulation of matters and that of Augustine in City of God.

insertions transform the Mishnah's statement into one of considerably enhanced dimensions and depth. None more admirably matched their capacities of deep reflection on the inner structure of Israel's history with the promise and potential of a subject of absolutely primary urgency. My earlier remarks, in Chapter Two, on the Torah, Oral and Written, do not here require repetition. One criterion that governs is, can we explain how the Oral Torah has not only responded to, but completed, the theological exposition set forth in the Written Torah? Here is an example of what is to be done.

IV. THE TRANSFORMATION OF THE DAY OF ATONEMENT BY BAVLI-TRACTATE YOMA: FROM THE CULTIC PURIFICATION OF THE PRIEST TO THE MORAL PURIFICATION OF HOLY ISRAEL

In a more abbreviated presentation, we once more ask, How do the topical composites fit into the Talmud-tractate Yoma and what do they contribute that the Mishnah-tractate of the same name would lack without them? The tractate is formidable in size, and it carries with it a large and important component of free-standing composites, some of which intersect with the Mishnah in topic, others of which bear upon the theme of the tractate but make no contribution to the amplification of anything that the Mishnah-tractate has to say about that theme. We know that the compilers undertake an initiative of weight when we find jarring juxtapositions. We may suppose that the compilers mean only to provide information, not an occasion for reflection through startling points of intersection, when a topic introduced in the Mishnah in a tangential way is given an exposition lacking all argument or coherent point. The difference then is the mixing of things ordinarily kept distinct as against the provision of information on a subject. This becomes clear in the exposition that follows.

I.A: The framers begin with a remarkable conception, which is to compare the rite of the Day of Atonement with another rite, so placing Leviticus Sixteen into relationship with other systematic Pentateuchal expositions of the most distinguish offerings of the cultic calendar. In selecting another rite for comparison, what guided them? I see three distinct considerations. First is the formal one, which is articulated: rites that demand that the high priest prepare for a week in advance. But there are more than formal considerations. For, second, the compilers surely reflected on critical cultic occasions that brought the cult outside the walls of the Temple. Since a major step in the order of service here is to send forth the scapegoat, it is quite natural to take up a comparable occasion on which a sacrifice is made outside of the Temple. For that purpose, the rite of burning the red cow to produce ashes for purification water, in line with the rite described at Numbers Chapter Nineteen, comes to mind; that offering is not in the Temple but on Mount of Olives. What draws these two offerings into alignment is a third quality. The scapegoat carries with it the sins of the people; the purification-water bears the classification of *hat'at,* translated both purification- and sin. In the present context, therefore, by raising the question of how rites compare, two rites of atonement, one for uncleanness, the other for sin, are drawn into alignment for purposes of comparison and contrast. But having moved beyond the limits of the Talmud's presentation, I note at the end the formal consideration obviously governs, even though the substantive effect — introducing the notion of rites that take up conduct outside of the cult — is to direct attention from the inner to the outer dimensions of the Day. This initiative at the formal level finds its counterpart in substantive ways, as we shall see, when the Talmud insists in its re-presentation of the topic of the Day of Atonement upon asking about considerations external to the Temple and its cult but critical to the life of Israel and its sanctification and salvation.

I.B: The initiative at the opening composite is carried forward on a still larger scale at I.B: what makes the requirement of the Day of Atonement unique, and how we relate the rules governing that day with those governing another comparable occasion, the consecration of the Tent of Meeting. The upshot is that in the majestic opening reading, the Mishnah's simple, factual account is left behind, as the topic, the rite of the Day of Atonement, is addressed in its own, much larger setting of comparable rites, first, the burning of the red cow, second, the consecration of the tent of meeting. Only at I.C, D, do we come back to the high priesthood.

I.E: As if I.A, B, did not suffice to draw attention from the Mishnah's facts to the context, I.E really revises the entire matter, and the composite does so in a dramatic way. Now the entire face of the presentation by the Mishnah changes. From purification of sin and uncleanness, on the one side, and the formation of the tabernacle/Temple, on the other, we proceed to what is always the critical issue in the Rabbinic system, the destruction of the Temple. This is now set forth as the result of the corruption of the priesthood, particularly the high priesthood. So the Day of Atonement calls to mind [1] sin, [2] the Temple and its cult, and [3] the power of sin to destroy the Temple and its cult. The treatment of the third theme seems to me miscellaneous, and the upshot is, what we have is the theme alone, not an exposition that makes some stunning point in the way that I.A, and B do. The upshot, however, is the same, and that is, the definition of an entirely fresh context in which the theme of the Mishnah-tractate, the Day of Atonement, is going to be expounded. Indeed, once we have worked our way through I.A and B, we can scarcely see as definitive for the topic the Mishnah-tractate's identification of its program of exposition — Leviticus Chapter Sixteen, point by point. What the Mishnah-tractate's authors found important about the Day of Atonement the Bavli-tractate's compilers chose to treat as subsidiary and incidental to the points they wished to register at the very beginning of their tractate.

I.G: Why should the topic of the councillors' chamber, I.F, should call to mind the requirement of putting a mezuzah on the doorposts of all Israelites' houses — gates of houses, courts, provinces, cities? The juxtaposition of subjects is jarring. But if we remember where we started — finding contexts in which to interpret the order of service of the Day of Atonement — the answer presents itself quite readily. We begin by moving from the Temple outward: rites comparable in that preparation outside of the cult (the high priest's separation) and beyond the limits of the Temple (the scapegoat, the red cow). We proceeded to a clear statement that the reason the Temple was destroyed was the sins of the priesthood and of Israel. Now we treat as comparable the sanctity of the dwellings of all Israel and the sanctity of the Temple and its chambers. The mezuzah marks off Israel's dwellings as holy, a counterpart to the Temple's very walls and hangings. The presentation, by contrast with the topic, proves once more miscellaneous; I see no point at which anything is said, beyond the introduction of the topic itself, that bears meaning, let alone a clear and relevant proposition.

VII.D: Saul is introduced because he violated the prohibition of taking a census; but then he provides the occasion to underscore the power of sin, however small, to yield weighty consequences. Still, it seems to me this topical appendix does not vastly change the face of the setting in which it is presented.

VIII.A: The exposition of the general procedure of the lottery simply spells out details of the Mishnah's topic.

XII.G: The secondary amplification of facts and rules relevant to the Mishnah's topic seems to me inert.

XIV.B: The wonderful composite at XIV.B really clarifies the presentation of the Mishnah's topic; it does not introduce an unanticipated topic, let alone a problem out of alignment with the Mishnah's, but only works in its own way through the very information that the Mishnah has already given. The improvement upon the Mishnah's presentation nonetheless is particularly talmudic: a more systematic and orderly account of what has already been laid out in a systematic manner.

XIV.D: The richly glossed account of the proper order of the daily priestly rites — by contrast to that of the Day of Atonement — enriches in a factual way the Mishnah's own presentation. I do not discern a single point at which a not-to-be-predicted subject makes an appearance.

XV.E: Now we come to a small but important insertion. We have been told that priests could spend their own money on enhancing the rites. Now we are told, in a huge composition of obvious artistic merit, how riches and poverty and good looks are fundamentally irrelevant to Torah-study. Whether one is rich or poor, handsome or ugly, all are obligated to Torah-study.

This composition forms a subtle but powerful comment on the topic of the Mishnah-composite before us, the kind of editorial insertion that changes the face of the whole.

XVIII.F: Once more, we have a startling juxtaposition, one that the Mishnah-composite accommodates but hardly requires. That is, the exposition of the Mishnah-composition is complete in its own terms. Then we have a massive composite on the righteous and the wicked in general. But while in the Mishnah, attention focuses upon those who contributed to the cult or refused to do so, here we deal with issues of personal morality, on the one side, and the power of the righteous to save the world, on the other. The conduct in the cult now recedes into the background, and conduct in the social order of holy Israel comes to the fore. The comment made by placing this remarkable composite here is then unmistakable. Virtue in everyday affairs forms the primary consideration, and Israelites who wish to do what is right take priority over those whose virtue involves only cultic activities. Since the Mishnah has cited Prov. 10:7 in the setting of those who were remembered favorably or unfavorably for their activities in the Temple, while the Talmud wishes to read the same verse in the setting of Israel's everyday life, the intent is obvious. Here is a fine example of how the Talmud's compositors make their statement through the juxtaposition of distinct composites, and the comparison and contrast of those composites' themes or even propositions, respectively.

XIX.C: I see this entry as topical; nothing is jarring here, since we have dealt with the outcome of the lottery, and the composite on Simeon begins with that subject. The composite has been assembled for its own purpose, which is to present Simeon the Righteous, but fits in quite well as a supplement to the Mishnah's rule, nothing more.

XIX.E: The question of whether the rite under discussion is essential or merely recommended in no way changes the Mishnah's presentation of the subject.

XX.B: Here we find a reprise of the opening exercise in comparison of the rite of the Day of Atonement, the rite of burning the Red Cow, and other, cognate rituals, now the purification rite involving thread. The composite is a very sizable one, but I am unable to identify in it any proposition, or even a theme, that leads us to take up a position outside of the framework of the factual repertoire of the Mishnah. Here is a lost occasion for theological reflection, sharpening by contrast the quite remarkable character of the juxtapositions that make their own, fresh statement.

XXXV.B: The topic of the Mishnah — the high priest's garments — accounts for the inclusion of this composite.

XXXV.C: The same goes for this composite. But the next items change the picture.

XXXV.D: We move from rules on the disposition of the sacred objects to moral lessons to be drawn from verses that deal with the utensils and furniture of the Temple. The moral lessons are commonplaces; what is interesting is only that at this point a set of sayings is introduced to impart to the Mishnah's topic a set of meanings that the Mishnah does not require.

XXXV.E: Here we find the jarring juxtaposition that bears the Talmud's statement upon the Mishnah's topic or proposition, not only the Talmud's re-statement thereof. We move from moral lessons deriving from Scripture's account of the Temple's appurtenances to Torah-study sayings pertinent to those same matters. The moral sayings now are recast as lessons for disciples of sages, and the important lesson is that the sage's disciple must be sincere in his convictions and conduct, his inside corresponding to his outside.

XXXV.G: Here we have a topical composite to supplement the Mishnah's exposition.

XXXVI.B: Now we come to Talmud's most remarkable theological statement. We begin with a preparatory composite on the affliction of souls through fasting. This is important because it introduces the theme of hunger as affliction. And that raises to the surface a question that invites the stunning juxtaposition of the next entry.

XXXVI.C: A verse invites our interest in manna, which is, "Who fed you in the wilderness with manna...that he might afflict you" (Dt. 8:16). So we turn to a huge and coherent exposition of manna as a form of affliction, on the one side, but grace, on the other. What happens when the subject of manna is introduced? The issue of fasting for Heaven is given its counterpart: Heaven feeding Israel. So the topic, fasting on the Day of Atonement, is given a new dimension of meaning, we give to Heaven, but Heaven has fed us, and feeds us, so the transaction is reciprocal. When humanity fasts and shows its humility and contrition, Heaven responds with the realization of grace that is provided through supernatural food. Fasting, a deed in the natural world, evokes in Heaven a supernatural response. Now the activities of the Day of Atonement are set into a fresh context and recast in cosmic dimensions. The cultic program for the Day recedes in consequence; the activities of the private person take over. God's interest and response address what all Israel does. Nothing in the Mishnah's presentation of the holy day, it goes without saying, has prepared us for such an amazing interjection of a theme that is at once unanticipated and alien, and, once introduced, also quite natural.

XXXVI.H: What we have here is a repertoire of relevant facts.

XXXVI.I: The same is so here. The face of the Mishnah is unaffected.

XL.C: This brief appendix treats the topic of the Mishnah.

XLI.D: The composite on repentance carries forward the Mishnah's theme; I see
          here nothing that will have surprised the Mishnah's own framers in con-
          text. Nor do I find any proposition that vastly revises the standard picture
          of the subject. We therefore see how critical to the making of the Talmud's
          own statement is the intrusion of the unanticipated topic — that princi-
          pally, possible even, that alone.

XLI.H: This composite stands out of all relationship to the Mishnah-paragraph
          that stands at the head of its Talmud-unit. It is rare in the Talmud to come
          across a discussion so out of phase with the Mishnah-context as the present
          item. The real question is, why has the compositor of XVI.D not in-
          cluded the composite in his presentation of the high priest's confession.
          If I were making the Talmud over, that is the point to which I would move
          XLI.H. As it is, it is not only out of place but also fails to make the point
          that, in the right position, it can have made. It suffices to observe that, in
          the dozen and a half tractates to date, I have found no other composite
          that both stands out of relationship to its larger context, whether Mishnaic
          or Talmudic, and also fails to make the contribution that it ought to have
          made in its proper context, in the way that this one does. That exception
          to the rule of brilliant composition forms a mark of the Talmud's com-
          positors' amazing intellectual rigor.

        Can we state what the compilers of this document propose to accomplish
in producing this complete, organized piece of writing? To understand what our
compilers have accomplished, as in the case of tractate Abodah Zarah in the Mishnah
and the Talmud of Babylonia, we have to call to mind the fundamental program of
the Mishnah-tractate. Even a simple glance at the Mishnah-tractate suffices to
show that all chapters but the final one are devoted to an exposition of the Temple
rite on the Day of Atonement. Only the last chapter of the Mishnah-tractate
addresses the situation of the individual Israelite, not in the Temple cult, and how
he observes the occasion. The Mishnah-tractate therefore closely follows the
presentation of the Day of Atonement at Leviticus Chapter Sixteen, which carefully
catalogues the activities of the high priest on the holy day, but in a sentence or two
suffices to tell ordinary folk how they are to conduct themselves. The challenge
facing the Talmud-tractate framers, therefore, is to place the facts of the Mishnah's
first seven chapters into a framework that accords proportion and balance to the re-
presentation of the Mishnah-tractate. That is to say, along with the exposition of
the facts of Leviticus Chapter Sixteen as the Mishnah lays them out and
complements them, the meaning of the Day of Atonement in the holy life of Israel
the people has to be set forth.

        Now, when the compilers of the Bavli address the Mishnah, they define
for themselves three tasks. First and paramount, they identify what they deemed
to be the Mishnah's problematic, that is, what the Mishnah states that they deem to

require amplification. So they clarify the Mishnah's words and phrases; they find Scriptural bases for the Mishnah's rules; they ask about the authority behind an anonymous ruling and make an effort to show that rulings belonging to a given authority may be accepted even by those who oppose his position on a parallel matter. Second, they add some sizable complexes of materials that address a topic of the Mishnah, rather than the problematic thereof, and as we now have seen, they organize sizable compositions into composites that supplement the Mishnah's inclusion of a topic with more information about that topic. These composites so far as I can see lack any proposition and accomplish little more than the recapitulation of marginally interesting facts. They fill space, they do not impart structure or add sense. And, third, as we now have seen, the Bavli's framers make us see the Mishnah's topic in a very different way from the way that we would understand that topic absent their work. This they do at critical points in the tractate.

Let us quickly review the main points that we derive from the massive composites that stand wholly outside of the exposition of our Mishnah-tractate and even of our Mishnah-tractate's topic:

1.   the rites of the Day of Atonement fall into the larger framework of Israel's rites of purification and atonement for sin; these take place outside of the cult, as much as inside the Temple; they require of the high priest a higher level of sanctification through purification than the Temple's internal cult requires

2.   the rite of sanctification of the tent of meeting — also in the world beyond the Temple walls — is comparable to the rite of the Day of Atonement

3.   the world intruded on the Temple by reason of Israel's (unatoned-for) sin, which brought about the destruction of the Temple and the cessation of its cult — all the more reason to atone for sin on the Day of Atonement

4.   the Temple's points of domestic sanctity, its special chambers, are comparable in their holiness to Israel's points of sanctity, its homes, towns, and cities, all of which are encompassed in the signs of sanctification that apply both in the holy place and also in the homes and towns of holy Israel

5.   the Temple requires high priests who can invest their own funds in its rites; the study of Torah is obligatory on all Israel equally, without regard to wealth or poverty, beauty or ugliness

6.   Righteous people in this world strengthen their capacity to do what is right; they can avoid the influence of wicked neighbors; even on account of a single righteous man is the world created; a righteous man does not take his leave from the world before another righteous man like him is created the Holy One, blessed be he, saw that the righteous are few. He went and planted some of them in every generation; even for the sake of a single righteous man the world endures; when a man has lived out the better part of his years and has not sinned, he will not likely sin again. And we are responsible for what we make of ourselves, specifically: if someone comes to make himself unclean, they open the way to him, but if he comes to purify himself, they assist him, but transgression dulls the heart of man.;

if a person makes himself a bit unclean, he is made very unclean; if someone sanctifies himself a bit, he is made abundantly sanctified.

7. The propositions prominent in the exposition of the theme of the manna treats the manna as Heaven's response to self-affliction for sin. Thus "Who fed you in the wilderness with manna...that he might afflict you" (Dt. 8:16): Just as the prophet told the Israelites what was to be found in clefts or holes, so manna would reveal to Israelites what was in the clefts and holes. Meat, for which they asked not in the right way, was given to them at the wrong time. Bread, for which they asked in the right way, was given to them at the right time. "While the meat was yet between their teeth" (Num. 11:33). And it is written, "But a whole month" (Num. 11:20) — The middling folk died on the spot, the wicked suffered pain for a whole month. When the righteous eat the quail, it is at ease, but when the wicked eat it, it is like thorns for them. "Man did eat the bread of the mighty" (Ps. 78:25) — "It is the bread that the ministering angels eat." The manna marked Israel as supernatural — and so does its fasting.

These important additions, in the form of large-scale composites, introduce into the representation of the theme of the Day of Atonement conceptions and considerations of which the Mishnah scarcely takes cognizance. While the conception of Heaven's response to afflicting oneself by fasting is providing manna in the wilderness — the bread that the angels eat! — strikes me as the single most remarkable initiative, the other propositions before us prove equally striking.

Seen as a group, they yield the following proposition: the Day of Atonement, which the Torah lays out as principally a Temple occasion, overspreads the world. That is not a merely-moral statement but one of cultic consequence, since we see the rite itself as one affecting the world beyond the Temple walls in the way in which the one analogous in its careful concern for the high priest's purification, the burning of the red cow, does. Israel's sin in the world intrudes into the cult, because the Temple, the mark of divine favor, was lost on account of Israel's sin. But Israel's virtue, the virtue of self-affliction through fasting, can win Heaven's cordial response, analogous to the provision of manna in the wilderness. That is because Israel's ordinary life compares with the Temple's sanctification; even as the Temple space is sanctified, so Israel's space is marked off by signs of the holy. Just as the Temple's priests display their riches in the ample cult, so Israel's sages display their resources of virtue and intellect in the service of the mind and heart, study of the Torah. And, it must follow, the righteousness represented by a life fearful of sin and rich in repentance, which comes to its climax on the Day of Atonement, infuses the entire people of Israel, not only the priesthood in the Temple on that same holy day.

The upshot is, the Mishnah's presentation of the Day of Atonement and its recapitulation of the themes of Leviticus Chapter Sixteen in the proportions of Scripture's treatment of that topic are both replicated and revised. What for Leviticus and Mishnah-tractate Yoma forms a cultic occasion, in which Israel participates as bystanders, emerges in Bavli-tractate Yoma as an event in the life of holy Israel, in which all Israel bears tasks of the weight and consequence that, on that holy day, the High Priest uniquely carries out. On the Day of Atonement, holy Israel joins the high priest in the Holy of Holies; this they do on that day by afflicting themselves through fasting and other forms of abstinence, recalling how with Heaven's favor they would eat the bread of angels; this they do on the other days of the year by entering into the disciplines of the Torah; this they do through their lives of virtue. The Day of Atonement, the occasion on which the high priest conducts the rite in the privacy of the Holy of Holies, emerges transformed: the rites are private, but the event is public; the liturgy is conducted in the holy Temple, with sins sent forth through the scapegoat, but the event bears its consequences in holy Israel, where sins are atoned for in the setting of the everyday and and the here and now. What is singular and distinct — the rites of atonement on the holiest day of the year in the holiest place in the world — now makes its statement about what takes place on every day of the year in the ordinary life of holy Israel.

And that is how the Day of Atonement would make its way through time, not the sacrificial rite of the high priest in the Temple, but the atonement-celebration of all Israel in the world. What mattered to the compilers of Leviticus and the Mishnah alike was the timeless rite of atonement through the bloody rites of the Temple What captured the attention of the framers of the Bavli-tractate, by contrast, was the personal discipline of atonement through repentance on the Day of Atonement and a life of virtue and Torah-learning on the rest of the days of the year. They took out of the Holy of Holies and brought into the homes and streets of the holy people that very mysterious rite of atonement that the Day of Atonement called forth. When the compilers of our Talmud moved beyond the limits of the Mishnah-tractate, they transformed the presentation the day and its meaning, transcending its cultic limits. And it was their vision, and not the vision of Leviticus Sixteen and the Mishnah's tractate, that would prove definitive.

The irony comes to expression in the fact that, from antiquity to our own day, the Day of Atonement would enjoy the loyalty of holy Israel come what may, and everywhere, gaining the standing of Judaism's single most widely observed occasion. That fact attests to the power of the distinctive ideas set forth by the framers of the Bavli to transform a sacerdotal narrative into a medium of the inner, moral sanctification for Israel, the holy people in utopia entering into the status of the holy priest and the locus of the Temple's inner sanctum. But that re-framing of the rite defines the Bavli-tractate's compilers intent, since, after all, it turns out to form the very first point that the framers of the Bavli make when they commence their exposition of the Mishnah-tractate. The opening composite turns out to bear the entire message, just as it should, just as it does in tractate Abodah Zarah.

V. THE GLORY OF THE TORAH REPRESENTED BY THE SAGE: TRANSVALUATION OF VALUES BY BAVLI-TRACTATE MAKKOT

How do the topical composites fit into the Talmud-tractate Makkot and what do they contribute that the Mishnah-tractate of the same name would lack without them? We turn directly to each specific item.

IX.D:　　This item introduces the complication of the suitability of testimony of witnesses. It may be that the intent is to carry forward the introduction of the rules of testimony into the matter at hand, but that is not a compelling consideration.

XVI.B:　　The introduction of the matter of relationships of disciples and masters — a general point, of enormous interest — into the rules governing going into exile reshapes the topic by adding a profound observation. It is that while someone may go into exile from his home town and family, the Torah never leaves him; if his master goes into exile, he goes along; if he goes into exile, his master goes along. The point then is that exile affects the natural relationships, but not supernatural ones. In a case of manslaughter, God knows that there has been no murder and does not inflict the penalty of separation from the Torah upon the surviving party to a tragic accident. The Torah legislates for this world, allowing for a penalty to manslaughter, since, after all, the victim has died; but the Torah also distinguishes this world's penalties, which are painful but can be endured, from those of Heaven. Exile from the Torah would be a penalty that cannot be endured and may not be inflicted. So XVI.B recasts the rules at hand into a very original point.

XVI.C:　　In light of the foregoing, we cannot find surprising the explicit statement of what is implicit, which is, the Torah is the sole source of authentic, enduring wealth. This world's rewards are transient; Torah-study with a multitude of disciples forms the reward of eternity. So XVI.C forms an essential step in a carefully-wrought statement. Then the topic, exile, provides the occasion for making a statement that the framers of the Talmud wish to make, not only in its own terms, therefore abstractly, but also in terms of one topic after another, and so in a very concrete way.

XVI.F:　　Since an "elder" is a sage, the addition here makes the same point once more: a city that lacks elders, or sages, is not a suitable city of refuge. This addition is now predictable: the dimension of Torah-learning, which is supernatural, completely recasts our perception of the topic, its issues, and its messages.

XXII.D:　　The curse of a sage takes effect even when it is not justified. The passage to which this propositional composite is attached concerns the curse of the mother of the manslayer. Once more, therefore, we know why the passage has been included: it is to recast the topic in a new dimension, one in which the supernatural enters in. The mother's curse may not take effect; the sage's curse will.

XXX.C: Here we find a systematic set of reflections on Israel's history, which make a striking point. A quick review of the reflections shows us what that point is. To restate the main propositions laid out in sequence: The statement maintains that [1] the sage succeeds to prophecy, because now the sage, through master of the Torah, can convey Heaven's statement to Israel; [2] the Holy Spirit appears to Israel, but the upshot is the same as that of Torah-learning; and Moses our rabbi made decrees, but sages annulled them. This last point yields the proposition that the sage is the master of prophecy, because the sages know how to read prophecy in the correct way.

Let me now give an entire topical composite, so as to show in detail how a statement outside the course of Mishnah-exegesis places the Mishnah-tractate into a different light altogether, as I have alleged in the foregoing summary:

REFLECTIONS ON ISRAEL'S LIFE WITHIN HISTORY

2.   A.   Said R. Yosé bar Hanina, "Four decrees did our lord, Moses, make against Israel. Four prophets came along and annulled them.

B.   "Moses said, 'And Israel dwells in safety alone at the fountain of Jacob' (Dt. 33:28). Amos came and annulled it: 'Then I said, O Lord God, stop, I ask you, how shall Jacob stand alone, for he is small,' and it goes on, 'The Lord repented concerning this: This also shall not be, says the Lord god' (Amos 7:5-6).

C.   "Moses said, 'And among those nations you shall have no repose' (Dt. 28:65). Jeremiah came and annulled it: 'Thus says the Lord, the people that were left of the sword have found grace in the wilderness, even Israel, when I go to provide him rest' (Jer. 31:1).

D.   "Moses said, 'The Lord...visits the sin of the fathers upon the children and upon the children's children to the third and to the fourth generation' (Ex. 34:7), but Ezekiel said, 'the soul that sins it shall die' (Ez. 18:3-4).

E.   "Moses said, 'And you shall perish among the nations' (Lev. 26:38), but Isaiah said, 'And it shall come to pass in that day that a great horn shall sound and they shall come who were lost in the land of Assyria' (Is. 27:13)."

3.   A.   Said Rab, "I am troubled by this verse: 'And you shall
            perish among the nations' (Lev. 26:38)."

      B.   *To this objected R. Pappa,* "Perhaps the meaning is,
            something that was lost and searched for, in line with
            this usage: 'I have gone astray like a lost sheep, seek
            your servant' (Ps. 119:176)?"

      C.   *At issue for Rab was the end of the same verse:* "And
            the land of your enemies shall eat you up" (Lev.
            26:38).

      D.   *To this objected Mar Zutra, "But perhaps the meaning
            is, in the way in which cucumbers and pumpkins are
            eaten [that is, slice by slice]."*

4.   A.   Once upon a time Rabban Gamaliel, R. Eleazar b.
            Azariah, R. Joshua, and R. Aqiba were walking along
            the way and heard the roar of Rome all the way from
            Puteoli, at a distance of a hundred and twenty miles.
            They began to cry, but R. Aqiba brightened up.

      B.   They said to him, "Why so cheerful?"

      C.   He said to them, "Why so gloomy?"

      D.   They said to him, "These Cushites worship sticks and
            stones and burn incense to idolatry but live in safety
            and comfort, while as to us, the house that was the
            footstool for our God is burned **[24B]** with fire! Why
            shouldn't we cry?!"

      E.   He said to them, "But that's precisely why I rejoice.
            If those who violate his will have it so good, those
            who do his will all the more so!"

5.   A.   Once again, they were going up to Jerusalem. When
            they got to Mount Scopus, they tore their garments.
            When they reached the Temple mount, they saw a
            fox emerge from the house of the Holy of Holies.
            They began to cry, but R. Aqiba brightened up.

      B.   They said to him, "Why so cheerful?"

      C.   He said to them, "Why so gloomy?"

      D.   They said to him, "The place of which it once was
            said, 'And the non-priest who draws near shall be
            put to death' (Num. 1:51) has become a fox hole, so
            shouldn't we weep?"

      E.   He said to them, "But that's precisely why I rejoice.
            It is written, 'And I will take to me faithful witnesses
            to record, Uriah the priest and Zechariah son of
            Jeberechiah' (Is. 8:2). And what has Uriah the priest

to do with Zechariah? Uriah lived during the first Temple, and Zechariah during the second, but Scripture had linked the prophesy of Zechariah to the prophecy of Uriah. In the case of Uriah: 'Therefore shall Zion for your sake be ploughed as a field' (Mic. 3:12). Zechariah: 'Thus says the Lord of hosts, there shall yet old men and old women sit in the broad places of Jerusalem' (Zech. 8:4). Until the prophecy of Uriah was fulfilled, I was afraid that the prophecy of Zechariah might not be fulfilled. Now that the prophecy of Uriah has come about, we may be certain that the prophecy of Zechariah will be fulfilled word for word."

F. They said to him, "Aqiba, you have given us comfort, Aqiba, you have given us comfort."

Readers can judge for themselves whether my reading of matters is sustained by the data.

Can we state what the compilers of this document propose to accomplish in producing this complete, organized piece of writing? With the sole exception of IX.D, we can account for the intruded compositions and composites in one of two ways. One set of materials portrays legal topics by organizing teachings of named masters. Then the named master, not the topic, forms the source of coherence. The other set of materials portrays the topic of our tractate in a quite fresh way, by introducing a dimension of all law that the Mishnah ordinarily does not portray, namely, how the intrusion of the sage imparts a supernatural character to the affairs of this world. [1] The Torah does not abandon a person, but accompanies the disciple into exile; that means the supernatural family of master and disciples forms a unit subject to the judgment of the law; the Torah is the sole enduring and reliable form of wealth; a city without "elders," that is, sages, cannot afford the refuge that the Torah has provided for the manslayer; the sage is the heir to prophecy, has direct access through his powers of analytical learning, to Heaven's wishes, and disposes of prophecy much as the prophets were able to dispose of even the teachings of Moses.

The Mishnah-tractate that concerns flogging and exile has been transformed into a statement about the glory of the Torah as represented by the sage, who may be subject to flogging and exile, but who always represents that transcendent reality that the Torah conveys in this world. The topic is now seen from a different perspective altogether, and though the Mishnah has been faithfully set forth, through the introduction of topics not required for Mishnah-exegesis, and through the juxtaposition of those topical presentations with the exposition of the Mishnah, all things have changed. It is probably extending matters beyond the limits to observe that in a tractate bearing such a message, the presentation of composites formed around the names of sages delivers the message of the priority of the sage over prophecy, as much as the power of the sage to transcend exile and the power of the Torah to secure a permanent endowment, that other intruded compositions and composites deliver as well. That observation about the appropriateness even of what is least coherent in the most definitive and formal traits must, for the moment, form a mere footnote. But the text and its message leave no grounds for doubt on how the Talmud-tractate has recast the Mishnah-tractate and made the Mishnah-tractate into a medium for the message that the Talmud's system, and not the Mishnah's, wishes to set forth.

VI. THE HERE AND NOW IN GOD'S PERSPECTIVE SET FORTH BY BAVLI-TRACTATE BABA BATRA: THE SACRED CONTEXT OF SECULAR AFFAIRS

How do the topical composites fit into the Talmud-tractate and what do they contribute that the Mishnah-tractate of the same name would lack without them? In the following I indent the entries that carry forward in large-scale composites the theme or problem or proposition of the Mishnah, and I focus upon those composites that treat topics not relevant to the Mishnah; further, I underline items that fall into neither category. That procedure allows for a refinement of the presentation, encompassing topical composites of diverse classifications.

I.D: The sizable composite about dismantling synagogue buildings, shading over into the distinct composite on the Temple of Herod. The discussion of dismantling synagogue buildings is fully articulated; it has no relationship I can discern to the context defined by the Mishnah.

I.E: The Temple that Herod Built.

    III.C: The introduction at the Mishnah, III.B, of the consideration of assumptions as to facts where we cannot prove the facts leads to a secondary exercise on the presumptive rights signified by established usage. The composite, while autonomous, is situated in a relevant context.

    IV.D: Once we deal with forcing neighbors to contribute to the common defense, the special rules that pertain to sages are worked out; sages represent an exception to the Mishnah's rule.

    IV.F: Philanthropic obligations that apply to residents of a town, shading over into a discussion of how the funds are collected and distributed, remains well within the established framework of the exposition of common obligations of citizens of a community. This is a massive composite with its own interests, but viewed whole, it remains within the classification of a secondary topical supplement to an exposition of the Mishnah. Its insertion here is not jarring, though its dimensions and full articulation certainly are not to have been predicted on the basis of comparable insertions.

V.C: The composite on prophecy and sagacity is inserted whole because of the casual reference at V.B.II.3 to the status of a statement of a prophet as having no legal standing. Then the exposition takes up the subject in its own terms; but the six items are scarcely more than a long footnote.

    V.D: Special problems here do not vastly change the face of the Mishnah-exposition.

V.G: Dividing up Sacred Scriptures, V.F, to which the Mishnah makes reference, draws in its wake an enormous exposition about the rules of joining, and dividing, Sacred Scriptures. This carries us forward to the correct order of the books of Scripture, and that continues with

V.H: who wrote various books of Scripture.

V.I: The composite on Job is added because V.I invites further discussion of that subject. So the first three items of this composite pursue the systematic exposition of the theme, and the penultimate one is an add-on,

V.J: as is the final item, the theme of Abraham, often compared to Job and treated as Job's counterpart. This continues the foregoing, these latter two items being footnotes to the foundation-set.

    VI.G: This is inserted because it intersects with the interests of the Mishnah to the exposition of this it is attached.

    VIII.B: The discussion of the rights and rules of shop-keeping invites the secondary exposition of rules governing limitation on competition. The connection is at the opening item, which is in detail an appropriate amplification of the Mishnah's principle, but the exposition of which shades over into the larger issue treated here.

    XV.B: The basic theme here is the four winds and what each brings, and that surely forms a valid amplification of the Mishnah's interest in keeping noxious odors out of town. The ubiquity of God's presence certainly is not a topic introduced by an explanation of how we must keep carrion, graves, and tanneries away from a town. We can readily see how the gloss of the opening item, which does amplify the Mishnah's rule, yields a secondary point on the meaning of "constant," and once we are told that only God's Presence is "constant," the rest follows.

    XX.B: This is a massive compilation of cases that illustrate the general principles of the Mishnah on settling conflicting claims.

XXV.B: The set on Benaah is introduced because it glosses a detail of the prior composite; but it is free-standing. It makes a variety of points, and the whole holds together only around the named authority.

XXX.E: This important compilation is tacked on because it makes the point that, in mourning for the Temple, one does not fully stucco his house but leaves a bare spot, which intersects with a detail of the foregoing. But the composite stands on its own and in no way serves to amplify a detail let alone a principle pertinent to the Mishnah.

> XXXI.C: The meaning of the language used in selling real estate carries forward the Mishnah's interest in interpreting the language that describes commercial transactions of sale.

XL.E: The composite of sailors' and other travellers' tales begins with those of Rabbah bar bar Hannah, moving on to

XL.F: other travellers' tales, yielding an interest in

XL.G: sea monsters in general, and Leviathan in particular,

XL.H: bearing a brief insertion on the character and sources of the waters of the sea,

XL.I: then reverting to the theme of Leviathan again.

XL.J: Since Leviathan serves as the meal for the Messianic banquet, the theme of the coming of the Messianic age once more intrudes.

> XL.K: This item reverts to the Mishnah's topic and problematic.
>
> L.C: Interest in just weights and measures shades over into an exposition of the penalty for falsifying weights and measures.
>
> L.E: The same theme as above is worked out here.
>
> L.F: The same theme as above is worked out here.
>
> L.G: From one form of unjust market practices, we move on to the next, which is, price manipulation and hoarding.

L.H: Once the theme of market crises enters, we turn to the correct response to shortages, which is not migration from the Land of Israel. That introduces the case of Ruth's family, which migrated because of famine.

L.I: From famine we move on to plenty.

> LII.C: The theme of the Mishnah invites a free-standing complement of important information.
>
> LIV.E: As above, this item simply provides information invited by the Mishnah's own topic.
>
> LXII.B: The problem of the Mishnah's rule is here extended by introducing some further details.
>
> LXIV.B: As above.
>
> LXIV.H: As above.
>
> LXV.C: The theme of the Mishnah, how others inherit the estate of someone who does not have sons, explains the introduction of the composite on dying without sons and what it means. It is a sign of divine wrath.
>
> LXVI.C: The fact that on the fifteenth of Ab, the tribes were permitted to intermarry, which forms the background for the problem of the Mishnah's case, accounts for this and the next entry.
>
> LXVI.D: As above.

LXVII.C: The general theme of the Mishnah, the disposition of the birth-right, the division of an estate among the sons, is amplified by the case of Jacob and his sons.

LXVII.D: As above: the special claim of the firstborn of a priest and other special cases of inheritance.

LXVIII.B: A secondary problem, how we deal with special problems of inheritance, explains the intrusion of this small st.

LXVIII.C: Here is another special problem on inheritance, namely, the father's right to deprive the firstborn of his special portion.

LXVIII.D: This is a formal intrusion, based on a shared formula, and I see no substantive reason for inserting the entire composite except the one that accounts for its intersection with the immediately preceding item — a substantive intersection, bearing in its wake a formal intrusion.

LXXIII.D: This composite does not amplify the particular law of the Mishnah but it does pursue its main theme and interests.

LXXVII.C: The Mishnah's own interests invites the addition of this autonomous composite.

LXXVII.D: As above.

LXXX.C: This brief appendix does not greatly affect the context in which it is introduced; it is nothing more than a secondary exposition of a tangential theme.

LXXXII.B: The Mishnah's own interests invites the addition of this autonomous composite.

LXXXII.E: Once we deal with gifts of real estate and movables, we turn to the question of the status of a slave: how is he classified?

LXXXII.F: The matter of gifts shades over into a discussion of the form of gifts, with special attention to gifts that are made in writing.

LXXXVIII.C: The Mishnah's principle is illustrated by a distinct case.

Can we state what the compilers of this document propose to accomplish in producing this complete, organized piece of writing? When we examine the program of our Mishnah-tractate and compare it with the topics of the composites that the compilers introduced on their own, not in response to the task of Mishnah-exegesis, we can readily reconstruct their reading of the Mishnah. Eliminating the numerous free-standing composites that serve to amplify the Mishnah's own propositions or introduce principles to reshape the Mishnah's topics, what topics do we find our Talmud's framers have added on their own?

The single most obvious insertion is their attention to the special rights and status of the sages themselves. But that is only the starting pint Beyond lie the items on the familiar list of historical-Messianic and transcendent themes: the Temple of Herod; prophecy in the present age; the dimensions of the various books of Scripture and their correct order and their authors; Job and Abraham; mourning for the Temple; travellers' tales, shading over into a large-scale composite on Leviathan and on the Messianic age; remaining in the Holy Land at all costs and famine and plenty.

Now with this simple and compelling result in hand, we have little difficulty in answering the question, what did the compilers of the Talmud find lacking in the Mishnah's repertoire of cases and principles? What they missed in the Mishnah was attention to precisely those issues that the Mishnah-tractate ignored, which is, the theological dimension, specifically, the historical-Messianic context in which the everyday conflicts over inheritances and estates, property and land, and the conduct of the civil order took place. It is as though the compilers of the Talmud wished to remind those engaged in the secular and everyday matters on which this tractate centers that in the end God will resolve the mundane issues taken up here. History intrudes on the eternal present of home and family, inheritance and estates, the continuities of the private life. A public world intervenes, one for which the Temple on the one side, and Scripture on the other, form the media and provide the motive. So what makes our Mishnah-tractate insufficient — its very success in disposing of the everyday problems of property and conflict over property, cheating customers and overreaching in prices for example — forms the program of the compilers of the Talmud when they work on their own.

Their expansion of the Talmud's boundaries far beyond the limits of Mishnah-exegesis in my view now proves purposive and turns out to make its own comment on the Mishnah, once that the Mishnah's exegetes in no way can have conceived. Specifically, the inclusion of a range of topics omitted by the Mishnah, the sometimes quite jarring introduction of themes entirely out of phase with what is being discussed — from stuccoing a house to leaving off stucco in memorial to the destruction of the Temple, for example! — leave no doubt in our minds concerning the compilers' perception of the Mishnah-tractate. And how they wished us to conceive the Mishnah-tractate's topics and concerns, the dimensions in which they wished to recast these matters, the perspective they proposed to introduce — these form the particular statement of the Talmud's compilers. What counts, what really counts in the perspective of eternity, is precisely what is omitted by the Mishnah's program, and, furthermore, demands its proper place in any consideration of what the Mishnah's framers have set forth as their principal message for the civil order.

VII. THE DEATH OF DEATH IN BAVLI-TRACTATE SANHEDRIN

How do the topical composites fit into the Talmud-tractate Sanhedrin and what do they contribute that the Mishnah-tractate of the same name would lack without them? As above, In the following, as before, I indent the entries that carry forward in large-scale composites the theme or problem or proposition of the Mishnah, and I focus upon those composites that treat topics not relevant to the Mishnah; further, I underline items that fall into neither category.

I.C: The judgment of cases by fewer than three judges is simply a question invited by the law of the Mishnah.

I.D: Arbitration as an alternative to a legal contest falls into the same category as the foregoing.

I.E: In praise of justice and true judges: This entry is invited by the general theme and premise of the Mishnah-rule and does not vastly change our impression of the Mishnah's topic, which is, the judgment of cases and the fair conduct of trials.

> VI.D Composite on the Writing and Revelation of the Torah: This is a thematic composite, inserted because of the discussion, by the Mishnah, of the King's writing out a scroll of the Torah and carrying it about with him. I do not see how this composite vastly changes our perception of the Mishnah's rule or its context.

> VII.B The evils of divorce, particularly of an aging wife: This composite is inserted without any clear relationship to the Mishnah;'s rule. Including the set has probably been provoked by the story of Abishad and Bath Sheba.

XVI.F: The creation of man, the minim, debates with unbelievers, the emperor and the patriarch. This is a vast and important composite on a variety of topics. It is added as a complement to the Mishnah's statement that God put his mint-mark on everyone, yet not one is like another. While this passage moves in a variety of directions, it seems to me wholly complementary to the Mishnah's interests and statements and in no way does the composite (or, really, set of composites) reshape the setting or context in which we are to read the Mishnah's statements. To the contrary, what we have is a rich and dense extension of what the Mishnah clearly wishes to emphasize.

XVI.H: The exegesis of the story of Ahab's death illustrates the statement of the Mishnah immediately preceding, which is, "When the wicked perish there is rejoicing." This item then illustrates that point. But of course, the composite moves in its own direction, guided by the requirements of the theme that it pursues.

XVII.H: Topical appendix on reciting the blessing over the New Moon. The Mishnah's statement introduces this theme, which is then a compendium of useful information, nothing more.

XXIV.E: Burial as the preferred mode of disposition. This is a clear appendix to the statement that one may not leave the deceased to stay unburied overnight. The composite simply reenforces the Mishnah's premise.

XXXI.B: The religious obligations of the children of Noah: idolators and slaves. This composite begins with the statement that idolators as much as Israelites are admonished not to curse God, which is precisely the topic that the Mishnah has introduced. The composite goes off in its own direction, but blasphemy remains a principal consideration throughout, even though the governing topic is now not blasphemy but the obligations of non-Israelites.

XLI.B: The evils of wine: This is a topical composite added after a reference to the rebellious son's drinking a half-log of Italian wine. The Mishnah's general interests thus are advanced, and the premise of Scripture and the Mishnah, that drunkenness is evil, is reenforced.

XLIX.B: Marrying off one's children in the proper manner: This item forms a positive side to the Mishnah's negative, that is, those put to death for incest and similar sexual crimes. Now we are given the opposite: how matters should be carried on.

LVII.C: The zealotry of Phineas: This is a first-rate illustration of the Mishnah's interest in how zealots may enforce the law outside the normal framework of court procedures.

LXV.B: Topical Appendix on Gebiha and Alexander: This is added because of the reference in the foregoing to Gebiha's proof for the resurrection of the dead.

LXV.C: Topical Appendix on Antoninus and Rabbi: My best guess is that this composite was joined to the foregoing as part of a set on sages and emperors; I see no point of topical, let alone propositional, intersection with our Mishnah.

LXV.D: The death of Death: Here we really do have a point of extension, beyond the limits of the Mishnah, so as to recast the Mishnah's topic and set forth a proposition that the exegesis of the Mishnah does not require and that greatly changes our sense of the Mishnah's meaning. The Mishnah's interest in the resurrection of the dead is now shown to be part of a larger proposition, which is, in time to come, death itself will die.

LXV.E: How on the basis of the Torah do we know about the resurrection of the dead. This large composite carries forward the exegesis of the Mishnah, proving in various ways on the strength of Scripture the facticity of the Mishnah's claim.

LXV.F: Topical appendix on Hananiah, Mishael, and Azariah: Here is an example of how death is overcome.

LXV.G: The Messiah. Pharaoh, Sennacherib, Hezekiah, and other Players in the Messianic drama. Here is the point in our tractate at which the Mishnah's program really comes under considerable revision. The Talmud treats as self-evident the link between the Messiah and the resurrection of the dead, but the Mishnah has not done so, indeed, has no introduced the Messiah-theme at all. The Talmud then wants to know how the Messiah's coming relates to the resurrection of the dead. Various salvific occasions are then introduced, Pharaoh and Moses; Sennacherib and Hezekiah. These form secondary expositions of the general theme of the Messiah.

LXV.H: When will the Messiah come? Here is yet another major revision in the presentation of the Mishnah, a systematic recasting of matters to link the resurrection to that other, and quite separate, issue. The upshot is that Israel's historical fate and its salvation at the end of time form a component in the exposition of the theme of the resurrection of the dead. Since this passage of the Mishnah does not introduce the Messiah-theme, the radical re-presentation of matters emerges with great force.

LXV.R: Wicked monarchs who nonetheless merit a portion in the world to come: This is a clear extension of the Mishnah, since the point of interest is to form a catalogue of kings who, despite their evil, will inherit the world to come.

LXV.S: The special case of Hezekiah. The Exegesis of Lamentations. Since Hezekiah is designated as a player in the Messianic drama, and since the exegesis of Lamentations is introduced as if out of nowhere, it seems to me we should regard this composite, mostly devoted to Lamentations, as a further treatment of the Messiah-theme. Here is why Israel requires the Messiah: the city sits solitary.

LXV.T: Summary judgments. What we have here is yet another secondary amplification of the Mishnah's topic. The composite is situated where it belongs for the purpose of Mishnah-commentary, precisely at the end of the account of the kings who do not merit the world to come, and at the outset of the account of the commoners who likewise lose out.

LXV.W: After Doeg we deal with David, who is matched against Doeg. I am somewhat puzzled by the introduction of this composite, but it does seem to me continuous in its general proposition with the preceding one.

LXVIII.K: Jericho in Particular. Here we have a fine illustration of the one case in which a town really was treated in accord with the law of the Torah governing the apostate city.

Can we state what the compilers of this document propose to accomplish in producing this complete, organized piece of writing? The first ten chapters of the tractate conform to the general rules of sustained, analytical investigation that govern in the Talmud in general. Chapter Eleven contains much information, many well-crafted compositions and purposive composites, and, while it exhibits singular deficiencies in the analytical process to which we become accustomed, the rules of large-scale conglomeration remain firm.

When we take a second look at Chapter Eleven, we find a sustained effort at recasting the Mishnah's topic by introducing themes that the Mishnah either omits altogether or treats in a casual way. These emerge in unit LXV: the death of death; the coming of the Messiah — past time; the coming of the Messiah — future time; the special case of Hezekiah and the pertinence of the book of Lamentations. Here in a single set of composites we find introduced a set of propositions concerning the Messiah and Israel's history that the Mishnah has neglected. The Mishnah, after all, has focused upon private persons — specific kings and commoners who have lost the world to come. The Talmud, by contrast, introduces the dimension of the Israelite community seen whole. The Mishnah tells us how individuals lose out, e.g., by denying that the Torah itself teaches that the dead will be raised. The Talmud turns to the more profound question of the death of death, which itself then comes as the prologue to the advent of the Messiah. As though to underscore the main point — the issue is Israel the holy people, not merely individual players in Israelite life — the exegesis of Lamentations is inserted, whole and in no clear connection to what has preceded. The result of this analysis leaves no doubt that the framers of the Talmud have both commented upon the Mishnah in a rich and remarkably profound way but also recast the context in which the Mishnah is to be received and understood. The Talmud truly forms the re-presentation of the Mishnah. And what the Talmud's framers find self-evident in the exposition of the Mishnah's statements that the Mishnah's authors treated casually or not at all speaks for itself: the death of death, of which the Mishnah's account of the Messiah's time knows nothing, but to which the Talmud's jarring juxtaposition calls attention.

VIII. CATEGORY-FORMATION, LOCATION, PROPORTION

That the topical composites define for us category-formations that are native to the Oral Torah forms an axiom of our inquiry, and that they also point to the location at which a given category-formation is given its authoritative exposition hardly requires demonstration. The question of proportion cannot find a ready answer in the kinds of materials at hand, though we may say, as a preliminary hypothesis, that where a given category-formation imposes a completely new perspective on a large and important disquisition of the Mishnah — the case of Yoma suffices to exemplify the matter — we deal with an important component of the system as a whole. Not only so, but the recurrent themes and points of stress and tension underscore the paramount paradigms of which the theology of the Oral Torah will, in due course, be comprised.

VIII

Paradigm and Symbol:
Decoding Another Mode of Theological Speech

I. SYMBOLIC VOCABULARY AND THEOLOGICAL STRUCTURE

Symbols in verbal form — sets of opaque words strung into lists that induce meaning through recombinancy — constitute the third of the three modes of the study of the theology of the Oral Torah, after [1] documents and their theological category-formations, and [2] systematic expositions in the form of free-standing composites. The manipulation of opaque symbols for conveying sense and meaning requires attention in its own terms. That is because symbols, lacking explicit and articulated propositions but bearing implicit and unmediated sense and meaning, play an active role in conveying the theological structure and system that the Oral Torah embodies.

Before proceeding, let me set forth one example of what I conceive to be a fine statement of the symbolic structure of Judaism as symbols in verbal form set forth such a structure. This will serve as an example of the kinds of symbols we find in general in symbolic discourse in verbal form. The character of the passage will explain why I have chosen it as representative:

GENESIS RABBAH LXX:VIII

2. A. "As he looked, he saw a well in the field:"
   B. R. Hama bar Hanina interpreted the verse in six ways [that is, he divides the verse into six clauses and systematically reads each of the clauses in light of the others and in line with an overriding theme:
   C. "'As he looked, he saw a well in the field:' this refers to the well [of water in the wilderness, Num. 21:17].
   D. "'...and lo, three flocks of sheep lying beside it:' specifically, Moses, Aaron, and Miriam.

    E. "'...for out of that well the flocks were watered:' from from there each one drew water for his standard, tribe, and family."

    F. "And the stone upon the well's mouth was great:"

    G. Said R. Hanina, "It was only the size of a little sieve."

    H. [Reverting to Hama's statement:] "'...and put the stone back in its place upon the mouth of the well:' for the coming journeys. [Thus the first interpretation applies the passage at hand to the life of Israel in the wilderness.]

3.   A. "'As he looked, he saw a well in the field:' refers to Zion.

    B. "'...and lo, three flocks of sheep lying beside it:' refers to the three festivals.

    C. "'....for out of that well the flocks were watered:' from there they drank of the holy spirit.

    D. "'...The stone on the well's mouth was large:' this refers to the rejoicing of the house of the water-drawing."

    E. Said R. Hoshaiah, "Why is it called 'the house of the water drawing'? Because from there they drink of the Holy Spirit."

    F. [Resuming Hama b. Hanina's discourse:] "'...and when all the flocks were gathered there:' coming from 'the entrance of Hamath to the brook of Egypt' (1 Kgs. 8:66).

    G. "'...the shepherds would roll the stone from the mouth of the well and water the sheep:' for from there they would drink of the Holy Spirit.

    H. "'...and put the stone back in its place upon the mouth of the well:' leaving it in place until the coming festival. [Thus the second interpretation reads the verse in light of the Temple celebration of the Festival of Tabernacles.]

4.   A. "'...As he looked, he saw a well in the field:' this refers to Zion.

    B. "'...and lo, three flocks of sheep lying beside it:' this refers to the three courts, concerning which we have learned in the Mishnah: **There were three courts there, one at the gateway of the Temple mount, one at the gateway of the courtyard, and one in the chamber of the hewn stones [M. San. 11:2].**

C. "'...for out of that well the flocks were watered:' for from there they would hear the ruling.

D. "The stone on the well's mouth was large:' this refers to the high court that was in the chamber of the hewn stones.

E. "'...and when all the flocks were gathered there:' this refers to the courts in session in the Land of Israel.

F. "'...the shepherds would roll the stone from the mouth of the well and water the sheep:' for from there they would hear the ruling.

G. "'...and put the stone back in its place upon the mouth of the well:' for they would give and take until they had produced the ruling in all the required clarity." [The third interpretation reads the verse in light of the Israelite institution of justice and administration.]

5. A. "'As he looked, he saw a well in the field:' this refers to Zion.

B. "'...and lo, three flocks of sheep lying beside it:' this refers to the first three kingdoms [Babylonia, Media, Greece].

C. "'...for out of that well the flocks were watered:' for they enriched the treasures that were laid upon up in the chambers of the Temple.

D. "'...The stone on the well's mouth was large:' this refers to the merit attained by the patriarchs.

E. "'...and when all the flocks were gathered there:' this refers to the wicked kingdom, which collects troops through levies over all the nations of the world.

F. "'...the shepherds would roll the stone from the mouth of the well and water the sheep:' for they enriched the treasures that were laid upon up in the chambers of the Temple.

G. "'...and put the stone back in its place upon the mouth of the well:' in the age to come the merit attained by the patriarchs will stand [in defense of Israel].' [So the fourth interpretation interweaves the themes of the Temple cult and the domination of the four monarchies.]

6. A. "'As he looked, he saw a well in the field:' this refers to the sanhedrin.

B. "'...and lo, three flocks of sheep lying beside it:' this alludes to the three rows of disciples of sages that would go into session in their presence.

C. "for out of that well the flocks were watered:' for from
there they would listen to the ruling of the law.

D. "'...The stone on the well's mouth was large:' this
refers to the most distinguished member of the court,
who determines the law-decision.

E. "'...and when all the flocks were gathered there:' this
refers to disciples of the sages in the Land of Israel.

F. "'...the shepherds would roll the stone from the mouth
of the well and water the sheep:' for from there they
would listen to the ruling of the law.

G. "'...and put the stone back in its place upon the mouth
of the well:' for they would give and take until they
had produced the ruling in all the required clarity."
[The fifth interpretation again reads the verse in light
of the Israelite institution of legal education and
justice.]

7.   A. "'As he looked, he saw a well in the field:' this refers
to the synagogue.

B. "'...and lo, three flocks of sheep lying beside it:' this
refers to the three who are called to the reading of
the Torah on weekdays.

C. "'...for out of that well the flocks were watered:' for
from there they hear the reading of the Torah.

D. "'...The stone on the well's mouth was large:' this
refers to the impulse to do evil.

E. "'...and when all the flocks were gathered there:' this
refers to the congregation.

F. "'...the shepherds would roll the stone from the mouth
of the well and water the sheep:' for from there they
hear the reading of the Torah.

G. "'...and put the stone back in its place upon the mouth
of the well:' for once they go forth [from the hearing
of the reading of the torah] the impulse to do evil
reverts to its place." [The sixth and last interpretation
turns to the twin themes of the reading of the Torah
in the synagogue and the evil impulse, temporarily
driven off through the hearing of the Torah.]

GENESIS RABBAH LXX:IX

1.   A. R. Yohanan interpreted the statement in terms of Sinai:

B. "'As he looked, he saw a well in the field:' this refers
to Sinai.

C. "'...and lo, three flocks of sheep lying beside it:' these stand for the priests, Levites, and Israelites.

D. "'...for out of that well the flocks were watered:' for from there they heard the Ten Commandments.

E. "'...The stone on the well's mouth was large:' this refers to the Presence of God."

F. "...and when all the flocks were gathered there:"

G. R. Simeon b. Judah of Kefar Akum in the name of R. Simeon: "All of the flocks of Israel had to be present, for if any one of them had been lacking, they would not have been worthy of receiving the Torah."

H. [Returning to Yohanan's exposition:] "'...the shepherds would roll the stone from the mouth of the well and water the sheep:' for from there they heard the Ten Commandments.

I. "'...and put the stone back in its place upon the mouth of the well:' 'You yourselves have seen that I have talked with you from heaven' (Ex. 20:19)."

The six themes read in response to the verse cover (1) Israel in the wilderness, (2) the Temple cult on festivals with special reference to Tabernacles, (3) the judiciary and government, (4) the history of Israel under the four kingdoms, (5) the life of sages, and (6) the ordinary folk and the synagogue. The whole is an astonishing repertoire of fundamental themes of the life of the nation, Israel: at its origins in the wilderness, in its cult, in its institutions based on the cult, in the history of the nations, and, finally, in the twin social estates of sages and ordinary folk, matched by the institutions of the master-disciple circle and the synagogue. The vision of Jacob at the well thus encompassed the whole of the social reality of Jacob's people, Israel. Yohanan's exposition adds what was left out, namely, reference to the revelation of the Torah at Sinai. The reason I have offered the present passage as a fine instance of symbolic discourse is now clear. For a catalogue of the kinds of topics addressed in passages of symbolic, as distinct from propositional, discourse, the present catalogue proves compendious and complete. It embodies symbolic discourse in verbal form, to which we now turn.

That symbols serve to convey structures and working systems of thought is expressed, for Christianity, with special attention to iconic symbols, when Gerhart Ladner states,

...in early Christianity the Middle Ages...the relationship of the image and the symbol to what they depict rests on an experience of a world pervaded by the divine; that is to say, this world was still a good order...animated by the breath of God, in which everything was given a spiritual meaning. For the people of that time everything in the world could be a symbol of God...What is important is the

human ability to experience the reality of symbols and...by means of symbols to
see a reality in which individual things are always connected with a world-view
that is experienced and recognized as a totality.[1]

For Rabbinic Judaism, too, opaque verbal symbols that occur throughout the literary
evidence serve in the same way, to convey through other-than-propositional speech
that reality that shows how things are connected, and indicates what conclusions
are to be drawn from the connection. And that result stands for theology as I have
defined the task of theology: to describe the structure and system that permeates
the documents of the Oral Torah and renders them cogent. That is hardly surprising,
since symbols, whether expressed in iconic or verbal form, convey conceptions of
God, the cosmos, and the nature of Man and the human community.[2] Standing for
themselves and also for what transcends themselves, symbols form a medium of
speech in other than propositional form, a mode of conveying sense and meaning
— normative emotions and attitudes — other than through declarative statements.
Because in the documents of the Oral Torah certain words serve a symbolic function,
being combined with other such words into lists that, seen whole, on their own
form statements of significance, even propositional formulations, we turn finally
to theological discourse in the medium of verbal symbols that pervade the
documents.

Our task to begin with is first to demonstrate that the Oral Torah sets forth
a set of symbols in verbal form and then — a somewhat more complicated venture
— to show that these aniconic symbols make a statement distinctive to the Oral
Torah, particular to its writings, and readily distinguished from the iconic
symbolism, for example, of synagogue art. Now, where to look? Raw materials
for symbolic speech prove abundant, such words as "Torah," "Sinai," "at the Sea,"
"David," "Babylonia-Medea [or: Persia]-Greece-Rome," "mezuzah," "phylacteries,"
and the like standing for salvific knowledge, revelation, divine intervention, Messiah,
the pattern of the history of the nations and Israel, holy object, and holy action,
respectively. And that list only symbolizes much that is not mentioned. Readers
already have encountered a considerable symbolic vocabulary — references to
events, persons, activities — that permeates discourse throughout the documents.
That vocabulary, more than the explicit theological paradigms of documents, the
articulated propositions of topical expositions in the Bavli — everywhere presents
itself as a medium for expressing theological positions and convictions that permeate
the documents of the Oral Torah.

---

[1] Ladner, *op. cit.,* p. 2.

[2] Cf. Gerhart B. Ladner, *God, Cosmos, and Humankind. The World of Early Christian
Symbolism* (Berkeley, 1995: University of California Press, p. 1. Ladner deals with
theological, cosmological, and anthropological symbolism, all expressed in iconic form,
but also takes up language-symbolism. But most of his discussion turns on iconic symbols.

II. THEOLOGICAL DISCOURSE IN VERBAL SYMBOLS

Within verbal communication, theological statements come about in the form of propositions and yield syllogisms: God is this, God does that, God wants the other thing. In paradigmatic speech, patterns or models of organization and explanation yield the same conclusion. In symbolic discourse, by contrast, are conveyed and evoked attitudes and emotions, rather than propositions: faith as confidence in God, rather than faith as the statement of truth about God.[3] In the Oral Torah, moreover, various symbols would be used to combine and recombine so as — in their combinations — to make normative theological statements, in some composites of attitudes that are to be encouraged, in others of propositions that are to be accepted and believed. Symbolic discourse took place not only in the iconic, but also in the literary medium. Both media were meant to serve to elicit right attitudes and approved emotions in the meeting with God, whether in synagogue worship or in Torah-study among sages. These attitudes and emotions brought to expression within their mode of thought and expression propositions readily identified in intellectual form. That is how symbolic discourse served the theology vocation.

How does symbolic discourse take place in the Oral Torah? Lists of names that bore meaning apart from any propositions associated with them formed a familiar medium of communication. Those names, correctly selected and ordered, communicated intelligible thought in symbolic, as distinct from propositional, signs. These symbols, whether represented in iconographical or verbal media, were relied upon to elicit, if not articulated right thoughts, then besought attitudes. The names — words out of all syntactic context, words not assembled to set forth syllogisms and prove propositions — communicated because they brought up attitudes and imparted their self-evident truth. Names listed in catalogues but otherwise opaque in any denotative sense, such as Abel, Enoch, Noah, Abraham and Sarah, Isaac, Jacob, Moses, the people crossing the Red Sea, Rahab, Gideon, Barak, Samson, Jephthah, David, Samuel, properly selected and rightly ordered could be expected to communicate, conveying sense if not proposition. When joined with the words "by faith," the names just given indeed powerfully served the purposes of the author of Hebrews 11 — and they did so as much as the arguments and propositions on the same matter, set forth in Romans and Thessalonians about salvation by faith, conveyed the meaning of the apostle Paul. Not only so, but standard lists of names of heroes , on their own convey the right attitude or even lead to the correct conclusion, and that can be without regard to an associated, verbal proposition. As much as Washington and Lincoln and Eisenhower and Reagan for one party, or

---

[3] Compare *Goodenough's Jewish Symbols. An Abridged Edition.* Princeton, 1988: Princeton University Press, which I edited to summarize Goodenough's work on symbolism of Judaism. Goodenough's key-treatment of the theory of religious symbolism is in his *Jewish Symbols of the Graeco-Roman Period* Volume IV Part I, reproduced in my condensation.

Jefferson, Wilson, Roosevelt for the other — communicate symbolically, as a kind of short-hand, for "what we stand for" in political contexts, so names rightly chosen and properly ordered bore meaning, if not explicit messages.

How does this symbolic communication take place, even alongside propositional discourse? To take a familiar example, for Ben Sira, the well-known catalogue of "famous men" of Sirah Chapter 44 makes a point that is never articulated — but does not have to be. The catalogue encompasses these names: Enoch, Noah, Abraham, Moses, Aaron, Phinehas son of Eleazar, Joshua son of Nun, Judges, Samuel, Nathan, David, Solomon, Elijah, Hezekiah, Josiah, Ezekiel, Zerubbabel, and finally, *Simon the high priest son of Onias*. Now as the catalogue of Hebrews indicates, some of these names prove commonplace. They routinely appear, also on counterpart lists in rabbinic writings. But of others that is not true. The inclusion, in particular, of Simon the high priest and the positioning of that name at the end, in contrast to other such catalogues of names, is so jarring as to suggest that including him was the point of making the list. Ben Sira says much about the names he lists, but what he says merely by mentioning his ancestor's name, without an articulated proposition, proves his most eloquent and powerful medium of communication.

Composites of names serve in the same way in Rabbinic documents. As we noticed in Chapter One, there is another list of names, compiled in the opening chapter of tractate Abot: Moses, Joshua, elders, prophets, the men of the great assembly, Simeon the Righteous, Antigonos of Sokho, Yosé b. Yoezer of Seredah and Yosé b. Yohanan of Jerusalem, Joshua b. Perahiah and Nittai the Arbelite, Judah b. Tabbai and Simeon b. Shatah, Shemaiah and Abtalion, Hillel and Shammai, Rabban Gamaliel, Simeon his son, Rabban Simeon b. Gamaliel. The names on their own connect to Sinai the Pharisaic authorities of the first century, Gamaliel and Simeon b. Gamaliel, and their predecessors, principals of the Mishnah, Shammai and Hillel. The list makes the point that the Mishnah's authorities stand in a chain of tradition back to Moses at Sinai — there is no missing the point, which is expressed in the choice and ordering of the names. The contrast to Ben Sira's list emerges at their point of intersection: Simeon the Righteous = Simeon the High Priest!

It follows that controlling the agenda governs communication, in which case one need not dictate what actually is said about the items that are on the agenda. Wildly disparate statements assigned to the authorities of the list from Moses to Simeon b. Gamaliel have slight bearing on the message that is communicated by the list. Communication takes place on its own, without articulation in propositions. Then lists that omit that name, or Zerubbabel, or "Judges," or "Nathan," will represent other principles of selection, convey other meanings or attitudes. Then the ordering of lists that encompass Abraham, Moses, and David will clearly mean to convey some message other than the one Ben Sira's list so casually imparts. Symbolic discourse takes diverse forms; it may form the only medium of communication, or it may work within the infrastructure of articulated thought; it may appeal to iconic representations, or to verbally-formulations, of symbols.

Now, in the rabbinic writings, certain words stand for opaque symbols, not for specific and determined propositions; they may denote, but, used for symbols, they only connote. And the connotations are conveyed through the manipulations of several such symbols, also in verbal form — hence, for instance, the lists of opaque symbols, such as, I maintain, Ben Sira and the author of Hebrews use to make points important to their compositions. True, artists in fiction and poetry have for all times spoken to us in just that way. But that passages in rabbinic literature of late antiquity communicate in symbols in verbal form, rather than through the conventional representation of proposition has not been understood in accounts of the theology of Rabbinic Judaism.

III. LOCATING SYMBOLS

Precisely what do I mean by "symbol," and how do I know that a sign or cognitive representation, whether verbal or artistic, is "symbolic"? An ostensive definition suffices. By symbol I refer to that which speaks beyond its own particularity, so "symbol" here signifies one thing that says many things. So while a symbol may denote, it always must connote. Within this simple definition a symbol is a thing that may or may not stand for itself but that must always stand for something more than itself. Whether to soul or to heart or to mind, whether to intellect or to intuition, whether to change attitudes or to reshape emotions or to impart convictions or to express ideas, the symbol makes its statement by moving beyond the bounds of its own character.

But can the name of a person — not just a drawing of a lamb or a scroll — serve as a symbol? The "historical Moses" for instance may denote an individual and stand for himself in all his particularity. But "Moses our rabbi" connotes something that transcends a particular person at a given moment; it is then (among diverse possibilities) Moses in relationship to the Torah, so that "Moses our rabbi" connotes God's giving the Torah to Israel. What about an object? The ram's horn denotes a particular object. But, represented on the floor or wall of a synagogue, the ram's horn connotes (and may evoke) sentiments, intuitions, feelings, or propositions that vastly transcend the representation of the hardened excrescence on the head of the ram: the binding of Isaac, for one thing, Moriah and the Temple, for a second, the judgment of the New Year, for a third, the great trumpet that heralds the coming of the Messiah, for a fourth. In all of these cases the "thing" may or may not stand for itself. But to be symbolic, a "thing" must stand for something beyond itself — many things, that are far beyond itself, as a matter of fact.

What about events? A symbol, for example, may derive from and stand for an event, which, when represented however crudely, will bear self-evident implications that transcend what actually happened on that particular day on which the singular event took place. An event reduced to a sign, such as a battle won or lost, becomes symbolic when, to the sign for the battle are attached meanings or consequences that extend far beyond what actually happened, or what took place on account of what happened, in the battle itself: the signs, here, mere names of places, such as Hastings or Agincourt, Gettysburg or Pearl Harbor or Midway, for instance. In the case of a Judaism the *shofar,* or ram's horn, may signify the binding of Isaac, hence a a singular event; the penitential season encompassing the New Year, hence a recurrent event; the altar of Moriah, hence the Temple in Jerusalem; and a variety of other things. It can stand, also, for Abraham and Isaac, for a symbol may be a person, and a person may be made symbolic, exemplifying in himself or herself an obvious attitude, virtue, or value. A gesture, such as kneeling, dancing, a motion of the hand or the head that evokes whether thought or attitude or feeling serves as a symbol, speaking, as it does, beyond its own contents; or it may have no contents to begin with: an action that bears meaning beyond the physical movement of torso or knee that on its own is inert, neutral, without implicit or self-evident meaning.

What about the representation of symbols by opaque words — words not formed into sentences that contribute to a syllogism? Here we come to a much more difficult matter: to identify out of all the words of a given document the particular ones that serve as signs and therefore represent symbolic "things" in written form? The same components of the definition that has applied to symbols in iconic form must pertain. But the content of those components will shift. Can I identify the rather particular parts of the literary evidence that seem to me to speak through symbols rather than through sentences? How will I know when, in reading a document, a set of things portrayed through words, clearly, by an objective criterion, serves to speak not for itself alone but also (or only) beyond itself? The answer to that question derives to begin with from certain formal traits of the literary evidence. When I have set forth these traits, I shall be able to explain how, in documents of a given type, some words portray symbols, rather than convey propositions: *so that symbolic discourse is underway.* We begin with familiar definitions of operative criteria.

First, symbols represented in words are those "things" (or signs) that transcend their particularity and signify, that is, deliver a message — verbal or intuitive — beyond themselves. These we must distinguish from the things that in context stand for themselves alone and that bear meanings restricted to their own characteristics, e.g., the verbal explanations associated with them, or the specific, explicit message conveyed along with them.

Second, symbols conveyed in words must represent a highly restricted vocabulary, so that some few words recur in symbolic, as distinct from restricted, senses. Only a few words ought to occur, time and again, in such a way as to warrant classification as symbolic, as distinct from propositional, discourse.

Third and most important, I must be able to specify why I think the verbal representation of a symbol functions along with other such verbal representations to make a statement that is of a symbolic, not a propositional or syllogistic, character. I have to offer a theory to explain not why a word is symbolic in its context, but how sets of such symbols combine to convey meaning in a different medium of thought from the meaning conveyed through propositional constructions of words used in a sense restricted by their own traits or significance. Here, again, therefore, I want to identify not the words but the syntax and grammar of symbolic discourse.

In certain documents within the Oral Torah some composites of compositions that utilize a particular form and that join together things that clearly are meant, in combination with other things, to transcend their particular meaning. The two elements of that somewhat opaque sentence forthwith require definition: [1] the particular forms, [2] the things that I maintain are meant in combination to bear meanings that, not in combination, they do not necessarily convey (connote or denote). When I have clarified the evidence that seems to me to testify to symbolic discourse, this exploration of the symbolic structure of Judaism, conveyed in both iconic and literary form, can commence.

[1] There is a particular form that, in my view, means to conduct symbolic, as distinct from propositional and syllogistic discourse. The form is based upon the repeated citation, in disciplined parsing, of a verse of Scripture, and the successive imputation of various meanings, entirely cogent with one another, to each component of that verse. The form requires disciplined repetition of the parsed verse together with presentation of a repertoire of distinct meanings to be imputed to those components. The parsed verse then is explained in terms other than those specified by the verse when it is not parsed. When parsed, element by element, the verse is given a whole new set of meanings or reference points. And when this process is repeated, these new meanings prove multiple. If not repeated, the form is not present; not surprisingly, the form involved ordinarily bears a rhetorical signal, "another matter."

[2] The key-words that are utilized in that "another-matter"-composite form bear meaning only in combination, having in that context no denotative sense whatsoever outside of the combination with other such verbal-signs. Our task is to recognize symbolic discourse when it occurs.

How is the form just now described pertinent to our inquiry into the use of language for the representation of symbols, so that, within the cited form in particular, I can adduce evidence that words are utilized *solely* to portray symbols? Two considerations pertain, and both of them run parallel to the ones that apply to evidence of an iconic character concerning the symbolic structure of Judaism.

First is the matter of repetition, integral to the execution of the form just now introduced, just as the repeated use of iconic representations in the same circumstance (synagogue decoration) indicates that we have in those re-repeated presentations of the same few objects not mute decoration but transcendent symbols.

Second and concomitantly comes the consideration of a restricted vocabulary, which signals the utilization of a restricted, privileged code. How do these traits of symbolic discourse in iconic form pertain in the verbal medium? In our sequences of three or more representations of the same parsed verse, each with its own "other matter," we shall see that a restricted vocabulary of verbal representations of symbolic things recurs, with the same matter signified many times over. When we gather all of the "things" — the signs — that serve in an entire collection of these kinds of compositions, we shall see that a strikingly limited repertoire of persons, events, or actions comprise all of the lists of these "other matters." That fact standing by itself will prove only that a restricted vocabulary characterizes the "another-matter"-compositions and composites.

But why are these words opaque signs, to be interpreted by appeal to a syntax and grammar that pertains to signs whether in verbal or iconic form, and why are they not to be classified as narrowly substantive and to be read by appeal to the conventional rules of the syntax and grammar of propositional discourse? The answer brings us to the consideration already introduced for the identification of symbols in iconic form: a symbol is a sign that transcends the details of its own representation. But can that same trait also characterize words, which surely denote, whether or not they also connote? Indeed so, in the present context at least. Let me give a theoretical instance and then state what I conceive to be the rule.

In the context of the "another-matter"-composition, "Moses" or "David" or "Israel at the sea" serve no propositional purpose at all — conveying no faith that, belief that — as (mere) signs, but are available for combination with other signs into aggregates meant to bear meaning, even to make points, in accord with the syntax and grammar solely of symbolic discourse. "David" or "Moses" in symbolic discourse bear no determinate meaning at all; when we see "Moses" or "the Exodus" we do not know the subject of the signification that symbolic discourse will set forth, let alone the proposition (if any) that will be laid out. Only in combination does "David" or "Moses" or "shofar" or "menorah" gain any signification at all. And then the sense that is desired by the composer of the discourse will emerge not from the words that are used, but from the combinations that are accomplished: combinations of the (otherwise senseless) parsed components of the verse at hand, along with the (otherwise senseless) symbolic signs that are used. When, therefore, is a symbol symbolic? When the item meets these criteria:

[1] the thing (represented here by the word, "David" or by the verbal expression of the event, "Israel at the Sea," for instance) signifies beyond its particularity;

[2] in this context the thing bears sense *only* in combination with other things;

[3] the "thing" (sign) is one of some few things, among many candidates supplied, e.g., by Scripture, that can have been used, to be repeated many times.

Whether the picture of a *menorah* on the wall of a synagogue, or the reference to Abraham, Moses, and David, or the Exodus from Egypt, the destruction of the Temple, and the coming of the Messiah in strings of words joined with parsed verses of Scripture, the upshot is the same. We deal with symbols, representations of objects that bear meaning beyond the details, verbal evocations of things that bear meaning beyond their particularities.

In "another-matter"-composites the figure of Moses, or the Exodus from Egypt, or Sennacherib, Nebuchadnezzar, and Belshazzar, occur over and over again, in one combination or another. In these combinations the restricted vocabulary of symbolic discourse makes a virtually limitless number of points. In this regard, therefore, these things occur not as denotative words, where sense is limited to particular circumstance. Nor do they appear bearing determinate sense, e.g., as solely connotative words, evoking a less-determinate sense, e.g., a particular emotion or an attitude that we can predict when a given word occurs. That explains why, as a matter of fact, the components of the "another-matter"-compositions and composites, when seen in the aggregate, require classification as not words bearing determinate meaning (however broadly constructed) as symbols in verbal, rather than iconic, representation. The reason for that claim requires emphasis: *whatever the words mean in particular has no bearing upon their utilization in symbolic discourse.*

We know that is the fact because with the words alone in hand, we cannot predict the range of signification that they will be made to communicate: there is no clear limit to the possibilities of the sign, "David," or "Israel at the Sea" when those "things" stand by themselves. We do not know what they may be permitted to signify and we also do not know what they may not be permitted to signify. In the combinations formed to comprise an "another-matter"-composition and composite, however, they conform to a syntax and grammar that impose determinate meaning upon them: each joined to the other, sign after sign after sign, bears all together a very specific sense or significance. So it is not only that, viewed one by one, these words that serve in the "another-matter"-compositions bear meanings that transcend their own particularities. It is the simple fact that, standing alone they have no determinate and conventional, predictable meanings but are opaque; they take on meaning only in combination. These "things" are signs and only signs and yield symbolic discourse and only that.

The compositor of a given "another-matter" composition therefore accomplishes his goal through the combinations of things that he assembles to make his point: these things together signify this, not that. It follows that, whether in iconic or verbal form, we deal with signs: words that used as symbols as much as icons that are used as symbols. Whence significance? In symbolic discourse it must derive from combinations of one kind or another. How do these "things" — iconic, verbal alike — then serve as symbols within the definition offered at the outset? First, their sense (whether propositional, intuitive, emotional) transcends their immediate limits; or they have no intrinsic sense at all. Second, they bear their meanings only in combination, and not on their own; the rules of grammar and syntax of propositional communication do not pertain at all. The words at hand — "the Sea," "Sinai," "David," "Abraham," "the Torah" — serve as written-down symbols not in bearing meaning that is transcended but *in bearing no meaning within themselves at all*. In the kind of rhetoric represented by "another matter"-composites, very often, verbal representations of symbols are lucid *only as words serving a symbolic purpose*,.

IV. VERBAL SYMBOLS AND THE SYMBOLIC DISCOURSE OF RECOMBINANCY

The identification of how a word may serve as a symbol — connoting a meaning that transcends its own particularity, combining with other such verbal-symbols to convey a meaning that emerges not through syllogistic speech — now requires demonstration. I am going to show at some length, and in rich detail, that some few things — again: persons, actions, conceptions, events — in a restricted repertoire and in a clearly-defined and conventional manner — serves as signs as they combine and recombine in written evidence of a particular kind. These signs in this evidence never occur by themselves, but always in combination with other such "things." They very commonly refer to scriptural persons, events, actions, or attitudes, deriving from the Israelite Scriptures. They always combine with parsed verses of Scripture. (They never join together in discourse assigned to particular, named sages.[4]) It is in the combination of the opaque symbols in verbal form with the opaque clauses of a verse of Scripture that the signification of the whole take place: that is what I mean by recombinancy.

So symbolic discourse undertaken in verbal form proves recombinant. Only in context, in combinations with other such opaque signs, do symbols represented in verbal form begin to bear meaning, whether propositional or intuitive or emotional. The sole medium for conveying significance of any kind is to combine otherwise opaque symbols, whether conveyed in words or in iconic representation. The set of objects represented on the wall or floor of a synagogue, a list, e.g., Abraham, Isaac, Jacob, Sinai, made up of words that, in context, do not transcend meaning but have no fixed mean, — either constitutes symbolic discourse. Iconic

---

[4] Eli Ungar, in J. Neusner, *Approaches to Ancient Judaism* (Atlanta, 1990: Scholars Press for Brown Judaic Studies) VII.. I am not entirely certain what that fact means, but it is an established trait of the "another-matter" form that "another matter" never is used as a rhetorical signal in connection with sets of name-bearing rabbinical statements on a given theme or problem — or even, verse of Scripture, properly parsed. It serves in the Midrash-compilations to connect statements that commence with exegeses of parsed verses of Scripture. Ungar's discovery raises the question of where and how statements are assigned to named authorities, why that is done, and what attributions mean in a given context by comparison to their use in some other. Up until now, I have assumed that things were attributed because they were attributed, and I did not realize that the very resort to attributions itself constituted a convention and a significant trait. The cogency of composites of "another matter"s is not critical to my argument, but does serve it.

symbols, of course, bear their signification only in combination. But the same is so for those words that serve only as signs, and it takes place, when, in association with the parsed components of a given verse of Scripture, the opaque symbols combine to make sense, evoke an attitude, even convey a message. As my example stated in abstract terms has shown, the recombinancy therefore is in two aspects: [1] the joining in a single list of several opaque symbols, on the one side, [2] the joining of those opaque verbal signs with the parsed components of the cited verse of Scripture, on the other. The combinations are then two and distinct; the recombinancy forms the whole into a single statement, a discourse that is wholly carried on in the syntax and grammar of symbols, not in the syntax and grammar of words at all.

That is why I claim "Abraham" or "the destruction of the Temple" constitutes not a concept but simply a sign in the form of a word. It is a word that is opaque until made lucid by utilization in the syntactic and grammatical ways buy which symbolic discourse is carried on, and the meanings imputed to those words derive from the grammar and syntax of their utilization. Just as "king" or "child" or "murder" or "love" may serve in one sentence to convey one proposition or one sentiment, and in another, a quite different proposition or sentiment, so "Abraham" or "Sennacherib," "the pig" or "the lamb" may serve an evidently-unlimited range of propositional purposes. Then how are we to interpret "Abraham" or "Sinai" or "the destruction of the Temple"? It can only be the way in which we interpret any other word: in the context defined by syntax and grammar. But in the present sort of evidence, where are we to uncover that context? It can only be in the setting of the "sentences" formed by sets of these symbols that are expressed in the form of words — opaque words, until, like all other words, they are used to make sentences. But the sentences then are comprised of sets of opaque symbols, and to make sense of the word-symbols, we have to learn how to decipher the sentences that form of those word-symbols intelligible thought, whether propositional or intuitive or attitudinal. The issue, as with the visual symbols of the synagogue, then is the same: *how things combine, how we are to decipher the combinations.*

But the matter does not rest even there. In fact a well-crafted "another-matter" composition so functions as to join a vast range and variety of things (now: verbal symbols, in the sense just now spelled out) to make a single point. For as a matter of fact, in a set of three or five or eight "another-matter"-compositions formed into a single composite, we find in point of fact the same matter stated many times. So the medium of communication within the several compositions, which is combining and recombining symbols in verbal form, effects the formation of the entire set of compositions into a still larger, cogent statement, a statement made up of numerous statements, all of them effected through combining what are in fact words turned into symbols: recombinant symbolic speech. So much for locating symbols.

The rhetorical form that signals the utilization of words as symbols, bearing meaning only in combination with other, otherwise opaque symbols, ordinarily requires two or three statements, joined by the formula, "another matter," to effect intelligible communication of a message. Now, in general, "another matter" signals "another way of saying the same thing;" or the formula bears the sense, "these two distinct things add up to one thing," with the further proviso that both are necessary to make one point that transcends each one. That formula, in formal terms, serves as a signifier that the signs by themselves bear no meaning; the signs when joined together in one way, rather than another, make this statement, rather than that. Accordingly, the author of a composition gives way to the authorship of a composite. If individual authors made up the compositions, viewed as singletons, in which discrete elements of a parsed verse are joined with otherwise unconnected words ("theological things"), their work is null. For the "another-matter"-composite makes its statement *only* by joining together a variety of treatments of a given verse of Scripture. A single combination of parsed elements of a verse and discrete and unconnected words may bear implications of a message; the repetition of different combinations — the same parsed elements of a verse, other discrete words — brings the message to the surface. Communication here takes place only in series.

Hence only when we have in hand the entire repertoire of "another-matter"-compositions do we gain access to the statement that the compositor wishes to make. In the first illustrative case, drawn from Song of Songs Rabbah, the fixed formula of the *"another-matter"*—compilation points toward what I call "theological things," that is, fixed formulas of theological thought. These comprise sets of otherwise-opaque verbal-symbols, which, when juxtaposed on a given list in a given order, do cohere and do work together to form a statement within symbolic discourse. In their aggregation the statement that the framer wishes to make emerges. But what sorts of words may function as these "theological things"?

As a matter of fact, these "things" — theological signs — encompass time, space, person and object, action and attitude. I cannot think of a single person, event, or noteworthy locale in Scripture that in theory cannot serve, just as, in theory, Ben Sira and the author of Hebrews had available for their argument and proposition the entire Hebrew Scriptures. The very diversity of the signs, which may, in our categories, stand for persons, places, or things, proves their opacity; they do not on their own, by reason of their intrinsic traits of function in the form at hand, form taxa of their own, e.g., lists only of objects, only of signifiers of time, only of signs of space, or of persons of one kind or another, or of actions of a given classification. The deliberate confusion of categories that the intrinsic characteristics of the things listed *ought* to dictate — the mixing of persons, places, things for instance — underlines my claim that the things listed when viewed on their own are opaque. They gain sense only when joined together, that is, when combined and recombined. David, Solomon, Messiah at the end of time; this age, the age to come; the Exodus from Egypt, Sinai, the age to come all may appear together within a single list. That means the persons, David, Solomon, Messiah, the significations of time, this age, the age to come, events, the Exodus and "Sinai" — all are homogenized. Without regard to their own traits, then, the form a list because of traits extrinsic to the things listed; or because the things listed have no traits — except as their positioning on the list imputes to them traits.

Here is a concrete example of the symbolic discourse that, I maintain, the canonical writings of Judaism in its formative age present:

SONG OF SONGS RABBAH TO SONG 1:5

V:i.1   A.   "I am very dark, but comely, [O daughters of Jerusalem, like the tents of Kedar, like the curtains of Solomon]" (Song 1:5):

         B.   "I am dark" in my deeds.

         C.   "But comely" in the deeds of my forebears.

2.   A.   "I am very dark, but comely:"

         B.   Said the Community of Israel, "'I am dark' in my view, 'but comely' before my Creator."

         C.   For it is written, "Are you not as the children of the Ethiopians to Me, O children of Israel, says the Lord" (Amos 9:7):

         D.   "as the children of the Ethiopians" — in your sight.

         E.   But "to Me, O children of Israel, says the Lord."

3.   A.   Another interpretation of the verse, "'I am very dark:'" in Egypt.

         B.   "but comely:" in Egypt.

         C.   "I am very dark" in Egypt: "But they rebelled against me and would not hearken to me" (Ez. 20:8).

         D.   "but comely" in Egypt: with the blood of the Passover offering and circumcision, "And when I passed by you and saw you wallowing in your blood, I said to you, In your blood live" (Ez. 16:6) — in the blood of the Passover.

         E.   "I said to you, In your blood live" (Ez. 16:6) — in the blood of the circumcision.

4.   A.   Another interpretation of the verse, "I am very dark:" at the sea, "They were rebellious at the sea, even the Red Sea" (Ps. 106:7).

         B.   "but comely:" at the sea, "This is my God and I will be comely for him" (Ex. 15:2).

5.   A.   "I am very dark:" at Marah, "And the people murmured against Moses, saying, What shall we drink" (Ex. 15:24).

    B. "but comely:" at Marah, "And he cried to the Lord and the Lord showed him a tree, and he cast it into the waters and the waters were made sweet" (Ex. 15:25).

6.   A. "I am very dark:" at Rephidim, "And the name of the place was called Massah and Meribah" (Ex. 17:7).

    B. "but comely:" at Rephidim, "And Moses built an altar and called it by the name 'the Lord is my banner' (Ex. 17:15).

7.   A. "I am very dark:" at Horeb, "And they made a calf at Horeb" (Ps. 106:19).

    B. "but comely:" at Horeb, "And they said, All that the Lord has spoken we will do and obey" (Ex. 24:7).

8.   A. "I am very dark:" in the wilderness, ""How often did they rebel against him in the wilderness" (Ps. 78:40).

    B. "but comely:" in the wilderness at the setting up of the tabernacle, "And on the day that the tabernacle was set up" (Num. 9:15).

9.   A. "I am very dark:" in the deed of the spies, "And they spread an evil report of the land" (Num. 13:32).

    B. "but comely:" in the deed of Joshua and Caleb, ""Save for Caleb, the son of Jephunneh the Kenizzite" (Num. 32:12).

10.   A. "I am very dark:" at Shittim, "And Israel abode at Shittim and the people began to commit harlotry with the daughters of Moab" (Num. 25:1).

    B. "but comely:" at Shittim, "Then arose Phinehas and wrought judgment" (Ps. 106:30).

11.   A. "I am very dark:" through Achan, "But the children of Israel committed a trespass concerning the devoted thing" (Josh. 7:1).

    B. "but comely:" through Joshua, "And Joshua said to Achan, My son, give I pray you glory" (Josh. 7:19).

12.   A. "I am very dark:" through the kings of Israel.

    B. "but comely:" through the kings of Judah.

    C. If with my dark ones that I had, it was such that "I am comely," all the more so with my prophets.

V:ii.5. A. [As to the verse, "I am very dark, but comely," R. Levi b. R. Haita gave three interpretations:

    B. "'I am very dark:' all the days of the week.

    C. "'but comely:' on the Sabbath.

    D. "'I am very dark:' all the days of the year.

E. "'but comely:' on the Day of Atonement.
F. "'I am very dark:' among the Ten Tribes.
G. "'but comely:' in the tribe of Judah and Benjamin.
H. "'I am very dark:' in this world.
I. "'but comely:' in the world to come."

This is surely an easy example, for the message is communicated through contrasts, and if we had to specify the rule of intelligible discourse, it is: we convey our message by contrasting opposed cases. That is not the sole, or even the most paramount, mode of discourse, but it does establish the fact that communication is taking place through combining parsed elements of a verse of Scripture with lists of "theological things."

The formal traits of this composite prove blatant. The base-verse is parsed in three clauses, and the same parsing recurs throughout. Then in each sequence, a different set of meanings is imputed: deeds, deeds of forebears; my view, my Creator's view; rebellion in Egypt, obedience in Egypt; rebellion at the Sea, obedience at the sea; and so on. The items that are listed, time and again, by themselves bear no meaning that on its own is necessarily cogent with the other items on the same list. *But by effecting a pattern over and over again, — just as in the manner of paradigmatic speech — the various items are made to deliver a single message: the contrast of rebellion and obedience.* Do the several components bear that message? Horeb, Egypt, the Sea, the spies, the days of the week and the Sabbath — none of these on its own bears the meaning that, all together, they convey. Is then some other message delivered by the listed items, Horeb, Egypt, the Sea? I see none. To the contrary, the words, Horeb, Egypt, the Sea, by themselves stand for nothing that the composite contains; the words in combination with other words — again, Horeb, Egypt, the Sea — likewise bear no clear sense. It is the joining of two sets of words, the components of the base-verse, "I am dark" "but comely" together with the sequences, Horeb, Egypt, the Sea that contains the message. The combinancy is Horeb, Egypt, the Sea; that produces no symbolic speech. The recombinancy is Horeb, Egypt, the Sea, in the pattern with "I am dark" "but comely" — and that produces a powerful and well-crafted message. Why do I classify the delivery of the message as symbolic discourse? Because at no point is the message made explicit, e.g., propositionally let alone syllogistically. The message is contained within the recombinant contrasts; it is fully exposed through the symbols that gain meaning in the recombinancy and contrast; and the message then is conveyed wholly through the manipulation of otherwise-opaque words: hence, symbols in verbal form.

Let us now turn from the general theory of discourse to the details. The contrast of dark and comely yields a variety of applications; in all of them the same situation that is the one also is the other, and the rest follows in a wonderfully well-crafted composition. What is the repertoire of items? Dark in deeds but comely in ancestry; dark in my view but comely before God; dark when rebellious, comely when obedient, a point made at Nos. 3, for Egypt, 4, for the sea, and 5 for Marah, 6, for Massah and Meribah, 7 for Horeb, 8 for the wilderness, 9 for the spies in the Land, 10 for Shittim, 11 for Achan/Joshua and the conquest of the Land, 12 for Israel and Judah. But look what follows: the week as against the Sabbath, the weekdays as against the Day of Atonement, the Ten Tribes as against Judah and Benjamin, this world as against the world to come. Whatever classification these next items demand for themselves, it surely will not be that of events. Indeed, if by event we mean something that happened once, as in "once upon a time," then Sabbath as against weekday, Day of Atonement as against ordinary day form a different category; the Ten Tribes as against Judah and Benjamin constitute social entities, not divisions of time; and this age and the age to come form utterly anti-historical taxa altogether.

Events not only do not form a taxon, they also do not present a vast corpus of candidates for inclusion in some other taxon. The lists in the document at hand form selections from a most limited repertoire of candidates. If we were to catalogue all of the exegetical repertoire encompassed by *"another matter"*--constructions in this document, we should not have a very long list of candidates for inclusion in any list. And among the candidates, events are few indeed. They encompass Israel at the Sea and at Sinai, the destruction of the first Temple, the destruction of the second Temple, events as defined by the actions of some holy men such as Abraham, Isaac, and Jacob (treated not for what they did but for who they were), Daniel, Mishael, Hananiah and Azariah, and the like. .It follows that the restricted repertoire of candidates for taxonomic study encompasses remarkably few events, remarkably few for a literary culture that is commonly described as quintessentially historical!

Now we shall deal with composites in which symbolic discourse takes place within the propositional kind, so that there are two messages, one that is made explicit and that involves syllogistic demonstration, another that is left implicit and that involves evocative images, set forth in the medium of symbolic discourse I have described. Let me give an example of how, through both propositional and also symbolic discourse, a compositor may make his desired point.

LEVITICUS RABBAH XXVII:V

1. A. "God seeks what has been driven away" (Qoh. 3:15).
    B. R. Huna in the name of R. Joseph said, "It is always the case that 'God seeks what has been driven away' [favoring the victim].
    C. "You find when a righteous man pursues a righteous man, 'God seeks what has been driven away.'
    D. "When a wicked man pursues a wicked man, 'God seeks what has been driven away.'

E. "All the more so when a wicked man pursues a righteous man, 'God seeks what has been driven away.'

F. "[The same principle applies] even when you come around to a case in which a righteous man pursues a wicked man, 'God seeks what has been driven away.'"

2. A. R. Yosé b. R. Yudan in the name of R. Yosé b. R. Nehorai says, "It is always the case that the Holy One, blessed be he, demands an accounting for the blood of those who have been pursued from the hand of the pursuer.

B. "Abel was pursued by Cain, and God sought [an accounting for] the pursued: 'And the Lord looked [favorably] upon Abel and his meal offering' [Gen. 4:4].

C. "Noah was pursued by his generation, and God sought [an accounting for] the pursued: 'You and all your household shall come into the ark' [Gen. 7:1]. And it says, 'For this is like the days of Noah to me, as I swore [that the waters of Noah should no more go over the earth]' [Is. 54:9].

D. "Abraham was pursued by Nimrod, 'and God seeks what has been driven away': 'You are the Lord, the God who chose Abram and brought him out of Ur' [Neh. 9:7].

E. "Isaac was pursued by Ishmael, 'and God seeks what has been driven away': 'For through Isaac will seed be called for you' [Gen. 21:12].

F. "Jacob was pursued by Esau, 'and God seeks what has been driven away': 'For the Lord has chosen Jacob, Israel for his prized possession' [Ps. 135:4].

G. "Moses was pursued by Pharaoh, 'and God seeks what has been driven away': 'Had not Moses His chosen stood in the breach before Him' [Ps. 106:23].

H. "David was pursued by Saul, 'and God seeks what has been driven away': 'And he chose David, his servant' [Ps. 78:70].

I. "Israel was pursued by the nations, 'and God seeks what has been driven away': 'And you has the Lord chosen to be a people to him' [Deut. 14:2].

J. "And the rule applies also to the matter of offerings. A bull is pursued by a lion, a sheep is pursued by a wolf, a goat is pursued by a leopard.

      K.   "Therefore the Holy One, blessed be he, has said,
          'Do not make offerings before me from those animals
          that pursue, but from those that are pursued: 'When
          a bull, a sheep, or a goat is born'"" (Lev. 22:27).

The theological point is made very powerfully — and in two distinct modes of discourse. It is that God favors the persecuted over the persecutor, the pursued over the pursuer. This point is made in an abstract way at No. 1, and then through a review of the sacred history of Israel at No. 2. By listing the figures that are given, we see, the framer has made his point; had he wished to speak solely through opaque symbols, he would have omitted No. 1 and given us only No. 2. If, then, we knew the key to decipher the opaque symbols, laid out in the way that they are, we should have been able to discern the message wholly by our response to the opaque symbols consisting of lists of names of persons, in a given order and hence contrast: Abel/Cain, Noah/his generation, Abraham/Nimrod.

    v. THEOLOGY THROUGH SYMBOLIC DISCOURSE: ANOTHER MODE OF LIST-MAKING

    As a matter of simple fact, the vast majority of cases of symbolic discourse in the canonical writings deal with God's relationship with Israel and Israel's relationship with God. Hence symbolic discourse serves the particular task of working out theological themes. It yields no so much propositions as attitudes, evokes sentiment and right feeling — love for God, for example, or the feeling of being loved by God. The theological tableau or diorama relies upon combinations of words that on their own have no meaning — the parsed verse, the "theological theme" and, as I have explained, it may be called recombinant, in that combinations are worked out again and again, all with the same purpose in view. Before us a medium of theology, in which the framer ("the theologian") selects from a restricted repertoire a few items for combination in one way, rather than some other, with this verse's parsed components, rather than those of some other. The theologian through recombinant representation of symbols intends sometimes to make a point (e.g., the contrast of obedient and disobedient Israel we saw just now), sometimes not. So I should call symbolic discourse in Judaism a medium for the working out of recombinant theology.

    My insistence that this sector of Judaic theological expression resorts to symbolic discourse requires me to return to the question, when is a symbol symbolic? In the case of history, can we define what taxic indicator dictates which happenings will be deemed events bearing symbolic messages beyond articulation — and which not? As a matter of fact, the events that are listed throughout the example just now presented are not data of nature or history but of *theology:* God's relationship with Israel, expressed in such facts as the three events, the first two in the past, the third in the future, namely, the three redemptions of Israel, the three patriarchs, and holy persons, actions, events, what-have-you. The symbols expressed in verbal form all pertain to theological facts, all of them provided by the written

Torah or Scripture. The theological facts are manipulated in such a way as to conduct discourse, portrayed in such a way that the discourse is effected through symbolic media, so crafted as to set forth, through verbal symbols, a theological tableau. Then the symbols bear no message of a dynamic, syllogistic character, because they bear a message of a different order: theological truth set forth, not theological proposition subjected to argument and analysis. These are facts that are assembled and grouped; in our sample, drawn from Song of Songs Rabbah, the result is not propositional at all, or, if propositional, then essentially the repetition of familiar propositions through unfamiliar data.

To make this point concrete, here is a survey of sequences of components of such lists in Song of Songs Rabbah, that is, those combinations of "theological things" that, by themselves, bear no clear meaning whatsoever, but, in relationship to the elements of a parsed verse, convey a quite explicit theological message, delivered entirely symbolically in the recombinant manner I have now explained:

> Joseph, righteous men, Moses, and Solomon;
>
> patriarchs as against princes, offerings as against merit, and Israel as against the nations; those who love the king, proselytes, martyrs, penitents;
>
> first, Israel at Sinai; then Israel's loss of God's presence on account of the golden calf; then God's favoring Israel by treating Israel not in accord with the requirements of justice but with mercy;
>
> Dathan and Abiram, the spies, Jeroboam, Solomon's marriage to Pharaoh's daughter, Ahab, Jezebel, Zedekiah;
>
> Israel is feminine, the enemy (Egypt) masculine, but God the father saves Israel the daughter;
>
> Moses and Aaron, the Sanhedrin, the teachers of Scripture and Mishnah, the rabbis;
>
> the disciples; the relationship among disciples, public recitation of teachings of the Torah in the right order; lections of the Torah;
>
> the spoil at the Sea = the Exodus, the Torah, the Tabernacle, the ark;
>
> the patriarchs, Abraham, Isaac, Jacob, then Israel in Egypt, Israel's atonement and God's forgiveness;
>
> the Temple where God and Israel are joined, the Temple is God's resting place, the Temple is the source of Israel's fecundity;
>
> Israel in Egypt, at the Sea, at Sinai, and subjugated by the gentile kingdoms, and how the redemption will come;
>
> Rebecca, those who came forth from Egypt, Israel at Sinai, acts of loving kindness, the kingdoms who now rule Israel, the coming redemption;
>
> fire above, fire below, meaning heavenly and altar fires; Torah in writing, Torah in memory; fire of Abraham, Moriah, bush, Elijah, Hananiah, Mishael, and Azariah;
>
> the Ten Commandments, show-fringes and phylacteries, recitation of the Shema and the Prayer, the tabernacle and the cloud of the Presence of God, and the mezuzah;

the timing of redemption, the moral condition of those to be redeemed, and the past religious misdeeds of those to be redeemed;

Israel at the sea, Sinai, the Ten Commandments; then the synagogues and school houses; then the redeemer;

the Exodus, the conquest of the Land, the redemption and restoration of Israel to Zion after the destruction of the first Temple, and the final and ultimate salvation;

the Egyptians, Esau and his generals, and, finally, the four kingdoms;

Moses's redemption, the first, to the second redemption in the time of the Babylonians and Daniel;

the litter of Solomon: the priestly blessing, the priestly watches, the sanhedrin, and the Israelites coming out of Egypt;

Israel at the sea and forgiveness for sins effected through their passing through the sea; Israel at Sinai; the war with Midian; the crossing of the Jordan and entry into the Land; the house of the sanctuary; the priestly watches; the offerings in the Temple; the sanhedrin; the Day of Atonement;

God redeemed Israel without preparation; the nations of the world will be punished, after Israel is punished; the nations of the world will present Israel as gifts to the royal messiah, and here the base-verse refers to Abraham, Isaac, Jacob, Sihon, Og, Canaanites;

the return to Zion in the time of Ezra, the Exodus from Egypt in the time of Moses;

the patriarchs and with Israel in Egypt, at the Sea, and then before Sinai;

Abraham, Jacob, Moses;

Isaac, Jacob, Esau, Jacob, Joseph, the brothers, Jonathan, David, Saul, man, wife, paramour;

Abraham in the fiery furnace and Shadrach Meshach and Abednego, the Exile in Babylonia, now with reference to the return to Zion

This list suffices to make the simple point under discussion. The "another matter"-composites yield no fixed order of items or even commonly-repeated list of items, though some do recur as sets, e.g., first redemption (the sea), second redemption (the return to Zion), third redemption (the end of time or the Messiah); Abraham, Isaac, Jacob; Moses, Aaron, Miriam; Moses, David, Messiah; and so on. But if we were to set side by side and then catalogue all of the exegetical repertoire encompassed by "another matter"-constructions, we should have a very long list of candidates for inclusion in any list, and nearly as long a list of groups of candidates that are included in some list.

The upshot is simple. List-making — the counterpart in symbolic discourse to the making of jarring connections and the drawing of self-evidently valid conclusions in propositional discourse in the Bavli examined in Chapter Seven — is accomplished within a restricted repertoire of items; the list-making presents interesting combinations of an essentially small number of candidates for the exercise. But then, when making lists, one can do pretty much anything with the items that are combined; the taxic indicators are unlimited, but the data studied, severely limited. Take for example the case of history, meaning, events or happenings. Forming part of the *dabar-aher* or "another-matter"-construction, history constitutes one among a variety of what I have been calling theological "things" but what we might call (mere) signs. These by themselves comprise names, places, events, actions deemed to bear theological weight and to affect attitude and action. The play is worked out by a reprise of available materials, composed in some fresh and interesting combination. Events or happenings do not form random possibilities but comprise highly selected lists; but combining and recombining items on those lists with the parsed elements of a verse, one can say pretty much anything.

The same is so of anything Scripture affords. When three or more such theological "things" — whether person, whether event, whether action, whether attitude — are combined, they form a theological structure, and, viewed all together, all of the theological "things" in a given document constitute the components of the entire theological structure that the document affords. The propositions portrayed visually, through metaphors of sight, or dramatically, through metaphors of action and relationship, or in attitude and emotion, through metaphors that convey or provoke feeling and sentiment, when translated into language prove familiar and commonplace. The work of the theologian in this context is not to say something new or even persuasive, for the former is unthinkable by definition, the latter unnecessary in context. It is rather to display theological "things" in a fresh and interesting way, to accomplish a fresh exegesis of the canon of theological "things."

The combinations and recombinations identify some events as facts sharing the paramount taxic indicators of a variety of other facts, comprising a theological structure within a larger theological system: a reworking of canonical materials. An event is therefore reduced to a "thing," losing all taxic autonomy, requiring no distinct indicator of an intrinsic order. It is simply something else to utilize in composing facts into knowledge; the event does not explain, it does not define, indeed, it does not even exist within its own framework at all. Judaism by "an event" means, in a very exact sense, nothing in particular. It is a component in a culture that combines and recombines facts into structures of its own design, an aspect of what I should call a culture that comes to full expression in recombinant theology.

VI. THE ART OF THE SYNAGOGUES AND SYMBOLIC DISCOURSE IN THE ORAL TORAH: COMPARISONS AND CONTRASTS

Then the question arises, do not the same symbols in iconic form characterize the extant synagogue art of late antiquity? Certainly the sages for whom the Rabbinic writings speak are not alone in invoking the name of David, the icon of the shofar or ram's horn, or the figure of the menorah. Any claim to examine verbal symbols in the examination of the theology of the Oral Torah has to address that question.

If, as most people now understand, the Oral Torah (a.k.a., Rabbinic Judaism) stands for one Judaism among a menu of Judaisms, surely the identification of such ubiquitous symbols as the figure of David and doctrines as the Messianic person and age points to a single encompassing Judaism, not to the specific and particular theology of the Oral Torah that I pursue. How to differentiate verbal symbols of the books of the Oral Torah from the visual symbols of synagogue art? To show that these verbal systems serve particularly for the Oral Torah I identify principal synagogue-symbols in iconic form, those paramount in synagogue decoration, and ask whether and how they correlate with their counterparts in literary form through which symbolic discourse is effected. At stake is whether or not the two distinct bodies of evidence, when they communicate within precisely the same realm of signification, the symbolic, say the same thing or different things. The evidence analyzed here yields the result that iconic symbolic discourse resorted to one set of symbols to say its thing, verbal symbolic discourse to a different set of symbols to say something else.

Why insist that the recombinant lists form statements of the Oral Torah in particular, when, as a matter of fact, the preserved walls and mosaic floors of synagogues of the fourth through sixth centuries also reveal an active symbolic vocabulary? Substantial evidence that a restricted symbolic vocabulary characterized both the literary and the archaeological sources of Judaism in late antiquity. The same few objects, but no others, repeatedly appear in iconic form; the same limited repertoire of symbolic representations in literary form of certain persons, events, or actions, but no others, constantly makes up the probative lists. An inventory, based on the Hebrew Scriptures for instance, of the objects that can have been represented or of the scriptural heroes or miracles or objects that can have been invoked, vastly outweighs the incomparably shorter list of those iconic or verbal symbolic representations of the scriptural persons, events, objects, or actions that do appear. Ben Sira's list in comparison with counterpart lists in the rabbinic writings show that fact. Drawing upon a limited vocabulary of only a few things that occur nearly everywhere, synagogues present iconic decorations that clearly are so selected as to convey messages or connote meanings. In the writings of the sages of the Judaism taking shape in that same period, recurrent allusions to a restricted catalogue of only certain events, persons, or actions alert us to the presence of an implicit symbolic repertoire.

Most synagogues built from the third to the seventh century, both in the land of Israel and abroad, had decorated floors or walls. Some symbols out of the religious life of Judaism or of Graeco-Roman piety occur nearly everywhere. Other symbols, available, for example, from the repertoire of items mentioned in Scripture, or from the Graeco-Roman world, never make an appearance at all. A *shofar*, a *lulab* and *etrog*, a *menorah*, all of them Jewish in origin, but also such pagan symbols as a Zodiac, with symbols difficult to find in Judaic written sources — all of these form part of the absolutely fixed symbolic vocabulary of the synagogues of late antiquity. By contrast, symbols of other elements of the calendar year, at least as important as those that we do find, turn out never to make an appearance. And, obviously, a vast number of pagan symbols proved useless to Judaic synagogue artists. It follows that the artists of the synagogues spoke through a certain set of symbols and ignored other available ones. That simple fact makes it highly likely that the symbols they did use meant something to them, represented a set of choices, delivered a message important to the people who worshipped in those synagogues.

The synagogues bearing an ample repertoire of symbolic discourse were built in the time that the Talmud of Babylonia and Song of Songs Rabbah were coming to closure. We recall that in writings addressing the relationship of God and Israel, Israel and God, symbolic discourse went forward within, and along side, propositional-analytical and narrative discourse. Symbolic discourse proved distinctively important in Song of Songs Rabbah, generally assigned a date in the sixth century. So a mode of discourse formerly unimportant among the writers of documents later deemed canonical now served in a quite specific context. It was for the expression of religious feeling, the communication, in words, of religious sentiments. Synagogue decoration in the fourth, fifth, and sixth centuries likewise utilized symbols for the communication of religious sentiments. A restricted vocabulary of symbols served. A single mode of discourse came to prominence in the same age and for the same purpose, so it will appear. We have now to ask, do we have other evidence about means of communication for sentiments or attitudes of the same order? And, if we do, does that evidence also point toward the resort, among Judaic believers, to symbolic discourse for the expression of those sentiments?

The answer to both questions is affirmative. Synagogues, ordinarily left without symbolic decoration prior to the period under discussion — the fourth, fifth, and sixth centuries — at this time were commonly given symbolic decoration. And, we shall see, a strikingly limited repertoire of symbols predominated. I earlier stipulated that, to be symbolic, a sign must prove, if not ubiquitous, then commonplace, that is, appear in more than a single venue. Second, to be symbolic signs must represent a highly restricted vocabulary, so that some few recur very broadly, and many possible ones (out of the same corpus) not at all. Signs meant to serve as symbols are therefore distinguished, in iconic form, by three traits: [1] the function and provenance, within a synagogue; [2] the combination or relationship with other representations of things; [3] the selection of those few things among many that can have been represented. We shall now see that these conditions are met by synagogue iconic representation in the fourth, fifth and sixth centuries, so it would appear that symbolic discourse as a medium for the expression of religious feeling served not only the authors of compositions and compilers of composites but also the patrons and artists responsible for the decoration of synagogues. A brief survey of the data, summarily reviewed, validates that claim.

Elsewhere[5] I have established three facts: [1] If synagogues were decorated at all before the fifth and sixth centuries (and many were), they exhibited diverse iconic representations, and, so far as we can see, no severely limited repertoire of iconic items governed. By contrast, [2] most synagogues were decorated in the fifth and sixth centuries, and among them, [3] most utilized a severely restricted symbolic vocabulary. By the criteria just now set forth, therefore, the marks of symbolic discourse then are exhibited by the iconic evidence of Judaism in the fifth and sixth centuries. As to the specific iconic symbols, the facts are these:

1. the *etrog* and *lulab* and *shofar* travel together, and the *menorah* goes with them. Among the sites in which the *etrog, lulab,* and *shofar* occur, the *menorah* is always portrayed. Where there is an *etrog* and a *lulab,* there is ordinarily a *shofar* as well (18 sites for the *etrog* and *lulab,* 18 sites for the *shofar,* with only two discrepancies).

2. While, by my rough guess, any "other"-symbol may occur at two or at most three sites by chance or randomly, the grouping of *etrog* and *lulab, shofar,* and *menorah* is very unlikely to have occurred by chance alone. If the *etrog, lulab,* and *shofar* occur, it will always be with a *menorah.*

It follows that, by the same criteria imposed on the literary evidence, we may conclude that [1] symbolic discourse did go forward through utilization of combinations of symbols in iconic form; [2] single combination of iconic symbols did circulate very broadly; and [3] that set of symbols in iconic form does represent a clear-cut selection among a much larger repertoire of available symbols. Whether or not those 97 other objects that are represented in synagogue art (a rough count at best!) were symbolic and not decorative I do not claim to know. But the *etrog* and *lulab, shofar,* and *menorah* do form a repertoire of icons that clearly served to carry on symbolic discourse.

Now to bring the restricted iconic vocabulary of the synagogue into juxtaposition, for purposes of comparison and contrast, with that of the canonical books. Effecting that comparison of course requires us to frame in the same medium the two sets of symbols. But which medium — the visual (in our imagination at least) or the verbal? If it is to be the verbal, then we have to put into words the symbolic discourse portrayed for us on the walls and floors of synagogues. That is to say, we have to set forth in a manner parallel to symbolic discourse in words the symbols of the *etrog* and *lulab, shofar,* and *menorah.* And we have to do so in accord with the rhetoric forms that sustain symbolic discourse in verbal media. But by definition that cannot be done. First, symbolic discourse in verbal form requires us to identify and parse a verse of Scripture. But which verse for the items at hand? Second, we should require a clear notion of the meanings of the iconic symbols. But among the possible meanings, e.g., for the *shofar* — the New Year and Day of Atonement, Abraham binding Isaac on the altar, the coming of the

---

[5] *Symbol and Theology in Formative Judaism.*

Messiah, Moriah and the Temple — which are we to choose? And, third, since the symbolic discourse in iconic form obviously joins the the *etrog* and *lulab, shofar,* and *menorah,* translating the three (or four) into words demands a theory about what those symbols mean when they are joined in order, arrangement, and context. What do the symbols mean together that they do not mean when apart? The key is why certain combinations yield meaning, others, gibberish (Moses and Sennacherib on the same list, for example). Since we do not have that key for symbolic discourse in iconic form, we had best consider the alternative.

Since we cannot meet any one of those three conditions, we take the other road, which is open. That is, we must proceed (in our imagination) to translate into visual images the symbols in verbal form that we have. Here, by definition, we have access to the context defined by a parsed verse of Scripture. We have a fairly explicit statement of the meanings imputed to the symbols, that is, the use in communication that is made of them. And, finally, the combinations of symbols for symbolic discourse are defined for us by our documents — again by definition. So we can turn to written evidence and ask whether, in verbal form, symbolic discourse seems to converge with the counterpart discourse in the iconic medium. To satisfy ourselves that the distinctive combination of symbols — the *etrog* and *lulab, shofar,* and *menorah* — does not occur in the literary form of discourse (whether symbolic or otherwise) I present a brief account of how the Midrash-compilations treat two of the three items, the first and second. Here we shall see that the persistent manipulation of the three symbols as a group finds no counterpart in writing. The connections are different.

We begin with the *lulab* and ask whether representation of that symbol provokes discourse pertinent, also, to the symbols of the *shofar* and of the *menorah,* or even only of the menorah. The answer is negative. Other matters, but not those matters, are invoked. Leviticus Rabbah Parashah XXX treats the festival of Tabernacles (*Sukkot*), the sole point in the liturgical calendar at which the *etrog* and *lulab* pertain. The base-verse that is treated is Lev. 23:39-40: "You shall take on the first day the fruit of goodly trees, branches of palm trees and boughs of leafy trees and willows of the brook," and that statement is taken to refer, specifically, to the *lulab*. When sages read that verse, they are provoked to introduce the consideration of Torah-study; the opening and closing units of the pertinent unit tell us what is important:

LEVITICUS RABBAH XXX:I

1. A. "[On the fifteenth day of the seventh month, when you have gathered in the produce of the land, you shall keep the feast of the Lord seven days . . .] And you shall take on the first day [the fruit of goodly trees, branches of palm trees and boughs of leafy trees and willows of the brook, and you shall rejoice before the Lord your God for seven days]" (Lev. 23:39-40).

B.   R. Abba bar Kahana commenced [discourse by citing
     the following verse]: "Take my instruction instead
     of silver, [and knowledge rather than choice gold]"
     (Prov. 8:10).

C.   Said R. Abba bar Kahana, "Take the instruction of
     the Torah instead of silver.

D.   "'Why do you weigh out money? Because there is
     no bread' (Is. 55:2).

E.   "'Why do you weigh out money to the sons of Esau
     [Rome]? [It is because] "there is no bread," because
     you did not sate yourselves with the bread of the
     Torah.

F.   "'And [why] do you labor? Because there is no
     satisfaction' [Is. 55:2].

G.   "'Why do you labor while the nations of the world
     enjoy plenty? 'Because there is no satisfaction,' that
     is, because you have not sated yourselves with the
     wine of the Torah.

H.   "For it is written, 'Come, eat of my bread, and drink
     of the wine I have mixed'" (Prov. 9:5).

6.   A.   Said R. Abba bar Kahana, "On the basis of the reward
          paid for one act of 'taking,' you may assess the reward
          for [taking] the palm branch [on the festival of
          Tabernacles].

     B.   "There was an act of taking in Egypt: 'You will take
          a bunch of hyssop' [Ex. 12:22].

     C.   "And how much was it worth? Four *manehs*.

     D.   "Yet that act of taking is what made Israel inherit the
          spoil at the sea, the spoil of Sihon and Og, and the
          spoil of the thirty-one kings.

     E.   "Now the palm-branch, which costs a person such a
          high price, and which involves so many religious
          duties — how much the more so [will a great reward
          be forthcoming on its account]!"

F.   Therefore Moses admonished Israel, saying to them, "And
     you shall take on the first day . . . " (Lev. 23:40).

Whatever the sense of *lulab* to synagogue artists and their patrons, the combination
with the *etrog, menorah,* and *shofar* was critical; nothing in these words invokes
any of those other symbols. What would have led us to suppose some sort of
interchange between iconic and verbal symbols? If we had an association, in iconic
combinations, of the Torah-shrine and the *etrog* and *lulab*, we might have grounds

on which to frame the hypothesis that some sort of association — comparison, contrast for instance — between the symbols of the festival of Tabernacles and Torah-study was contemplated. Here there is no basis for treating the iconic symbols as convergent with the manipulation of those same symbols in propositional discourse. It suffices to say that nowhere in Leviticus Rabbah Parashah Thirty do we find reason to introduce the other iconic symbols.

What about the *shofar?* If we speak of that object, do we routinely introduce the *etrog, lulab, menorah?* The answer is negative. We introduce other things, but not those things. Pesiqta deRab Kahana *pisqa* 23 addresses the New Year as described at Lev. 23:24: "In the seventh month on the first day of the month you shall observe a day of solemn rest, a memorial proclaimed with blast of trumpets." The combination of judgment and the end of days is evoked in the following. I give two distinct statements of the same point, to show that it is in context an important motif.

PESIQTA DERAB KAHANA XXIII:II

2.   A. *For I will make a full end of all the nations* (Jer. 30:11): As to the nations of the world, because they make a full end (when they harvest even the corner of) their field, concerning them Scripture states: *I will make a full end of all the nations among whom I scattered you.*

   B. But as to Israel, because they do not make a full end (when they harvest, for they leave the corner of) their field, therefore: *But of you I will not make a full end* (Jer. 30:11).

   C. *I will chasten you in just measure, and I will by no means leave you unpunished* (Jer. 30:11). I shall chasten you through suffering in this world, so as to leave you unpunished in the world to come.

   D. When?

   E. *In the seventh month, [on the first day of the month]* (Lev. 23:24).

PESIQTA DERAB KAHANA XXIII:V

1.   A. R. Jeremiah commenced [[discourse by citing the following verse]: *"The wise man's path of life leads upward, that he may avoid Sheol beneath* (Prov. 15:24).

   B. *"The path of life*: The path of life refers only to the words of the Torah, for it is written, as it is written, *It is a tree of life* (Prov. 3:18).

C. "Another matter: *The path of life*: The path of life
    refers only to suffering, as it is written, *The way of
    life is through rebuke and correction* (Prov. 6:23).

D. "[*The wise man's path*] . . . *leads upward* refers to
    one who looks deeply into the Torah's religious duties,
    [learning how to carry them out properly].

E. "What then is written just prior to this same matter
    (of the New Year)?

F. "*When you harvest your crop of your land, you will
    not make a full end of the corner of your field* (Lev.
    23:22).

G. "The nations of the world, because they make a full
    end when they harvest even the corner of their
    field,[and the rest of the matter is as is given above: *I
    will make a full end of all the nations among whom I
    have driven you* (Jer. 30:11). But Israel, because they
    do not make a full end when they harvest, for they
    leave the corner of their field, therefore, *But of you I
    will not make a full end* (Jer. 30:11). *I will chasten
    you in just measure, and I will by no means leave
    you unpunished* (Jer. 30:11)." When? *In the seventh
    month, on the first day of the month, [you shall
    observe a day of solemn rest, a memorial proclaimed
    with blast of trumpets]* (Lev. 23:24)].

What is now linked is Israel's leaving the corner of the field for the poor, Lev.
23:22, the connection between that verse and the base-verse here is what is
expounded. Then there is no evocation of the menorah or the *lulab* and *etrog* — to
state the obvious. We can explain what is combined, and we also can see clearly
that the combination is deliberate. That means what joined elsewhere but not here
bears another message but not this one. An elaborate investigation of the role of
lulab and *etrog, shofar* and *menorah* in the literary evidence of the Midrash-
compilations hardly is required to demonstrate what we now know: we find no
evidence of interest in the combination of those items in literary evidence.

VII. SYMBOLIC DISCOURSE IN ICONIC AND IN VERBAL FORM: CONVERGENCE OR
DIVERGENCE?

A simple set of indicators will now permit us to compare the character of
symbolic discourse in verbal form with that in iconic form. The question is now a
simple one. Let us represent the Judaism — way of life, world view, theory of who
or what is "Israel"? — set forth by symbolic discourse in iconic form effected by
the *lulab* and *etrog, shofar,* and *menorah*. Let us further represent the Judaism set
forth by symbolic discourse in verbal form, treating as exemplary a discourse that

will appeal to visual images appropriate to the themes of Israel in the wilderness, the Temple cult, the judiciary and government, Israel under the four kingdoms and at the end of time, the life of sages, ordinary folk and the synagogue. How do these statements relate?

The shared program will cover the standard topics that any symbolic structure of representing a religion should treat: holy day, holy space, holy word, holy man (or: person), and holy time or the division of time.

	ICONIC SYMBOLS	VERBAL SYMBOLS
Holy day	New Year/Tabernacles/Hanukkah	
	Tabernacles/Pentecost/Passover	
Holy space	Temple	Temple/Zion
Holy man/person	No evidence[6]	the sage and disciple
Holy time	Messiah (shofar)	Four kingdoms/Israel's rule
Holy event	Not clear[7]	Exodus from Egypt/Sinai

The important point of convergence is unmistakable: holy space for both symbolic structures is defined as the Temple and Mount Zion. That is hardly surprising; no Judaic structure beyond 70 ignored the Temple, and all Judaisms, both before and after 70, found it necessary to deal in some way with, to situate themselves in relationship to, that paramount subject. So the convergence proves systemically inert, indeed trivial.

Whether or not we classify the treatment of holy time as convergent or divergent is not equally obvious to me. Both structures point toward the end of time; but they speak of it differently. So far as the *shofar* means to refer to the coming of the Messiah the gathering of the exiles, and the restoration of the Temple, as, in the synagogue liturgy, it does, then the iconic representation of the messianic topic and the verbal representation of the same topic diverge. For the latter, we see in our case and in much of the evidence surveyed earlier, frames the messianic topic in terms of Israel's relationship with the nations, and the principal interest is in Israel's rule over the world as the fifth and final monarchy. That theme is repeated in symbolic discourse in verbal form, and, if the *shofar* stands in synagogue iconography for what the synagogue liturgy says, then the message, if not an utterly different one, is not identical with that delivered by symbols in verbal form. So here matters are ambiguous.

---

[6] At the Dura Synagogue, we do have evidence: Moses/Heracles, Aaron, David/Orpheus, Mordecai, and other heroic figures who saved Israel are portrayed and clearly signified through differentiating indicators.

[7] At Dura the events portrayed in the book of Esther take a prominent place, and in synagogue mosaics the binding of Isaac recurs. But we have nothing to compare to the ubiquitous shofar, lulab, and ethrog, for the synagogue, or the sage and disciple or the four kingdoms/ Israel's rule motif, for aniconic symbolism.

The unambiguous points of divergence are equally striking. The most important comes first. Symbolic discourse in verbal form privileges the three festivals equally and utterly ignores Hanukkah. So far as the menorah stands for Hanukkah — and in the literary evidence, the association is firm — we may suppose that, just as the *lulab* and *etrog* mean to evoke Tabernacles, and the *shofar,* the New Year and Day of Atonement, so the *menorah* speaks of Hanukkah. Then we find a clear and striking divergence. That the menorah serves, also, as an astral symbol, is well established, and if that is the fact, then another point of divergence is registered. In symbolic discourse in verbal form I find not one allusion to an astral ascent accessible to an Israelite, e.g., through worship or Torah-study. A survey of the cited passages yields not a trace of the theme of the astral ascent.

The second point of divergence seems similarly unambiguous. Critical to the symbolic vocabulary of the rabbinic Midrash-compilations is study of the Torah, on the one side, and the figure of the sage and disciple, on the other. I do not find in the extant literary sources a medium for identifying the figure of the sage and the act of Torah study with the symbols of the *lulab, etrog, shofar,* or *menorah.* Quite to the contrary, the example given above from Leviticus Rabbah counterpoises the *lulab* with words of Torah. The fact that these are deemed opposites, with the former not invoking, but provoking, the latter, by itself means little. But it does not sustain the proposition that the combined symbols before us, the *lulab, etrog, shofar,* and menorah, somehow mean to speak of Torah-study and the sage.

Thus far we see marks of convergence and also of divergence. What happens if we present a sizable repertoire of the combinations of symbols in verbal form that we find in Song of Songs Rabbah? We wonder whether a sizable sample of combinations of symbols in verbal form intersects, or even coincides, with the simple vocabulary, in combination, paramount in iconic representations of symbolic discourse in synagogues. We recall in this connection the list drawn from combinations of symbols in verbal form found in Song of Songs Rabbah, cited just now. Examining the entire list once more, let us ask ourselves some very simple questions: is there a single combination of symbols in verbal form in this catalogue that joins the same symbols as are combined in the symbolic vocabulary in iconic form that we have identified? No, not a single combination coincides. Is there a paramount role assigned to Tabernacles at all? No, in this catalogue the principal holy day must be Passover, commemorating the Exodus, which occurs throughout, and not Tabernacles, commemorating the life in the wilderness, which occurs not at all. Is there a single set of symbols in verbal form that can be served by the *shofar*? No, not one. Whatever the sense or meaning that we assign to the shofar, if the shofar stands for Isaac on the altar with Abraham ready to give him up, if it stands for the New Year and Day of Atonement, or if it stands for the coming of the Messiah and the ingathering of the exiles, makes no difference.

On the list before us, I see no point at which the *shofar* in any of these senses will have served uniquely well or even served at all. Whatever the sense of the *menorah,* whether invoking Hanukkah or an astral ascent, makes no difference; it is not a useful symbol, in verbal form, for any of the combinations before us; it cannot have served in a single recombinant statement. The *lulab* and *etrog* so far as I can see can have claimed no place, in verbal form, in any of our combinations. While, therefore, at certain points the symbolic discourse in verbal form surely intersects with the same mode of discourse in iconic form, in the aggregate, symbolic discourse represented in one medium bears one set of symbols — singly or in combination! — and symbolic discourse in another medium appeals to a quite different set of symbols altogether.

VIII. THE WAY FORWARD: SYMBOLIC DISCOURSE AND THE DESCRIPTION OF THE THEOLOGY OF THE ORAL TORAH

The theology of the Oral Torah then comes to expression in not only in propositional but also in symbolic discourse. The "another-matter"-construction, constitutes a play on what I have been calling theological "things," — names, places, events, actions deemed to bear theological weight and to affect attitude and action. The play is worked out by a reprise of available materials, composed in some fresh and interesting combination. When three or more such theological "things" are combined, they form a theological structure, and, viewed all together, all of the theological "things" in a given document constitute the components of the entire theological structure that the document affords. The propositions portrayed visually, through metaphors of sight, or dramatically, through metaphors of action and relationship, or in attitude and emotion, through metaphors that convey or provoke feeling and sentiment, when translated into language prove familiar and commonplace. The work of the theologian in this context is not to say something new or even persuasive, for the former is unthinkable by definition, the latter unnecessary in context. It is rather to display theological "things" in a fresh and interesting way, to accomplish a fresh exegesis of the canon of theological "things."

What is at stake in focusing upon aniconic symbolism? Until now, in my judgment, we have had no method of description of theology in the Oral Torah that is both coherent with the character of the documents and also cogent with the tasks of theological description. The problem has been the character of the documents and their mode of theological discourse. It is not that the writers speak only in concrete terms; we could readily move from their detail to our abstraction and speak in general terms about the coherence of prevailing principles of a theological order. The problem has been much more profound. We face a set of writings that clearly mean to tell us about God and God's relationship to Israel and Israel and Israel's relationship to God. The authorships *a priori* exhibit the conviction that the thoughts of the whole are cogent and coherent, since they prove deeply concerned to identify contradiction, disharmony, and incoherence, and remove it. But we have not known how to find the connections between what they have written and the structure or system of thought that leads them to say, in detail, the things that they say. In working out a theory of the symbolic discourse, I hope to make possible the description of the symbolic structure set forth by that discourse, and, thereby, I further mean to open the way to the description of the theology.

The reason that I think we must begin with the elementary analysis of how discourse proceeds is simple. The kind of evidence before us offers little alternative. When we propose to describe the theological system to which a piece of well-crafted writing testifies, our task is easy when the writing to begin with discusses in syllogistic logic and within an appropriate program of propositions what we conceive to be theological themes or problems. Hence — it is generally conceded — we may legitimately translate the topically-theological writings of Paul, Augustine, or Luther into the systematic and coherent theologies of those three figures, respectively: finding order and structure in materials of a cogent theological character. But what about a literature that to begin with does not set forth theological propositions in philosophical form, even while using profoundly religious language for self-evidently religious purposes? And how shall we deal with a literature that conducts theological thought without engaging in analytical inquiry in the way in which the philosophers and theologians of Christianity have done, and did in that period?

Surely the Oral Torah testifies to an orderly structure or system of thought, for the alternative is to impute to the contents of those writings the status of mere episodic and unsystematic observations about this and that. True, profound expressions of piety may exhibit the traits of intellectual chaos and disorder, and holy simplicity may mask confusion. But such a description of the rabbinic literature of late antiquity, which I call the canon of the Judaism of the dual Torah, defies the most definitive and indicative traits of the writings. These are order, system, cogency, coherence, proportion, fine and well-crafted thought.

To begin with, we have to justify the theological inquiry, through analysis of symbolism, into literature that self-evidently does not conform to the conventions of theological discourse to which Western civilization in its Graeco-Roman heritage and Christian (and, as a matter of fact, Muslim) civilization in its philosophical formulation has made us accustomed. The Muslim and Christian theological heritage, formulated within the conventions of philosophical argument, joined by a much smaller Judaic theological corpus to be sure, does not allow us to read as a theological statement a single canonical writing of the Judaism of the dual Torah of late antiquity. So if the literary canons of Western theology are to govern, then to begin with the literature of Judaism in its formative age by definition can present no theological order and system at all.

But that proposition on the face of it hardly proves compelling. For it is difficult for us to imagine a mental universe so lacking in structure, form, and order as to permit everything and its opposite to be said about God, to imagine a God so confused and self-contradictory as to yield a revelation lacking all cogency and truly unintelligible. The very premises of all theology — that there is order, structure, and composition, proportion, and form, in God's mind, which in fact is intelligible to us through the medium of revelation properly construed — *a priori* render improbable the hypothesis that the canonical writings of the Judaism of the dual Torah violate every rule of intelligible discourse concerning the principal and foundation of all being. If, after all, we really cannot speak intelligibly about God, the Torah, holy Israel, and what God wants of us, then why write all those books to begin with?

While theology may comprise propositions well-crafted into a cogent structure, about fundamental questions of God and revelation, the social entity that realizes that revelation, the attitudes and deeds that God, through revelation, requires of humanity, there is another way entirely. Theology — the structure and system, the perception of order and meaning of God, in God, through God — these may make themselves known otherwise than through the media of thought and expression that yield belief that; theology can deliver its message to and through sentiment and emotion, heart as much as mind; it can be conviction as much as position, and conviction for its part also is orderly, proportioned, compelling of mind and intellect by reason of right attitude, rather than right proposition or position. That is to say, theology may set forth a system of thought in syllogistic arguments concerning the normative truths of the world-view, social entity, and way of life of a religious system. But theology may speak in other than dynamic and compelling argument, and theologians may accomplish their goal of speaking truth about God through other than the statements made by language and in conformity with the syntax of reasoned thought.

Theology may also address vision and speak in tactile ways; it may utilize a vocabulary of not proposition but opaque symbol (whether conveyed in visual or verbal media), and through portraying symbol, theology may affect attitude and emotion, speak its truth through other media than those of philosophy and proposition. From the time of Martin Buber's *Two Types of Faith*, now nearly four decades ago, people have understood that this other type of theology, the one that lives in attitude and sentiment and that evokes and demands trust, may coexist, or even compete, with the philosophical type to the discourse of which, in general, we are accustomed. Since, as a matter of fact, in the Oral Torah we do not have a single sustained theological treatise, while — as I have now shown in each succeeding chapter — we do have a monument to a faith that is choate and subject to fully-accessible expression, we must teach ourselves how to describe the theology of the Oral Torah out of its fully-exposed and complete, systemic documents. What we now realize brings us to the end of our work, though to no weighty conclusion: some documents utilize certain forms to make theological statements in symbolic discourse, the recombinant symbolic ones such as that which we have now examined. These documents communicate through symbolic discourse. They therefore point toward the symbolic structure that, for the Judaism of the dual Torah, constitutes the theological statement and message.

IX. **WHY NO CONCLUSION AND WHAT COMES NEXT?**

Now this book draws no conclusions and offers none. It simply has now to stop. The reason is contained within the word "prolegomenon." I have offered here a first word, but not a last word. Three different ways — in the setting of the documents of the Oral Torah[8] I can think of no others — to describe the encompassing and governing theology of the Oral Torah will serve. These are [1] identification of the paradigms set forth by specific documents, [2] analysis of systematic propositional composites set forth by the Talmud of Babylonia and certain other compilations, and [3] examination of the recombinancy of opaque verbal symbols. Each has been shown to point out significant theological structures and to identify their systemic workings. A set of three experiments in method has signalled, also, significant points of convergence, results of one method that coincide with those of another or of both of the others. Paradigms in their context correspond to topical compositions in theirs and to aniconic symbolic discourse as well.

We now anticipate three distinct sources of category-formations: paradigms that some documents expose, systematic expositions of a given category-formation and even of a proposition contained therein, and the recombinant formations of "another-matter." We also can identify three separate locations for inquiry into such formations, entire documents, clearly-delineated topical composites (not only those of the Talmud of Babylonia, but also those of other compilations as well), and compositions and composites comprised by lists of opaque symbols in verbal form. As to the matter of proportion, we may hope, at some point in the future, to gain a vision of the whole: paradigms, propositions, statements in symbolic form. So far — no further can we go.

---

[8] When we take account of the kinds of data available to those who propose to describe the theology of catholic Christianity in the same period — creeds and decrees of Church councils, a near-universal consensus on liturgy, systematic and fully articulated writings by individual figures who enjoyed a solid hearing — we can understand the qualification required here. I have tried to invent methods suitable for discerning the theological structure and system that inheres in writings of a particular set of traits. Writings that exhibit other traits — more philosophical ones, for instance — will sustain other methods altogether. Much depends, to be sure, on what we classify as belonging to the Oral Torah and what we exclude. Once we have solid results of descriptive theology based on documents assuredly belonging to the Oral Torah — from the Mishnah through the Bavli — we may address documents that may or may not belong to those responsible for the Oral Torah. To take the obvious case of liturgical forms, that sages legislated in liturgical matters and even contributed liturgies is clear; that liturgy originates with, speaks in particular for, sages forms another set of questions awaiting investigation. Once we have solid data of the theology sages deemed their own, we shall have framed a criterion of authenticity to the Oral Torah in particular and then may take up documents the status of which is not equivalently clear. We have to work from within and move outward.

What is at stake? First, I have pointed toward modes of reliable and accurate description of category-formations, where they are defined, how they are framed into significant statements. Consequently, we may expect to produce solid results, points on which diverse documents, compositions or composites, producing authoritative statements, concur. Second, out of those points of concurrence we may construct a formidable, reliable account of the theological structure of the Oral Torah. Third, and from the long perspective most important, seeing the components all together and all at once, we may also formulate a theory on how the structure holds together and therefore sustains through its own syntax the formulation new statements out of its established vocabulary. When we know the vocabulary, grammar, and syntax of the Oral Torah as a language of theological discourse, we may hope to join in the discourse, speaking that same language, even, about another age, another world altogether.

The matter of theological vocabulary properly identified, accurately defined awaits. What is needed now is a vast exercise in defining the theological facts of the matter, that is to say, systematic entries designed ultimately for *the theological grammar of the Oral Torah,* to which I now turn.

South Florida Studies in the History of Judaism

South Florida Academic Commentary Series

243062	The Two Talmuds Compared, I. Tractate Berakhot and the Division of Appointed Times in the Talmud of the Land of Israel and the Talmud of Babylonia, Volume C, Tractate Erubin	Neusner
243063	The Two Talmuds Compared, I. Tractate Berakhot and the Division of Appointed Times in the Talmud of the Land of Israel and the Talmud of Babylonia, Volume D, Tractates Yoma and Sukkah	Neusner
243064	The Two Talmuds Compared, I. Tractate Berakhot and the Division of Appointed Times in the Talmud of the Land of Israel and the Talmud of Babylonia, Volume E, Tractate Pesahim	Neusner
243065	The Two Talmuds Compared, I. Tractate Berakhot and the Division of Appointed Times in the Talmud of the Land of Israel and the Talmud of Babylonia, Volume F, Tractates Besah, Taanit and Megillah	Neusner
243066	The Two Talmuds Compared, I. Tractate Berakhot and the Division of Appointed Times in the Talmud of the Land of Israel and the Talmud of Babylonia, Volume G, Tractates Rosh Hashanah and Moed Qatan	Neusner
243067	The Talmud of Babylonia, An Academic Commentary, Volume XXII, Bavli Tractate Baba Batra, B. Chapters VII through XI	Neusner
243068	The Talmud of Babylonia, An Academic Commentary, Volume XXIII, Bavli Tractate Sanhedrin, B. Chapters VIII through XII	Neusner
243069	The Talmud of Babylonia, An Academic Commentary, Volume XIV, Bavli Tractate Ketubot, B. ChaptersVII through XIV	Neusner
243070	The Talmud of Babylonia, An Academic Commentary, Volume IV, Bavli Tractate Pesahim, B. Chapters VIII through XI	Neusner
243071	The Talmud of Babylonia, An Academic Commentary, Volume XXIX, Bavli Tractate Menahot, B. Chapters VII through XIV	Neusner
243072	The Talmud of Babylonia, An Academic Commentary, Volume XXVIII, Bavli Tractate Zebahim B. Chapters VIII through XV	Neusner
243073	The Talmud of Babylonia, An Academic Commentary, Volume XXI, Bavli Tractate Baba Mesia, B. Chapters VIII through XI	Neusner
243074	The Talmud of Babylonia, An Academic Commentary, Volume III, Bavli Tractate Erubin, A. ChaptersVI through XI	Neusner

South Florida-Rochester-Saint Louis
Studies on Religion and the Social Order

245001	Faith and Context, Volume 1	Ong
245002	Faith and Context, Volume 2	Ong
245003	Judaism and Civil Religion	Breslauer

South Florida International Studies in Formative Christianity and Judaism